MW01144603

The Holy Roman Empire

James Bryce

Nabu Public Domain Reprints:

You are holding a reproduction of an original work published before 1923 that is in the public domain in the United States of America, and possibly other countries. You may freely copy and distribute this work as no entity (individual or corporate) has a copyright on the body of the work. This book may contain prior copyright references, and library stamps (as most of these works were scanned from library copies). These have been scanned and retained as part of the historical artifact.

This book may have occasional imperfections such as missing or blurred pages, poor pictures, errant marks, etc. that were either part of the original artifact, or were introduced by the scanning process. We believe this work is culturally important, and despite the imperfections, have elected to bring it back into print as part of our continuing commitment to the preservation of printed works worldwide. We appreciate your understanding of the imperfections in the preservation process, and hope you enjoy this valuable book.

Professor E. W. Gurney

With the author's kind regards

THE HOLY ROMAN EMPIRE.

THE

HOLY ROMAN EMPIRE

BY

JAMES BRYCE, D.C.L.

FELLOW OF ORIEL COLLEGE

and

PROFESSOR OF CIVIL LAW IN THE UNIVERSITY OF OXFORD

THIRD EDITION REVISED

London

MACMILLAN AND CO.

1871

13536.8.2

A

Harvard College Library
From the Estate of
PROF. E. W. GURNEY
1 July, 1902

BOUND 9 FEB 1912

OXFORD:

By T. Combe, M.A., E. B. Gardner, and E. Pickard Hall,

PRINTERS TO THE UNIVERSITY.

PREFACE TO THE THIRD EDITION.

THE object of this treatise is not so much to give a narrative history of the countries included in the Romano-Germanic Empire—Italy during the middle ages; Germany from the ninth century to the nineteenth—as to describe the Holy Empire itself as an institution or system, the wonderful offspring of a body of beliefs and traditions which have almost wholly passed away from the world. Such a description, however, would not be intelligible without some account of the great events which accompanied the growth and decay of imperial power; and it has therefore appeared best to give the book the form rather of a narrative than of a dissertation; and to combine with an exposition of what may be called the theory of the Empire an outline of the political history of Germany, as well as some notices of the affairs of mediæval Italy. To make the succession of events clearer, a Chronological List of Emperors and Popes has been prefixed*.

The present edition has been carefully revised and corrected throughout; and a good many additions have been made to both text and notes.

LINCOLN'S INN,
August 11, 1870.

* The author has in preparation, and hopes before long to complete and publish, a set of chronological tables which may be made to serve as a sort of skeleton history of mediæval Germany and Italy.

CONTENTS.

CHAPTER I.

Introductory.

CHAPTER II.

The Roman Empire before the Invasion of the Barbarians.

CHAPTER III.

The Barbarian Invasions.

CHAPTER IV.

Restoration of the Empire in the West.

CHAPTER V.

Empire and Policy of Charles.

CHAPTER VI.

Carolingian and Italian Emperors.

CHAPTER VII.

Theory of the Mediæval Empire.

CHAPTER VIII.

The Roman Empire and the German Kingdom.

CHAPTER IX.

Saxon and Franconian Emperors.

CHAPTER X.

Struggle of the Empire and the Papacy.

CHAPTER XI.

The Emperors in Italy : Frederick Barbarossa.

CHAPTER XII.

Imperial Titles and Pretensions.

CHAPTER XIII.

Fall of the Hohenstaufen.

CHAPTER XIV.

The Germanic Constitution—the Seven Electors.

CHAPTER XV.

The Empire as an International Power.

CHAPTER XVI.

The City of Rome in the Middle Ages.

CHAPTER XVII.

The Renaissance: Change in the Character of the Empire.

CHAPTER XVIII.

The Reformation and its Effects upon the Empire.

CHAPTER XIX.

The Peace of Westphalia: Last Stage in the Decline of the Empire.

CHAPTER XX.

Fall of the Empire.

CHAPTER XXI.

Conclusion: General Summary.

APPENDIX.

DATES OF

SEVERAL IMPORTANT EVENTS

IN THE HISTORY OF THE EMPIRE.

	B.C.
Battle of Pharsalia	48

	A.D.
Council of Nicæa	325
End of the separate Western Empire	476
Revolt of the Italians from the Iconoclastic Emperors	728 754
Coronation of Charles the Great	800
End of the Carolingian Empire	888
Coronation of Otto the Great	962
Final Union of Italy to the Empire	1014
Quarrel between Henry IV and Gregory VII	1076
The First Crusade	1096
Battle of Legnano	1176
Death of Frederick II	1250
League of the three Forest Cantons of Switzerland	1308
Career of Rienzi	1347–1354
The Golden Bull	1356
Council of Constance	1415
Extinction of the Eastern Empire	1453
Discovery of America	1492
Luther at the Diet of Worms	1521

CHRONOLOGICAL TABLE

OF

EMPERORS AND POPES.

Year of Accession.	Bishops of Rome.	Emperors.	Year of Accession.
A. D.			B. C.
		Augustus.	27
			A. D.
		Tiberius.	14
		Caligula.	37
		Claudius.	41
42	St. Peter, (according to Jerome).		
		Nero.	54
67	Linus, (according to Jerome, Irenæus, Eusebius).		
68	Clement, (according to Tertullian and Rufinus).	Galba, Otho, Vitellius, Vespasian.	68
78	Anacletus (?).		
		Titus.	79
		Domitian.	81
91	Clement, (according to later writers).		
		Nerva.	96
		Trajan.	98
100	Evaristus (?).		
109	Alexander (?).		
		Hadrian.	117
119	Sixtus I.		
129	Telesphorus.		
		Antoninus Pius.	138
139	Hyginus.		
143	Pius I.		

b

Year of Accession.	Bishops of Rome.	Emperors.	Year of Accession.
A. D.			A. D.
157	Anicetus.		
		Marcus Aurelius.	161
168	Soter.		
177	Eleutherius.		
		Commodus.	180
		Pertinax.	190
		Didius Julianus.	191
		Niger.	192
193	Victor (?).	Septimius Severus.	193
202	Zephyrinus (?).		
		Caracalla, Geta, Diadumenian.	211
		Opilius Macrínus.	217
		Elagabalus.	218
219	Calixtus I.		
		Alexander Severus.	222
223	Urban I.		
230	Pontianus.		
235	Anterius or Anteros.	Maximin.	235
236	Fabianus.		
		The two Gordians, Maximus Pupienus, Balbinus.	237
		Gordian the Younger.	238
		Philip.	244
		Decius.	249
251	Cornelius.	Gallus.	251
252	Lucius I.	Volusian.	252
253	Stephen I.	Æmilian, Valerian, Gallienus.	253
257	Sixtus II.		
259	Dionysius.		
		Claudius II.	268
269	Felix.		
		Aurelian.	270
275	Eutychianus.	Tacitus.	275
		Probus.	276
		Carus.	282
283	Caius.		
		Carinus, Numerian, Diocletian.	284
		Maximian, joint Emperor with Diocletian.	286
296	Marcellinus.		[305 (?)
304	Vacancy.	Constantius, Galerius.	304 (?) or
		Licinius.	307]

Year of Accession.	Bishops of Rome.	Emperors.	Year of Accession.
A. D.			A. D.
308	Marcellus I.	Maximin.	308
		Constantine, Galerius, Licinius, Maximin, Maxentius, and Maximian reigning jointly.	309
310	Eusebius.		
311	Melchiades.		
314	Sylvester I.		
		Constantine (the Great) alone.	323
336	Marcus I.		
337	Julius I.	Constantine II, Constantius II, Constans.	337
		Magnentius.	350
352	Liberius.		
		Constantius alone.	353
356	Felix (Anti-pope).		
		Julian.	361
		Jovian.	363
		Valens and Valentinian I.	364
366	Damasus I.		
		Gratian and Valentinian I.	367
		Valentinian II and Gratian.	375
		Theodosius.	379
384	Siricius.		
		Arcadius (in the East), Honorius (in the West).	395
398	Anastasius I.		
402	Innocent I.		
		Theodosius II. (E)	408
417	Zosimus.		
418	Boniface I.		
418	Eulalius (Anti-pope).		
422	Celestine I.		
		Valentinian III. (W)	424
432	Sixtus III.		
440	Leo I (the Great).		
		Marcian. (E)	450
		Maximus, Avitus. (W)	455
		Majorian. (W)	455
		Leo I. (E)	457
461	Hilarius.	Severus. (W)	461
		Vacancy. (W)	465

Year of Accession.	Bishops of Rome, or Popes.	Emperors.	Year of Accession.
A. D.			A. D.
		Anthemius. (W)	467
468	Simplicius.		
		Olybrius. (W)	472
		Glycerius. (W)	473
		Julius Nepos. (W)	474
		Leo II, Zeno, Basiliscus (all E.)	474
		Romulus Augustulus. (W)	475
		(End of the Western Line in Romulus Augustus.	476)
		(*Henceforth, till* A.D. 800, *Emperors reigning at Constantinople*).	
483	Felix III *.		
		Anastasius I.	491
492	Gelasius I.		
496	Anastasius II.		
498	Symmachus.		
498	Laurentius (Anti-pope).		
514	Hormisdas.		
		Justin I.	518
523	John I.		
526	Felix IV.		
		Justinian.	527
530	Boniface II.		
530	Dioscorus (Anti-pope).		
532	John II.		
535	Agapetus I.		
536	Silverius.		
537	Vigilius.		
555	Pelagius I.		
560	John III.		
		Justin II.	565
574	Benedict I.		
578	Pelagius II.	Tiberius II.	578
		Maurice.	582
590	Gregory I (the Great).		
		Phocas.	602
604	Sabinianus.		
607	Boniface III.		
607	Boniface IV.		
		Heraclius.	610
615	Deus dedit.		
618	Boniface V.		

* Reckoning the Anti-pope Felix (A.D. 356) as Felix II.

Year of Accession.	Popes.	Emperors.	Year of Accession.
A. D.			A. D.
625	Honorius I.		
638	Severinus.		
640	John IV.		
		Constantine III, Heracleonas, Constans II.	641
642	Theodorus I.		
649	Martin I.		
654	Eugenius I.		
657	Vitalianus.		
		Constantine IV (Pogonatus).	668
672	Adeodatus.		
676	Domnus or Donus I.		
678	Agatho.		
682	Leo II.		
683 (?)	Benedict II.		
685	John V.	Justinian II.	685
685 (?)	Conon.		
687	Sergius I.		
687	Paschal (Anti-pope).		
687	Theodorus (Anti-pope).		
		Leontius.	694
		Tiberius.	697
701	John VI.		
705	John VII.	Justinian II restored.	705
708	Sisinnius.		
708	Constantine.		
		Philippicus Bardanes.	711
		Anastasius II.	713
715	Gregory II.		
		Theodosius III.	716
		Leo III (the Isaurian).	718
731	Gregory III.		
741	Zacharias.	Constantine V (Copronymus).	741
752	Stephen (II).		
752	Stephen II (or III).		
757	Paul I.		
767	Constantine (Anti-pope).		
768	Stephen III (IV).		
772	Hadrian I.		
		Leo IV.	775
		Constantine VI.	780
795	Leo III.		
		Deposition of Constantine VI by Irene.	797

Year of Accession.	Popes.	Emperors.	Year of Accession.
A.D.			A.D.
		Charles I (the Great). *(Following henceforth the new Western line).*	800
		Lewis I (the Pious).	814
816	Stephen IV.		
817	Paschal I.		
824	Eugenius II.		
827	Valentinus.		
827	Gregory IV.		
		Lothar I.	840
844	Sergius II.		
847	Leo IV.		
855	Benedict III.	Lewis II.	855
855	Anastasius (Anti-pope).		
858	Nicholas I.		
867	Hadrian II.		
872	John VIII.		
		Charles II (the Bald).	875
		Charles III (the Fat).	881
882	Martin II.		
884	Hadrian III.		
885	Stephen V.		
891	Formosus.	Guido.	891
		Lambert.	894
896	Boniface VI.	Arnulf.	896
896	Stephen VI.		
897	Romanus.		
897	Theodore II.		
898	John IX.		
		Lewis (the Child). †	899
900	Benedict IV.		
		Lewis III (of Provence).	901
903	Leo V.		
903	Christopher.		
904	Sergius III.		
911	Anastasius III.		
		Conrad I.	912(?)
913	Lando.		
914	John X.		
		Berengar.	915
		Henry I (the Fowler).	918
928	Leo VI.		

† The names in italics are those of German kings who never made any claim to the imperial title.

THE HOLY ROMAN EMPIRE.

CHAPTER I.

INTRODUCTORY.

Of those who in August, 1806, read in the English newspapers that the Emperor Francis II had announced to the Diet his resignation of the imperial crown, there were probably few who reflected that the oldest political institution in the world had come to an end. Yet it was so. The Empire which a note issued by a diplomatist on the banks of the Danube extinguished, was the same which the crafty nephew of Julius had won for himself, against the powers of the East, beneath the cliffs of Actium; and which had preserved almost unaltered, through eighteen centuries of time, and through the greatest changes in extent, in power, in character, a title and pretensions from which all meaning had long since departed. Nothing else so directly linked the old world to the new—nothing else displayed so many strange contrasts of the present and the past, and summed up in those contrasts so much of European history. From the days of Constantine till far down into the middle ages it was, conjointly with the Papacy, the recognised centre and head of Christendom,

B

exercising over the minds of men an influence such as its material strength could never have commanded. It is of this influence and of the causes that gave it power rather than of the external history of the Empire, that the following pages are designed to treat. That history is indeed full of interest and brilliance, of grand characters and striking situations. But it is a subject too vast for any single canvas. Without a minuteness of detail sufficient to make its scenes dramatic and give us a lively sympathy with the actors, a narrative history can have little value and still less charm. But to trace with any minuteness the career of the Empire, would be to write the history of Christendom from the fifth century to the twelfth, of Germany and Italy from the twelfth to the nineteenth; while even a narrative of more restricted scope, which should attempt to disengage from a general account of the affairs of those countries the events that properly belong to imperial history, could hardly be compressed within reasonable limits. It is therefore better, declining so great a task, to attempt one simpler and more practicable though not necessarily inferior in interest; to speak less of events than of principles, and endeavour to describe the Empire not as a State but as an Institution, an institution created by and embodying a wonderful system of ideas. In pursuance of such a plan, the forms which the Empire took in the several stages of its growth and decline must be briefly sketched. The characters and acts of the great men who founded, guided, and overthrew it must from time to time be touched upon. But the chief aim of the treatise will be to dwell more fully on the inner nature of the Empire, as the most signal instance of the fusion of Roman and Teutonic elements in modern civilization : to shew how such a combination was possible ; how Charles and Otto were led to revive the imperial title in the West; how far during the reigns of their successors it preserved the memory of its origin, and influenced the European commonwealth of nations.

Strictly speaking, it is from the year 800 A.D., when a King of the Franks was crowned Emperor of the Romans by Pope Leo III, that the beginning of the Holy Roman Empire must be dated. But in history there is nothing isolated, and just as to explain a modern Act of Parliament or a modern conveyance of lands we must go back to the feudal customs of the thirteenth century, so among the institutions of the Middle Ages there is scarcely one which can be understood until it is traced up either to classical or to primitive Teutonic antiquity. Such a mode of inquiry is most of all needful in the case of the Holy Empire, itself no more than a tradition, a fancied revival of departed glories. And thus, in order to make it clear out of what elements the imperial system was formed, we might be required to scrutinize the antiquities of the Christian Church ; to survey the constitution of Rome in the days when Rome was no more than the first of the Latin cities; nay, to travel back yet further to that Jewish theocratic polity whose influence on the minds of the mediæval priesthood was necessarily so profound. Practically, however, it may suffice to begin by glancing at the condition of the Roman world in the third and fourth centuries of the Christian era. We shall then see the old Empire with its scheme of absolutism fully matured; we shall mark how the new religion, rising in the midst of a hostile power, ends by embracing and transforming it; and we shall be in a position to understand what impression the whole huge fabric of secular and ecclesiastical government which Roman and Christian had piled up made upon the barbarian tribes who pressed into the charmed circle of the ancient civilization.

CHAPTER II.

THE ROMAN EMPIRE BEFORE THE INVASIONS OF THE BARBARIANS.

THAT ostentation of humility which the subtle policy of Augustus had conceived, and the jealous hypocrisy of Tiberius maintained, was gradually dropped by their successors, till despotism became at last recognised in principle as the government of the Roman Empire. With an aristocracy decayed, a populace degraded, an army no longer recruited from Italy, the semblance of liberty that yet survived might be swept away with impunity. Republican forms had never been known in the provinces at all, and the aspect which the imperial administration had originally assumed there, soon reacted on its position in the capital. Earlier rulers had disguised their supremacy by making a slavish senate the instrument of their more cruel or arbitrary acts. As time went on, even this veil was withdrawn; and in the age of Septimius Severus, the Emperor stood forth to the whole Roman world as the single centre and source of power and political action. The warlike character of the Roman state was preserved in his title of General; his provincial lieutenants were military governors; and a more terrible enforcement of the theory was found in his dependence on the army, at once the origin and support of all authority. But, as he united in himself every function of government, his sovereignty was civil as well as military. Laws emanated from him; all officials acted under his commission; the sanctity of his person bordered on divinity. This increased concentration of power was mainly required by the necessities of frontier defence, for within there was more decay than disaffection. Few troops were quartered through the country: few fortresses checked the march of armies in the struggles which placed Vespasian and Severus on the throne. The distant crash of war from the Rhine or the Euphrates was scarcely heard or heeded in the profound quiet of the Mediterranean coasts, where, with piracy, fleets had disappeared. No quarrels of race or religion disturbed that calm, for all national distinctions were becoming merged in the idea of a common Empire. The gradual extension of Roman citizenship through the *coloniæ*, the working of the equalized and equalizing Roman law, the even pressure of the government on all subjects, the movement of population caused by commerce and the slave traffic, were steadily assimilating the various peoples. Emperors who were for the most part natives of the provinces cared little to cherish Italy or conciliate Rome: it was their policy to keep open for every subject a career by whose freedom they had themselves risen to greatness, and to recruit the senate from the most illustrious families in the cities of Gaul, Spain, and Asia. The edict by which Caracalla extended to all natives of the Roman world the rights of Roman citizenship, though prompted by no motives of kindness, proved in the end a boon. Annihilating legal distinctions, it completed the work which trade and literature and toleration

Obliteration of national distinctions.

to all beliefs but one were already performing, and left,
so far as we can tell, only two nations still cherishing
a national feeling. The Jew was kept apart by his
religion: the Greek boasted his original intellectual superiority. Speculative philosophy lent her aid to this
general assimilation. Stoicism, with its doctrine of a
universal system of nature, made minor distinctions between man and man seem insignificant: and by its
teachers the idea of cosmopolitanism was for the first
time proclaimed. Alexandrian Neo-Platonism, uniting
the tenets of many schools, first bringing the mysticism
of the East into connection with the logical philosophies
of Greece, had opened up a new ground of agreement
or controversy for the minds of all the world. Yet
Rome's commanding position was scarcely shaken. Her
actual power was indeed confined within narrow limits.
Rarely were her senate and people permitted to choose
the sovereign: more rarely still could they control his
policy; neither law nor custom raised them above other
subjects, or accorded to them any advantage in the career
of civil or military ambition. As in time past Rome had
sacrificed domestic freedom that she might be the mistress
of others, so now to be universal, she, the conqueror, had
descended to the level of the conquered. But the sacrifice had not wanted its reward. From her came the
laws and the language that had overspread the world:
at her feet the nations laid the offerings of their labour:
she was the head of the Empire and of civilization, and
in riches, fame, and splendour far outshone as well the
cities of that time as the fabled glories of Babylon or
Persepolis.

Scarcely had these slowly working influences brought
about this unity, when other influences began to threaten

it. New foes assailed the frontiers; while the loosening of the structure within was shewn by the long struggles for power which followed the death or deposition of each successive emperor. In the period of anarchy after the fall of Valerian, generals were raised by their armies in every part of the Empire, and ruled great provinces as monarchs apart, owning no allegiance to the possessor of the capital.

The founding of the kingdoms of modern Europe might have been anticipated by two hundred years, had the barbarians been bolder, or had there not arisen in Diocletian a prince active and politic enough to bind up the fragments before they had lost all cohesion, meeting altered conditions by new remedies. By dividing and localizing authority, he confessed that the weaker heart could no longer make its pulsations felt to the body's extremities. He parcelled out the supreme power among four persons, and then sought to give it a factitious strength, by surrounding it with an oriental pomp which his earlier predecessors would have scorned. The sovereign's person became more sacred, and was removed further from the subject by the interposition of a host of officials. The prerogative of Rome was menaced by the rivalry of Nicomedia, and the nearer greatness of Milan. Constantine trod in the same path, extending the system of titles and functionaries, separating the civil from the military, placing counts and dukes along the frontiers and in the cities, making the household larger, its etiquette stricter, its offices more important, though to a Roman eye degraded by their attachment to the monarch's person. The crown became, for the first time, the fountain of honour. These changes brought little good. Heavier taxation depressed the aristocracy[a]: population decreased, agriculture withered, serfdom spread: it was found more difficult to raise native troops and to pay any troops whatever. The removal of the seat of power to Byzantium, if it prolonged the life of a part of the Empire, shook it as a whole, by making the separation of East and West inevitable. By it Rome's self-abnegation that she might Romanize the world, was completed; for though the new capital preserved her name, and followed her customs and precedents, yet now the imperial sway ceased to be connected with the city which had created it. Thus did the idea of Roman monarchy become more universal; for, having lost its local centre, it subsisted no longer historically, but, so to speak, naturally, as a part of an order of things which a change in external conditions seemed incapable of disturbing. Henceforth the Empire would be unaffected by the disasters of the city. And though, after the partition of the Empire had been confirmed by Valentinian, and finally settled on the death of Theodosius, the seat of the Western government was removed first to Milan and then to Ravenna, neither event destroyed Rome's prestige, nor the notion of a single imperial nationality common to all her subjects. The Syrian, the Pannonian, the Briton, the Spaniard, still called himself a Roman[b].

[a] According to the vicious financial system that prevailed, the *curiales* in each city were required to collect the taxes, and when there was a deficit, to supply it from their own property.

[b] See the eloquent passage of Claudian, *In secundum consulatum Stilichonis*, 129, *sqq.*, from which the following lines are taken (150–60):—

'Hæc est in gremio victos quæ sola recepit,
Humanumque genus communi nomine fovit,
Matris, non dominæ, ritu; civesque vocavit
Quos domuit, nexuque pio longinqua revinxit.
Hujus pacificis debemus moribus omnes
Quod veluti patriis regionibus utitur hospes:

For that nationality was now beginning to be supported by a new and vigorous power. The Emperors
had indeed opposed it as disloyal and revolutionary: had
more than once put forth their whole strength to root it
out. But the unity of the Empire, and the ease of communication through its parts, had favoured the spread of
Christianity: persecution had scattered the seeds more
widely, had forced on it a firm organization, had given it
martyr-heroes and a history. When Constantine, partly
perhaps from a genuine moral sympathy, yet doubtless
far more in the well-grounded belief that he had more
to gain from the zealous sympathy of its professors than
he could lose by the aversion of those who still cultivated
a languid paganism, took Christianity to be the religion
of the Empire, it was already a great political force, able,
and not more able than willing, to repay him by aid and
submission. Yet the league was struck in no mere mercenary spirit, for the league was inevitable. Of the evils
and dangers incident to the system then founded, there
was as yet no experience: of that antagonism between
Church and State which to a modern appears so natural,
there was not even an idea. Among the Jews, the State
had rested upon religion; among the Romans, religion
had been an integral part of the political constitution, a
matter far more of national or tribal or family feeling
than of personal[c]. Both in Israel and at Rome the
mingling of religious with civic patriotism had been har-

> Quod sedem mutare licet: quod cernere Thulen
> Lusus, et horrendos quondam penetrare recessus:
> Quod bibimus passim Rhodanum, potamus Oronten,
> Quod cuncti gens una sumus. Nec terminus unquam
> Romanæ ditionis erit.'

[c] In the Roman jurisprudence, *ius sacrum* is a branch of *ius
publicum.*

monious, giving strength and elasticity to the whole body politic. So perfect a union was now no longer possible in the Roman Empire, for the new faith had already a governing body of her own in those rulers and teachers whom the growth of sacramentalism, and of sacerdotalism its necessary consequence, was making every day more powerful, and marking off more sharply from the mass of the Christian people. Since therefore the ecclesiastical organization could not be identical with the civil, it became its counterpart. Suddenly called from danger and ignominy to the seat of power, and finding her inexperience perplexed by a sphere of action vast and varied, the Church was compelled to frame herself upon the model of the secular administration. Where her own machinery was defective, as in the case of doctrinal disputes affecting the whole Christian world, she sought the interposition of the sovereign; in all else she strove not to sink in, but to reproduce for herself the imperial system. And just as with the extension of the Empire all the independent rights of districts, towns, or tribes had disappeared, so now the primitive freedom and diversity of individual Christians and local Churches, already circumscribed by the frequent struggles against heresy, was finally overborne by the idea of one visible catholic Church, uniform in faith and ritual; uniform too in her relation to the civil power and the increasingly oligarchical character of her government. Thus, under the combined force of doctrinal theory and practical needs, there shaped itself a hierarchy of patriarchs, metropolitans, and bishops, their jurisdiction, although still chiefly spiritual, enforced by the laws of the State, their provinces and dioceses usually corresponding to the administrative divisions of the Empire. As no

patriarch yet enjoyed more than an honorary supremacy,
the head of the Church—so far as she could be said
to have a head—was virtually the Emperor himself.
The inchoate right to intermeddle in religious affairs
which he derived from the office of Pontifex Maximus
was readily admitted ; and the clergy, preaching the
duty of passive obedience now as it had been preached
in the days of Nero and Diocletian[d], were well pleased
to see him preside in councils, issue edicts against
heresy, and testify even by arbitrary measures his zeal
for the advancement of the faith and the overthrow of
pagan rites. But though the tone of the Church remained humble, her strength waxed greater, nor were
occasions wanting which revealed the future that was
in store for her. The resistance and final triumph of
Athanasius proved that the new society could put forth
a power of opinion such as had never been known before : the abasement of Theodosius the Emperor before
Ambrose the Archbishop admitted the supremacy of
spiritual authority. In the decrepitude of old institutions, in the barrenness of literature and the feebleness
of art, it was to the Church that the life and feelings
of the people sought more and more to attach themselves ; and when in the fifth century the horizon grew
black with clouds of ruin, those who watched with despair or apathy the approach of irresistible foes, fled for
comfort to the shrine of a religion which even those foes
revered.

But that which we are above all concerned to remark

---

[d] Tertullian, writing circ. A.D.
200, says : ‘Sed quid ego amplius
de religione atque pietate Chris-
tiana in imperatorem quem necesse
est suspiciamus ut eum quem Dominus noster elegerit. Et merito
dixerim, noster est magis Cæsar, ut
a nostro Deo constitutus.’—*Apolo-
get.* cap. 34.

here is, that this church system, demanding a more rigid uniformity in doctrine and organization, making more and more vital the notion of a visible body of worshippers united by participation in the same sacraments, maintained and propagated afresh the feeling of a single Roman people throughout the world. Christianity as well as civilization became conterminous with the Roman Empire[e].

CHAP. II.

It embraces and preserves the imperial idea.

[e] See the book of Optatus, bishop of Milevis, *Contra Donatistas.* 'Non enim respublica est in ecclesia, sed ecclesia in republica, id est, in imperio Romano, cum super imperatorem non sit nisi solus Deus:' (p. 999 of vol. ii. of Migne's *Patrologiæ Cursus completus.*) The treatise of Optatus is full of interest, as shewing the growth of the idea of the visible Church, and of the primacy of Peter's chair, as constituting its centre and representing its unity.

CHAPTER III.

THE BARBARIAN INVASIONS.

UPON a world so constituted did the barbarians of the North descend. From the dawn of history they shew as a dim background to the warmth and light of the Mediterranean coast, changing little while kingdoms rise and fall in the South: only thought on when some hungry swarm comes down to pillage or to settle. It is always as foes that they are known. The Romans never forgot the invasion of Brennus; and their fears, renewed by the irruption of the Cimbri and Teutones, could not let them rest till the extension of the frontier to the Rhine and the Danube removed Italy from immediate danger. A little more perseverance under Tiberius, or again under Hadrian, would probably have reduced all Germany as far as the Baltic and the Oder. But the politic or jealous advice of Augustus[a] was followed, and it was only along the frontiers that Roman arts and culture affected the Teutonic races. Commerce was brisk; Roman envoys penetrated the forests to the courts of rude chieftains; adventurous barbarians entered the provinces, sometimes to admire, oftener, like the brother of Arminius[b], to take service under the Roman flag, and rise to a distinction in the legion which some feud denied them at home. This

[a] 'Addiderat consilium coercendi intra terminos imperii.' — Tac. *Ann.* i. 2.　　　　　　　　　　[b] Tac. *Ann.* ii. 9.

was found even more convenient by the hirer than by the
employed; till by degrees barbarian mercenaries came
to form the largest, or at least the most effective, part of
the Roman armies. The body-guard of Augustus had
been so composed; the prætorians were generally selected
from the bravest frontier troops, most of them German;
the practice could not but increase with the extinction of
the free peasantry, the growth of villenage, and the ef-
feminacy of all classes. Emperors who were, like Maximin, themselves foreigners, encouraged a system by
whose means they had risen, and whose advantages they
knew. After Constantine, the barbarians form the majority of the troops; after Theodosius, a Roman is the
exception. The soldiers of the Eastern Empire in the
time of Arcadius are almost all Goths, vast bodies of
whom had been settled in the provinces; while in the
West, Stilicho [c] can oppose Rhodogast only by summoning the German auxiliaries from the frontiers. Along
with this practice there had grown up another, which did
still more to make the barbarians feel themselves members
of the Roman state. Whatever the pride of the old republic might assert, the maxim of the Empire had always
been that birth and race should exclude no subject from
any post which his abilities deserved. This principle,
which had removed all obstacles from the path of the
Spaniard Trajan, the Pannonian Maximin, the Numidian
Philip, was afterwards extended to the conferring of
honour and power on persons who did not even profess
to have passed through the grades of Roman service, but
remained leaders of their own tribes. Ariovistus had been
soothed by the title of Friend of the Roman People; in

CHAP. III.

*Admitted
to Roman
titles and
honours.*

[c] Stilicho, the bulwark of the Empire, seems to have been himself
a Vandal by extraction.

the third century the insignia of the consulship [d] were conferred on a Herulian chief: Crocus and his Alemanni entered as an independent body into the service of Rome; along the Rhine whole tribes received, under the name of Laeti, lands within the provinces on condition of military service; and the foreign aid which the Sarmatian had proffered to Vespasian against his rival, and Marcus Aurelius had indignantly rejected in the war with Cassius, became the usual, at last the sole support of the Empire, in civil as well as in external strife.

Thus in many ways was the old antagonism broken down—Romans admitting barbarians. to rank and office, barbarians catching something of the manners and culture of their neighbours.   And thus when the final movement came, and the Teutonic tribes slowly established themselves through the provinces, they entered not as savage strangers, but as colonists knowing something of the system into which they came, and not unwilling to be considered its members ; despising the degenerate provincials who struck no blow in their own defence, but full of respect for the majestic power which had for so many centuries confronted and instructed them.

Their feelings towards the Roman Empire.

Great during all these ages, but greatest when they were actually traversing and settling in the Empire, must have been the impression which its elaborate machinery of government and mature civilization made upon the minds of the Northern invaders.   With arms whose fabrication they had learned from their foes, these dwellers in the forest conquered well-tilled fields, and entered towns whose busy workshops, marts stored with the productions of distant countries, and palaces rich in monuments of art, equally roused their wonder.   To the beauty of

[d] Of course not the consulship itself, but the *ornamenta consularia.*

statuary or painting they might often be blind, but the
rudest mind must have been awed by the massive piles
with which vanity or devotion, or the passion for amusement, had adorned Milan and Verona, Arles, Treves, and
Bordeaux. A deeper awe would strike them as they
gazed on the crowding worshippers and stately ceremonial of Christianity, most unlike their own rude sacrifices.
The exclamation of the Goth Athanaric, when led into
the market-place of Constantinople, may stand for the
feelings of his nation: 'Without doubt the Emperor is a
God upon earth, and he who attacks him is guilty of his
own blood [e].'

The social and political system, with its cultivated language and literature, into which they came, would impress
fewer of the conquerors, but by those few would be admired beyond all else. Its regular organization supplied
what they most needed and could least construct for
themselves, and hence it was that the greatest among
them were the most desirous to preserve it. The Mongol
Attila excepted, there is among these terrible hosts no
destroyer; the wish of each leader is to maintain the existing order, to spare life, to respect every work of skill
and labour, above all to perpetuate the methods of
Roman administration, and rule the people as the deputy
or successor of their Emperor. Titles conferred by him
were the highest honours they knew: they were also the
only means of acquiring something like a legal claim to
the obedience of the subject, and of turning a patriarchal
or military chieftainship into the regular sway of an
hereditary monarch. Civilis had long since endeavoured
to govern his Batavians as a Roman general [f]. Alaric

*Their desire
to preserve
its institu-
tions.*

---

[e] Jornandes, *De Rebus Geticis*, cap. 28.
[f] Tac. *Hist.* i. and iv.

C

became master-general of the armies of Illyricum. Clovis exulted in the consulship; his son Theodebert received Provence, the conquest of his own battle-axe, as the gift of Justinian. Sigismund the Burgundian king, created count and patrician by the Emperor Anastasius, professed the deepest gratitude and the firmest faith to that Eastern court which was absolutely powerless to help or to hurt him. 'My people is yours,' he writes, 'and to rule them delights me less than to serve you; the hereditary devotion of my race to Rome has made us account those the highest honours which your military titles convey; we have always preferred what an Emperor gave to all that our ancestors could bequeath. In ruling our nation we hold ourselves but your lieutenants: you, whose divinely-appointed sway no barrier bounds, whose blessed beams shine from the Bosphorus into distant Gaul, employ us to administer the remoter regions of your Empire: your world is our fatherland ᵍ.' A contemporary historian has recorded the remarkable disclosure of his own thoughts and purposes, made by one of the ablest

---

ᵍ 'Vester quidem est populus meus sed me plus servire vobis quam illi præesse delectat. Traxit istud a proavis generis mei apud vos decessoresque vestros semper animo Romana devotio, ut illa nobis magis claritas putaretur, quam vestra per militiæ titulos porrigeret celsitudo : cunctisque auctoribus meis semper magis ambitum est quod a principibus sumerent quam quod a patribus attulissent. Cumque gentem nostram videamur regere, non aliud nos quam milites vestros credimus ordinari. . . . Per nos administratis remotarum spatia regionum : patria nostra vester orbis est. Tangit Galliam suam lumen orientis, et radius qui illis partibus oriri creditur, hic refulget. Dominationem vobis divinitus præstitam obex nulla concludit, nec ullis provinciarum terminis diffusio felicium sceptrorum limitatur. Salvo divinitatis honore sit dictum.'— Letter printed among the works of Avitus, Bishop of Vienne. (Migne's *Patrologia*, vol. lix. p. 285.)

This letter, as its style shews, is the composition not of Sigismund himself, but of Avitus, writing on Sigismund's behalf. But this makes it scarcely less valuable evidence of the feelings of the time.

of the barbarian chieftains, Athaulf the Visigoth, the brother-in-law and successor of Alaric. 'It was at first my wish to destroy the Roman name, and erect in its place a Gothic empire, taking to myself the place and the powers of Cæsar Augustus. But when experience taught me that the untameable barbarism of the Goths would not suffer them to live beneath the sway of law, and that the abolition of the institutions on which the state rested would involve the ruin of the state itself, I chose the glory of renewing and maintaining by Gothic strength the fame of Rome, desiring to go down to posterity as the restorer of that Roman power which it was beyond my power to replace. Wherefore I avoid war and strive for peace [h].'

Historians have remarked how valuable must have been the skill of Roman officials to princes who from leaders of tribes were become rulers of wide lands; and in particular how indispensable the aid of the Christian bishops, the intellectual aristocracy of their new subjects, whose advice could alone guide their policy and conciliate the vanquished. Not only is this true; it is but a small part of the truth; one form of that manifold and overpowering influence which the old system exercised over its foes not less than its own children. For it is hardly too much to say that the thought of antagonism to the Empire and the

[h] 'Referre solitus est (*sc.* Ataulphus) se in primis ardenter inhiasse: ut obliterato Romanorum nomine Romanum omne solum Gothorum imperium et faceret et vocaret: essetque, ut vulgariter loquar, Gothia quod Romania fuisset; fieretque nunc Ataulphus quod quondam Cæsar Augustus. At ubi multa experientia probavisset, neque Gothos ullo modo parere legibus posse propter effrenatam barbariem, neque reipublicæ interdici leges oportere sine quibus respublica non est respublica; elegisse se saltem, ut gloriam sibi de restituendo in integrum augendoque Romano nomine Gothorum viribus quæreret, habereturque apud posteros Romanæ restitutionis auctor postquam esse non potuerat immutator. Ob hoc abstinere a bello, ob hoc inhiare paci nitebatur.'—Orosius, vii. 43.

CHAP. III.

wish to extinguish it never crossed the mind of the barbarians[i]. The conception of that Empire was too universal, too august, too enduring. It was everywhere around them, and they could remember no time when it had not been so. It had no association of people or place whose fall could seem to involve that of the whole fabric; it had that connection with the Christian Church which made it all-embracing and venerable.

The belief in its eternity.

There were especially two ideas whereon it rested, and from which it obtained a peculiar strength and a peculiar direction. The one was the belief that as the dominion of Rome was universal, so must it be eternal. Nothing like it had been seen before. The empire of Alexander had lasted a short lifetime; and within its wide compass were included many arid wastes, and many tracts where none but the roving savage had ever set foot. That of the Italian city had for fourteen generations embraced all the most wealthy and populous regions of the civilized world, and had laid the foundations of its power so deep that they seemed destined to last for ever. If Rome moved slowly for a time, her foot was always planted firmly: the ease and swiftness of her later conquests proved the solidity of the earlier; and to her, more justly than to his own city, might the boast of the Athenian historian be applied: that she advanced farthest in prosperity, and in adversity drew back the least. From the end of the republican period her poets, her orators, her jurists, ceased not to repeat the claim of world-dominion, and confidently predict its eternity[k]. The proud belief of

[i] Athaulf formed only to abandon it.

[k] See, among other passages, Varro, *De lingua Latina*, iv. 34;

Cic., *Pro Domo*, 33; and in the *Corpus Iuris Civilis*, Dig. i. 5, 17; l. 1, 33; xiv. 2, 9; quoted by Ægidi, *Der Fürstenrath nach dem*

his countrymen which Virgil had expressed—

> 'His ego nec metas rerum, nec tempora pono:
> Imperium sine fine dedi'—

was shared by the early Christians when they prayed for the persecuting power whose fall would bring Antichrist upon earth. Lactantius writes: 'When Rome the head of the world shall have fallen, who can doubt that the end is come of human things, aye, of the earth itself. She, she alone is the state by which all things are upheld even until now; wherefore let us make prayers and supplications to the God of heaven, if indeed his decrees and his purposes can be delayed, that that hateful tyrant come not sooner than we look for, he for whom are reserved fearful deeds, who shall pluck out that eye in whose extinction the world itself shall perish [1].' With the

Luneviller Frieden. The phrase 'urbs æterna' appears in a novel issued by Valentinian III.

Tertullian speaks of Rome as 'civitas sacrosancta.'

[1] Lact. *Divin. Instit.* vii. 25: 'Etiam res ipsa declarat lapsum ruinamque rerum brevi fore: nisi quod incolumi urbe Roma nihil istiusmodi videtur esse metuendum. At vero cum caput illud orbis occiderit, et ῥύμη esse cœperit quod Sibyllæ fore aiunt, quis dubitet venisse iam finem rebus humanis, orbique terrarum? Illa, illa est civitas quæ adhuc sustentat omnia, precandusque nobis et adorandus est Deus cœli si tamen statuta eius et placita differri possunt, ne citius quam putemus tyrannus ille abominabilis veniat qui tantum facinus moliatur, ac lumen illud effodiat cuius interitu mundus ipse lapsurus est.'

Cf. Tertull. *Apolog.* cap. xxxii:

' Est et alia maior necessitas nobis orandi pro imperatoribus, etiam pro omni statu imperii rebusque Romanis, qui vim maximam universo orbi imminentem ipsamque clausulam sæculi acerbitates horrendas comminantem Romani imperii commeatu scimus retardari.' Also the same writer, *Ad Scapulam*, cap. ii: ' Christianus sciens imperatorem a Deo suo constitui, necesse est ut ipsum diligat et revereatur et honoret et salvum velit cum toto Romano imperio quousque sæculum stabit: tamdiu enim stabit.' So too the author—now usually supposed to be Hilary the Deacon—of the Commentary on the Pauline Epistles ascribed to S. Ambrose: ' Non prius veniet Dominus quam regni Romani defectio fiat, et appareat antichristus qui interficiet sanctos, reddita Romanis libertate, sub suo tamen nomine.'—Ad II Thess. ii. 4, 7.

triumph of Christianity this belief had found a new basis. For as the Empire had decayed, the Church had grown stronger; and now while the one, trembling at the approach of the destroyer, saw province after province torn away, the other, rising in stately youth, prepared to fill her place and govern in her name, and in doing so, to adopt and sanctify and propagate anew the notion of a universal and unending state.

Sanctity of the imperial name.

The second chief element in this conception was the association of such a state with one irresponsible governor, the Emperor. The hatred to the name of King, which their earliest political struggles had left in the Romans, by obliging their ruler to take a new and strange title, marked him off from all the other sovereigns of the world. To the provincials especially he became an awful impersonation of the great machine of government which moved above and around them. It was not merely that he was, like a modern king, the centre of power and the dispenser of honour: his pre-eminence, broken by no comparison with other princes, by the ascending ranks of no aristocracy, had in it something almost supernatural. The right of legislation had become vested in him alone: the decrees of the people, and resolutions of the senate, and edicts of the magistrates were, during the last three centuries, replaced by imperial constitutions; his domestic council, the consistory, was the supreme court of appeal; his interposition, like that of some terrestrial Providence, was invoked, and legally provided so to be, to reverse or overleap the ordinary rules of law[m]. From the time of Julius and Augustus his person had been

---

[m] For example, by the 'restitutio natalium,' and the 'adrogatio per rescriptum principis,' or, as it is expressed, 'per sacrum oraculum.'

hallowed by the office of chief pontiff[n] and the tribunician power; to swear by his head was considered the most solemn of all oaths[o]; his effigy was sacred[p], even on a coin; to him or to his Genius temples were erected and divine honours paid while he lived[q]; and when, as it was expressed, he ceased to be among men, the title of Divus was accorded to him, after a solemn consecration[r]. In the confused multiplicity of mythologies, the worship of the Emperor was the only worship common to the whole Roman world, and was therefore that usually proposed as a test to the Christians on their trial. Under the new religion the form of adoration vanished, the sentiment of reverence remained: the right to control Church as well as State, admitted at Nicæa, and habitually exercised by the sovereigns of Constantinople, made the Emperor hardly less essential to the new conception of a world-wide Christian monarchy than he had been to the military despotism of old. These considerations explain why the men of the fifth century, clinging to preconceived ideas, refused to believe in that dissolution of the Empire which they saw with their own eyes.

325

[n] Even the Christian Emperors took the title of Pontifex Maximus, till Gratian refused it: ἀθέμιστον εἶναι Χριστιανῷ τὸ σχῆμα νομίσας. —Zosimus, lib. iv. cap. 36.

[o] 'Maiore formidine et callidiore timiditate Cæsarem observatis quam ipsum ex Olympo Iovem, et merito, si sciatis. . . . Citius denique apud vos per omnes Deos quam per unum genium Cæsaris peieratur.'—Tertull. *Apolog.* c. xxviii.

Cf. Zos. v. 51: εἰ μὲν γὰρ πρὸς τὸν θεὸν τετυχήκει διδόμενος ὅρκος, ἦν ἂν ὡς εἰκὸς παριδεῖν ἐνδίδοντας τῇ τοῦ θεοῦ φιλανθρωπίᾳ τὴν ἐπὶ

τῇ ἀσεβείᾳ συγγνώμην. ἐπεὶ δὲ κατὰ τὴν τοῦ βασιλέως ὁμωμόκεσαν κεφαλῆς, οὐκ εἶναι θεμιτὸν αὐτοῖς εἰς τὸν τοσοῦτον ὅρκον ἐξαμαρτεῖν.

[p] Tac. *Ann.* i. 73; iii. 38, etc.

[q] It is curious that this should have begun in the first years of the Empire. See, among other passages that might be cited from the Augustan poets, Virg. *Georg.* i. 42; iv. 462; Hor. *Od.* iii. 3, 11; Ovid, *Epp. ex Ponto,* iv. 9. 105.

[r] Hence Vespasian's dying jest, 'Ut puto, deus fio.'

Because it could not die, it lived. And there was in the slowness of the change and its external aspect, as well as in the fortunes of the capital, something to favour the illusion. The Roman name was shared by every subject; the Roman city was no longer the seat of government, nor did her capture extinguish the imperial power, for the maxim was now accepted, Where the Emperor is, there is Rome[s]. But her continued existence, not permanently occupied by any conqueror, striking the nations with an awe which the history or the external splendours of Constantinople, Milan, or Ravenna could nowise inspire, was an ever new assertion of the endurance of the Roman race and dominion. Dishonoured and defenceless, the spell of her name was still strong enough to arrest the conqueror in the moment of triumph. The irresistible impulse that drew Alaric was one of glory or revenge, not of destruction: the Hun turned back from Aquileia with a vague fear upon him: the Ostrogoth adorned and protected his splendid prize.

Last days of the Western Empire.

In the history of the last days of the Western Empire, two points deserve special remark: its continued union with the Eastern branch, and the way in which its ideal dignity was respected while its representatives were despised. After Stilicho's death, and Alaric's invasion, its fall was a question of time. While one by one the provinces were abandoned by the central government, left either to be occupied by invading tribes or to maintain a precarious independence, like Britain and Armorica[t], by means of municipal unions, Italy lay at the mercy of the barbarian auxiliaries and was governed by their leaders. The degenerate line of Theodosius might

[s] ὅπου ἂν ὁ βασιλεὺς ᾖ, ἐκεῖ ἡ Ῥώμη.——Herodian.
[t] If the accounts we find of the Armorican republic can be trusted.

have seemed to reign by hereditary right, but after their extinction in Valentinian III each phantom Emperor—Maximus, Avitus, Majorian, Anthemius, Olybrius—received the purple from the haughty Ricimer, general of the troops, only to be stripped of it when he presumed to forget his dependence. Though the division between Arcadius and Honorius had definitely severed the two realms for administrative purposes, they were still supposed to constitute a single Empire, and the rulers of the East interfered more than once to raise to the Western throne princes they could not protect upon it. Ricimer's insolence quailed before the shadowy grandeur of the imperial title: his ambition, and Gundobald his successor's, were bounded by the name of patrician. The bolder genius of Odoacer[u], general of the barbarian auxiliaries, resolved to abolish an empty pageant, and extinguish the title and office of Emperor of the West. Yet over him too the spell had power; and as the Gaulish warrior had gazed on the silent majesty of the senate in a deserted city, so the Herulian revered the power before which the world had bowed, and though there was no force to check or to affright him, shrank from grasping in his own barbarian hand the sceptre of the Cæsars. When, at Odoacer's bidding, Romulus Augustulus, the boy whom a whim of fate had chosen to be the last native

[u] Odoacer or Odovaker, as it seems his name ought to be written, is usually, but incorrectly, described as a King of the Heruli, who led his people into Italy and overthrew the Empire of the West; others call him King of the Rugii, or Skyrri, or Turcilingi. The truth seems to be that he was not a king at all, but the son of a Skyrrian chieftain (Edecon, known as one of the envoys whom Attila sent to Constantinople), whose personal merits made him chosen by the barbarian auxiliaries to be their leader. The Skyrri were a small tribe, apparently akin to the more powerful Heruli, whose name is often extended to them.

Cæsar of Rome, had formally announced his resignation to the senate, a deputation from that body proceeded to the Eastern court to lay the insignia of royalty at the feet of the Eastern Emperor Zeno. The West, they declared, no longer required an Emperor of its own; one monarch sufficed for the world; Odoacer was qualified by his wisdom and courage to be the protector of their state, and upon him Zeno was entreated to confer the title of patrician and the administration of the Italian provinces[x]. The Emperor granted what he could not refuse, and Odoacer, taking the title of King[y], continued the consular office, respected the civil and ecclesiastical institutions of his subjects, and ruled for fourteen years as the nominal vicar of the Eastern Emperor. There was thus legally no extinction of the Western Empire at all, but only a reunion of East and West. In form, and to some extent also in the belief of men, things now reverted to their state during the first two centuries of the Empire, save that Byzantium instead of Rome was the centre of the civil government. The joint tenancy which had been conceived by Diocletian, carried further by Constantine, renewed under Valentinian I and again at the death of Theodosius, had come to an end; once more did a single Emperor sway

---

[x] Αὔγουστος ὁ Ὀρέστου υἱὸς ἀκούσας Ζήνωνα πάλιν τὴν βασιλείαν ἀνακεκτῆσθαι τῆς ἔω. . . . ἠνάγκασε τὴν βουλὴν ἀποστεῖλαι πρεσβείαν Ζήνωνι σημαίνουσαν ὡς ἰδίας μὲν αὐτοῖς βασιλείας οὐ δέοι, κοινὸς δὲ ἀποχρήσει μόνος ὢν αὐτοκράτωρ ἐπ' ἀμφοτέροις τοῖς πέρασι. τὸν μέντοι Ὀδόαχον ὑπ' αὐτῶν προβεβλῆσθαι ἱκανὸν ὄντα σώζειν τὰ παρ' αὐτοῖς πράγματα πολιτικὴν ἐχὼν νοῦν καὶ σύνεσιν ὁμοῦ καὶ μάχιμον. καὶ δεῖσθαι τοῦ Ζήνωνος πατρικίου τε αὐτῷ ἀποστεῖλαι ἀξίαν καὶ τὴν τῶν Ἰτάλων τουτῷ ἐφεῖναι διοίκησιν.— Malchus ap. Photium in *Corp. Hist. Byzant.*

[y] Not king of Italy, as is often said. The barbarian kings did not for several centuries employ territorial titles; the title 'king of France,' for instance, was first used by Henry IV. Jornandes tells us that Odoacer never so much as assumed the insignia of royalty.

the sceptre of the world, and head an undivided Catholic Church[z]. To those who lived at the time, this year (476 A.D.) was no such epoch as it has since become, nor was any impression made on men's minds commensurate with the real significance of the event. For though it did not destroy the Empire in idea, nor wholly even in fact, its consequences were from the first great. It hastened the development of a Latin as opposed to Greek and Oriental forms of Christianity: it emancipated the Popes: it gave a new character to the projects and government of the Teutonic rulers of the West. But the importance of remembering its formal aspect to those who witnessed it will be felt as we approach the era when the Empire was revived by Charles the Frank.

Odoacer's monarchy was not more oppressive than those of his neighbours in Gaul, Spain, and Africa. But the mercenary *fœderati* who supported it were a loose swarm of predatory tribes: themselves without cohesion, they could take no firm root in Italy. During the eighteen years of his reign no progress seems to have been made towards the re-organization of society; and the first real attempt to blend the peoples and maintain the traditions of Roman wisdom in the hands of a new and vigorous race was reserved for a more famous chieftain, the greatest of all the barbarian conquerors, the forerunner of the first barbarian Emperor, Theodoric the Ostrogoth. The aim of his reign, though he professed allegiance to the Eastern court which had favoured his invasion[a], was the establishment of a national monarchy in Italy. Brought up as a hostage in the court of Byzan-

CHAP. III.

Odoacer.

Theodoric.

---

[z] Sismondi, *Histoire de la Chute de l'Empire Occidentale.*

[a] 'Nil deest nobis imperio vestro famulantibus.'—Theodoric to Zeno: Jornandes, *De Rebus Geticis*, cap. 57.

tium, he learnt to know the advantages of an orderly and cultivated society and the principles by which it must be maintained; called in early manhood to roam as a warrior-chief over the plains of the Danube, he acquired along with the arts of command a sense of the superiority of his own people in valour and energy and truth. When the defeat and death of Odoacer had left the peninsula at his mercy, he sought no further conquest, easy as it would have been to tear away new provinces from the Eastern realm, but strove only to preserve and strengthen the ancient polity of Rome, to breathe into her decaying institutions the spirit of a fresh life, and without endangering the military supremacy of his own Goths, to conciliate by indulgence and gradually raise to the level of their masters the degenerate population of Italy. The Gothic nation appears from the first less cruel in war and more prudent in council than any of their Germanic brethren[b]: all that was most noble among them shone forth now in the rule of the greatest of the Amali. From his palace at Verona[c], commemorated in the song of the Nibelungs, he

[b] 'Unde et pæne omnibus barbaris Gothi sapientiores exstiterunt Græcisque pæne consimiles.' — Jorn. cap. 5.

[c] Theodoric (Thiodorich) seems to have resided usually at Ravenna, where he died and was buried; a remarkable building which tradition points out as his tomb stands a little way out of the town, near the railway station, but the porphyry sarcophagus, in which his body is supposed to have lain, has been removed thence, and may be seen built up into the wall of the building called his palace, situated close to the church of Sant' Apollinare, and not far from the tomb of Dante. There does not appear to be any sufficient authority for attributing this building to Ostrogothic times; it is very different from the representation of Theodoric's palace which we have in the contemporary mosaics of Sant' Apollinare in urbe.

In the German legends, however, Theodoric is always the prince of Verona (Dietrich von Berne), no doubt because that city was better known to the Teutonic nations, and because it was thither that he moved his court when transalpine affairs required his attention. His castle there stood in the old town on the left bank of the Adige, on the height now occupied by the citadel;

issued equal laws for Roman and Goth, and bade the intruder, if he must occupy part of the lands, at least respect the goods and the person of his fellow-subject. Jurisprudence and administration remained in native hands: two annual consuls, one named by Theodoric, the other by the Eastern monarch, presented an image of the ancient state; and while agriculture and the arts revived in the provinces, Rome herself celebrated the visits of a master who provided for the wants of her people and preserved with care the monuments of her former splendour. With peace and plenty men's minds took hope, and the study of letters revived. The last gleam of classical literature gilds the reign of the barbarian. By the consolidation of the two races under one wise government, Italy might have been spared six hundred years of gloom and degradation. It was not so to be. Theodoric was tolerant, but toleration was itself a crime in the eyes of his orthodox subjects: the Arian Goths were and remained strangers and enemies among the Catholic Italians. Scarcely had the sceptre passed from the hands of Theodoric to his unworthy offspring, when Justinian, who had viewed with jealousy the greatness of his nominal lieutenant, determined to assert his dormant rights over Italy; its people welcomed Belisarius as a deliverer, and in the struggle that followed the race and name of the Ostrogoths perished for ever. Thus again reunited in fact, as it had been all the while united in name, to the Roman Empire, the peninsula was divided into counties and dukedoms, and obeyed the exarch of Ravenna, viceroy of the Byzantine court, till the arrival of the Lombards in A.D. 568

Italy reconquered by Justinian.

it is doubtful whether any traces of it remain, for the old foundations which we now see may have belonged to the fortress erected by Gian Galeazzo Visconti in the fourteenth century.

*The Trans-
alpine pro-
vinces.*

drove him from some districts, and left him only a feeble
authority in the rest.

Beyond the Alps, though the Roman population had
now ceased to seek help from the Eastern court, the
Empire's rights still subsisted in theory, and were never
legally extinguished. As has been said, they were admitted by the conquerors themselves: by Athaulf, when
he reigned in Aquitaine as the vicar of Honorius, and
recovered Spain from the Suevi to restore it to its ancient
masters; by the Visigothic kings of Spain, when they
permitted the Mediterranean cities to send tribute to
Byzantium; by Clovis, when, after the representatives of
the old government, Syagrius and the Armorican cities,
had been overpowered or absorbed, he received with delight from the Eastern emperor Anastasius the grant of a
Roman dignity to confirm his possession. Arrayed like a
Fabius or Valerius in the consul's embroidered robe, the
Sicambrian chieftain rode through the streets of Tours,
while the shout of the provincials hailed him Augustus [d].
They already obeyed him, but his power was now legal-
ised in their eyes, and it was not without a melancholy
pride that they saw the terrible conqueror himself yield to
the spell of the Roman name, and do homage to the
enduring majesty of their legitimate sovereign [e].

*Lingering
influences
of Rome.*

Yet the severed limbs of the Empire forgot by degrees

[d] 'Igitur Chlodovechus ab imperatore Anastasio codicillos de
consulatu accepit, et in basilica
beati Martini tunica blatea indutus
est et chlamyde, imponens vertici
diadema . . . et ab ea die tanquam
consul aut (= et) Augustus est voci-
tatus.'—Gregory of Tours, ii. 58.

[e] Sir F. Palgrave (*English Commonwealth*) considers this grant as

equivalent to a formal ratification
of Clovis' rule in Gaul. Hallam
rates its importance lower (*Middle
Ages*, note iii. to chap. i.). Taken
in connection with the grant of
south-eastern Gaul to Theodebert
by Justinian, it may fairly be held
to shew that the influence of the
Empire was still felt in these distant provinces.

their original unity. As in the breaking up of the old
society, which we trace from the sixth to the eighth
century, rudeness and ignorance grew apace, as language
and manners were changed by the infiltration of Teutonic
settlers, as men's thoughts and hopes and interests were
narrowed by isolation from their fellows, as the organization of the Roman province and the Germanic tribe alike
dissolved into a chaos whence the new order began to
shape itself, dimly and doubtfully as yet, the memory of
the old Empire, its symmetry, its sway, its civilization,
must needs wane and fade. It might have perished altogether but for the two enduring witnesses Rome had left
—her Church and her Law. The barbarians had at first
associated Christianity with the Romans from whom they
learned it: the Romans had used it as their only bulwark
against oppression. The hierarchy were the natural leaders
of the people, and the necessary councillors of the king.
Their power grew with the extinction of civil government
and the spread of superstition; and when the Frank found
it too valuable to be abandoned to the vanquished people,
he insensibly acquired the feelings and policy of the order
he entered.

As the Empire fell to pieces, and the new kingdoms
which the conquerors had founded themselves began to
dissolve, the Church clung more closely to her unity of
faith and discipline, the common bond of all Christian men. That unity must have a centre, that centre
was Rome. A succession of able and zealous pontiffs
extended her influence (the sanctity and the writings of
Gregory the Great were famous through all the West):
never occupied by barbarians, she retained her peculiar
character and customs, and laid the foundations of a
power over men's souls more durable than that which she

CHAP. III.

Religion.

*Jurispru-
dence.*

CHAP. III.

had lost over their bodies [f]. Only second in importance to this influence was that which was exercised by the permanence of the old law, and of its creature the municipality. The barbarian invaders retained the customs of their ancestors, characteristic memorials of a rude people, as we see them in the Salic law or in the ordinances of Ina and Alfred. But the subject population and the clergy continued to be governed by that elaborate system which the genius and labour of many generations had raised to be the most lasting monument of Roman greatness.

The civil law had maintained itself in Spain and Southern Gaul, nor was it utterly forgotten even in the North, in Britain, on the borders of Germany. Revised editions of the Theodosian code were issued by the Visigothic and Burgundian princes. For some centuries it was the patrimony of the subject population everywhere, and in Aquitaine and Italy has outlived feudalism. The presumption in later times was that all men were to be judged by it who could not be proved to be subject to some other [g]. Its phrases, its forms, its courts, its subtlety and precision, all recalled the strong and refined society which had produced it. Other motives, as well as those of kindness to their subjects, made the new kings favour it; for it exalted their prerogative, and the submission enjoined by it on one class of their subjects soon

[f] Even so early as the middle of the fifth century, S. Leo the Great could say to the Roman people, 'Isti (sc. Petrus et Paulus) sunt qui te ad hanc gloriam provexerunt ut gens sancta, populus electus, civitas sacerdotalis et regia, per sacram B. Petri sedem caput orbis effecta latius præsideres religione divina quam dominatione terrena.' — *Sermon on the feast of SS. Peter and Paul.* (Opp. *ap.* Migne tom. i. p. 336.)

[g] 'Ius Romanum est adhuc in viridi observantia et eo iure præsumitur quilibet vivere nisi adversum probetur.'—Maranta, quoted by Marquard Freher.

came to be demanded from the other, by their own laws the equals of the prince. Considering attentively how many of the old institutions continued to subsist, and studying the feelings of that time, as they are faintly preserved in its scanty records, it seems hardly too much to say that in the eighth century the Roman Empire still existed in the West: existed in men's minds as a power weakened, delegated, suspended, but not destroyed.

It is easy for those who read the history of an age in the light of those that followed it, to perceive that in this men erred; that the tendency of events was wholly different; that society had entered on a new phase, wherein every change did more to localize authority and strengthen the aristocratic principle at the expense of the despotic. We can see that other forms of life, more full of promise for the distant future, had already begun to shew themselves: they—with no type of power or beauty, but that which had filled the imagination of their forefathers, and now loomed on them grander than ever through the mist of centuries—mistook, as it has been said of Rienzi in later days, memories for hopes, and sighed only for the renewal of its strength. Events were at hand by which these hopes seemed destined to be gratified.

D

CHAPTER IV.

RESTORATION OF THE WESTERN EMPIRE.

It was towards Rome as their ecclesiastical capital that the thoughts and hopes of the men of the sixth and seventh centuries were constantly directed. Yet not from Rome, feeble and corrupt, nor on the exhausted soil of Italy, was the deliverer to arise. Just when, as we may suppose, the vision of a renewal of imperial authority in the Western provinces was beginning to vanish away, there appeared in the furthest corner of Europe, sprung of a race but lately brought within the pale of civilization, a line of chieftains devoted to the service-of the Holy See, and among them one whose power, good fortune, and heroic character pointed him out as worthy of a dignity to which doctrine and tradition had attached a sanctity almost divine.

The Franks. Of the new monarchies that had risen on the ruins of Rome, that of the Franks was by far the greatest. In the third century they appear, with Saxons, Alemanni, and Thuringians, as one of the greatest German tribe leagues. The Sicambri (for it seems probable that this famous race was a chief source of the Frankish nation) had now laid aside their former hostility to Rome, and her future representatives were thenceforth, with few intervals, her faithful allies. Many of their chiefs rose to high place: Malarich receives from Jovian the charge of the Western provinces; Bauto and Mellobaudes figure in the days of Theodosius and his sons; Meroveus (if Meroveus be a real name) fights under Aetius against Attila in the great battle of Chalons; his countrymen endeavour in vain to save Gaul from the Suevi and Burgundians. Not till the Empire was evidently helpless did they claim a share of the booty; then Clovis, or Chlodovech, chief of the Salian tribe, leaving his kindred the Ripuarians in their seats on the lower Rhine, advances from Flanders to wrest Gaul from the barbarian nations which had entered it some sixty years before. Few conquerors have had a career of more unbroken success. By the defeat of the Roman governor Syagrius he was left master of the northern provinces: the Burgundian kingdom in the valley of the Rhone was in no long time reduced to dependence: last of all, the Visigothic power was overthrown in one great battle, and Aquitaine added to the dominions of Clovis. Nor were the Frankish arms less prosperous on the other side of the Rhine. The victory of Tolbiac led to the submission of the Alemanni: their allies the Bavarians followed, and when the Thuringian power had been broken by Theodorich I (son of Clovis), the Frankish league embraced all the tribes of western and southern Germany. The state thus formed, stretching from the Bay of Biscay to the Inn and the Ems, was of course in no sense a French, that is to say, a Gallic monarchy. Nor, although the widest and strongest empire that had yet been founded by a Teutonic race, was it, under the Merovingian kings, a united kingdom at. all, but rather a congeries of principalities, held together by the predominance of a single nation and a single family, who ruled in Gaul as masters over a subject race, and in Germany exercised a sort of hegemony among kindred and scarcely inferior tribes. But towards the middle of the eighth century a change began. Under the rule of Pipin of Herstal and his son

Charles Martel, mayors of the palace to the last feeble Merovingians, the Austrasian Franks in the lower Rhineland became acknowledged heads of the nation, and were able, while establishing a firmer government at home, to direct its whole strength in projects of foreign ambition. The form those projects took arose from a circumstance which has not yet been mentioned. It was not solely or even chiefly to their own valour that the Franks owed their past greatness and the yet loftier future which awaited them, it was to the friendship of the clergy and the favour of the Apostolic See. The other Teutonic nations, Goths, Vandals, Burgundians, Suevians, Lombards, had been most of them converted by Arian missionaries who proceeded from the Roman Empire during the short period when Arian doctrines were in the ascendant. The Franks, who were among the latest converts, were Catholics from the first, and gladly accepted the clergy as their teachers and allies. Thus it was that while the hostility of their orthodox subjects destroyed the Vandal kingdom in Africa and the Ostrogothic kingdom in Italy, the eager sympathy of the priesthood enabled the Franks to vanquish their Burgundian and Visigothic enemies, and made it comparatively easy for them to blend with the Roman population in the provinces. They had done good service against the Saracens of Spain; they had aided the English Boniface in his mission to the heathen of Germany [a]; and at length, as the most powerful among Catholic nations, they attracted the eyes of the ecclesiastical head of the West, now sorely bested by domestic foes.

Since the invasion of Alboin, Italy had groaned under

---

[a] ' Denique gens Francorum multos et fœcundissimos fructus Domino attulit, non solum credendo, sed et alios salutifere convertendo,' says the emperor Lewis II in A.D. 871.

a complication of evils. The Lombards who had entered along with that chief in A.D. 568 had settled in considerable numbers in the valley of the Po, and founded the duchies of Spoleto and Benevento, leaving the rest of the country to be governed by the exarch of Ravenna as viceroy of the Eastern crown. This subjection was, however, little better than nominal. Although too few to occupy the whole peninsula, the invaders were yet strong enough to harass every part of it by inroads which met with no resistance from a population unused to arms, and without the spirit to use them in self-defence. More cruel and repulsive, if we may believe the evidence of their enemies, than any other of the Northern tribes, the Lombards were certainly singular in their aversion to the clergy, never admitting them to the national councils. Tormented by their repeated attacks, Rome sought help in vain from Byzantium, whose forces, scarce able to repel from their walls the Avars and Saracens, could give no support to the distant exarch of Ravenna. The Popes were the Emperor's subjects; they awaited his confirmation, like other bishops; they had more than once been the victims of his anger [b]. But as the city became more accustomed in independence, and the Pope rose to a predominance, real if not yet legal, his tone grew bolder than that of the Eastern patriarchs. In the controversies that had raged in the Church, he had had the wisdom or good fortune to espouse (though not always from the first) the orthodox side: it was now by another quarrel of religion that his deliverance from an unwelcome yoke was accomplished [c].

[b] Martin, as in earlier times Sylverius.

[c] A singular account of the origin of the separation of the Greeks and Latins occurs in the treatise of Radulfus de Columna (Ralph Colonna, or, as some think, de Coloumelle), *De translatione Imperii Romani* (circ. 1300). 'The tyranny of Heraclius,' says he,

The Emperor Leo, born among the Isaurian mountains, where a purer faith may yet have lingered, and stung by the Mohammedan taunt of idolatry, determined to abolish the worship of images, which seemed fast obscuring the more spiritual part of Christianity. An attempt sufficient to cause tumults among the submissive Greeks, excited in Italy a fiercer commotion. The populace rose with one heart in defence of what had become to them more than a symbol: the exarch was slain: the Pope, though unwilling to sever himself from the lawful head and protector of the Church, must yet excommunicate the prince whom he could not reclaim from so hateful a heresy. Liudprand, king of the Lombards, improved his opportunity: falling on the exarchate as the champion of images, on Rome as the minister of the Greek Emperor, he overran the one, and all but succeeded in capturing the other. The Pope escaped for the moment, but saw his peril; placed between a heretic and a robber, he turned his gaze beyond the Alps, to a Catholic chief who had just achieved a signal deliverance for Christendom on the field of Poitiers. Gregory II had already opened communications with Charles Martel, mayor of the palace, and virtual ruler of the Frankish realm[d]. As the crisis

'provoked a revolt of the Eastern nations. They could not be reduced, because the Greeks at the same time began to disobey the Roman Pontiff, receding, like Jeroboam, from the true faith. Others among these schismatics (apparently with the view of strengthening their political revolt) carried their heresy further and founded Mohammedanism.' Similarly, the Franciscan Marsilius of Padua (circa 1324) says that Mohammed, 'a rich Persian,' invented his religion to keep the East from returning to allegiance to Rome. It is worth remarking that few, if any, of the earlier historians (from the tenth to the fifteenth century) refer to the Emperors of the West from Constantine to Augustulus: the very existence of this Western line seems to have been even in the eighth or ninth century altogether forgotten.

[d] Anastasius, *Vitæ Pontificum Romanorum* i. *ap.* Muratori.

becomes more pressing, Gregory III finds in the same
quarter his only hope, and appeals to him, in urgent
letters, to haste to the succour of Holy Church [e]. Some
accounts add that Charles was offered, in the name of the
Roman people, the office of consul and patrician. It is
at least certain that here begins the connection of the old
imperial seat with the rising German power : here first
the pontiff leads a political movement, and shakes off the
ties that bound him to his legitimate sovereign. Charles
died before he could obey the call ; but his son Pipin
(surnamed the Short) made good use of the new friendship with Rome. He was the third of his family who had
ruled the Franks with a monarch's full power : it seemed
time to abolish the pageant of Merovingian royalty ; yet
a departure from the ancient line might shock the feelings
of the people. A course was taken whose dangers no
one then foresaw : the Holy See, now for the first time
invoked as an international power, pronounced the deposition of Childeric, and gave to the royal office of his
successor Pipin a sanctity hitherto unknown ; adding to
the old Frankish election, which consisted in raising the
chief on a shield amid the clash of arms, the Roman
diadem and the Hebrew right of anointing. The compact between the chair of Peter and the Teutonic throne
was hardly sealed, when the latter was summoned to discharge its share of the duties. Twice did Aistulf the
Lombard assail Rome, twice did Pipin descend to the
rescue : the second time at the bidding of a letter written
in the name of St. Peter himself [f]. Aistulf could make no

---

[e] Letter in *Codex Carolinus*, in
Muratori's *Scriptores Rerum Italicarum*, vol. iii. (part 2nd), addressed ' Subregulo Carolo.'

[f] Letter in *Cod. Carol.* (Mur.
R. S. I. iii. [2.] p. 96), a strange
mixture of earnest adjurations,
dexterous appeals to Frankish

CHAP. IV.

*Pipin pa-
trician of
the Romans,*
A.D. 754.

*Import of
this title.*

resistance; and the Frank bestowed on the Papal chair all that belonged to the exarchate in North Italy, receiving as the meed of his services the title of Patrician[g].

As a foreshadowing of the higher dignity that was to follow, this title requires a passing notice. Introduced by Constantine at a time when its original meaning had been long forgotten, it was designed to be, and for awhile remained, the name not of an office but of a rank, the highest after those of emperor and consul. As such, it was usually conferred upon provincial governors of the first class, and in time also upon barbarian potentates whose vanity the Roman court might wish to flatter. Thus Odoacer, Theodoric, the Burgundian king Sigismund, Clovis himself, had all received it from the Eastern emperor; so too in still later times it was given to Saracenic and Bulgarian princes[h]. In the sixth and seventh centuries an invariable practice seems to have attached it to the Byzantine viceroys of Italy, and thus, as we may conjecture, a natural confusion of ideas had made men take it to be, in some sense, an official title, conveying an extensive though undefined authority, and implying in par-

---

pride, and long scriptural quotations: 'Declaratum quippe est quod super omnes gentes vestra Francorum gens prona mihi Apostolo Dei Petro exstitit, et ideo ecclesiam quam mihi Dominus tradidit vobis per manus Vicarii mei commendavi.'

[g] The exact date when Pipin received the title cannot be made out. Pope Stephen's next letter (p. 96 of Mur. iii.) is addressed 'Pipino, Carolo et Carolomanno patriciis.' And so the *Chronicon Casinense* (Mur. iv. 273) says it was first given to Pipin. Gibbon

can hardly be right in attributing it to Charles Martel, although one or two documents may be quoted in which it is used of him. As one of these is a letter of Pope Gregory II's, the explanation may be that the title was offered or intended to be offered to him, although never accepted by him.

[h] The title of Patrician appears even in the remote West: it stands in a charter of Ina the West Saxon king, and in one given by Richard of Normandy in A.D. 1015. Ducange, *s. v.*

ticular the duty of overseeing the Church and promoting her temporal interests. It was doubtless with such a meaning that the Romans and their bishop bestowed it upon the Frankish kings, acting quite without legal right, for it could emanate from the emperor alone, but choosing it as the title which bound its possessor to render to the Church support and defence against her Lombard foes. Hence the phrase is always ' *Patricius Romanorum ;*' not, as in former times, ' *Patricius*' alone : hence it is usually associated with the terms ' *defensor*' and '*protector.*' And since 'defence' implies a corresponding measure of obedience on the part of those who profit by it, there must have been conceded to the new patrician more or less of the positive authority in Rome, although not such as to extinguish the supremacy of the Emperor.

So long indeed as the Franks were separated by a hostile kingdom from their new allies, this control remained little better than nominal. But when on Pipin's death the restless Lombards again took up arms and menaced the possessions of the Church, Pipin's son Charles or Charlemagne swept down like a whirlwind from the Alps at the call of Pope Hadrian, seized king Desiderius in his capital, assumed himself the Lombard crown, and made northern Italy thenceforward an integral part of the Frankish empire. Proceeding to Rome at the head of his victorious army, the first of a long line of Teutonic kings who were to find her love more deadly than her hate, he was received by Hadrian with distinguished honours, and welcomed by the people as their leader and deliverer. Yet even then, whether out of policy or from that sentiment of reverence to which his ambitious mind did not refuse to bow, he was moderate in claims of jurisdiction, he yielded to the pontiff the

Extinction of the Lombard kingdom by Charles king of the Franks.

*Charles and
Hadrian.*

place of honour in processions, and renewed, although in the guise of a lord and conqueror, the gift of the Exarchate and Pentapolis, which Pipin had made to the Roman Church twenty years before.

It is with a strange sense, half of sadness, half of amusement, that in watching the progress of this grand historical drama, we recognise the meaner motives by which its chief actors were influenced. The Frankish king and the Roman pontiff were for the time the two most powerful forces that urged the movement of the world, leading it on by swift steps to a mighty crisis of its fate, themselves guided, as it might well seem, by the purest zeal for its spiritual welfare. Their words and acts, their whole character and bearing in the sight of expectant Christendom, were worthy of men destined to leave an indelible impress on their own and many succeeding ages. Nevertheless in them too appears the undercurrent of vulgar human desires and passions. The lofty and fervent mind of Charles was not free from the stirrings of personal ambition : yet these may be excused, if not defended, as almost inseparable from an intense and restless genius, which, be it never so unselfish in its ends, must in pursuing them fix upon everything its grasp and raise out of everything its monument. The policy of the Popes was prompted by motives less noble. Ever since the extinction of the Western Empire had emancipated the ecclesiastical potentate from secular control, the first and most abiding object of his schemes and prayers had been the acquisition of territorial wealth in the neighbourhood of his capital. He had indeed a sort of justification—for Rome, a city with neither trade nor industry, was crowded with poor, for whom it devolved on the bishop to provide. Yet the pursuit was

one which could not fail to pervert the purposes of the
Popes and give a sinister character to all they did. It
was this fear for the lands of the Church far more than
for religion or the safety of the city—neither of which
were really endangered by the Lombard attacks—that
had prompted their passionate appeals to Charles Martel
and Pipin ; it was now the well-grounded hope of having
these possessions confirmed and extended by Pipin's
greater son that made the Roman ecclesiastics so forward
in his cause. And it was the same lust after worldly
wealth and pomp, mingled with the dawning prospect
of an independent principality, that now began to seduce
them into a long course of guile and intrigue. For this
is probably the very time, although the exact date cannot
be established, to which must be assigned the extraordinary forgery of the Donation of Constantine, whereby
it was pretended that power over Italy and the whole
West had been granted by the first Christian Emperor to
Pope Sylvester and his successors in the Chair of the
Apostle.

For the next twenty-four years Italy remained quiet.
The government of Rome was carried on in the name
of the Patrician Charles, although it does not appear that
he sent thither any official representative; while at the
same time both the city and the exarchate continued to
admit the nominal supremacy of the Eastern Emperor,
employing the years of his reign to date documents.
In A.D. 796 Leo, the Third succeeded Pope Hadrian, and
signalized his devotion to the Frankish throne by sending
to Charles the banner of the city and the keys of the
holiest of all Rome's shrines, the confession of St. Peter,
asking that some officer should be deputed to the city
to receive from the people their oath of allegiance to the

Patrician. He had soon need to seek the Patrician's help for himself. In A.D. 798 a sedition broke out: the Pope, going in solemn procession from the Lateran to the church of S. Lorenzo in Lucina, was attacked by a band of armed men, headed by two officials of his court, nephews of his predecessor; was wounded and left for dead, and with difficulty succeeded in escaping to Spoleto, whence he fled northward into the Frankish lands. Charles had led his army against the revolted Saxons: thither Leo following overtook him at Paderborn in Westphalia. The king received with respect his spiritual father, entertained and conferred with him for some time, and at length sent him back to Rome under the escort of Angilbert, one of his trustiest ministers; promising to follow ere long in person. After some months peace was restored in Saxony, and in the autumn of 799 Charles descended from the Alps once more, while Leo revolved deeply the great scheme for whose accomplishment the time was now ripe.

Belief in the Roman Empire not extinct.

Three hundred and twenty-four years had passed since the last Cæsar of the West resigned his power into the hands of the senate, and left to his Eastern brother the sole headship of the Roman world. To the latter Italy had from that time been nominally subject; but it was only during one brief interval between the death of Totila the last Ostrogothic king and the descent of Alboin the first Lombard, that his power had been really effective. In the further provinces, Gaul, Spain, Britain, it was only a memory. But the idea of a Roman Empire as a necessary part of the world's order had not vanished: it had been admitted by those who seemed to be destroying it; it had been cherished by the Church; was still recalled by laws and customs; was dear to the subject populations, who fondly looked back to the days when slavery was at least mitigated by peace and order. We have seen the Teuton endeavouring everywhere to identify himself with the system he overthrew. As Goths, Burgundians, and Franks sought the title of consul or patrician, as the Lombard kings when they renounced their Arianism styled themselves Flavii, so even in distant England the fierce Saxon and Anglian conquerors used the names of Roman dignities, and before long began to call themselves *imperatores* and *basileis* of Britain. Within the last century and a half the rise of Mohammedanism [1] had brought out the common Christianity of Europe into a fuller relief. The false prophet had left one religion, one Empire, one Commander of the faithful: the Christian commonwealth needed more than ever an efficient head and centre. Such leadership it could nowise find in the Court of the Bosphorus, growing ever feebler and more alien to the West. The name of 'respublica,' permanent at the elder Rome, had never been applied to the Eastern Empire. Its government was from the first half Greek, half Asiatic; and had now drifted away from its ancient traditions into the forms of an Oriental despotism. Claudian had already sneered at 'Greek Quirites [j]:' the general use, since Heraclius's reign, of the Greek tongue, and the difference of manners and usages, made the taunt now more deserved. The Pope had no reason to wish well to the Byzantine princes, who while insulting his weakness had given him no help against the savage Lombards, and who for nearly seventy

Motives of the Pope.

[1] After the *translatio ad Francos* of A.D. 800, the two Empires corresponded exactly to the two Khalifates of Bagdad and Cordova.

[j] 'Plaudentem cerne senatum
Et Byzantinos proceres, Graiosque Quirites.'
In Eutrop. ii. 135.

years [k] had been contaminated by a heresy the more odious that it touched not speculative points of doctrine but the most familiar usages of worship. In North Italy their power was extinct : no pontiff since Zacharias had asked their confirmation of his election : nay, the appointment of the intruding Frank to the patriciate, an office which it belonged to the Emperor to confer, was of itself an act of rebellion. Nevertheless their rights subsisted : they were still, and while they retained the imperial name, must so long continue, titular sovereigns of the Roman city. Nor could the spiritual head of Christendom dispense with the temporal; without the Roman Empire there could not be a Roman, nor by necessary consequence a Catholic and Apostolic Church [l]. For, as will be shewn more fully hereafter, men could not separate in fact what was indissoluble in thought : Christianity must stand or fall along with the great Christian state : they were but two names for the same thing. Thus urged, the Pope took a step which some among his predecessors are said to have already contemplated [m], and towards

[k] Several Emperors during this period had been patrons of images, as was Irene at the moment of which I write : the stain nevertheless adhered to their government as a whole.

[l] I should not have thought it necessary to explain that the sentence in the text is meant simply to state what were (so far as can be made out) the sentiments and notions of the ninth century, if a writer in the *Tablet* (reviewing a former edition) had not understood it as an expression of the author's own belief.

To a modern eye there is of course no necessary connection between the Roman Empire and a catholic and apostolic Church; in fact, the two things seem rather, such has been the impression made on us by the long struggle of church and state, in their nature mutually antagonistic. The interest of history lies not least in this, that it shews us how men have at different times entertained wholly different notions respecting the relation to one another of the same ideas or the same institutions.

[m] Monachus Sangallensis, *De Gestis Karoli;* in Pertz, *Monumenta Germaniæ Historica.*

which the events of the last fifty years had pointed. The moment was opportune. The widowed empress Irene, equally famous for her beauty, her talents, and her crimes, had deposed and blinded her son Constantine VI : a woman, an usurper, almost a parricide, sullied the throne of the world. By what right, it might well be asked, did the factions of Byzantium impose a master on the original seat of empire ? It was time to provide better for the most august of human offices : an election at Rome was as valid as at Constantinople—the possessor of the real power should also be clothed with the outward dignity. Nor could it be doubted where that possessor was to be found. The Frank had been always faithful to Rome : his baptism was the enlistment of a new barbarian auxiliary. His services against Arian heretics and Lombard marauders, against the Saracen of Spain and the Avar of Pannonia, had earned him the title of Champion of the Faith and Defender of the Holy See. He was now unquestioned lord of Western Europe, whose subject nations, Keltic and Teutonic, were eager to be called by his name and to imitate his customs [n]. In Charles, the hero who united under one sceptre so many races, who ruled all as the vicegerent of God, the pontiff might well see—as later ages saw—the new golden head of a second image [o], erected on the ruins of that whose mingled iron and clay seemed crumbling to nothingness behind the impregnable bulwarks of Constantinople.

[n] Monachus Sangallensis; *ut supra*. So Pope Gregory the Great two centuries earlier : ' Quanto cæteros homines regia dignitas antecedit, tanto cæterarum gentium regna regni Francorum culmen excellit.' Ep. v. 6.

[o] Alciatus, *De Formula imperii Romani*.

At length the Frankish host entered Rome. The Pope's cause was heard; his innocence, already vindicated by a miracle, was pronounced by the Patrician in full synod; his accusers condemned in his stead. Charles remained in the city for some weeks; and on Christmas-day, A.D. 800[p], he heard mass in the basilica of St. Peter. On the spot where now the gigantic dome of Bramante and Michael Angelo towers over the buildings of the modern city, the spot which tradition had hallowed as that of the Apostle's martyrdom, Constantine the Great had erected the oldest and stateliest temple of Christian Rome. Nothing could be less like than was this basilica to those northern cathedrals, shadowy, fantastic, irregular, crowded with pillars, fringed all round by clustering shrines and chapels, which are to most of us the types of mediæval architecture. In its plan and decorations, in the spacious sunny hall, the roof plain as that of a Greek temple, the long rows of Corinthian columns, the vivid mosaics on its walls, in its brightness, its sternness, its simplicity, it had preserved every feature of Roman art, and had remained a perfect expression of the Roman character[q]. Out of the transept, a flight of steps led up to the high altar underneath and just beyond the great arch, the arch of triumph as it was called: behind in the semicircular apse sat the clergy, rising tier above tier around its walls; in the midst, high above the rest, and looking down past the altar over the multitude, was placed the bishop's throne[r], itself the curule chair of some

[p] Or rather, according to the then prevailing practice of beginning the year from Christmas-day, A.D. 801.

[q] An elaborate description of old St. Peter's may be found in Bunsen's and Platner's *Beschreibung der Stadt Rom;* with which compare Bunsen's work on the Basilicas of Rome.

[r] The primitive custom was for the bishop to sit in the centre of

forgotten magistrate[s]. From that chair the Pope now rose, as the reading of the Gospel ended, advanced to where Charles—who had exchanged his simple Frankish dress for the sandals and the chlamys of a Roman patrician[t]—knelt in prayer by the high altar, and as in the sight of all he placed upon the brow of the barbarian chieftain the diadem of the Cæsars, then bent in obeisance before him, the church rang to the shout of the multitude, again free, again the lords and centre of the world, 'Karolo Augusto a Deo coronato magno et pacifico imperatori vita et victoria[u].' In that shout, echoed by the Franks without, was pronounced the union, so long in preparation, so mighty in its consequences, of the Roman and the Teuton, of the memories and the civilization of the South with the fresh energy of the North, and from that moment modern history begins.

the apse, at the central point of the east end of the church (or, as it would be more correct to say, the end furthest from the door) just as the judge had done in those law courts on the model of which the first basilicas were constructed. This arrangement may still be seen in some of the churches of Rome, as well as elsewhere in Italy; nowhere better than in the churches of Ravenna, particularly the beautiful one of Sant' Apollinare in Classe, and in the cathedral of Torcello, near Venice.

[s] On this chair were represented the labours of Hercules and the signs of the zodiac. It is believed at Rome to be the veritable chair of the Apostle himself, and whatever may be thought of such an antiquity as this, it can be satisfactorily traced back to the third

or fourth century of Christianity. (The story that it is inscribed with verses from the Koran is, I believe, without foundation.) It is now enclosed in a gorgeous casing of gilded wood (some say, of bronze), and placed aloft at the extremity of St. Peter's, just over the spot where a bishop's chair would in the old arrangement of the basilica have stood. The sarcophagus in which Charles himself lay, till the French scattered his bones abroad, had carved on it the rape of Proserpine. It may still be seen in the gallery of the basilica at Aachen.

[t] Eginhard, *Vita Karoli.*

[u] The coronation scene is described in all the annals of the time, to which it is therefore needless to refer more particularly.

CHAPTER V.

EMPIRE AND POLICY OF CHARLES.

THE coronation of Charles is not only the central event of the Middle Ages, it is also one of those very few events of which, taking them singly, it may be said that if they had not happened, the history of the world would have been different. In one sense indeed it has scarcely a parallel. The assassins of Julius Cæsar thought that they had saved Rome from monarchy, but monarchy came inevitable in the next generation. The conversion of Constantine changed the face of the world, but Christianity was spreading fast, and its ultimate triumph was only a question of time. Had Columbus never spread his sails, the secret of the western sea would yet have been pierced by some later voyager: had Charles V broken his safe-conduct to Luther, the voice silenced at Wittenberg would have been taken up by echoes elsewhere. But if the Roman Empire had not been restored in the West in the person of Charles, it would never have been restored at all, and the inexhaustible train of consequences for good and for evil that followed could not have been. Why this was so may be seen by examining the history of the next two centuries. In that day, as through all the Dark and Middle Ages, two forces were striving for the mastery. The one was the instinct of separation, disorder, anarchy, caused by the ungoverned impulses and barbarous ignorance of the great bulk of mankind; the other was that passionate longing of the better minds for a formal unity of government, which had its historical basis in the memories of the old Roman Empire, and its most constant expression in the devotion to a visible and catholic Church. The former tendency, as everything shews, was, in politics at least, the stronger, but the latter, used and stimulated by an extraordinary genius like Charles, achieved in the year 800 a victory whose results were never to be lost. When the hero was gone, the returning wave of anarchy and barbarism swept up violent as ever, yet it could not wholly obliterate the past: the Empire, maimed and shattered though it was, had struck its roots too deep to be overthrown by force, and when it perished at last, perished from inner decay. It was just because men felt that no one less than Charles could have won such a triumph over the evils of the time, by framing and establishing a gigantic scheme of government, that the excitement and hope and joy which the coronation evoked were so intense. Their best evidence is perhaps to be found not in the records of that time itself, but in the cries of lamentation that broke forth when the Empire began to dissolve towards the close of the ninth century, in the marvellous legends which attached themselves to the name of Charles the Emperor, a hero of whom any exploit was credible[a], in the devout admiration wherewith his German successors looked back to, and strove in all things to imitate, their all but superhuman prototype.

[a] Before the end of the tenth century we find the monk Benedict of Soracte ascribing to Charles an expedition to Palestine, and other marvellous exploits. The romance which passes under the name of Archbishop Turpin is well known. All the best stories about Charles—and some of them are very good—may be found in the book of the Monk of St. Gall. Many refer to his dealings with the bishops, towards whom he is described as acting like a good-humoured schoolmaster.

As the event of A.D. 800 made an unparalleled impression on those who lived at the time, so has it engaged the attention of men in succeeding ages, has been viewed in the most opposite lights, and become the theme of interminable controversies. It is better to look at it simply as it appeared to the men who witnessed it. Here, as in so many other cases, may be seen the errors into which jurists have been led by the want of historical feeling. In rude and unsettled states of society men respect forms and obey facts, while careless of rules and principles. In England, for example, in the eleventh and twelfth centuries, it signified very little whether an aspirant to the throne was next lawful heir, but it signified a great deal whether he had been duly crowned and was supported by a strong party. Regarding the matter thus, it is not hard to see why those who judged the actors of A.D. 800 as they would have judged their contemporaries should have misunderstood the nature of that which then came to pass. Baronius and Bellarmine, Spanheim and Conring, are advocates bound to prove a thesis, and therefore believing it; nor does either party find any lack of plausible arguments[b]. But civilian and canonist alike proceed upon strict legal principles, and no such principles can be found in the case, or applied to it. Neither the instances cited by the Cardinal from the Old Testament of the power of priests to set up and pull down princes, nor those which shew the earlier Emperors controlling the bishops of Rome, really meet the question. Leo acted not as having alone the right to transfer the crown; the practice of hereditary succession and the theory of popular election

[b] Baronius, *Ann.*, ad ann. 800; Bellarminus, *De translatione imperii Romani adversus Illyricum*; Spanhemius, *De ficta translatione imperii*; Conringius, *De imperio Romano Germanico.*

would have equally excluded such a claim; he was the
spokesman of the popular will, which, identifying itself
with the sacerdotal power, hated the Greeks and was
grateful to the Franks. Yet he was also something more.
The act, as it specially affected his interests, was mainly
his work, and without him would never have been brought
about at all. It was natural that a confusion of his secular
functions as leader, and his spiritual as consecrating priest,
should lay the foundation of the right claimed afterwards
of raising and deposing monarchs at the will of Christ's
vicar. The Emperor was passive throughout; he did
not, as in Lombardy, appear as a conqueror, but was received by the Pope and the people as a friend and ally.
Rome no doubt became his capital, but it had already
obeyed him as Patrician, and the greatest fact that stood
out to posterity from the whole transaction was that the
crown was bestowed, was at least imposed, by the hands
of the pontiff. He seemed the trustee and depositary of
the imperial authority[c].

The best way of shewing the thoughts and motives of
those concerned in the transaction is to transcribe the
narratives of three contemporary, or almost contemporary
annalists, two of them German and one Italian. The
Annals of Lauresheim say:—

'And because the name of Emperor had now ceased
among the Greeks, and their Empire was possessed by a
woman, it then seemed both to Leo the Pope himself, and
to all the holy fathers who were present in the selfsame
council, as well as to the rest of the Christian people, that
they ought to take to be Emperor Charles king of the
Franks, who held Rome herself, where the Cæsars had
always been wont to sit, and all the other regions which

CHAP. V.

*Contempo-
rary ac-
counts.*

[c] See especially Greenwood, *Cathedra Petri*, vol. iii. p. 109.

he ruled through Italy and Gaul and Germany; and inasmuch as God had given all these lands into his hand, it seemed right that with the help of God and at the prayer of the whole Christian people he should have the name of Emperor also. Whose petition king Charles willed not to refuse, but submitting himself with all humility to God, and at the prayer of the priests and of the whole Christian people, on the day of the nativity of our Lord Jesus Christ he took on himself the name of Emperor, being consecrated by the lord Pope Leo[d].'

Very similar in substance is the account of the Chronicle of Moissac (ad ann. 801):—

'Now when the king upon the most holy day of the Lord's birth was rising to the mass after praying before the confession of the blessed Peter the Apostle, Leo the Pope, with the consent of all the bishops and priests and of the senate of the Franks and likewise of the Romans, set a golden crown upon his head, the Roman people also shouting aloud. And when the people had made an end of chanting the Laudes, he was adored by the Pope after the manner of the emperors of old. For this also was done by the will of God. For while the said Emperor abode at Rome certain men were brought unto him, who said that the name of Emperor had ceased among the Greeks, and that among them the Empire was held by a woman called Irene, who had by guile laid hold on her son the Emperor, and put out his eyes, and taken the Empire to herself, as it is written of Athaliah in the Book of the Kings; which when Leo the Pope and all the assembly of the bishops and priests and abbots heard, and the senate of the Franks and all the elders of the Romans, they took counsel with the rest of the Christian people,

[d] *Ann. Lauresb. ap.* Pertz, *M. G. H.* i.

that they should name Charles king of the Franks to be
Emperor, seeing that he held Rome the mother of empire
where the Cæsars and Emperors were always used to sit;
and that the heathen might not mock the Christians if
the name of Emperor should have ceased among the
Christians[e].'

These two accounts are both from a German source:
that which follows is Roman, written probably within
some fifty or sixty years of the event. It is taken from
the Life of Leo III in the *Vitæ Pontificum Romanorum*,
compiled by Anastasius the papal librarian.

'After these things came the day of the birth of our
Lord Jesus Christ, and all men were again gathered together in the aforesaid basilica of the blessed Peter the
Apostle: and then the gracious and venerable pontiff did
with his own hands crown Charles with a very precious
crown. Then all the faithful people of Rome, seeing the
defence that he gave and the love that he bare to the holy
Roman Church and her Vicar, did by the will of God and
of the blessed Peter, the keeper of the keys of the kingdom
of heaven, cry with one accord with a loud voice, ' To
Charles, the most pious Augustus, crowned of God, the
great and peacegiving Emperor, be life and victory.'
While he, before the holy confession of the blessed Peter
the Apostle, was invoking divers saints, it was proclaimed
thrice, and he was chosen by all to be Emperor of the
Romans. Thereon the most holy pontiff anointed Charles
with holy oil, and likewise his most excellent son to be
king, upon the very day of the birth of our Lord Jesus
Christ; and when the mass was finished, then after the
mass the most serene lord Emperor offered gifts[f].'

[e] *Apud* Pertz, *M. G. H.* i.
[f] *Vitæ Pontif.* in Mur. *S. R. I.*

Anastasius in reporting the shout
of the people omits the word

In these three accounts there is no serious discrepancy as to the facts, although the Italian priest, as is natural, heightens the importance of the part played by the Pope, while the Germans are too anxious to rationalize the event, talking of a synod of the clergy, a consultation of the people, and a formal request to Charles, which the silence of Eginhard, as well as the other circumstances of the case, forbid us to accept as literally true. Similarly Anastasius passes over the adoration rendered by the Pope to the Emperor, upon which most of the Frankish records insist in a way which puts it beyond doubt. But the impression which the three narratives leave is essentially the same. They all shew how little the transaction

Impression which they convey.

can be made to wear a strictly legal character. The Frankish king does not of his own might seize the crown, but rather receives it as coming naturally to him, as the legitimate consequence of the authority he already enjoyed. The Pope bestows the crown, not in virtue of any right of his own as head of the Church : he is merely the instrument of God's providence, which has unmistakeably pointed out Charles as the proper person to defend and lead the Christian commonwealth. The Roman people do not formally elect and appoint, but by their applause accept the chief who is presented to them. The act is conceived of as directly ordered by the Divine Providence which has brought about a state of things that admits of but one issue, an issue which king, priest, and people have only to recognise and obey; their personal ambitions, passions, intrigues, sinking and vanishing in reverential awe at what seems the immediate interposition of Heaven. And as the result is desired by all parties

'Romanorum,' which the other annalists insert after 'imperatori.'

The balance of probability is certainly in his favour.

alike, they do not think of inquiring into one another's rights, but take their momentary harmony to be natural and necessary, never dreaming of the difficulties and conflicts which were to arise out of what seemed then so simple. And it was just because everything was thus left undetermined, resting not on express stipulation but rather on a sort of mutual understanding, a sympathy of beliefs and wishes which augured no evil, that the event admitted of being afterwards represented in so many different lights. Four centuries later, when Papacy and Empire had been forced into the mortal struggle by which the fate of both was decided, three distinct theories regarding the coronation of Charles will be found advocated by three different parties, all of them plausible, all of them to some extent misleading. The Swabian Emperors held the crown to have been won by their great predecessor as the prize of conquest, and drew the conclusion that the citizens and bishop of Rome had no rights as against themselves. The patriotic party among the Romans, appealing to the early history of the Empire, declared that by nothing but the voice of their senate and people could an Emperor be lawfully created, he being only their chief magistrate, the temporary depositary of their authority. The Popes pointed to the indisputable fact that Leo imposed the crown, and argued that as God's earthly vicar it was then his, and must always continue to be their right to give to whomsoever they would an office which was created to be the handmaid of their own. Of these three it was the last view that eventually prevailed, yet to an impartial eye it cannot claim, any more than do the two others, to contain the whole truth. Charles did not conquer, nor the Pope give, nor the people elect. As the act was unprecedented so was it illegal; it was a revolt of the ancient

CHAP. V.

Later theories respecting the coronation.

N.B.

Western capital against a daughter who had become a mistress; an exercise of the sacred right of insurrection, justified by the weakness and wickedness of the Byzantine princes, hallowed to the eyes of the world by the sanction of Christ's representative, but founded upon no law, nor competent to create any for the future.

Was the coronation a surprise?

It is an interesting and somewhat perplexing question, how far the coronation scene, an act as imposing in its circumstances as it was momentous in its results, was prearranged among the parties. Eginhard tells us that Charles was accustomed to declare that he would not, even on so high a festival, have entered the church had he known of the Pope's intention. Even if the monarch had uttered, the secretary would hardly have recorded a falsehood long after the motive that might have prompted it had disappeared. Of the existence of that motive which has been most commonly assumed, a fear of the discontent of the Franks who might think their liberties endangered, little or no proof can be brought from the records of the time, wherein the nation is represented as exulting in the new dignity of their chief as an accession of grandeur to themselves. Nor can we suppose that Charles's disavowal was meant to soothe the offended pride of the Byzantine princes, from whom he had nothing to fear, and who were none the more likely to recognise his dignity, if they should believe it to be not of his own seeking. Yet it is hard to suppose the whole affair a surprise; for it was the goal towards which the policy of the Frankish kings had for many years pointed, and Charles himself, in sending before him to Rome many of the spiritual and temporal magnates of his realm, in summoning thither his son Pipin from the war against the Lombards of Benevento, had shewn that he expected some more than ordinary result from this journey to the imperial city. Alcuin moreover, Alcuin of York, the prime minister of Charles in matters religious and literary, appears from one of his extant letters to have sent as a Christmas gift to his royal pupil a carefully corrected and superbly adorned copy of the Scriptures, with the words ' ad splendorem imperialis potentiæ.' This has commonly been taken for conclusive evidence that the plan had been settled beforehand, and such it would be were there not some reasons for giving the letter an earlier date, and looking upon the word 'imperialis'· as a mere magniloquent flourish ᵍ. More weight is therefore to be laid upon the arguments supplied by the nature of the case itself. The Pope, whatever his confidence in the sympathy of the people, would never have ventured on so momentous a step until previous conferences had assured him of the feelings of the king, nor could an act for which the assembly were evidently prepared have been kept a secret. Nevertheless, the declaration of Charles himself can neither be evaded nor set down to mere dissimulation. It is more just to him, and on the whole more reasonable, to suppose that Leo, having satisfied himself of the wishes of the Roman clergy and people as well as of the Frankish magnates, resolved to seize an occasion and place so eminently favourable to his long-cherished plan, while Charles, carried away by the enthusiasm of the moment and seeing in the pontiff the prophet and instrument of the divine will, accepted a dignity which he might have wished to receive at some later time or in some other way. If, therefore, any positive conclusion be adopted, it would seem to be that Charles, although he had probably given a more or less vague consent to the pro-

ᵍ Lorentz, *Leben Alcuins.* And cf. Döllinger, *Das Kaiserthum Karls des Grossen und seiner Nachfolger.*

ject, was surprised and disconcerted by a sudden fulfilment which interrupted his own carefully studied designs.
And although a deed which changed the history of the
world was in any case no accident, it may well have worn
to the Frankish and Roman spectators the air of a surprise.   For there were no preparations apparent in the
church; the king was not, like his Teutonic successors in
aftertime, led in procession to the pontifical throne: suddenly, at the very moment when he rose from the sacred
hollow where he had knelt among the ever-burning lamps
before the holiest of Christian relics—the body of the
prince of the Apostles—the hands of that Apostle's representative placed upon his head the crown of glory and
poured upon him the oil of sanctification. There was something in this to thrill the beholders with the awe of a divine
presence, and make them hail him whom that presence
seemed almost visibly to consecrate, the 'pious and
peace-giving Emperor, crowned of God.'

Theories of the motives of Charles.

The reluctance of Charles to assume the imperial title
is ascribed by Eginhard to a fear of the jealous hostility of
the Greeks, who could not only deny his claim to it, but
might disturb by their intrigues his dominions in Italy.
Accepting this statement, the problem remains, how is
this reluctance to be reconciled with those acts of his
which clearly shew him aiming at the Roman crown? An
ingenious and probable, if not certain solution, is suggested by a recent historian[h], who argues from a minute
examination of the previous policy of Charles, that while
it was the great object of his reign to obtain the crown of
the world, he foresaw at the same time the opposition of

[h] See a very learned and interesting tract entitled *Das Kaiserthum
Karls des Grossen und seiner Nach-*
folger, recently published by Dr. v.
Döllinger of Munich.

the Eastern Court, and the want of legality from which his title would in consequence suffer. He was therefore bent on getting from the Byzantines, if possible, a transference of their crown; if not, at least a recognition of his own: and he appears to have hoped to win this by the negotiations which had been for some time kept on foot with the Empress Irene. Just at this moment came the coronation by Pope Leo, interrupting these deep-laid schemes, irritating the Eastern Court, and forcing Charles into the position of a rival who could not with dignity adopt a soothing or submissive tone. Nevertheless, he seems not even then to have abandoned the hope of obtaining a peaceful recognition. Irene's crimes did not prevent him, if we may credit Theophanes[i], from seeking her hand in marriage. And when the project of thus uniting the East and West in a single Empire, baffled for a time by the opposition of her minister Ætius, was rendered impossible by her subsequent dethronement and exile, he did not abandon the policy of conciliation until a surly acquiescence in rather than admission of his dignity had been won from the Byzantine sovereigns Michael and Nicephorus[j].

Whether, supposing Leo to have been less precipitate, a cession of the crown, or an acknowledgment of the right of the Romans to confer it, could ever have been obtained by Charles is perhaps more than doubtful. But it is clear that he judged rightly in rating its importance high, for the want of it was the great blemish in his own and his successors' dignity. To shew how this was so, reference

CHAP. V.

Defect in the title of the Teutonic Emperors.

---

[i] Ἀποκρισιάριοι παρὰ Καρούλλου καὶ Λέοντος αἰτούμενοι ζευχθῆναι αὐτὴν τῷ Καρούλλῳ πρὸς γάμον καὶ ἐνῶσαι τὰ Ἑῷα καὶ τὰ Ἑσπερία. —Theoph. *Chron.* in *Corp. Scriptt. Hist. Byz.*

[j] Their ambassadors at last saluted him by the desired title 'Laudes ei dixerunt imperatorem eum et basileum appellantes.' Eginh. *Ann.*, ad ann. 812.

must be made to the events of A.D. 476. Both the extinction of the Western Empire in that year and its revival in A.D. 800 have been very generally misunderstood in modern times, and although the mistake is not, in a certain sense, of practical importance, yet it tends to confuse history and to blind us to the ideas of the people who acted on both occasions. When Odoacer compelled the abdication of Romulus Augustulus, he did not abolish the Western Empire as a separate power, but caused it to be reunited with or sink into the Eastern, so that from that time there was, as there had been before Diocletian, a single undivided Roman Empire. In A.D. 800 the very memory of the separate Western Empire, as it had stood from the death of Theodosius till Odoacer, had, so far as appears, been long since lost, and neither Leo nor Charles nor any one among their advisers dreamt of reviving it. They too, like their predecessors, held the Roman Empire to be one and indivisible, and proposed by the coronation of the Frankish king not to proclaim a severance of the East and West, but to reverse the act of Constantine, and make Old Rome again the civil as well as the ecclesiastical capital of the Empire that bore her name. Their deed was in its essence illegal, but they sought to give it every semblance of legality : they professed and partly believed that they were not revolting against a reigning sovereign, but legitimately filling up the place of the deposed Constantine the Sixth; the people of the imperial city exercising their ancient right of choice, their bishop his right of consecration.

Their purpose was but half accomplished. They could create but they could not destroy : they set up an Emperor of their own, whose representatives thenceforward ruled the West, but Constantinople retained her sovereigns as of yore; and Christendom saw henceforth two imperial lines, not as in the time before A.D. 476, the conjoint heads of a single realm, but rivals and enemies, each denouncing the other as an impostor, each professing to be the only true and lawful head of the Christian Church and people. Although therefore we must in practice speak during the next seven centuries (down till A.D. 1453, when Constantinople fell before the Mohammedan) of an Eastern and a Western Empire, the phrase is in strictness incorrect, and was one which either court ought to have repudiated. The Byzantines always did repudiate it; the Latins usually; although, yielding to facts, they sometimes condescended to employ it themselves. But their theory was always the same. Charles was held to be the legitimate successor, not of Romulus Augustulus, but of Basil, Heraclius, Justinian, Arcadius, and all the Eastern line; and hence it is that in all the annals of the time and of many succeeding centuries, the name of Constantine VI, the sixty-seventh in order from Augustus, is followed without a break by that of Charles, the sixty-eighth.

The maintenance of an imperial line among the Greeks was a continuing protest against the validity of Charles's title. But from their enmity he had little to fear, and in the eyes of the world he seemed to step into their place, adding the traditional dignity which had been theirs to the power that he already enjoyed. North Italy and Rome ceased for ever to own the supremacy of Byzantium; and while the Eastern princes paid a shameful tribute to the Mussulman, the Frankish Emperor—as the recognised head of Christendom—received from the patriarch of Jerusalem the keys of the Holy Sepulchre and the banner of Calvary; the gift of the Sepulchre

Government of Charles as Emperor.

*His author-
ity in mat-
ters eccle-
siastical.*

N³

itself, says Eginhard, from Aaron king of the Persians[k]. Out of this peaceful intercourse with the great Khalif the romancers created a crusade. Within his own dominions his sway assumed a more sacred character. Already had his unwearied and comprehensive activity made him throughout his reign an ecclesiastical no less than a civil ruler, summoning and sitting in councils, examining and appointing bishops, settling by capitularies the smallest points of church discipline and polity. A synod held at Frankfort in A.D. 794 condemned the decrees of the second council of Nicæa, which had been approved by Pope Hadrian, censured in violent terms the conduct of the Byzantine rulers in suggesting them, and without excluding images from churches, altogether forbade them to be worshipped or even venerated. Not only did Charles preside in and direct the deliberations of this synod, although legates from the Pope were present—he also caused a treatise to be drawn up stating and urging its conclusions; he pressed Hadrian to declare Constantine VI a heretic for enouncing doctrines to which Hadrian had himself consented. There are letters of his extant in which he lectures Pope Leo in a tone of easy superiority, admonishes him to obey the holy canons, and bids him pray earnestly for the success of the efforts which it is the monarch's duty to make for the subjugation of pagans and the establishment of sound doctrine throughout the Church. Nay, subsequent Popes themselves[l] admitted and applauded the despotic superintendence of matters spiritual which he was wont to exercise, and which led some one to give him playfully a

[k] Harun erl Rashid; Eginh. *Vita Karoli*, c. 16.
[l] So Pope John VIII in a document quoted by Waitz, *Deutsche Verfassungs-geschichte*, iii.

title that had once been applied to the Pope himself, 'Episcopus episcoporum.'

Acting and speaking thus when merely king, it may be thought that Charles needed no further title to justify his power. The inference is in truth rather the converse of this. Upon what he had done already the imperial title must necessarily follow: the attitude of protection and control which he held towards the Church and the Holy See belonged, according to the ideas of the time, especially and only to an Emperor. Therefore his coronation was the fitting completion and legitimation of his authority, sanctifying rather than increasing it. We have, however, one remarkable witness to the importance that was attached to the imperial name, and the enhancement which he conceived his office to have received from it. In a great assembly held at Aachen, A.D. 802, the lately-crowned Emperor revised the laws of all the races that obeyed him, endeavouring to harmonize and correct them, and issued a capitulary singular in subject and tone[m]. All persons within his dominions, as well ecclesiastical as civil, who have already sworn allegiance to him as king, are thereby commanded to swear to him afresh as Cæsar; and all who have never yet sworn, down to the age of twelve, shall now take the same oath. 'At the same time it shall be publicly explained to all what is the force and meaning of this oath, and how much more it includes than a mere promise of fidelity to the monarch's person. Firstly, it binds those who swear it to live, each and every one of them, according to his strength and knowledge, in the holy service of God; since the lord Emperor cannot extend over all his care and discipline. Secondly, it binds them neither by force nor fraud to seize or molest

The imperial office in its ecclesiastical relations.

Capitulary of A.D. 802.

[m] Pertz, *M. G. H.* iii. (legg. I.)

F

any of the goods or servants of his crown. Thirdly, to do no violence nor treason towards the holy Church, or to widows, or orphans, or strangers, seeing that the lord Emperor has been appointed, after the Lord and his saints, the protector and defender of all such.' Then in similar fashion purity of life is prescribed to the monks; homicide, the neglect of hospitality, and other offences are denounced, the notions of sin and crime being intermingled and almost identified in a. way to which no parallel can be found, unless it be in the Mosaic code. There God, the invisible object of worship, is also, though almost incidentally, the judge and political ruler of Israel; here the whole cycle of social and moral duty is deduced from the obligation of obedience to the visible autocratic head of the Christian state.

In most of Charles's words and deeds, nor less distinctly in the writings of his adviser Alcuin. may be discerned the working of the same theocratic ideas. Among his intimate friends he chose to be called by the name of David, exercising in reality all the powers of the Jewish king; presiding over this kingdom of God upon earth rather as a second Constantine or Theodosius than in the spirit and traditions of the Julii or the Flavii. Among his measures there are two which in particular recall the first Christian Emperor. As Constantine founds so Charles erects on a firmer basis the connection of Church and State. Bishops and abbots are as essential a part of rising feudalism as counts and dukes. Their benefices are held under the same conditions of fealty and the service in war of their vassal tenants, not of the spiritual person himself: they have similar rights of jurisdiction, and are subject alike to the imperial *missi*. The monarch tries often to restrict the clergy, as persons, to spiritual duties; quells the insubordination of the monasteries; endeavours to bring the seculars into a monastic life by instituting and regulating chapters. But after granting wealth and power, the attempt was vain; his strong hand withdrawn, they laughed at control. Again, it was by him first that the payment of tithes, for which the priest-hood had long been pleading, was made compulsory in Western Europe, and the support of the ministers of religion entrusted to the laws of the state.

In civil affairs also Charles acquired, with the imperial title, a new position. Later jurists labour to distinguish his power as Roman Emperor from that which he held already as king of the Franks and their subject allies: they insist that his coronation gave him the capital only, that it is absurd to talk of a Roman Empire in regions whither the eagles had never flown[n]. In such expressions there seems to lurk either confusion or misconception. It was not the actual government of the city that Charles obtained in A.D. 800 : that his father had already held as Patrician and he had constantly exercised in the same capa-city: it was far more than the titular sovereignty of Rome which had hitherto been supposed to be vested in the Byzantine princes: it was nothing less than the headship of the world, believed to appertain of right to the lawful Roman Emperor, whether he reigned on the Bosphorus, the Tiber, or the Rhine. As that headship, although never denied, had been in abeyance in the West for several centuries, its bestowal on the king of so vast a realm was a change of the first moment, for it made the coronation not merely a transference of the seat of Empire, but a renewal of the Empire itself, a bringing back of it from

Influence of the imperial title in Germany and Gaul.

[n] Putter, *Historical Development of the German Constitution;* so too

Conring, and esp. David Blondel, *Adv. Chiffletium.*

faith to sight, from the world of belief and theory to the world of fact and reality.   And since the powers it gave were autocratic and unlimited, it must swallow up all minor claims and dignities: the rights of Charles the Frankish king were merged in those of Charles the successor of Augustus, the lord of the world.   That his imperial authority was theoretically irrespective of place is clear from his own words and acts, and from all the monuments of that time.   He would not, indeed, have dreamed of treating the free Franks as Justinian had treated his half-Oriental subjects, nor would the warriors who followed his standard have brooked such an attempt. Yet even to German eyes his position must have been altered by the halo of vague splendour which now surrounded him;   for all, even the Saxon and the Slave, had heard of Rome's glories, and revered the name of Cæsar.   And in his effort to weld discordant elements into one body, to introduce regular gradations of authority, to control the Teutonic tendency to localization by his *missi*—officials commissioned to traverse each some part of his dominions, reporting on and redressing the evils they found—and by his own oft-repeated personal progresses, Charles was guided by the traditions of the old Empire.   His sway is the revival of order and culture, fusing the West into a compact whole, whose parts are never thenceforward to lose the marks of their connection and their half-Roman character, gathering up all that is left in Europe of spirit and wealth and knowledge, and hurling it with the new force of Christianity on the infidel of the South and the masses of untamed barbarism to the North and East. Ruling the world by the gift of God, and the transmitted rights of the Romans and their Cæsar whom God had chosen to conquer it, he renews the original aggressive

Action of Charles on Europe.

.movement of the Empire: the civilized world has subdued her invader[o], and now arms him against savagery and heathendom. Hence the wars, not more of the sword than of the cross, against Saxons, Avars, Slaves, Danes, Spanish Arabs, where monasteries are fortresses and baptism the badge of submission. The overthrow of the Irminsûl[p], in the first Saxon campaign[q], sums up the changes of seven centuries. The Romanized Teuton destroys the monument of his country's freedom, for it is also the emblem of paganism and barbarism. The work of Arminius is undone by his successor.

This, however, is not the only side from which Charles's policy and character may be regarded. If the unity of the Church and the shadow of imperial prerogative was one pillar of his power, the other was the Frankish nation. The Empire was still military, though in a sense strangely different from that of Julius or Severus. The warlike Franks had permeated Western

His position as Frankish king.

[o] 'Græcia capta ferum victorem cepit,' is repeated in this conquest of the Teuton by the Roman.

[p] The notion that once prevailed that the Irminsûl was the 'pillar of Hermann,' set up on the spot of the defeat of Varus, is now generally discredited. Some German antiquaries take the pillar to be a rude figure of the native god Irmin; but nothing seems to be known of this alleged deity: and it is more probable that the name Irmin is after all merely an altered form of the Keltic word which appears in Welsh as Hir Vaen, the long stone (*Maen*, a stone). Thus the pillar, so far from being the monument of the great Teutonic victory, would commemorate a pre-Teutonic race, whose name for it the invading tribes adopted. The Rev. Dr. Scott, of Westminster, to whose kindness I am indebted for this explanation, informs me that a rude ditty recording the destruction of the pillar by Charles was current on the spot a few years ago. It ran thus:—

'Irmin slad Irmin
Sla Pfeifen sla Trommen
Der Kaiser wird kommen
Mit Hammer und Stangen
Wird Irmin uphangen.'

[q] Eginhard, *Ann.*

Europe; their primacy was admitted by the kindred tribes of Lombards, Bavarians, Thuringians, Alemannians, and Burgundians; the Slavic peoples on the borders trembled and paid tribute; Alfonso of Asturias found in the Emperor a protector against the infidel foe. His influence, if not his exerted power, crossed the ocean: the kings of the Scots sent gifts and called him lord[r]: the restoration of Eardulf to Northumbria, still more of Egbert to Wessex, might furnish a better ground for the claim of suzerainty than many to which his successors had afterwards recourse. As it was by Frankish arms that this predominance in Europe which the imperial title adorned and legalized had been won, so was the government of Charles Roman in semblance rather than in fact. It was not by restoring the effete mechanism of the old Empire, but by his own vigorous personal action and that of his great officers, that he strove to administer and reform. With every effort for a strong central government, there is no despotism; each nation retains its laws, its hereditary chiefs, its free popular assemblies. The conditions granted to the Saxons after such cruel warfare, conditions so favourable that in the next century their dukes hold the foremost place in Germany, shew how little he desired to make the Franks a dominant caste.

General results of his Empire.

He repeats the attempt of Theodoric to breathe a Teutonic spirit into Roman forms. The conception was magnificent; great results followed its partial execution. Two causes forbade success. The one was the ecclesiastical, especially the Papal power, apparently subject to the temporal, but with a strong and undefined prerogative which only waited the occasion to trample on

[r] Most probably the Scots of Ireland—Eginhard, *Vita Karoli*, cap. 16.

what it had helped to raise. The Pope might take away the crown he had bestowed, and turn against the Emperor the Church which now·obeyed him. The other was to be found in the discordance of the component parts of the Empire. The nations were not ripe for settled life or extensive schemes of polity; the differences of race, language, manners, over vast and thinly-peopled lands baffled every attempt to maintain their connection: and when once the spell of the great mind was withdrawn, the mutually repellent forces began to work, and the mass dissolved into that chaos out of which it had been formed. Nevertheless, the parts separated not as they met, but having all of them undergone influences which continued to act when political connection had ceased. For the work of Charles—a genius pre-eminently creative—was not lost in the anarchy that followed: rather are we to regard his reign as the beginning of a new era, or as laying the foundations whereon men continued for many generations to build.

No claim can be more groundless than that which the modern French, the sons of the Latinized Kelt, set up to the Teutonic Charles. At Rome he might assume the chlamys and the sandals, but at the head of his Frankish host he strictly adhered to the customs of his country, and was beloved by his people as the very ideal of their own character and habits[s]. Of strength and stature almost superhuman, in swimming and hunting unsurpassed, steadfast and terrible in fight, to his friends gentle and condescending, he was a Roman, much less a Gaul, in nothing but his culture and his width of view, otherwise a Teuton. The centre of his realm was the

Personal habits and sympathies.

---

[s] Eginhard, *Vita Karoli*, cap. 23.

Rhine; his capitals Aachen[t] and Engilenheim[u]; his army Frankish; his sympathies as they are shewn in the gathering of the old hero-lays[x], the composition of a German grammar, the ordinance against confining prayer to the three languages,—Hebrew, Greek, and Latin,—were all for the race from which he sprang, and whose advance, represented by the victory of Austrasia, the true Frankish fatherland, over Neustria and Aquitaine, spread a second Germanic wave over the conquered countries.

His Empire and character generally.

There were in his Empire, as in his own mind, two elements; those two from the union and mutual action and reaction of which modern civilization has arisen. These vast domains, reaching from the Ebro to the Carpathian mountains, from the Eyder to the Liris, were all the conquests of the Frankish sword, and were still governed almost exclusively by viceroys and officers of Frankish blood. But the conception of the Empire, that which made it a State and not a mere mass of subject tribes like those great Eastern dominions which rise and perish in a lifetime, the realms of Sesostris, or Attila, or Timur, was inherited from an older and a grander system, was not Teutonic but Roman—Roman in its ordered rule, in its uniformity and precision, in its

---

[t] Aix-la-Chapelle. See the lines in Pertz (*M.G.H.* ii.), beginning,—

> ' Urbs Aquensis, urbs regalis,
> Sedes regni principalis,
> Prima regum curia.'

This city is commonly called Aken in English books of the seventeenth century, and probably that ought to be taken as its proper English name. That name has, however, fallen so entirely into disuse that I do not venture to use it; and as the employment of the French name Aix-la-Chapelle seems inevitably to produce the belief that the place is and was, even in Charles's time, a French town, there is nothing for it but to fall back upon the comparatively unfamiliar German name.

[u] Engilenheim, or Ingelheim, lies near the left shore of the Rhine between Mentz and Bingen.

[x] Eginhard, *Vita Karoli,* cap 29.

endeavour to subject the individual to the system—Roman in its effort to realize a certain limited and human perfection, whose very completeness shall exclude the hope of further progress. And the bond, too, by which the Empire was held together was Roman in its origin, although Roman in a sense which would have surprised Trajan or Severus, could it have been foretold them. The ecclesiastical body was already organized and centralized, and it was in his rule over the ecclesiastical body that the secret of Charles's power lay. Every Christian—Frank, Gaul, or Italian—owed loyalty to the head and defender of his religion: the unity of the Empire was a reflection of the unity of the Church.

Into a general view of the government and policy of Charles it is not possible here to enter. Yet his legislation, his assemblies, his administrative system, his magnificent works, recalling the projects of Alexander and Cæsar [y], the zeal for education and literature which he shewed in the collection of manuscripts, the founding of schools, the gathering of eminent men from all quarters around him, cannot be appreciated apart from his position as restorer of the Roman Empire. Like all the foremost men of our race, Charles was all great things in one, and was so great just because the workings of his genius were so harmonious. He was not a mere barbarian warrior any more than he was an astute diplomatist; there is none of all his qualities which would not be forced out of its place were we to characterize him chiefly by it. Comparisons between famous men of different ages are generally as worthless as they are easy: the circumstances among which Charles lived do

[y] Eginhard, *Vita Karoli*, cap. 17.

not permit us to institute a minute parallel between his greatness and that of those two to whom it is the modern fashion to compare him, nor to say whether he was or could have become as profound a politician as Cæsar, as skilful a commander as Napoleon[z]. But neither to the Roman nor to the Corsican was he inferior in that one quality by which both he and they chiefly impress our imaginations—that intense, vivid, unresting energy which swept him over Europe in campaign after campaign, which sought a field for its workings in theology, science, literature, no less than in politics and war. As it was this wondrous activity that made him the conqueror of Europe, so was it by the variety of his culture that he became her civilizer. From him, in whose wide deep mind the whole mediæval theory of the world and human life mirrored itself, did mediæval society take the form and impress which it retained for centuries, and the traces whereof are among us and upon us to this day.

The great Emperor was buried at Aachen, in that basilica which it had been the delight of his later years to erect and adorn with the treasures of ancient art. His tomb under the dome—where now we see an enormous slab, with the words 'Carolo Magno'—was inscribed, '*Magnus atque Orthodoxus Imperator*[a].' Poets,

[z] It is not a little curious that of the three whom the modern French have taken to be their national heroes all should have been foreigners, and two foreign conquerors.

[a] This basilica was built upon the model of the church of the Holy Sepulchre at Jerusalem, and as it was the first church of any size that had been erected in those regions for centuries past, it excited extraordinary interest among the Franks and Gauls. In many of its features it greatly resembles the beautiful church of San Vitale, at Ravenna (also modelled upon that of the Holy Sepulchre) which was begun by Theodoric, and completed under Justinian. Probably San Vitale was used as a pattern by Charles's architects: we know that he caused marble columns to be brought from Ravenna to deck

fostered by his own zeal, sang of him who had given to the Franks the sway of Romulus[h]. The gorgeous drapery of romance gradually wreathed itself round his name, till by canonization as a saint he received the highest glory the world or the Church could confer. For the Roman Church claimed then, as she claims still, the privilege which humanity in one form or another seems scarce able to deny itself, of raising to honours almost divine its great departed; and as in pagan times temples had risen to a deified Emperor, so churches were dedicated to St. Charlemagne. Between Sanctus Carolus and Divus Julius how strange an analogy and how strange a contrast!

the church at Aachen. Over the tomb of Charles, below the central dome (to which the Gothic choir we now see was added some centuries later), there hangs a huge chandelier, the gift of Frederick Barbarossa.

[b] 'Romuleum Francis præstitit imperium.' — Elegy of Ermoldus Nigellus, in Pertz; *M. G. H.*, t. i. So too Florus the Deacon,—

'Huic etenim cessit etiam gens Romula genti,
Regnorumque simul mater Roma inclyta cessit: .   ,
Huius ibi princeps regni diademata sumpsit
Munere apostolico, Christi munimine fretus.'

CHAPTER VI.

CAROLINGIAN AND ITALIAN EMPERORS.

LEWIS the Pious[a], left by Charles's death sole heir, had been some years before associated with his father in the Empire, and had been crowned by his own hands in a way which, intentionally or not, appeared to deny the need of Papal sanction. But it was soon seen that the strength to grasp the sceptre had not passed with it. Too mild to restrain his turbulent nobles, and thrown by over-conscientiousness into the hands of the clergy, he had reigned few years when dissensions broke out on all sides. Charles had wished the Empire to continue one, under the supremacy of a single Emperor, but with its several parts, Lombardy, Aquitaine, Austrasia, Bavaria, each a kingdom held by a scion of the reigning house. A scheme dangerous in itself, and rendered more so by the absence or neglect of regular rules of succession, could with difficulty have been managed by a wise and firm monarch. Lewis tried in vain to satisfy his sons (Lothar, Lewis, and Charles) by dividing and redividing: they rebelled; he was deposed, and forced by the bishops to do penance; again restored, but

[a] Usage has established this translation of 'Hludowicus Pius,' but 'gentle' or 'kind-hearted' would better express the meaning of the epithet.

without power, a tool in the hands of contending factions. On his death the sons flew to arms, and the first of the dynastic quarrels of modern Europe was fought out on the field of Fontenay. In the partition treaty of Verdun which followed, the Teutonic principle of equal division among heirs triumphed over the Roman one of the transmission of an indivisible Empire: the practical sovereignty of all three brothers was admitted in their respective territories, a barren precedence only reserved to Lothar, with the imperial title which he, as the eldest, already enjoyed. A more important result was the separation of the Gaulish and German nationalities. Their difference of feeling, shewn already in the support of Lewis the Pious by the Germans against the Gallo-Franks and the Church[b], took now a permanent shape: modern Germany proclaims the era of A.D. 843 the beginning of her national existence, and celebrated its thousandth anniversary twenty-seven years ago. To Charles the Bald was given Francia Occidentalis, that is to say, Neustria and Aquitaine; to Lothar, who as Emperor must possess the two capitals, Rome and Aachen, a long and narrow kingdom stretching from the North Sea to the Mediterranean, and including the northern half of Italy: Lewis (surnamed, from his kingdom, the German) received all east of the Rhine, Franks, Saxons, Bavarians, Austria, Carinthia, with possible supremacies over Czechs and Moravians beyond. Throughout these regions German was spoken; through Charles's kingdom a corrupt tongue, equally removed from Latin and from modern French. Lothar's, being mixed and

Partition of Verdun, A.D. 843.

CHAP. VI.

---

[b] Von Ranke discovers in this early traces of the aversion of the Germans to the pretensions of the spiritual power.—*History of Germany during the Reformation: Introduction.*

CHAP. VI.

having no national basis, was the weakest of the three, and soon dissolved into the separate sovereignties of Italy, Burgundy, and Lotharingia, or, as we call it, Lorraine.

On the tangled history of the period that follows it is not possible to do more than touch. After passing from one branch of the Carolingian line to another[c], the imperial sceptre was at last possessed and disgraced by Charles the Fat, who united all the dominions of his great-grandfather. This unworthy heir could not avail himself of recovered territory to strengthen or defend the expiring monarchy.

End of the Carolingian Empire of the West, A.D. 888.

He was driven out of Italy in A.D. 887, and his death in 888 has been usually taken as the date of the extinction of the Carolingian Empire of the West. The Germans, still attached to the ancient line, chose Arnulf, an illegitimate Carolingian, for their king: he entered Italy and was crowned Emperor by his partizan Pope Formosus, in 894. But Germany, divided and helpless, was in no condition to maintain her power over the southern lands: Arnulf retreated in haste, leaving Rome and Italy to sixty years of stormy independence.

That time was indeed the nadir of order and civilization. From all sides the torrent of barbarism which Charles the Great had stemmed was rushing down upon his empire. The Saracen wasted the Mediterranean coasts, and sacked Rome herself. The Dane and Norseman swept the Atlantic and the North Sea, pierced France and Germany by their rivers, burning, slaying, carrying off into captivity: pouring through the Straits

[c] Singularly enough, when one thinks of modern claims, the dynasty of France (Francia occidentalis) had the least share of it. Charles the Bald was the only West Frankish Emperor, and reigned a very short time.

of Gibraltar, they fell upon Provence and Italy. By land, while Wends and Czechs and Obotrites threw off the German yoke and threatened the borders, the wild Hungarian bands, pressing in from the steppes of the Caspian, dashed over Germany like the flying spray of a new wave of barbarism, and carried the terror of their battleaxes to the Apennines and the ocean. Under such strokes the already loosened fabric swiftly dissolved. No one thought of common defence or wide organization: the strong built castles, the weak became their bondsmen, or took shelter under the cowl: the governor—count, abbot, or bishop—tightened his grasp, turned a delegated into an independent, a personal into a territorial authority, and hardly owned a distant and feeble suzerain. The grand vision of a universal Christian empire was utterly lost in the isolation, the antagonism, the increasing localization of all powers: it might seem to have been but a passing gleam from an older and better world.

In Germany, the greatness of the evil worked at last its cure. When the male line of the eastern branch of the Carolingians had ended in Lewis (surnamed the Child), son of Arnulf, the chieftains chose and the people accepted Conrad the Franconian, and after him Henry the Saxon duke, both representing the female line of Charles. Henry laid the foundations of a firm monarchy, driving back the Magyars and Wends, recovering Lotharingia, founding towns to be centres of orderly life and strongholds against Hungarian irruptions. He had meant to claim at Rome his kingdom's rights, rights which Conrad's weakness had at least asserted by the demand of tribute; but death overtook him, and the plan was left to be fulfilled by Otto his son.

CHAP. VI.

The German Kingdom.

Henry the Fowler.

Otto the Great.

The Holy Roman Empire, taking the name in the sense which it commonly bore in later centuries, as denoting the sovereignty of Germany and Italy vested in a Germanic prince, is the creation of Otto the Great. Substantially, it is true, as well as technically, it was a prolongation of the Empire of Charles; and it rested (as will be shewn in the sequel) upon ideas essentially the same as those which brought about the coronation of A.D. 800. But a revival is always more or less a revolution: the one hundred and fifty years that had passed since the death of Charles had brought with them changes which made Otto's position in Germany and Europe less commanding and less autocratic than his predecessor's. With narrower geographical limits, his Empire had a less plausible claim to be the heir of Rome's universal dominion; and there were also differences in its inner character and structure sufficient to justify us in considering Otto (as he is usually considered by his countrymen) not a mere successor after an interregnum, but rather a second founder of the imperial throne in the West.

Before Otto's descent into Italy is described, something must be said of the condition of that country, where circumstances had again made possible the plan of Theodoric, permitted it to become an independent kingdom, and attached the imperial title to its sovereign.

Italian Emperors.

The bestowal of the purple on Charles the Great was not really that 'translation of the Empire from the Greeks to the Franks,' which it was afterwards described as having been. It was not meant to settle the office in one nation or one dynasty: there was but an extension of that principle of the equality of all Romans which had made Trajan and Maximin Emperors. The 'arcanum *imperii*,' whereof Tacitus speaks, '*posse principem alibi quam Romæ fieri*ᵈ,' had long before become *alium quam Romanum ;* and now, the names of Roman and Christian having grown co-extensive, a barbarian chieftain was, as a Roman citizen, eligible to the office of Roman Emperor. Treating him as such, the people and pontiff of the capital had in the vacancy of the Eastern throne asserted their ancient rights of election, and while attempting to reverse the act of Constantine, had re-established the division of Valentinian. The dignity was therefore in strictness personal to Charles; in point of fact, and by consent, hereditarily transmissible, just as it had formerly become in the families of Constantine and Theodosius. To the Frankish crown or nation it was by no means legally attached, though they might think it so; it had passed to their king only because he was the greatest European potentate, and might equally well pass to some stronger race, if any such appeared. Hence, when the line of Carolingian Emperors ended in Charles the Fat, the rights of Rome and Italy might be taken to revive, and there was nothing to prevent the citizens from choosing whom they would. At that memorable era (A.D. 888) the four kingdoms which this prince had united fell asunder; West France, where Odo or Eudes then began to reign, was never again united to Germany; East France (Germany) chose Arnulf; Burgundy ᵉ split up into two principalities, in one of which (Transjurane) Rudolf proclaimed himself king, while the other (Cisjurane with Provence) submitted to Boso ᶠ; while Italy

---

ᵈ Tac. *Hist.* i. 4.
ᵉ For an account of the various applications of the name Bur-

gundy, see Appendix, Note A.
ᶠ The accession of Boso took place in A.D. 877, eleven years

G

was divided between the parties of Berengar of Friuli and Guido of Spoleto. The former was chosen king by the estates of Lombardy; the latter, and on his speedy death his son Lambert, was crowned Emperor by the Pope. Arnulf's descent chased them away and vindicated the claims of the Franks, but on his flight Italy and the anti-German faction at Rome became again free. Berengar was made king of Italy, and afterwards Emperor. Lewis of Burgundy, son of Boso, renounced his fealty to Arnulf, and procured the imperial dignity, whose vain title he retained through years of misery and exile, till A.D. 928 [g]. None of these Emperors were strong enough to rule well even in Italy; beyond it they were not so much as recognized. The crown had become a bauble with which unscrupulous Popes dazzled the vanity of princes whom they summoned to their aid, and soothed the credulity of their more honest supporters. The demoralization and confusion of Italy, the shameless profligacy of Rome and her pontiffs during this period, were enough to prevent a true Italian kingdom from being built up on the basis of Roman choice and national unity. Italian indeed it can scarcely be called, for these Emperors

before Charles the Fat's death. But the new kingdom could not be considered legally settled until the latter date, and its establishment is at any rate a part of that general break-up of the great Carolingian empire whereof A.D. 888 marks the crisis. See Appendix A at the end.

It is a curious mark of the reverence paid to the Carolingian blood, that Boso, a powerful and ambitious prince, seems to have chiefly rested his claims on the fact that

he was husband of Irmingard, daughter of the Emperor Lewis II. Baron de Gingins la Sarraz quotes a charter of his (drawn up when he seems to have doubted whether to call himself king) which begins, 'Ego Boso Dei gratia id quod sum, et coniux mea Irmingardis proles imperialis.'

[g] Lewis had been surprised by Berengar at Verona, blinded, and forced to take refuge in his own kingdom of Provence.

were still in blood and manners Teutonic, and akin rather to their Transalpine enemies than their Romanic subjects. But Italian it might soon have become under a vigorous rule which should have organized it within and knit it together to resist attacks from without. And therefore the attempt to establish such a kingdom is remarkable, for it might have had great consequences; might, if it had prospered, have spared Italy much suffering and Germany endless waste of strength and blood. He who from the summit of Milan cathedral sees across the misty plain the gleaming turrets of its icy wall sweep in a great arc from North to West, may well wonder that a land which nature has so severed from its neighbours should, since history begins, have been always the victim of their intrusive tyranny.

In A.D. 924 died Berengar, the last of these phantom Emperors. After him Hugh of Burgundy, and Lothar his son, reigned as kings of Italy, if puppets in the hands of a riotous aristocracy can be so called. Rome was meanwhile ruled by the consul or senator Alberic [h], who had renewed her never-quite-extinct republican institutions, and in the degradation of the papacy was almost absolute in the city. Lothar dying, his widow Adelheid [i] was sought in marriage by Adalbert son of Berengar II, the new Italian monarch. A gleam of romance is shed on the Empire's revival by her beauty and her adventures. Rejecting the odious alliance, she was seized by Berengar, escaped with difficulty from the loathsome prison where his barbarity had confined her, and appealed

Adelheid Queen of Italy.

---

[h] Alberic is called variously senator, consul, patrician, and prince of the Romans.

[i] Adelheid was daughter of Ru-dolf, king of Trans-Jurane Burgundy. She was at this time in her nineteenth year.

*Otto's first
expedition
into Italy,
A.D. 951.*

*Invitation
sent by the
Pope to
Otto.*

*Motives for
reviving the
Empire.*

to Otto the German king, the model of that knightly
virtue which was beginning to shew itself after the fierce
brutality of the last age. He listened, descended into
Lombardy by the Adige valley, espoused the injured
queen, and forced Berengar to hold his kingdom as a
vassal of the East Frankish crown. That prince was
turbulent and faithless ; new complaints reached ere long
his liege lord, and envoys from the Pope offered Otto
the imperial title if he would re-visit and pacify Italy.
The proposal was well-timed. Men still thought, as they
had thought in the centuries before the Carolingians, that
the Empire was suspended, not extinct ; and the desire
to see its effective power restored, the belief that without
it the world could never be right, might seem better
grounded than it had been before the coronation of
Charles. Then the imperial name had recalled only the
faint memories of Roman majesty and order ; now it
was also associated with the golden age of the first
Frankish Emperor, when a single firm and just hand had
guided the state, reformed the church, repressed the excesses of local power : when Christianity had advanced
against heathendom, civilizing as she went, fearing neither
Hun nor Paynim. One annalist tells us that Charles was
elected ' lest the pagans should insult the Christians, if
the name of Emperor should have ceased among the
Christians [k].' The motive would be bitterly enforced
by the calamities of the last fifty years. In a time of
disintegration, confusion, strife, all the longings of every
wiser and better soul for unity, for peace and law, for
some bond to bring Christian men and Christian states
together against the common enemy of the faith, were

[k] *Chron. Moiss.*, in Pertz ; *M. G. H.* i. 305.

but so many cries for the restoration of the Roman Empire [1]. These were the feelings that on the field of Merseburg broke forth in the shout of 'Henry the Emperor:' these the hopes of the Teutonic host when after the great deliverance of the Lechfeld they greeted Otto, conqueror of the Magyars, as 'Imperator Augustus, Pater Patriæ [m].'

The anarchy which an Emperor was needed to heal was at its worst in Italy, desolated by the feuds of a crowd of petty princes. A succession of infamous Popes, raised by means yet more infamous, the lovers and sons of Theodora and Marozia, had disgraced the chair of the Apostle, and though Rome herself might be lost to decency, Western Christendom was roused to anger and alarm. Men had not yet learned to satisfy their consciences by separating the person from the office. The rule of Alberic had been succeeded by the wildest confusion, and demands were raised for the renewal of that imperial authority which all admitted in theory [n], and which nothing but the resolute opposition of Alberic himself had prevented Otto from claiming in 951. From the Byzantine Empire, whither Italy was more than once tempted to turn, nothing could be hoped; its dangers

CHAP. VI.

Condition of Italy.

[1] See especially the poem of Florus the Deacon (printed in the Benedictine collection and in Migne), a bitter lament over the dissolution of the Carolingian Empire. It is too long for quotation. I give four lines here:—

'Quid faciant populi quos ingens alluit Hister,
Quos Rhenus Rhodanusque rigant, Ligerisve, Padusve,
Quos omnes dudum tenuit concordia nexos,
Foedere nunc rupto divortia moesta fatigant.'

[m] Witukind, *Annales*, in Pertz. It may, however, be doubted whether the annalist is not here giving a very free rendering of the triumphant cries of the German army.

[n] Cf. esp. the '*Libellus de imperatoria potestate in urbe Roma,*' in Pertz.

from foreign enemies were aggravated by the plots of the court and the seditions of the capital; it was becoming more and more alienated from the West by the Photian schism and the question regarding the Procession of the Holy Ghost, which that quarrel had started. Germany was extending and consolidating herself, had escaped domestic perils, and might think of reviving ancient claims. No one could be more willing to revive them than Otto the Great. His ardent spirit, after waging a bold and successful struggle against the turbulent magnates of his German realm, had engaged him in wars with the surrounding nations, and was now captivated by the vision of a wider sway and a loftier world-embracing dignity. Nor was the prospect which the papal offer opened up less welcome to his people. Aachen, their capital, was the ancestral home of the house of Pipin : their sovereign, although himself a Saxon by race, titled himself king of the Franks, in opposition to the Frankish rulers of the Western branch, whose Teutonic character was disappearing among the Romans of Gaul ; they held themselves in every way the true representatives of the Carolingian power, and accounted the period since Arnulf's death nothing but an interregnum which had suspended but not impaired their rights over Rome. 'For so long,' says a writer of the time, 'as there remain kings of the Franks, so long will the dignity of the Roman Empire not wholly perish, seeing that it will abide in its kings [o].' The recovery of Italy was therefore to German

[o] ' Licet videamus Romanorum regnum in maxima parte jam destructum, tamen quamdiu reges Francorum duraverint qui Romanum imperium tenere debent, dignitas Romani imperii ex toto non peribit, quia stabit in regibus suis.'—*Liber de Antichristo*, addressed by Adso, abbot of Moutier-en-Der, to queen Gerberga (circa A.D. 950).

eyes a righteous as well as a glorious design : approved by the Teutonic Church which had lately been negotiating with Rome on the subject of missions to the heathen; embraced by the people, who saw in it an accession of strength to their young kingdom. Everything smiled on Otto's enterprise, and the connection which was destined to bring so much strife and woe to Germany and to Italy was welcomed by the wisest of both countries as the beginning of a better era.

Whatever were Otto's own feelings, whether or not he felt that he was sacrificing, as modern writers have thought that he did sacrifice, the greatness of his German kingdom to the lust of universal dominion, he shewed no hesitation in his acts. Descending from the Alps with an overpowering force, he was acknowledged as king of Italy at Pavia P; and, having first taken an oath to protect the Holy See and respect the liberties of the city, advanced to Rome. There, with Adelheid his queen, he was crowned by John XII, on the day of the Purification, the second of February, A.D. 962. The details of his election and coronation are unfortunately still more scanty than in the case of his great predecessor. Most of our authorities represent the act as of the Pope's favour q, yet it is plain that the

Descent of Otto the Great into Italy.

His coronation at Rome, A.D. 962.

P From the money which Otto struck in Italy, it seems probable that he did occasionally use the title of king of Italy or of the Lombards. That he was crowned can hardly be considered quite certain.

q 'A papa imperator ordinatur,' says Hermannus Contractus. 'Dominum Ottonem, ad hoc usque vocatum regem, non solum Romano sed et pœne totius Europæ populo acclamante imperatorem consecravit Augustum.' — *Annal. Quedlinb.*, ad. ann. 962. 'Benedictionem a domno apostolico Iohanne, cuius rogatione huc venit, cum sua coniuge promeruit imperialem ac patronus Romanæ effectus est ecclesiæ.'—Thietmar. 'Acclamatione totius Romani populi ab apostolico Iohanne, filio Alberici, imperator et Augustus vocatur et ordinatur.'—Continuator Reginonis. And similarly the other annalists.

consent of the people was still thought an essential part of the ceremony, and that Otto rested after all on his host of conquering Saxons. Be this as it may, there was neither question raised nor opposition made in Rome; the usual courtesies and promises were exchanged between Emperor and Pope, the latter owning himself a subject, and the citizens swore for the future to elect no pontiff without Otto's consent.

CHAPTER VII.

THEORY OF THE MEDIÆVAL EMPIRE.

THESE were the events and circumstances of the time: let us now look at the causes. The restoration of the Empire by Charles may seem to be sufficiently accounted for by the width of his conquests, by the peculiar connection which already subsisted between him and the Roman Church, by his commanding personal character, by the temporary vacancy of the Byzantine throne. The causes of its revival under Otto must be sought deeper. Making every allowance for the favouring incidents which have already been dwelt upon, there must have been some further influence at work to draw him and his successors, Saxon and Frankish kings, so far from home in pursuit of a barren crown, to lead the Italians to accept the dominion of a stranger and a barbarian, to make the Empire itself appear through the whole Middle Age not what it seems now, a gorgeous anachronism, but an institution divine and necessary, having its foundations in the very nature and order of things. The empire of the elder Rome had been splendid in its life, yet its judgment was written in the misery to which it had brought the provinces, and the helplessness that had invited the attacks of the barbarian. Now, as we at least can see, it had long been dead, and the course of events was adverse

CHAP. VII.

a more illusion

Mediæval
theories.

to its revival.   Its actual representatives, the Roman people, were a turbulent rabble, sunk in a profligacy notorious even in that guilty age.   Yet not the less for all this did men cling to the idea, and strive through long ages to stem the irresistible time-current, fondly believing that they were breasting it even while it was sweeping them ever faster and faster away from the old order into a region of new thoughts, new feelings, new forms of life.   Not till the days of the Reformation was the illusion dispelled.

The explanation is to be found in the state of the human mind during these centuries.   The Middle Ages were essentially unpolitical.   Ideas as familiar to the commonwealths of antiquity as to ourselves, ideas of the common good as the object of the State, of the rights of the people, of the comparative merits of different forms of government, were to them, though sometimes carried out in fact, in their speculative form unknown, perhaps incomprehensible.   Feudalism was the one great institution to which those times gave birth, and feudalism was a social and a legal system, only indirectly and by consequence a political one.   Yet the human mind, so far from being idle, was in certain directions never more active; nor was it possible for it to remain without general conceptions regarding the relation of men to each other in this world.   Such conceptions were neither made an expression of the actual present condition of things nor drawn from an induction of the past; they were partly inherited from the system that had preceded, partly evolved from the principles of that metaphysical theology which was ripening into scholasticism [a].   Now

[a] I do not mean to say that the system of ideas which it is endeavoured to set forth in the following pages was complete in this

the two great ideas which expiring antiquity bequeathed to the ages that followed were those of a World-Monarchy and a World-Religion.

Before the conquests of Rome, men, with little knowledge of each other, with no experience of wide political union [b], had held differences of race to be natural and irremovable barriers. Similarly, religion appeared to them a matter purely local and national; and as there were gods of the hills and gods of the valleys, of the land and of the sea, so each tribe rejoiced in its peculiar deities, looking on the natives of another country who worshipped other gods as Gentiles, natural foes, unclean beings. Such feelings, if keenest in the East, frequently shew themselves in the early records of Greece and Italy: in Homer the hero who wanders over the unfruitful sea glories in sacking the cities

CHAP. VII.

The World-Religion.

particular form, either in the days of Charles or in those of Otto, or in those of Frederick Barbarossa. It seems to have been constantly growing and decaying from the fourth century to the sixteenth, the relative prominence of its cardinal doctrines varying from age to age. But, just as the painter who sees the ever-shifting lights and shades play over the face of a wide landscape faster than his brush can place them on the canvas, in despair at representing their exact position at any single moment, contents himself with painting the effects that are broadest and most permanent, and at giving rather the impression which the scene makes on him than every detail of the scene itself, so here, the best and indeed the only practicable course seems to be that of setting forth in its most self-con-

sistent form the body of ideas and beliefs on which the Empire rested, although this form may not be exactly that which they can be asserted to have worn in any one century, and although the illustrations adduced may have to be taken sometimes from earlier, sometimes from later writers. As the doctrine of the Empire was in its essence the same during the whole Middle Age, such a general description as is attempted here may, I venture to hope, be found substantially true for the tenth as well as for the fourteenth century.

[b] Empires like the Persian did nothing to assimilate the subject races, who retained their own laws and customs, sometimes their own princes, and were bound only to serve in the armies and fill the treasury of the Great King.

of the stranger [c]; the primitive Latins have the same word for a foreigner and an enemy: the exclusive systems of Egypt, Hindostan, China, are only more vehement expressions of the belief which made Athenian philosophers look on a state of war between Greeks and barbarians as natural [d], and defend slavery on the same ground of the original diversity of the races that rule and the races that serve. The Roman dominion giving to many nations a common speech and law, smote this feeling on its political side; Christianity more effectually banished it from the soul by substituting for the variety of local pantheons the belief in one God, before whom all men are equal [e].

Coincides with the World-Empire.

It is on the religious life that nations repose. Because divinity was divided, humanity had been divided likewise; the doctrine of the unity of God now enforced the unity of man, who had been created in His image [f]. The first lesson of Christianity was love, a love that was to join in one body those whom suspicion and prejudice and pride of race had hitherto kept apart. There was thus formed by the new religion a community of the faithful, a Holy Empire, designed to gather all men into its bosom, and standing opposed to the manifold polytheisms of the older world, exactly as the universal sway of the Cæsars was

---

[e] Od. iii. 72 :—

　.... ἤ μαψιδίως ἀλάλησθε,
οἱά τε ληϊστῆρες, ὑπεὶρ ἅλα, τοίτ' ἀλόωνται
ψυχὰς παρθέμενοι, κακὸν ἀλλοδαποῖσι φέροντες;

Cf. Od. ix. 39 : and the Hymn to the Pythian Apollo, l. 274. So in Il. v. 214, ἀλλότριος φώς.

[d] Plato, in the beginning of the Laws, represents it as natural between all states: πολεμὸς φύσει ὑπάρχει πρὸς ἁπάσας τὰς πόλεις.

[e] See especially Acts xvii. 26; Gal. iii. 28; Eph. ii. 11, sqq.; iv. 3–6; Col. iii. 11.

[f] This is drawn out by Laurent, *Histoire du Droit des Gens;* and Ægidi, *Der Fürstenrath nach dem Luneviller Frieden.*

contrasted with the innumerable kingdoms and republics that had gone before it.. The analogy of the two made them appear parts of one great world-movement toward unity: the coincidence of their boundaries, which had begun before Constantine, lasted long enough after him to associate them indissolubly together, and make the names of Roman and Christian convertible [g]. Œcumenical councils, where the whole spiritual body gathered itself from every part of the temporal realm under the presidency of the temporal head, presented the most visible and impressive examples of their connection [h]. The language of civil government was, throughout the West, that of the sacred writings and of worship; the greatest mind of his generation consoled the faithful for the fall of their earthly commonwealth Rome, by describing to them its successor

[g] 'Romanos enim vocitant homines nostræ religionis.'—Gregory of Tours, quoted by Ægidi, from A. F. Pott, *Essay on the Words 'Rö-misch,' 'Romanisch,' 'Roman,' 'Romantisch.'* So in the Middle Ages, 'Ρωμαῖοι is used to mean Christians, as opposed to "Ελληνες, heathens.

Cf. Ducange, 'Romani olim dicti qui alias Christiani vel etiam Catholici.'

[h] As a reviewer in the *Tablet* (whose courtesy it is the more pleasant to acknowledge since his point of view is altogether opposed to mine) has understood this passage as meaning that 'people imagined the Christian religion was to last for ever because the Holy Roman Empire was never to decay,' it may be worth while to say that this is far from being the purport of the argument which this chapter was designed to state. The converse would be nearer the truth:—'people imagined the Holy Roman Empire was never to decay, because the Christian religion was to last for ever.'

The phenomen may perhaps be stated thus:—Men who were already disposed to believe the Roman Empire to be eternal for one set of reasons, came to believe the Christian Church to be eternal for another and, to them, more impressive set of reasons. Seeing the two institutions allied in fact, they took their alliance and connection to be eternal also; and went on for centuries believing in the necessary existence of the Roman Empire because they believed in its necessary union with the Catholic Church.

Preservation of the unity of the Church.

and representative, the 'city which hath foundations, whose builder and maker is God[i].'

Of these two parallel unities, that of the political and that of the religious society, meeting in the higher unity of all Christians, which may be indifferently called Catholicity or Romanism (since in that day those words would have had the same meaning), that only which had been entrusted to the keeping of the Church survived the storms of the fifth century. Many reasons may be assigned for the firmness with which she clung to it. Seeing one institution after another falling to pieces around her, seeing how countries and cities were being severed from each other by the irruption of strange tribes and the increasing difficulty of communication, she strove to save religious fellowship by strengthening the ecclesiastical organization, by drawing tighter every bond of outward union. Necessities of faith were still more powerful. Truth, it was said, is one, and as it must bind into one body all who hold it, so it is only by continuing in that body that they can preserve it. Thus with the growing rigidity of dogma, which may be traced from the council of Jerusalem to the council of Trent, there had arisen the idea of supplementing revelation by tradition as a source of doctrine, of exalting the universal conscience and belief above the individual, and allowing the soul to approach God only through the universal consciousness, represented by the sacerdotal order: principles still maintained by one branch of the Church, and for some at least of which far weightier reasons could be assigned then, in the paucity of written

Mediæval Theology requires One Visible Catholic Church.

[i] Augustine, in the *De Civitate Dei.* His influence, great through all the Middle Ages, was greater on no one than on Charles.—'Delectabatur et libris sancti Augustini, præcipueque his qui De Civitate Dei prætitulati sunt.'—Eginhard, *Vita Karoli,* cap. 24.

records and the blind ignorance of the mass of the people, than any to which their modern advocates have recourse. There was another cause yet more deeply seated, and which it is hard adequately to describe. It was not exactly a want of faith in the unseen, nor a shrinking fear which dared not look forth on the universe alone : it was rather the powerlessness of the untrained mind to realize the idea as an idea and live in it : it was the tendency to see everything in the concrete, to turn the parable into a fact, the doctrine into its most literal application, the symbol into the essential ceremony ; the tendency which intruded earthly Madonnas and saints between the worshipper and the spiritual Deity, and could satisfy its devotional feelings only by visible images even of these : which conceived of man's aspirations and temptations as the result of the direct action of angels and devils : which expressed the strivings of the soul after purity by the search for the Holy Grail : which in the Crusades sent myriads to win at Jerusalem by earthly arms the sepulchre of Him whom they could not serve in their own spirit nor approach by their own prayers. And therefore it was that the whole fabric of mediæval Christianity rested upon the idea of the Visible Church. Such a Church could be in nowise local or limited. To acquiesce in the establishment of National Churches would have appeared to those men, as it must always appear when scrutinized, contradictory to the nature of a religious body, opposed to the genius of Christianity, defensible, when capable of defence at all, only as a temporary resource in the presence of insuperable difficulties. Had this plan, on which so many have dwelt with complacency in later times, been proposed either to the primitive Church in its adversity or to the dominant Church of the ninth century, it would have been

CHAP. VII.

rejected with horror; but since there were as yet no nations, the plan was one which did not and could not present itself. The Visible Church was therefore the Church Universal, the whole congregation of Christian men dispersed throughout the world.

Idea of political unity upheld by the clergy.

Now of the Visible Church the emblem and stay was the priesthood; and it was by them, in whom dwelt whatever of learning and thought was left in Europe, that the second great idea whereof mention has been made—the belief in one universal temporal state—was preserved. As a matter of fact, that state had perished out of the West, and it might seem their interest to let its memory be lost. They, however, did not so calculate their interest. So far from feeling themselves opposed to the civil authority in the seventh and eighth centuries, as they came to do in the twelfth and thirteenth, the clergy were fully persuaded that its maintenance was indispensable to their own welfare. They were, be it remembered, at first Romans themselves living by the Roman law, using Latin as their proper tongue, and imbued with the idea of the historical connection of the two powers. And by them chiefly was that idea expounded and enforced for many generations, by none more earnestly than by Alcuin of York, the adviser of Charles [k]. The limits of those two powers had become confounded in practice: bishops were princes, the chief ministers of the sovereign, sometimes even the leaders of their flocks in war: kings were accustomed to summon ecclesiastical councils, and appoint to ecclesiastical offices.

---

[k] ' Quapropter universorum precibus fidelium optandum est, ut in omnem gloriam vestram extendatur imperium, ut scilicet catholica fides . . . veraciter in una confessione cunctorum cordibus infigatur, qua- tenus summi Regis donante pietate eadem sanctæ pacis et perfectæ caritatis omnes ubique regat et custodiat unitas.' Quoted by Waitz (*Deutsche Verfassungsgeschichte*, ii. 182) from an unprinted letter of Alcuin.

But, like the unity of the Church, the doctrine of a universal monarchy had a theoretical as well as an historical basis, and may be traced up to those metaphysical ideas out of which the system we call Realism developed itself. The beginnings of philosophy in those times were logical; and its first efforts were to distribute and classify: system, subordination, uniformity, appeared to be that which was most desirable in thought as in life. The search after causes became a search after principles of classification; since simplicity and truth were held to consist not in an analysis of thought into its elements, nor in an observation of the process of its growth, but rather in a sort of genealogy of notions, a statement of the relations of classes as containing or excluding each other. These classes, genera or species, were not themselves held to be conceptions formed by the mind from phenomena, nor mere accidental aggregates of objects grouped under and called by some common name; they were real things, existing independently of the individuals who composed them, recognized rather than created by the human mind. In this view, Humanity is an essential quality present in all men, and making them what they are: as regards it they are therefore not many but one, the differences between individuals being no more than accidents. The whole truth of their being lies in the universal property, which alone has a permanent and independent existence. The common nature of the individuals thus gathered into one Being is typified in its two aspects, the spiritual and the secular, by two persons, the World-Priest and the World-Monarch, who present on earth a similitude of the Divine unity. For, as we have seen, it was only through its concrete and symbolic expression that a thought could then be appre-

H

hended[1]. Although it was to unity in religion that the clerical body was both by doctrine and by practice attached, they found this inseparable from the corresponding unity in politics. They saw that every act of man has a social and public as well as a moral and personal bearing, and concluded that the rules which directed and the powers which rewarded or punished must be parallel and similar, not so much two powers as different manifestations of one and the same. That the souls of all Christian men should be guided by one hierarchy, rising through successive grades to a supreme head, while for their deeds they were answerable to a multitude of local, unconnected, mutually irresponsible potentates, appeared to them necessarily opposed to the Divine order. As they could not imagine, nor value if they had imagined, a communion of the saints without its expression in a visible Church, so in matters temporal they recognized no brotherhood of spirit without the bonds of form, no universal humanity save in the image of a universal State[m]. In this, as in so much

[1] A curious illustration of this tendency of mind is afforded by the descriptions we meet with of Learning or Theology (*Studium*) as a concrete existence, having a visible dwelling in the University of Paris. The three great powers which rule human life, says one writer, the Popedom, the Empire, and Learning, have been severally entrusted to the three foremost nations of Europe: Italians, Germans, French. 'His siquidem tribus, scilicet sacerdotio imperio et studio, tanquam tribus virtutibus, videlicet naturali vitali et scientiali, catholica ecclesia spiritualiter mirificatur, augmentatur et regitur. His itaque tribus, tanquam fundamento, pariete et tecto, eadem ecclesia tanquam materialiter proficit. Et sicut ecclesia materialis uno tantum fundamento et uno tecto eget, parietibus vero quatuor, ita imperium quatuor habet parietes, hoc est, quatuor imperii sedes, Aquisgranum, Arelatum, Mediolanum, Romam.'—*Jordanis Chronica; ap.* Schardius *Sylloge Tractatuum.* And see Döllinger, *Die Vergangenheit und Gegenwart der katholischen Theologie,* p. 8

[m] "Una est sola respublica totius populi Christiani, ergo de necessitate erit et unus solus princeps et rex illius reipublicæ, statutus et stabilitus ad ipsius fidei et populi Christiani dilatationem et defensionem."

else, the men of the Middle Ages were the slaves of the letter, unable, with all their aspirations, to rise out of the concrete, and prevented by the very grandeur and boldness of their conceptions from carrying them out in practice against the enormous obstacles that met them.

Deep as this belief had struck its roots, it might never have risen to maturity nor sensibly affected the progress of events, had it not gained in the pre-existence of the monarchy of Rome a definite shape and a definite purpose. It was chiefly by means of the Papacy that this came to pass. When under Constantine the Christian Church was framing her organization on the model of the state which protected her, the bishop of the metropolis perceived and improved the analogy between himself and the head of the civil government. The notion that the chair of Peter was the imperial throne of the Church had dawned upon the Popes very early in their history, and grew stronger every century under the operation of causes already specified. Even before the Empire of the West had fallen, St. Leo the Great could boast that to Rome, exalted by the preaching of the chief of the Apostles to be a holy nation, a chosen people, a priestly and royal city, there had been appointed a spiritual dominion wider than her earthly sway[n]. In A.D. 476 Rome ceased to be the political capital of the Western countries, and the Papacy, inheriting no small part of the Emperor's power,

The ideal state supposed to be embodied in the Roman Empire.

Ex qua ratione concludit etiam Augustinus (*De Civitate Dei*, lib. xix.) quod extra ecclesiam nunquam fuit nec potuit nec poterit esse verum imperium, etsi fuerint imperatores qualitercumque et secundum quid. non simpliciter, qui fuerunt extra fidem Catholicam et ecclesiam.'—Engelbert (abbot of Admont in Upper Austria), *De Ortu et Fine imperii Romani* (circ. 1310).

In this 'de necessitate' everything is included.

[n] See note f, p. 34.

H 2

CHAP. VII.

Constantine's Donation.

drew to herself the reverence which the name of the city still commanded, until by the middle of the eighth, or, at latest, of the ninth century she had perfected in theory a scheme which made her the exact counterpart of the departed despotism, the centre of the hierarchy, absolute mistress of the Christian world. The character of that scheme is best set forth in the singular document, most stupendous of all the mediæval forgeries, which under the name of the Donation of Constantine commanded for seven centuries the unquestioning belief of mankind [o]. Itself a portentous falsehood, it is the most unimpeachable evidence of the thoughts and beliefs of the priesthood which framed it, some time between the middle of the eighth and the middle of the tenth century. It tells how Constantine the Great, cured of his leprosy by the prayers of Sylvester, resolved, on the fourth day from his baptism, to forsake the ancient seat for a new capital on the Bosphorus, lest the continuance of the secular government should cramp the freedom of the spiritual, and how he bestowed therewith upon the Pope and his successors the sovereignty over Italy and the countries of the West. But this is not all, although this is what historians, in admiration of its splendid audacity, have chiefly dwelt upon. The edict proceeds to grant to the Roman pontiff and his clergy a series of dignities and privileges, all of them enjoyed by the Emperor and his senate, all of them shewing the same desire to make the pontifical a copy of the imperial office. The Pope is to inhabit the Lateran palace, to wear the diadem, the collar, the purple cloak, to carry

---

[o] This is admirably brought out by Ægidi, *Der Fürstenrath nach dem Luneviller Frieden.*

the sceptre, and to be attended by a body of chamberlains. Similarly his clergy are to ride on white horses and receive the honours and immunities of the senate and patricians P.

The notion which prevails throughout, that the chief of the religious society must be in every point conformed to his prototype the chief of the civil, is the key to all the thoughts and acts of the Roman clergy; not less plainly seen in the details of papal ceremonial than it is in the gigantic scheme of papal legislation. The Canon law was intended by its authors to reproduce and rival the imperial jurisprudence; a correspondence was traced

Interdependence of Papacy and Empire.

P See the original forgery (or rather the extracts which Gratian gives from it) in the *Corpus Iuris Canonici*, *Dist.* xcvi. cc. 13, 14. ‘Et sicut nostram terrenam imperialem potentiam, sic sacrosanctam Rómanam ecclesiam decrevimus veneranter honorari, et amplius quam nostrum imperium et terrenum thronum sedem beati Petri gloriose exaltari, tribuentes ei potestatem et gloriæ dignitatem atque vigorem et honorificentiam imperialem . . . . Beato Sylvestro patri nostro summo pontifici et universali urbis Romæ papæ, et omnibus eius successoribus pontificibus, qui usque in finem muudi in sede beati Petri erunt sessuri, de præsenti contradimus palatium imperii nostri Lateranense, deinde diadema, videlicet coronam capitis nostri, simulque phrygium, necnon et superhumerale, verum etiam et chlamydem purpuream et tunicam coccineam, et omnia imperialia indumenta, sed et dignitatem imperialem præsidentium equitum, conferentes etiam et imperialia sceptra, simulque cuncta signa atque banda et diversa ornamenta imperialia et omnem processionem imperialis culminis et gloriam potestatis nostrae. . . . . Et sicut imperialis militia ornatur ita et clerum sanctæ Romanæ ecclesiæ ornari decernimus. . . . Unde ut pontificalis apex non vilescat sed magis quam terreni imperii dignitas gloria et potentia decoretur, ecce tam palatium nostrum quam Romanam urbem et omnes Italiæ seu occidentalium regionum provincias loca et civitates beatissimo papæ Sylvestro universali papæ contradimus atque relinquimus. . . Ubi enim principatus sacerdotum et Christianæ religionis caput ab imperatore cœlesti constitutum est, iustum non est ut illic imperator terrenus habeat potestatem.’

The practice of kissing the Pope’s foot was adopted in imitation of the old imperial court. It was afterwards revived by the German Emperors.

between its divisions and those of the Corpus Juris Civilis, and Gregory IX, who was the first to consolidate it into a code, sought the fame and received the title of the Justinian of the Church. But the wish of the clergy was always, even in the weakness or hostility of the temporal power, to imitate and rival, not to supersede it; since they held it the necessary complement of their own, and thought the Christian people equally imperilled by the fall of either. Hence the reluctance of Gregory II to break with the Byzantine princes[q], and the maintenance of their titular sovereignty till A.D. 800: hence the part which the Holy See played in transferring the crown to Charles, the first sovereign of the West capable of fulfilling its duties; hence the grief with which its weakness under his successors was seen, the gladness when it descended to Otto as representative of the Frankish kingdom.

The Roman Empire revived in a new character.

Up to the era of A.D. 800 there had been at Constantinople a legitimate historical prolongation of the Roman Empire. Technically, as we have seen, the election of Charles, after the deposition of Constantine VI, was itself a prolongation, and maintained the old rights and forms in their integrity. But the Pope, though he knew it not, did far more than effect a change of dynasty when he rejected Irene and crowned the barbarian chief. Restorations are always delusive. As well might one hope to stop the earth's course in her orbit as to arrest that ceaseless change and movement in human affairs which forbids an old institution, sud-

---

[q] Döllinger has shewn in a recent work (*Die Papst-Fabeln des Mittelalters*) that the common belief that Gregory II excited the revolt against Leo the Iconoclast is unfounded.

So Anastasius, 'Ammonebat (*sc.* Gregorius Secundus) ne a fide vel amore Romani imperii desisterent.' —*Vitæ Pontif. Rom.*

denly transplanted into a new order of things, from filling its ancient place and serving its former ends. The dictatorship at Rome in the second Punic war was not more unlike the dictatorships of Sulla and Cæsar, nor the States-general of Louis XIII to the assembly which his unhappy descendant convoked in 1789, than was the imperial office of Theodosius to that of Charles the Frank; and the seal, ascribed to A.D. 800, which bears the legend 'Renovatio Romani Imperii [r],' expresses, more justly perhaps than was intended by its author, a second birth of the Roman Empire.

It is not, however, from Carolingian times that a proper view of this new creation can be formed. That period was one of transition, of fluctuation and uncertainty, in which the office, passing from one dynasty and country to another, had not time to acquire a settled character and claims, and was without the power that would have enabled it to support them. From the coronation of Otto the Great a new period begins, in which the ideas that have been described as floating in men's minds took clearer shape, and attached to the imperial title a body of definite rights and definite duties. It is this new phase, <u>the Holy Empire</u>, that we have now to consider.

[r] Of this curious seal, a leaden one, preserved at Paris, a figure is given upon the cover of this volume. There are very few monuments of that age whose genuineness can be considered altogether beyond doubt; but this seal has many respectable authorities in its favour. See, among others, Le Blanc, *Dissertation historique sur quelques Monnoies de Charlemagne*, Paris, 1689; J. M. Heineccius, *De Veteribus Germanorum aliarumque nationum sigillis*, Lips. 1709; Anastasius, *Vitœ Pontificum Romanorum*, ed. Vignoli, Romæ, 1752; Götz, *Deutschlands Kayser-Münzen des Mittelalters*, Dresden, 1827; and the authorities cited by Waitz, *Deutsche Verfassungs-geschichte*, iii. 179, n. 4.

The realistic philosophy, and the needs of a time when the only notion of civil or religious order was submission to authority, required the World-State to be a monarchy; tradition, as well as the continuance of certain institutions, gave the monarch the name of Roman Emperor. A king could not be universal sovereign, for there were many kings: the Emperor must be, for there had never been but one Emperor; he had in older and brighter days been the actual lord of the civilized world; the seat of his power was placed beside that of the spiritual autocrat of Christendom[s]. His functions will be seen most clearly if we deduce them from the leading principle of mediæval mythology, the exact correspondence of earth and heaven. As God, in the midst of the celestial hierarchy, ruled blessed spirits in paradise, so the Pope, His Vicar, raised above priests, bishops, metropolitans, reigned over the souls of mortal men below. But as God is Lord of earth as well as of heaven, so must he (the *Imperator cœlestis*[t]) be represented by a second earthly viceroy, the Emperor (*Imperator terrenus*[t]), whose authority shall be of and for this present life. And as in this present world the soul cannot act save through the

[s] 'Præterea mirari se dilecta fraternitas tua quod non Francorum set Romanorum imperatores nos appellemus; set scire te convenit quia nisi Romanorum imperatores essemus, utique nec Francorum. A Romanis enim hoc nomen et dignitatem assumpsimus, apud quos profecto primum tantæ culmen sublimitatis effulsit,' &c — *Letter of the Emperor Lewis II to Basil the Emperor at Constantinople,* from *Chron. Salernit. ap.* Murat. *S. R. I.*

[t] 'Illam (*sc.* Romanam ecclesiam) solus ille fundavit, et super petram fidei mox nascentis erexit, qui beato æternæ vitæ clavigero terreni simul et cœlestis imperii iura commisit.' — *Corpus Iuris Canonici, Dist.* xxii. c. I. The expression is not uncommon in mediæval writers. So 'unum est imperium Patris et Filii et Spiritus Sancti, cuius est pars ecclesia constituta in terris,' in Lewis II's letter.

body, while yet the body is no more than an instrument and means for the soul's manifestation, so must there be a rule and care of men's bodies as well as of their souls, yet subordinated always to the well-being of that which is the purer and the more enduring. It is under the emblem of soul and body that the relation of the papal and imperial power is presented to us throughout the Middle Ages [u]. The Pope, as God's vicar in matters spiritual, is to lead men to eternal life; the Emperor, as vicar in matters temporal, must so control them in their dealings with one another that they may be able to pursue undisturbed the spiritual life, and thereby attain the same supreme and common end of everlasting happiness. In the view of this object his chief duty is to maintain peace in the world, while towards the Church his position is that of Advocate, a title borrowed from the practice adopted by churches and monasteries, of choosing some powerful baron to protect their lands and lead their tenants in war [v]. The

---

[u] 'Merito summus Pontifex Romanus episcopus dici potest rex et sacerdos. Si enim dominus noster Iesus Christus sic appellatur, non videtur incongruum suum vocare successorem. Corporale et temporale ex spirituali et perpetuo dependet, sicut corporis operatio ex virtute animæ. Sicut ergo corpus per animam habet esse virtutem et operationem, ita et temporalis iurisdictio principum per spiritualem Petri et successorum eius.'—St. Thomas Aquinas, *De Regimine Principum.*

[v] 'Nonne Romana ecclesia tenetur imperatori tanquam suo patrono, et imperator ecclesiam fovere et defensare tanquam suus vere patronus? certe sic. . . . . Patronis vero concessum est ut prælatos in ecclesiis sui patronatus eligant. Cum ergo imperator onus sentiat patronatus, ut qui tenetur eam defendere, sentire debet honorem et emolumentum.' I quote this from a curious document in Goldast's collection of tracts (*Monarchia Imperii*), entitled 'Letter of the four Universities, Paris, Oxford, Prague, and the "Romana generalitas," to the Emperor Wenzel and Pope Urban,' A.D. 1380. The title can scarcely be right, but if the document is, as in all probability it is, not later than the fifteenth century, its being

functions of Advocacy are twofold: at home to make the Christian people obedient to the priesthood, and to execute their decrees upon heretics and sinners; abroad to propagate the faith among the heathen, not sparing to use carnal weapons[x]. Thus does the Emperor answer in every point to his antitype the Pope, his power being yet of a lower rank, created on the analogy of the papal, as the papal itself had been modelled after the elder Empire. The parallel holds good even in its details; for just as we have seen the churchman assuming the crown and robes of the secular prince, so now did he array the Emperor in his own ecclesiastical vestments, the stole and the dalmatic, gave him a clerical as well as a sacred character, removed his office from all narrowing associations of birth or country, inaugurated him by rites every one of which was meant to symbolize and enjoin duties in their essence religious. Thus the Holy Roman Church and the Holy Roman Empire are one and the same thing, in two aspects; and Catholicism, the principle of the universal Christian society, is also Romanism; that is, rests upon Rome as the origin and type of its universality; manifesting itself in a mystic

Correspondence and harmony of the spiritual and temporal powers.

---

misdescribed, or even its being a forgery, does not make it less valuable as an evidence of men's ideas.

[x] So Leo III in a charter issued on the day of Charles's coronation: '. . . . actum in præsentia gloriosi atque excellentissimi filii nostri Caroli quem auctore Deo in de-

fensionem et provectionem sanctæ universalis ecclesiæ hodie Augustum sacravimus.'—Jaffé *Regesta Pontificum Romanorum*, ad ann. 800.

So, indeed, Theodulf of Orleans, a contemporary of Charles, ascribes to the Emperor an almost papal authority over the Church itself :—

'Cœli habet hic (*sc.* Papa) claves, proprias te iussit habere;
 Tu regis ecclesiæ, nam regit ille poli;
 Tu regis eius opes, clerum populumque gubernas,
 Hic te cœlicolas ducet ad usque choros.'

In D. Bouquet, v. 415.

dualism which corresponds to the two natures of its
Founder. As divine and eternal, its head is the Pope,
to whom souls have been entrusted; as human and temporal, the Emperor, commissioned to rule men's bodies
and acts.

In nature and compass the government of these two
potentates is the same, differing only in the sphere of
its working; and it matters not whether we call the Pope
a spiritual Emperor or the Emperor a secular Pope.
Nor, though the one office is below the other as far
as man's life on earth is less precious than his life
hereafter, is therefore, on the older and truer theory,
the imperial authority delegated by the papal. For, as
has been said already, God is represented by the Pope
not in every capacity, but only as the ruler of spirits
in heaven: as sovereign of earth, He issues His commission directly to the Emperor. Opposition between
two servants of the same King is inconceivable, each
being bound to aid and foster the other: the co-operation
of both being needed in all that concerns the welfare
of Christendom at large. This is the one perfect and
self-consistent scheme of the union of Church and State;
for, taking the absolute coincidence of their limits to be
self-evident, it assumes the infallibility of their joint government, and derives, as a corollary from that infallibility, the duty of the civil magistrate to root out heresy
and schism no less than to punish treason and rebellion.
It is also the scheme which, granting the possibility of
their harmonious action, places the two powers in that
relation which gives each of them its maximum of
strength. But by a law to which it would be hard to
find exceptions, in proportion as the State became more
Christian, the Church, who to work out her purposes

*Union of
Church and
State.*

had assumed worldly forms, became by the contact worldlier, meaner, spiritually weaker; and the system which Constantine founded amid such rejoicings, which culminated so triumphantly in the Empire Church of the Middle Ages, has in each succeeding generation been slowly losing ground, has seen its brightness dimmed and its completeness marred, and sees now those who are most zealous on behalf of its surviving institutions feebly defend or silently desert the principle upon which all must rest.

The complete accord of the papal and imperial powers which this theory, as sublime as it is impracticable, requires, was attained only at a few points in their history[y]. It was finally supplanted by another view of their relation, which, professing to be a development of a principle recognized as fundamental, the superior importance of the religious life, found increasing favour in the eyes of fervent churchmen [z]. Declaring the Pope sole representative on earth of the Deity, it concluded that from him, and not directly from God, must the Empire be held— held feudally, it was said by many—and it thereby thrust down the temporal power, to be the slave instead of the sister of the spiritual [a]. Nevertheless, the Papacy in her

---

[y] Perhaps at no more than three: in the time of Charles and Leo; again under Otto III and his two Popes, Gregory V and Sylvester II; thirdly, under Henry III; certainly never thenceforth.

[z] *The Sachsenspiegel* (*Speculum Saxonicum*, circ. A.D. 1240), the great North-German law book, says, 'The Empire is held from God alone, not from the Pope. Emperor and Pope are supreme each in what has been entrusted to him: the Pope in what concerns the soul; the Emperor in all that belongs to the body and to knighthood.' *The Schwabenspiegel*, compiled half a century later, subordinates the prince to the pontiff: 'Daz weltliche Schwert des Gerichtes daz lihet der Babest dem Chaiser; daz geistlich ist dem Babest gesetzt daz er damit richte.'

[a] So Boniface VIII in the bull

meridian, and under the guidance of her greatest minds, of Hildebrand, of Alexander, of Innocent, not seeking to abolish or absorb the civil government, required only its obedience, and exalted its dignity against all save herself[b]. It was reserved for Boniface VIII, whose extravagant pretensions betrayed the decay that was already at work within, to show himself to the crowding pilgrims at the jubilee of A.D. 1300, seated on the throne of Constantine, arrayed with sword, and crown, and sceptre, shouting aloud, 'I am Cæsar—I am Emperor[c].'

The theory of an Emperor's place and functions thus sketched cannot be definitely assigned to any point of time; for it was growing and changing from the fifth century to the fifteenth. Nor need it surprise us that

---

Unam Sanctam, will have but one head for the Christian people. 'Igitur ecclesiæ unius et unicæ unum corpus, unum caput, non duo capita quasi monstrum.'

[b] St. Bernard writes to Conrad III: 'Non veniat anima mea in consilium eorum qui dicunt vel imperio pacem et libertatem ecclesiæ vel ecclesiæ prosperitatem et exaltationem imperii nocituram.' So in the *De Consideratione:* 'Si utrumque simul habere velis, perdes utrumque,' of the papal claim to temporal and spiritual authority, quoted by Gieseler.

[c] 'Sedens in solio armatus et cinctus ensem, habensque in capite Con-

stantini diadema, stricto dextra capulo ensis accincti, ait: "Numquid ego summus sum pontifex? nonne ista est cathedra Petri? Nonne possum imperii iura tutari? ego ego sum imperator."'—Fr. Pipinus (ap. Murat. *S. R. I.* ix.) l. iv. c 41. These words, however, are by this writer ascribed to Boniface, when receiving the envoys of the emperor Albert I, in A.D. 1299. I have not been able to find authority for their use at the jubilee, but give the current story for what it is worth.

It has been suggested that Dante may be alluding to this sword scene in a well-known passage of the Purgatorio (xvi. l. 106):—

'Soleva Roma, che 'l buon mondo feo
Duo Soli aver, che l' una e l' altra strada
Facean vedere, e del mondo e di Deo.
L' un l' altro ha spento, ed è giunta la spada
Col pastorale: e l' un coll altro insieme
Per viva forzu mal convien che vada.'

we do not find in any one author a statement of the grounds whereon it rested, since much of what seems strangest to us was then too obvious to. be formally explained. No one, however, who examines mediæval writings can fail to perceive, sometimes from direct words, oftener from allusions or assumptions, that such ideas as these are present to the minds of the authors [d]. That which it is easiest to prove is the connection of the Empire with religion, From every record, from chronicles and treatises; proclamations, laws, and sermons, passages may be adduced wherein the defence and spread of the faith, and the maintenance of concord among the Christian people, are represented as the function to which the Empire has been set apart. The belief expressed by Lewis II, 'Imperii dignitas non in vocabuli voce sed in gloriosæ pietatis culmine consistit [e],' appears again in the address of the Archbishop of Mentz to Conrad II [f], as Vicar of God; is reiterated by Frederick I [g], when he writes to the prelates of Germany, 'On earth God has placed no more than two powers, and as there is in heaven but one God, so is there here one Pope and one Emperor. Divine providence has specially appointed the Roman Empire to prevent the continuance

[d] See especially Peter de Andlo (*De Imperio Romano*); Ralph Colonna (*De translatione Imperii Romani*); Dante (*De Monarchia*); Engelbert (*De Ortu et Fine Imperii Romani*); Marsilius Patavinus (*De translatione Imperii Romani*); Æneas Sylvius Piccolomini (*De Ortu et Authoritate Imperii Romani*); Zoannetus (*De Imperio Romano atque ejus Iurisdictione*); and the writers in Schardius's *Sylloge*, and in Goldast's Collection of Tracts, entitled *Monarchia Imperii*.

[e] Letter of Lewis II to Basil the Macedonian, in *Chron. Salernit.* in Mur. *S.R.I.;* also given by Baronius, *Ann. Eccl.* ad ann. 871.

[f] 'Ad summum · dignitatis pervenisti: Vicarius es Christi.'—Wippo, *Vita Chuonradi (ap.* Pertz), c. 3.

[g] Letter in Radewic, *ap.* Murat, *S.R.I.*

of schism in the Church [h];' is echoed by jurists and divines down to the days of Charles V [i]. It was a doctrine which we shall find the friends and foes of the Holy See equally concerned to insist on, the one to make the transference (*translatio*) from the Greeks to the Germans appear entirely the Pope's work, and so establish his right of overseeing or cancelling his rival's election, the others by setting the Emperor at the head of the Church to reduce the Pope to the place of chief bishop of his realm [k]. His headship was dwelt upon chiefly in the two duties already noticed. As the counterpart of the Mussulman Commander of the Faithful, he was leader of the Church militant against her infidel foes, was in this capacity summoned to conduct crusades, and in later times recognized chief of the confederacies against the conquering Ottomans. As representative of the whole Christian people, it belonged to him to convoke General Councils, a right not without importance even when exercised concurrently with the Pope, but far more weighty when the object of the council was to settle a disputed election, or, as at Constance, to depose the reigning pontiff himself.

No better illustrations can be desired than those to

---

[h] Lewis IV is styled in one of his proclamations, ' Gentis humanæ, orbis Christiani custos, urbi et orbi a Deo electus præesse.'—Pfeffinger, *Vitriarius Illustratus.*

[i] In a document issued by the Diet of Speyer (A.D. 1529) the Emperor is called ' Oberst, Vogt, und Haupt der Christenheit.' Hieronymus Balbus, writing about the same time, puts the question whether all Christians are subject to the Emperor in temporal things, as they are to the Pope in spiritual, and answers it by saying, 'Cum ambo ex eodem fonte perfluxerint et eadem semita incedant, de utroque idem puto sentiendum.'

[k] 'Non magis ad Papam depositio seu remotio pertinet quam ad quoslibet regum prælatos, qui reges suos prout assolent, consecrant et inungunt.'—*Letter of Frederick II* (lib. i. c. 3).

be found in the office for the imperial coronation at
Rome, too long to be transcribed here, but well worthy
of an attentive study[1].   The rites prescribed in it are
rights of consecration to a religious office : the Emperor,
besides the sword, globe, and sceptre of temporal power,
receives a ring as the symbol of his faith, is ordained a
subdeacon, assists the Pope in celebrating mass, partakes
as a clerical person of the communion in both kinds, is
admitted a canon of St. Peter and St. John Lateran.
The oath to be taken by an elector begins, 'Ego N. volo
regem Romanorum in Cæsarem promovendum, temporale
caput populo Christiano eligere.'   The Emperor swears
to cherish and defend the Holy Roman Church and her
bishop : the Pope prays after the reading of the Gospel,
'Deus qui ad prædicandum æterni regni evangelium
Imperium Romanum præparasti, prætende famulo tuo
Imperatori nostro arma cœlestia.'   Among the Emperor's
official titles there occur these : 'Head of Christendom,'
'Defender and Advocate of the Christian Church,' 'Temporal Head of the Faithful,' 'Protector of Palestine and
of the Catholic Faith [m].'

Very singular are the reasonings used by which the
necessity and divine right of the Empire are proved out
of the Bible.   The mediæval theory of the relation of the
civil power to the priestly was profoundly influenced by
the account in the Old Testament of the Jewish theocracy, in which the king, though the institution of his
office was a derogation from the purity of the older

---

[1] *Liber Ceremonialis Romanus*,
lib. i. sect. 5 ; with which compare
the *Coronatio Romana* of Henry
VII, in Pertz, and Muratori's Dissertation in vol. i. of the *Antiqui-*
tates Italiæ Medii Ævi.

[m] See Goldast, *Collection of Im-*
perial Constitutions; and Moser,
Römische Kayser.

system, appears divinely chosen and commissioned, and stood in a peculiarly intimate relation to the national religion. From the New Testament the authority and eternity of Rome herself was established. Every passage was seized on where submission to the powers that be is enjoined, every instance cited where obedience had actually been rendered to imperial officials, a special emphasis being laid on the sanction which Christ Himself had given to Roman dominion by pacifying the world through Augustus, by being born at the time of the taxing, by paying tribute to Cæsar, by saying to Pilate, ' Thou couldest have no power at all against Me except it were given thee from above.'

More attractive to the mystical spirit than these direct arguments were those drawn from prophecy, or based on the allegorical interpretation of Scripture. Very early in Christian history had the belief formed itself that the Roman Empire—as the fourth beast of Daniel's vision, as the iron legs and feet of Nebuchadnezzar's image— was to be the world's last and universal kingdom. From Origen and Jerome downwards it found unquestioned acceptance[n], and that not unnaturally. For no new power had arisen to extinguish the Roman, as the Persian monarchy had been blotted out by Alexander, as the realms of his successors had fallen before the conquering republic herself. Every Northern conqueror, Goth, Lom-

---

[n] The abbot Engelbert (*De Ortu et Fine Imperii Romani*) quotes Origen and Jerome to this effect, and proceeds himself to explain, from 2 Thess. ii., how the falling away will precede the coming of Antichrist. There will be a triple ' discessio,' of the kingdoms of the earth from the Roman Empire, of the Church from the Apostolic See, of the faithful from the faith. Of these, the first causes the second; the temporal sword to punish heretics and schismatics being no longer ready to work the will of the rulers of the Church.

I

CHAP. VII.

bard, Burgundian, had cherished her memory and preserved her laws; Germany had adopted even the name of the Empire 'dreadful and terrible and strong exceedingly, and diverse from all that were before it.' To these predictions, and to many others from the Apocalypse, were added those which in the Gospels and Epistles foretold the advent of Antichrist [o]. He was to succeed the Roman dominion, and the Popes are more than once warned that by weakening the Empire they are hastening the coming of the enemy and the end of the world [p]. It is not only when groping in the dark labyrinths of prophecy that mediæval authors are quick in detecting emblems, imaginative in explaining them. Men were wont in those days to interpret Scripture in a singular fashion. Not only did it not occur to them to

[o] A full statement of the views that prevailed in the earlier Middle Age regarding Antichrist—as well as of the singular prophecy of the Frankish Emperor who shall appear in the latter days, conquer the world, and then going to Jerusalem shall lay down his crown on the Mount of Olives and deliver over the kingdom to Christ—may be found in the little treatise, *Vita Antichristi*, which Adso, monk and afterwards abbot of Moutier-en-Der, compiled (cir. 950) for the information of Queen Gerberga, wife of Louis d'Outremer. Antichrist is to be born a Jew of the tribe of Dan (Gen. xlix. 17), 'non de episcopo et monacha, sicut alii delirando dogmatizant, sed de immundissima meretrice et crudelissimo nebulone. Totus in peccato concipietur, in peccato generabitur, in peccato nascetur.' His birth-place is Babylon: he is to be brought up in Bethsaida and Chorazin.

Adso's book may be found printed in Migne, t. ci. p. 1290.

[p] S. Thomas explains the prophecy in a remarkable manner, shewing how the decline of the Empire is no argument against its fulfilment. 'Dicendum quod nondum cessavit, sed est commutatum de temporali in spirituale, ut dicit Leo Papa in sermone de Apostolis: et ideo discessio a Romano imperio debet intelligi non solum a temporali sed etiam a spirituali, scilicet a fide Catholica Romanæ Ecclesiæ. Est autem hoc conveniens signum nam Christus venit, quando Romanum imperium omnibus dominabatur: ita e contra signum adventus Antichristi est discessio ab eo.'— *Comment. ad 2 Thess.* ii.

ask what meaning words had to those to whom they were
originally addressed; they were quite as careless whether
the sense they discovered was one which the language
used would naturally and rationally bear to any reader at
any time. No analogy was too faint, no allegory too
fanciful, to be drawn out of a simple text; and, once
propounded, the interpretation acquired in argument all
the authority of the text itself. Thus the two swords of
which Christ said, 'It is enough,' became the spiritual
and temporal powers, and the grant of the spiritual to
Peter involves the supremacy of the Papacy q. Thus one
writer proves the eternity of Rome from the seventy-
second Psalm, 'They shall fear thee as long as the sun
and moon endure, throughout all generations;' the moon
being of course, since Gregory VII, the Roman Empire,
as the sun, or greater light, is the Popedom. Another
quoting, 'Qui tenet teneat donec auferatur r,' with Augustine's explanation thereof s, says, that when 'he who
letteth' is removed, tribes and provinces will rise in rebellion, and the Empire to which God has committed the
government of the human race will be dissolved. From
the miseries of his own time (he wrote under Frederick
III) he predicts that the end is near. The same spirit of
symbolism seized on the number of the electors: 'the
seven lamps burning in the unity of the sevenfold spirit

q See note z, page 119. The
Papal party sometimes insisted that
both swords were given to Peter,
while the imperialists assigned the
temporal sword to John. Thus a
gloss to the *Sachsenspiegel* says,
'Dat eine svert hadde Sinte Peter,
dat het nu de paves: dat andere hadde
Johannes, dat het nu de keyser.'

r 2 Thess. ii. 7.
s St. Augustine, however, though
he states the view (applying the
passage to the Roman Empire)
which was generally received in
the Middle Ages, is careful not
to commit himself positively to
it.

which illumine the Holy Empire [t].' Strange legends told
how Romans and Germans were of one lineage; how
Peter's staff had been found on the banks of the Rhine,
the miracle signifying that a commission was issued to
the Germans to reclaim wandering sheep to the one fold.
So complete does the scriptural proof appear in the
hands of mediæval churchmen, many holding it a mortal
sin to resist the power ordained of God, that we forget
they were all the while only adapting to an existing institution what they found written already; we begin to
fancy that the Empire was maintained, obeyed, exalted
for centuries, on the strength of words to which we
attach in almost every case a wholly different meaning..

*Illustra-
tions from
Mediæval
Art.*

It would be a task both pleasant and profitable to pass
on from the theologians to the poets and artists of the
Middle Ages, and endeavour to trace through their works
the influence of the ideas which have been expounded
above. But it is one far too wide for the scope of the
present treatise; and one which would demand an ac-
quaintance with those works themselves such as only
minute and long-continued study could give. For even
a slight knowledge enables any one to see how much
still remains to be interpreted in the imaginative literature
and in the paintings of those times, and how apt we are
in glancing over a piece of work to miss those seemingly
trifling indications of the artist's thought or belief which
are all the more precious that they are indirect or unconscious. Therefore a history of mediæval art which
shall evolve its philosophy from its concrete forms, if it
is to have any value at all, must be minute in description

[t] *Jordanis Chronica* (written towards the close of the thirteenth
century).

as well as subtle in method. But lest this class of illustrations should appear to have been wholly forgotten,
it may be well to mention here two paintings in which
the theory of the mediæval empire is unmistakeably set
forth. One of them is in Rome, the other in Florence ;
every traveller in Italy may examine both for himself.

The first of these is the famous mosaic of the Lateran
triclinium, constructed by Pope Leo III about A.D. 800,
and an exact copy of which, made by the order of Sextus
V, may still be seen over against the façade of St. John
Lateran. Originally meant to adorn the state banqueting-
hall of the Popes, it is now placed in the open air, in the
finest situation in Ròme, looking from the brow of a hill
across the green ridges of the Campagna to the olive-
groves of Tivoli and the glistering crags and snow-capped
summits of the Umbrian and Sabine Apennine. It represents in the centre Christ surrounded by the Apostles,
whom He is sending forth to preach the Gospel; one
hand is extended to bless, the other holds a book with
the words ' Pax Vobis.' Below and to the right Christ
is depicted again, and this time sitting : on his right hand
kneels Pope Sylvester, on his left the Emperor Constantine; to the one he gives the keys of heaven and
hell, to the other a banner surmounted by a cross. In
the group on the opposite, that is, on the left side of the
arch, we see the Apostle Peter seated, before whom in
like manner kneel Pope Leo III and Charles the Emperor; the latter wearing, like Constantine, his crown.
Peter, himself grasping the keys, gives to Leo the pallium of an archbishop, to Charles the banner of the
Christian army. The inscription is, ' Beatus Petrus dona
vitam Leoni PP et bictoriam Carulo regi dona;' while

CHAP. VII.

Mosaic of the Lateran Palace at Rome.

round the arch is written, ' Gloria in excelsis Deo, et in terra pax omnibus bonæ voluntatis.'

The order and nature of the ideas here symbolized is sufficiently clear. First comes the revelation of the Gospel, and the divine commission to gather all men into its fold. Next, the institution, at the memorable era of Constantine's conversion, of the two powers by which the Christian people is to be respectively taught and governed. Thirdly, we are shewn the permanent Vicar of God, the Apostle who keeps the keys of heaven and hell, re-establishing these same powers on a new and firmer basis [u]. The badge of ecclesiastical supremacy he gives to Leo as the spiritual head of the faithful on earth, the banner of the Church Militant to Charles, who is to maintain her cause against heretics and infidels.

Fresco in S. Maria Novella at Florence.

The second painting is of greatly later date. It is a fresco in the chapter-house of the Dominican convent of Santa Maria Novella [v] at Florence, usually known as the Capellone degli Spagnuoli. It has been commonly

[u] Compare with this the words which Pope Hadrian I. had used some twenty-three years before, of Charles as representative of Constantine : ' Et sicut temporibus Beati Sylvestri, Romani pontificis, a sanctæ recordationis piissimo Constantino magno imperatore, per eius largitatem sancta Dei catholica et apostolica Romana ecclesia elevata atque exaltata est, et potestatem in his Hesperiæ partibus largiri dignatus est, ita et in his vestris felicissimis temporibus atque nostris, sancta Dei ecclesia, id est, beati Petri apostoli germinet atque exsultet, ut omnes gentes quæ hæc audierint edicere valeant, ' Domine salvum fac regem, et exaudi nos in die in qua invocaverimus te ;' quia ecce novus Christianissimus Dei Constantinus imperator his temporibus surrexit, per quem omnia Deus sanctæ suæ ecclesiæ beati apostolorum principis Petri largiri dignatus est.'—*Letter XLIX of Cod. Carol.*, A.D. 777 (in Mur. *Scriptores Rerum Italicarum*).

This letter is memorable as containing the first allusion, or what seems an allusion, to Constantine's Donation.

The phrase ' sancta Dei ecclesia, id est, B. Petri apostoli,' is worth noting.

[v] The church in which the opening scene of Boccaccio's *Decameron* is laid.

ascribed, on Vasari's authority, to Simone Martini of Siena, but an examination of the dates of his life seems to discredit this view[x]. Most probably it was executed between A.D. 1340 and 1350. It is a huge work, covering one whole wall of the chapter-house, and filled with figures, some of which, but seemingly on no sufficient authority, have been taken to represent eminent persons of the tyme—Cimabue, Arnolfo, Boccaccio, Petrarch, Laura, and others. In it is represented the whole scheme of man's life here and hereafter—the Church on earth and the Church in heaven. Full in front are seated side by side the Pope and the Emperor: on their right and left, in a descending row, minor spiritual and temporal officials; next to the Pope a cardinal, bishops, and doctors; next to the Emperor, the king of France and a line of nobles and knights. Behind them appears the Duomo of Florence as an emblem of the Visible Church, while at their feet is a flock of sheep (the faithful) attacked by ravening wolves (heretics and schismatics), whom a pack of spotted dogs (the Dominicans[y]) combat and chase away. From this, the central foreground of the picture, a path winds round and up a height to a great gate where the Apostle sits on guard to admit true believers: they passing through it are met by choirs of seraphs, who lead them on through the delicious groves of Paradise. Above all, at the top of the painting and just over the spot where his two lieutenants, Pope and Emperor, are placed below, is the Saviour enthroned amid saints and angels[z].

---

[x] So Kugler (Eastlake's ed. vol. i. p. 144), and so also Messrs. Crowe and Cavalcaselle, in their *New History of Painting in Italy*, vol. ii. pp. 85 *sqq.*

[y] Domini canes. Spotted because of their black-and-white raiment.

[z] There is of course a great deal more detail in the picture, which

Here, too, there needs no comment. The Church Militant is the perfect counterpart of the Church Triumphant: her chief danger is from those who would rend the unity of her visible body, the seamless garment of her heavenly Lord; and that devotion to His person which is the sum of her faith and the essence of her being, must on earth be rendered to those two lieutenants whom He has chosen to govern in His name.

A theory such as that which it has been attempted to explain and illustrate, is utterly opposed to restrictions of place or person. The idea of one Christian people, all whose members are equal in the sight of God,—an idea so forcibly expressed in the unity of the priesthood, where no barrier separated the successor of the Apostle from the humblest curate,—and in the prevalence of one language for worship and government, made the post of Emperor independent of the race, or rank, or actual resources of its occupant. The Emperor was entitled to the obedience of Christendom, not as hereditary chief of a victorious tribe, or feudal lord of a portion of the earth's surface, but as solemnly invested with an office. Not only did he excel in dignity the kings of the earth: his power was different in its nature; and, so far from supplanting or rivalling theirs, rose above them to become the source and needful condition of their authority in their several territories, the bond which joined them in one harmonious body. The vast dominions and vigorous personal action of Charles the Great had concealed this distinction while

it does not appear necessary to describe. St. Dominic is a conspicuous figure.

It is worth remarking that the Emperor, who is on the Pope's left hand, and so made slightly inferior to him while superior to every one else, holds in his hand, instead of the usual imperial globe, a death's head, typifying the transitory nature of his power.

he reigned; under his successors the imperial crown appeared disconnected from the direct government of the kingdoms they had established, existing only in the form of an undefined suzerainty, as the type of that unity without which men's minds could not rest. It was characteristic of the Middle Ages, that demanding the existence of an Emperor, they were careless who he was or how he was chosen, so he had been duly inaugurated; and that they were not shocked by the contrast between unbounded rights and actual helplessness. At no time in the world's history has theory, pretending all the while to control practice, been so utterly divorced from it. Ferocious and sensual, that age worshipped humility and asceticism: there has never been a purer ideal of love, nor a grosser profligacy of life.

The power of the Roman Emperor cannot as yet be called international; though this, as we shall see, became in later times its most important aspect; for in the tenth century national distinctions had scarcely begun to exist. But its genius was clerical and old Roman, in nowise territorial or Teutonic: it rested not on armed hosts or wide lands, but upon the duty, the awe, the love of its subjects.

CHAPTER VIII.

THE ROMAN EMPIRE AND THE GERMAN KINGDOM.

THIS was the office which Otto the Great assumed in A.D. 962. But it was not his only office. He was already a German king; and the new dignity by no means superseded the old. This union in one person of two characters, a union at first personal, then official, and which became at last a fusion of the two into something different from either, is the key to the whole subsequent history of Germany and the Empire.

Of the German kingdom little need be said, since it differs in no essential respect from the other kingdoms of Western Europe as they stood in the tenth century. The five or six great tribes or tribe-leagues which composed the German nation had been first brought together under the sceptre of the Carolingians; and, though still retaining marks of their independent origin, were prevented from separating by community of speech and a common pride in the great Frankish Empire. When the line of Charles the Great ended in A.D. 911, by the death of Lewis the Child (son of Arnulf), Conrad, duke of the Franconians, and after him Henry (the Fowler), duke of the Saxons, was chosen to fill the vacant throne. By his vigorous yet conciliatory action, his upright character, his courage and good fortune in repelling the Hungarians,

Henry laid deep the foundations of royal power: under his more famous son it rose into a stable edifice. Otto's coronation feast at Aachen, where the great nobles of the realm did him menial service, where Franks, Bavarians, Suabians, Thuringians, and Lorrainers gathered round the Saxon manarch, is the inauguration of a true Teutonic realm, which, though it called itself not German but East Frankish, and claimed to be the lawful representative of the Carolingian monarchy, had a constitution and a tendency in many respects different.

There had been under those princes a singular mixture of the old German organization by tribes or districts (the so-called Gauverfassung), such as we find in the earliest records, with the method introduced by Charles of maintaining by means of officials, some fixed, others moving from place to place, the control of the central government. In the suspension of that government which followed his days, there grew up a system whose seeds had been sown as far back as the time of Clovis, a system whose essence was the combination of the tenure of land by military service with a peculiar personal relation between the landlord and his tenant, whereby the one was bound to render fatherly protection, the other aid and obedience. This is not the place for tracing the origin of feudality on Roman soil, nor for shewing how, by a sort of contagión, it spread into Germany, how it struck firm root in the period of comparative quiet under Pipin and Charles, how from the hands of the latter it took the impress which determined its ultimate form, how the weakness of his successors allowed it to triumph everywhere. Still less would it be possible here to examine its social and moral influence. Politically it might be defined as the system which made the owner of a piece of land,

CHAP. VIII.

Feudalism.

whether large or small, the sovereign of those who dwelt thereon : an annexation of personal to territorial authority more familiar to Eastern despotism than to the free races of primitive Europe. On this principle were founded, and by it are explained, feudal law and justice, feudal finance, feudal legislation, each tenant holding towards his lord the position which his own tenants held towards himself. And it is just because the relation was so uniform, the principle so comprehensive, the ruling class so firmly bound to its support, that feudalism has been able to lay upon society that grasp which the struggles of more than twenty generations have scarcely shaken off.

The feudal king.

Now by the middle of the tenth century, Germany, less fully committed than France to feudalism's worst feature, the hopeless bondage of the peasantry, was otherwise thoroughly feudalized. As for that equality of all the freeborn save the sacred line which we find in the Germany of Tacitus, there had been substituted a gradation of ranks and a concentration of power in the hands of a landholding caste, so had the monarch lost his ancient character as leader and judge of the people, to become the head of a tyrannical oligarchy. He was titular lord of the soil, could exact from his vassals service and aid in arms and money, could dispose of vacant fiefs, could at pleasure declare war or make peace. But all these rights he exercised far less as sovereign of the nation than as standing in a peculiar relation to the feudal tenants, a relation in its origin strictly personal, and whose prominence obscured the political duties of prince and subject. And great as these rights might become in the hands of an ambitious and politic ruler, they were in practice limited by the corresponding duties he owed to his vassals, and by the difficulty of enforcing them against a powerful offender. The king was not permitted to retain in his own hands escheated fiefs, must even grant away those he had held before coming to the throne; he could not interfere with the jurisdiction of his tenants in their own lands, nor prevent them from waging war or forming leagues with each other like independent princes. [Chief among the nobles stood the dukes, who, although their authority was now delegated, theoretically at least, instead of independent, territorial instead of personal, retained nevertheless much of that hold on the exclusive loyalty of their subjects which had belonged to them as hereditary leaders of the tribe under the ancient system.] They were, with the three Rhenish archbishops, by far the greatest subjects, often aspiring to the crown, sometimes not unable to resist its wearer. The constant encroachments which Otto made upon their privileges, especially through the institution of the Counts Palatine, destroyed their ascendancy, but not their importance. It was not till the thirteenth century that they disappeared with the rise of the second order of nobility. That order, at this period far less powerful, included the counts, margraves or marquises and landgraves, originally officers of the crown, now feudal tenants; holding their lands of the dukes, and maintaining against them the same contest which they in turn waged with the crown. Below these came the barons and simple knights, then the diminishing class of freemen, the increasing one of serfs. The institutions of primitive Germany were almost all gone; supplanted by a new system, partly the natural result of the formation of a settled from a half-nomad society, partly imitated from that which had arisen upon Roman soil, west of the Rhine and south of the Alps. The army was no longer the Heerban of the whole nation, which had been wont to

CHAP. VIII.

The nobility.

The Germanic feudal polity generally.

follow the king on foot in distant expeditions; but a cavalry militia of barons and their retainers, bound to service for a short period, and rendering it unwillingly where their own interest was not concerned. The frequent popular assemblies, whereof under the names of the Mallum, the Placitum, the Mayfield, we hear so much under Clovis and Charles, were now never summoned, and the laws that had been promulgated there were, if not abrogated, practically obsolete. No national council existed, save the Diet in which the higher nobility, lay and and clerical, met their sovereign, sometimes to decide on foreign war, oftener to concur in the grant of a fief or the proscription of a rebel. Every district had its own rude local customs administered by the court of the local lord: other law there was none, for imperial jurisprudence had in these lately civilized countries not yet filled the place left empty by the disuse of the barbarian codes.

This condition of things was indeed better than that utter confusion which had gone before, for a principle of order had begun to group and bind the tossing atoms; and though the union into which it drove men was a hard and narrow one, it was something that they should have learnt to unite themselves at all. Yet nascent feudality was but one remove from anarchy; and the tendency to isolation and diversity continued, despite the efforts of the Church and the Carolingian princes, to be all-powerful in Western Europe. The German kingdom was already a bond between the German races, and appears strong and united when we compare it with the France of Hugh Capet, or the England of Ethelred II; yet its history to the twelfth century is little else than a record of disorders, revolts, civil wars, of a ceaseless struggle on the part of the monarch to enforce his feudal rights, a resistance by

his vassals equally obstinate and more frequently successful. What the issue of the contest might have been if
Germany had been left to take her own course is matter
of speculation, though the example of every European
state except England and Norway may incline the balance
in favour of the crown./ But the strife had scarcely begun
when a new influence was interposed: the German king
became Roman Emperor. No two systems can be more
unlike than those whose headship became thus vested in
one person: the one centralized, the other local; the one
resting on a sublime theory, the other the rude offspring
of anarchy; the one gathering all power into the hands of
an irresponsible monarch, the other limiting his rights and
authorizing resistance to his commands; the one demanding the equality of all citizens as creatures equal before
Heaven, the other bound up with an aristocracy the
proudest, and in its gradations of rank the most exact,
that Europe had ever seen. Characters so repugnant
could not, it might be thought, meet in one person, or if
they met must strive till one swallowed up the other. It
was not so. In the fusion which began from the first,
though it was for a time imperceptible, each of the two
characters gave and each lost some of its attributes: the
king became more than German, the Emperor less than
Roman, till, at the end of six centuries, the monarch in
whom two 'persons' had been united, appeared as a third
different from either of the former, and might not inappro-
priately be entitled 'German Emperor[a].' The nature
and progress of this change will appear in the after history
of Germany, and cannot be described here without in

CHAP. VIII.

*The Roman
Empire
and the
German
kingdom.*

[a] Although this was of course
never his legal title. Till 1806
he was 'Romanorum Imperator
semper Augustus;' 'Römischer
Kaiser.'

some measure anticipating subsequent events. A word or two may indicate how the process of fusion began.

It was natural that the great mass of Otto's subjects, to whom the imperial title, dimly associated with Rome and the Pope, sounded grander than the regal, without being known as otherwise different, should in thought and speech confound them. The sovereign and his ecclesiastical advisers, with far clearer views of the new office and of the mutual relation of the two, found it impossible to separate them in practice, and were glad to merge the lesser in the greater. For as lord of the world, Otto was *Results of this union in one person.* Emperor north as well as south of the Alps. When he issued an edict, he claimed the obedience of his Teutonic subjects in both capacities; when as Emperor he led the armies of the gospel against the heathen, it was the standard of their feudal superior that his armed vassals followed; when he founded churches and appointed bishops, he acted partly as suzerain of feudal lands, partly as protector of the faith, charged to guide the Church in matters temporal. Thus the assumption of the imperial crown brought to Otto as its first result an apparent increase of domestic authority; it made his position by its historical associations more dignified, by its religious more hallowed; it raised him higher above his vassals and above other sovereigns; it enlarged his prerogative in ecclesiastical affairs, and by necessary consequence gave to ecclesiastics a more important place at court and in the administration of government than they had enjoyed before. Great as was the power of the bishops and abbots in all the feudal kingdoms, it stood nowhere so high as in Germany. There the Emperor's double position, as head both of Church and State, required the two organizations to be exactly parallel. In the eleventh century a full half of the land and wealth of the country, and no small part of its military strength, was in the hands of Churchmen: their influence predominated in the Diet; the archchancellorship of the Empire, highest of all offices, belonged of right to the archbishop of Mentz, as primate of Germany. It was by Otto, who in resuming the attitude must repeat the policy of Charles, that the greatness of the clergy was thus advanced. He is commonly said to have wished to weaken the aristocracy by raising up rivals to them in the hierarchy. It may have been so, and the measure was at any rate a disastrous one, for the clergy soon approved themselves not less rebellious than those whom they were to restrain. But in accusing Otto's judgment, historians have often forgotten in what position he stood to the Church, and how it behoved him, according to the doctrine received, to establish in her an order like in all things to that which he found already subsisting in the State.

The style which Otto adopted shewed his desire thus to merge the king in the Emperor [b]. Charles had called himself 'Imperator Cæsar Carolus rex Francorum invictissimus;' and again, 'Carolus serenissimus Augustus, Pius, Felix, Romanorum gubernans Imperium, qui et per misericordiam Dei rex Francorum atque Langobardorum.' Otto and his first successors, who until their coronation at Rome had used the titles of 'Rex Francorum,' or 'Rex Francorum Orientalium,' or oftener still 'Rex' alone, discarded after it all titles save the highest of 'Imperator Augustus;' seeming thereby, though they too had been crowned at Aachen and Milan, to claim the authority of

Changes in title.

[b] Pütter, *Dissertationes de Instauratione Imperii Romani;* cf. Goldast's *Collection of Constitutions;* and the proclamations and other documents collected in Pertz, *M.G.H.* legg. I.

K

Cæsar through all their dominions. Tracing as we are the history of a title, it is needless to dwell on the significance of the change [c]. Charles, son of the Ripuarian allies of Probus, had been a Frankish chieftain on the Rhine; Otto, the Saxon, successor of the Cheruscan Arminius, would rule his native Elbe with a power borrowed from the Tiber.

Imperial power feudalized.

Nevertheless, the imperial element did not in every respect predominate over the royal. The monarch might desire to make good against his turbulent barons the boundless prerogative which he acquired with his new crown, but he lacked the power to do so; and they, disputing neither the supremacy of that crown nor his right to wear it, refused with good reason to let their own freedom be infringed upon by any act of which they had not been the authors. So far was Otto from embarking on so vain an enterprise, that his rule was even more direct and more personal than that of Charles had been. There was no scheme of mechanical government, no claim of absolutism; there was only the resolve to make the energetic assertion of the king's feudal rights subserve the further aims of the Emperor. What Otto demanded he demanded as Emperor, what he received he received as king; the singular result was that in Germany the imperial office was itself pervaded and transformed by feudal ideas. Feudality needing, to make its theory complete, a lord paramount of the world, from whose grant all ownership in land must be supposed to have emanated, and finding such a suzerain in the Emperor, constituted him liege lord

[c] Pütter (*De Instauratione Imperii Romani*) will have it that upon this mistake, as he calls it, of Otto's, the whole subsequent history of the Empire turned; that if Otto had but continued to style himself 'Francorum Rex,' Germany would have been spared all her Italian wars.

of all kings and potentates, keystone of the feudal arch, himself, as it was expressed, 'holding' the world from God. There were not wanting Roman institutions to which these notions could attach themselves. Constantine, imitating the courts of the East, had made the dignitaries of his household great officials of the State: these were now reproduced in the cup-bearer, the seneschal, the marshal, the chamberlain of the Empire, so soon to become its electoral princes. The holding of land on condition of military service was Roman in its origin: the divided ownership of feudal law found its analogies in the Roman tenure of emphyteusis. Thus while Germany was Romanized the Empire was feudalized, and came to be considered not the antagonist but the perfection of an aristocratic system. And it was this adaptation to existing political facts that enabled it afterwards to assume an international character. Nevertheless, even while they seemed to blend, there remained between the genius of imperialism (if one may use a now perverted word) and that of feudalism a deep and lasting hostility. And so the rule of Otto and his successors was in a measure adverse to feudal polity, not from knowledge of what Roman government had been, but from the necessities of their position, raised as they were to an unapproachable height above their subjects, surrounded with a halo of sanctity as protectors of the Church. Thus were they driven to reduce local independence, and assimilate the various races through their vast territories. It was Otto who made the Germans, hitherto an aggregate of tribes, a single people, and welding them into a strong political body taught them to rise through its collective greatness to the consciousness of national life, never thenceforth to be extinguished.

K 2

One expedient against the land-holding oligarchy which Roman traditions as well as present needs might have suggested, it was scarcely possible for Otto to use. He could not invoke the friendship of the Third Estate, for as yet none existed. The Teutonic order of freemen, which two centuries earlier had formed the bulk of the population, was now fast disappearing, just as in England all who did not become thanes were classed as ceorls, and from ceorls sank for the most part, after the Conquest, into villeins. It was only in the Alpine valleys and along the shores of the ocean that free democratic communities maintained themselves. Town-life there was none, till Henry the Fowler forced his forest-loving people to dwell in fortresses that might repel the Hungarian invaders; and the burgher class thus beginning to form was too small to be a power in the state. But popular freedom, as it expired, bequeathed to the monarch such of its rights as could be saved from the grasp of the nobles; and the crown thus became what it has been wherever an aristocracy presses upon both, the ally, though as yet the tacit ally, of the people. More, too, than the royal could have done, did the imperial name invite the sympathy of the commons. For in all, however ignorant of its history, however unable to comprehend its functions, there yet lived a feeling that it was in some mysterious way consecrated to Christian brotherhood and equality, to peace and law, to the restraint of the strong and the defence of the helpless.

CHAPTER IX.

SAXON AND FRANCONIAN EMPERORS.

HE who begins to read the history of the Middle Ages is alternately amused and provoked by the seeming absurdities that meet him at every step. He finds writers proclaiming amidst universal assent magnificent theories which no one attempts to carry out. He sees men who are stained with every vice full of sincere devotion to a religion which, even when its doctrines were most obscured, never sullied the purity of its moral teaching. He is disposed to conclude that such people must have been either fools or hypocrites. Yet such a conclusion would be wholly erroneous. Every one knows how little a man's actions conform to the general maxims which he would lay down for himself, and how many things there are which he believes without realizing: believes sufficiently to be influenced, yet not sufficiently to be governed by them. Now in the Middle Ages this perpetual opposition of theory and practice was peculiarly abrupt. Men's impulses were more violent and their conduct more reckless than is often witnessed in modern society; while the absence of a criticizing and measuring spirit made them surrender their minds more unreservedly than they would now do to a complete and imposing theory. Therefore it was, that while everyone believed in the rights of the Empire as a part of divine truth, no one would yield to them where his own passions or interests interfered. Resistance to God's Vicar might be and indeed was admitted to be a deadly sin, but it was one which nobody hesitated to commit. Hence, in order to give this unbounded imperial prerogative any practical efficiency, it was found necessary to prop it up by the limited but tangible authority of a feudal king. And the one spot in Otto's empire on which feudality had never fixed its grasp, and where therefore he was forced to rule merely as emperor, and not also as king, was that in which he and his successors were never safe from insult and revolt. That spot was his capital. Accordingly an account of what befel the first Saxon emperor in Rome is a not unfitting comment on the theory expounded above, as well as a curious episode in the history of the Apostolic Chair.

Otto the Great in Rome.

After his coronation Otto had returned to North Italy, where the partizans of Berengar and his son Adalbert still maintained themselves in arms. Scarcely was he gone when the restless <u>John the Twelfth,</u> who found too late that in seeking an ally he had given himself a master, renounced his allegiance, opened negotiations with Berengar, and even scrupled not to send envoys pressing the heathen Magyars to invade Germany. The Emperor was soon informed of these plots, as well as of the flagitious life of the pontiff, a youth of twenty-five, the most profligate if not the most guilty of all who have worn the tiara. But he affected to despise them, saying, with a sort of unconscious irony, 'He is a boy, the example of good men may reform him.' When, however, Otto returned with a strong force, he found the city gates shut, and a party within furious against him. John the

Twelfth was not only Pope, but as the heir of Alberic, the head of a strong faction among the nobles, and a sort of temporal prince in the city. But neither he nor they had courage enough to stand a siege: John fled into the Campagna to join Adalbert, and Otto entering convoked a synod in St. Peter's. Himself presiding as temporal head of the Church, he began by inquiring into the character and manners of the Pope. At once a tempest of accusations burst forth from the assembled clergy. Liudprand, a credible although a hostile witness, gives us a long list of them :—'Peter, cardinal-priest, rose and witnessed that he had seen the Pope celebrate mass and not himself communicate. John, bishop of Narnia, and John, cardinal-deacon, declared that they had seen him ordain a deacon in a stable, neglecting the proper formalities. They said further that he had defiled by shameless acts of vice the pontifical palace; that he had openly diverted himself with hunting; had put out the eyes of his spiritual father Benedict; had set fire to houses; had girt himself with a sword, and put on a helmet and <u>hauberk</u>. All present, laymen as well as priests, cried out that he had drunk to the devil's health; that in throwing the dice he had invoked the help of Jupiter, Venus, and other demons; that he had celebrated matins at uncanonical hours, and had not fortified himself by making the sign of the cross. After these things the Emperor, who could not speak Latin, since the Romans could not understand his native, that is to say, the Saxon tongue, bade Liudprand bishop of Çremona interpret for him, and adjured the council to declare whether the charges they had brought were true, or sprang only of malice and envy. Then all the clergy and people cried with a loud voice, 'If John the Pope

hath not committed all the crimes which Benedict the
deacon hath read over, and even greater crimes than
these, then may the chief of the Apostles, the blessed
Peter, who by his word closes heaven to the unworthy
and opens it to the just, never absolve us from our sins,
but may we be bound by the chain of anathema, and on
the last day may we stand on the left hand along with
those who have said to the Lord God, "Depart from us,
for we will not know Thy ways." '

The solemnity of this answer seems to have satisfied
Otto and the council: a letter was despatched to John,
couched in respectful terms, recounting the charges
brought against him, and asking him to appear to clear
himself by his own oath and that of a sufficient number
of compurgators.   John's reply was short and pithy.

' John the bishop, the servant of the servants of God,
to all the bishops.   We have heard tell that you wish to
set up another Pope: if you do this, by Almighty God
I excommunicate you, so that you may not have power
to perform mass or to ordain no one [a].'

To this Otto and the synod replied by a letter of
humorous expostulation, begging the Pope to reform
both his morals and his Latin.   But the messenger who
bore it could not find John: he had repeated what seems
to have been thought his most heinous sin, by going into
the country with his bow and arrows; and after a search
had been made in vain, the synod resolved to take a

---

[a] ' Iohannes episcopus, servus ser-
vorum Dei, omnibus episcopis. Nos
audivimus dicere quia vos vultis
alium papam facere: si hoc facitis,
da Deum omnipotentem excommu-
nico vos, ut non habeatis licentiam
missam celebrare aut nullum ordi-
nare.'—Liudprand, *ut supra*. The
' da ' is curious, as shewing the
progress of the change from Latin
to Italian.   The answer sent by
Otto and the council takes exception to the double negative.

decisive step. Otto, who still led their deliberations, demanded the condemnation of the Pope ; the assembly deposed him by acclamation, 'because of his reprobate life,' and having obtained the Emperor's consent, proceeded in an equally hasty manner to raise Leo, the chief secretary and a layman, to the chair of the Apostle.

CHAP. IX.

Deposition of John XII.

Otto might seem to have now reached a position loftier and firmer than that of any of his predecessors. Within little more than a year from his arrival in Rome, he had exercised powers greater than those of Charles himself, ordering the dethronement of one pontiff and the installation of another, forcing a reluctant people to bend themselves to his will. The submission involved in his oath to protect the Holy See was more than compensated by the oath of allegiance to his crown which the Pope and the Romans had taken, and by their solemn engagement not to elect nor ordain any future pontiff without the Emperor's consent[b]. But he had yet to learn what this obedience and these oaths were worth. The Romans had eagerly joined in the expulsion of John ; they soon began to regret him. They were mortified to see their streets filled by a foreign soldiery, the habitual licence of their manners sternly repressed, their most cherished privilege, the right of choosing the universal bishop, grasped by the strong hand of a master who used it for purposes in which they did not sympathize. In a fickle and turbulent people, disaffection quickly turned to rebellion. One night, Otto's troops being most of them

[b] 'Cives fidelitatem promittunt hæc addentes et firmiter iurantes nunquam se papam electuros aut ordinaturos præter consensum atque electionem domini imperatoris Ottonis Cæsaris Augusti filiique ipsius Ottonis.'—Liudprand, *Gesta Ottonis*, lib. vi.

dispersed in their quarters at a distance, the Romans rose in arms, blocked up the Tiber bridges, and fell furiously upon the Emperor and his creature the new Pope. Superior valour and constancy triumphed over numbers, and the Romans were overthrown with terrible slaughter; yet this lesson did not prevent them from revolting a second time, after Otto's departure in pursuit of Adalbert. John the Twelfth returned to the city, and when his pontifical career was speedily closed by the sword of an injured husband[c], the people chose a new Pope in defiance of the Emperor and his nominee. Otto again subdued and again forgave them, but when they rebelled for a third time, in A.D. 966, he resolved to shew them what imperial supremacy meant. Thirteen leaders, among them the twelve tribunes, were executed, the consuls were banished, republican forms entirely suppressed, the government of the city entrusted to Pope Leo as viceroy. He, too, must not presume on the sacredness of his person to set up any claims to independence. Otto regarded the pontiff as no more than the first of his subjects, the creature of his own will, the depositary of an authority which must be exercised according to the discretion of his sovereign. The citizens yielded to the Emperor an absolute veto on papal elections in A.D. 963. Otto obtained from his nominee, Leo VIII, a confirmation of this privilege, which it was afterwards supposed that Hadrian I had granted to Charles, in a decree which may yet be read in the collec-

[c] 'In timporibus adeo a dyabulo est percussus ut infra dierum octo spacium eodem sit in vulnere mortuus,' says the chronicler, crediting with but little of his wonted cleverness the supposed author of John's death, who well might have desired a long life for so useful a servant.

He adds a detail too characteristic of the time to be omitted —'Sed eucharistiæ viaticum, ipsius instinctu qui eum percusserat, non percepit.'

tions of the canon law[d]. The vigorous exercise of such a power might be expected to reform as well as to restrain the apostolic see; and it was for this purpose, and in noble honesty, that the Teutonic sovereigns employed it. But the fortunes of Otto in the city are a type of those which his successors were destined to experience. Notwithstanding their clear rights and the momentary enthusiasm with which they were greeted in Rome, not all the efforts of Emperor after Emperor could gain any firm hold on the capital they were so proud of. Visiting it only once or twice in their reigns, they must be supported among a fickle populace by a large army of strangers, which melted away with terrible rapidity under the sun of Italy amid the deadly hollows of the Campagna[e]. Rome soon resumed her turbulent independence.

Causes partly the same prevented the Saxon princes from gaining a firm footing throughout Italy. Since Charles the Bald had bartered away for the crown all that made it worth having, no Emperor had exercised substantial authority there. The *missi dominici* had ceased to traverse the country; the local governors had thrown off control, a crowd of petty potentates had established principalities by aggressions on their weaker neighbours. Only in the dominions of great nobles, like the marquises of Tuscany and Spoleto, and in some of the cities where the supremacy of the bishop was paving

CHAP. IX.

Otto's rule in Italy.

---

[d] *Corpus Iuris Canonici*, Dist. lxiii., '*In synodo*.' A decree which is probably substantially genuine, although the form in which we have it is evidently of later date.

[e] Cf. St. Peter Damiani's lines—

'Roma vorax hominum domat ardua colla virorum,
Roma ferax febrium necis est uberrima frugum,
Romanæ febres stabili sunt iure fideles.'

CHAP. IX.

Italy was divided (handwritten note)

the way for a republican system, could traces of political order be found, or the arts of peace flourish. Otto, who, though he came as a conqueror, ruled legitimately as Italian king, found his feudal vassals less submissive than in Germany. While actually present he succeeded by progresses and edicts, and stern justice, in doing something to still the turmoil; on his departure Italy relapsed into that disorganization for which her natural features are not less answerable than the mixture of her races. Yet it was at this era, when the confusion was wildest, that there appeared the first rudiments of an Italian nationality, based partly on geographical position, partly on the use of a common language and the slow growth of peculiar customs and modes of thought. But though already jealous of the Tedescan, national feeling was still very far from disputing his sway. Pope, princes, and cities bowed to Otto as king and Emperor; nor did he bethink himself of crushing while it was weak a sentiment whose development threatened the existence of his empire. Holding Italy equally for his own with Germany, and ruling both on the same principles, he was content to keep it a separate kingdom, neither changing its institutions nor sending Saxons, as Charles had sent Franks, to represent his government[f].

Otto's foreign policy.

The lofty claims which Otto acquired with the Roman crown urged him to resume the plans of foreign conquest which had lain neglected since the days of Charles: the growing vigour of the Teutonic people, now definitely separating themselves from surrounding races (this is the era of the Marks—Brandenburg, Meissen, Schleswig), placed in his hands a force to execute those plans which

[f] There was a separate chancellor for Italy; as afterwards for the kingdom of Burgundy.

his predecessors had wanted. In this, as in his other
enterprises, the great Emperor was active, wise, successful. Retaining the extreme south of Italy, and unwilling to confess the loss of Rome, the Greeks had not
ceased to annoy her German masters by intrigue, and
might now, under the vigorous leadership of Nicephorus
and Tzimiskes, hope again to menace them in arms.
Policy, and the fascination which an ostentatiously *Towards*
legitimate court exercised over the Saxon stranger, made *Byzantium.*
Otto, as Napoleon wooed Maria Louisa, seek for his heir
the hand of the princess Theophano. Liudprand's account of his embassy represents in an amusing manner
the rival pretensions of the old and new Empires [g]. The
Greeks, who fancied that with the name they preserved
the character and rights of Rome, held it almost as
absurd as it was wicked that a Frank should insult their
prerogative by reigning in Italy as Emperor. They refused him that title altogether; and when the Pope
had, in a letter addressed '*Imperatori Græcorum*,' asked
Nicephorus to gratify the wishes of the Emperor of the
Romans, the Eastern was furious. 'You are no Romans,' said he, 'but wretched Lombards: what means
this insolent Pope? with Constantine all Rome migrated
hither.' The wily bishop appeased him by abusing the
Romans, while he insinuated that Byzantium could lay
no claim to their name, and proceeded to vindicate the
Francia and Saxonia of his master. '"Roman" is the
most contemptuous name we can use—it conveys the
reproach of every vice, cowardice, falsehood, avarice.
But what can be expected from the descendants of the
fratricide Romulus? to his asylum were gathered the
offscourings of the nations: thence came these κοσμο-

[g] Liudprand, *Legatio Constantinopolitana.*

κράτορες.' Nicephorus demanded the 'theme' or province of Rome as the price of compliance [h]; Tzimiskes was more moderate, and Theophano became the bride of Otto II.

Holding the two capitals of Charles the Great, Otto might vindicate the suzerainty over the West Frankish kingdom which it had been meant that the imperial title should carry with it. Arnulf had asserted it by making Eudes, the first Capetian king, receive the crown as his feudatory: Henry the Fowler had been less successful. Otto pursued the same course, intriguing with the discontented nobles of Louis d'Outremer, and receiving their fealty as Superior of Roman Gaul. These pretensions, however, could have been made effective only by arms, and the feudal militia of the tenth century was no such instrument of conquest as the hosts of Clovis and Charles had been. The star of the Carolingian of Laon was paling before the rising greatness of the Parisian Capets: a Romano-Keltic nation had formed itself, distinct in tongue from the Franks, whom it was fast absorbing, and still less willing to submit to a Saxon stranger. Modern France [i] dates from the accession of Hugh Capet, A.D. 987, and the claims of the Roman Empire were never afterwards formally admitted.

Of that France, however, Aquitaine was virtually inde

---

[h] 'Sancti imperii nostri olim servos principes, Beneventanum scilicet, tradat,' &c. The epithet is worth noticing.

[i] Liudprand calls the Eastern Franks 'Franci Teutonici' to distinguish them from the Romanized Franks of Gaul or 'Francigenæ,' as they were frequently called. The name 'Frank' seems even so early as the tenth century to have been used in the East as a general name for the Western peoples of Europe. Liudprand says that the Greek Emperor included ' sub Francorum nomine tam Latinos quam Teutonicos.' Probably this use dates from the time of Charles.

pendent. Lotharingia and Burgundy belonged to it as little as did England. The former of these kingdoms had adhered to the West Frankish king, Charles the Simple, against the East Frankish Conrad: but now, as mostly German in blood and speech, threw itself into the arms of Otto, and was thenceforth an integral part of the Empire. Burgundy, a separate kingdom, had, by seeking from Charles the Fat a ratification of Boso's election, by admitting, in the person of Rudolf the first Transjurane king, the feudal superiority of Arnulf, acknowledged itself to be dependent on the German crown. Otto governed it for thirty years, nominally as the guardian of the young king Conrad (son of Rudolf II).

Otto's conquests to the North and East approved him a worthy successor of the first Emperor. He penetrated far into Jutland, annexed Schleswig, made Harold the Blue-toothed his vassal. The Slavic tribes were obliged to submit, to follow the German host in war, to allow the free preaching of the Gospel in their borders. The Hungarians he forced to forsake their nomad life, and delivered Europe from the fear of Asiatic invasions by strengthening the frontier of Austria. Over more distant lands, Spain and England, it was not possible to recover the commanding position of Charles. Henry, as head of the Saxon name, may have wished to unite its branches on both sides the sea [k], and it was perhaps partly with this intent that he gained for Otto the hand of Edith, sister of the English Athelstan. But the claim of supremacy, if any there was, was repudiated by Edgar, when, exaggerating the lofty style assumed by some of his predecessors, he called himself 'Basileus and imperator of Britain[l],'

CHAP. IX.

Lorraine and Burgundy.

Denmark and the Slaves.

England.

---

[k] Conring, *De Finibus Imperii.*
[l] Basileus was a favourite title of the English kings before the Conquest. Titles like this used in these

thereby seeming to pretend to a sovereignty over all the nations of the island similar to that which the Roman Emperor claimed over the states of Christendom.

Extent of Otto's Empire.

This restored Empire, which professed itself a continuation of the Carolingian, was in many respects different. It was less wide, including, if we reckon strictly, only Germany proper and two-thirds of Italy; or counting in subject but separate kingdoms, Burgundy, Bohemia, Moravia, Poland, Denmark, perhaps Hungary. Its character

Comparison between it and that of Charles.

was less ecclesiastical. Otto exalted indeed the spiritual potentates of his realm, and was earnest in spreading Christianity among the heathen: he was master of the Pope and Defender of the Holy Roman Church. But religion held a less important place in his mind and his administration: he made fewer wars for its sake, held no councils, and did not, like his predecessor, criticize the discourses of bishops. It was also less Roman. We do not know whether Otto associated with that name anything more than the right to universal dominion and a certain oversight of matters spiritual, nor how far he believed himself to be treading in the steps of the Cæsars. He could not speak Latin, he had few learned men around him, he cannot have possessed the varied cultivation which had been so fruitful in the mind of Charles. Moreover, the conditions of his time were different, and did not permit similar attempts at wide organization. The local potentates would have submitted to no *missi dominici;* separate laws and jurisdictions would not have yielded to imperial capitularies; the

early English charters prove, it need hardly be said, absolutely nothing as to the real existence of any rights or powers of the English king beyond his own borders. What they do prove (over and above the taste for florid rhetoric in the royal clerks) is the impression produced by the imperial style, and by the idea of the emperor's throne as supported by the thrones of kings and other lesser potentates.

placita at which those laws were framed or published would not have been crowded, as of yore, by armed freemen. But what Otto could he did, and did it to good purpose. Constantly traversing his dominions, he introduced a peace and prosperity before unknown, and left everywhere the impress of an heroic character. Under him the Germans became not only a united nation, but were at once raised on a pinnacle among European peoples as the imperial race, the possessors of Rome and Rome's authority. While the political connection with Italy stirred their spirit, it brought with it a knowledge and culture hitherto unknown, and gave the newly-kindled energy an object. Germany became in her turn the instructress of the neighbouring tribes, who trembled at Otto's sceptre; Poland and Bohemia received from her their arts and their learning with their religion. If the revived Romano-Germanic Empire was less splendid than the Empire of the West had been under Charles, it was, within narrower limits, firmer and more lasting, since based on a social force which the other had wanted. It perpetuated the name, the language, the literature, such as it then was, of Rome; it extended her spiritual sway; it strove to represent that concentration for which men cried, and became a power to unite and civilize Europe.

The time of Otto the Great has required a fuller treatment, as the era of the Holy Empire's foundation: succeeding rulers may be more quickly dismissed. Yet Otto III's reign cannot pass unnoticed: short, sad, full of bright promise never fulfilled. His mother was the Greek princess Theophano; his preceptor, the illustrious Gerbert: through the one he felt himself connected with the old Empire, and had imbibed the absolutism of Byzantium; by the other he had been reared in the dream of a reno-

His ideas.
Fascination
exercised
over him by
the name of
Rome.

vated Rome, with her memories turned to realities. To accomplish that renovation, who so fit as he who with the vigorous blood of the Teutonic conqueror inherited the venerable rights of Constantinople? It was his design, now that the solemn millennial era of the founding of Christianity had arrived, to renew the majesty of the city and make her again the capital of a world-embracing Empire, victorious as Trajan's, despotic as Justinian's, holy as Constantine's. His young and visionary mind was too much dazzled by the gorgeous fancies it created to see the world as it was: Germany rude, Italy unquiet, Rome corrupt and faithless. In A.D. 994, at the age of sixteen, he took from his mother's hands the reins of government, and entered Italy to receive his crown, and quell the turbulence of Rome. There he put to death the rebel Crescentius, in whom modern enthusiasm has seen a patriotic republican, who, reviving the institutions of Alberic, had ruled as consul or senator, sometimes entitling himself Emperor [m]. The young monarch reclaimed, perhaps extended, the privilege of Charles and Otto the Great, by nominating successive pontiffs: first Bruno his cousin (Gregory V), then Gerbert, whose name of Sylvester II

Pope
Sylvester II,
A.D. 1000.

recalled significantly the ally of Constantine: Gerbert, to his contemporaries a marvel of piety and learning, in later legend the magician who, at the price of his own soul, purchased preferment from the Enemy, and by him was at last carried off in the body. With the substitution of these men for the profligate priests of Italy, began that Teutonic reform of the Papacy which raised it from the abyss of the tenth century to the point where Hildebrand

---

[m] The coins of Crescentius are said to exhibit the insignia of the old Empire.—Palgrave, *Normandy and England,* i. 715. But probably some at least of them are forgeries.

found it. The Emperors were working the ruin of their power by their most disinterested acts.

With his tutor on Peter's chair to second or direct him, Otto laboured on his great project in a spirit almost mystic. He had an intense religious belief in the Emperor's duties to the world—in his proclamations he calls himself 'Servant of the Apostles,' 'Servant of Jesus Christ [a]'—together with the ambitious antiquarianism of a fiery imagination, kindled by the memorials of the glory and power he represented. Even the wording of his laws witnesses to the strange mixture of notions that filled his eager brain. 'We have ordained this,' says an edict, 'in order that, the church of God being freely and firmly established, our Empire may be advanced and the crown of our knighthood triumph; that the power of the Roman people may be extended and the commonwealth be restored; so may we be found worthy after living righteously in the tabernacle of this world, to fly away from the prison of this life and reign most righteously with the Lord.' To exclude the claims of the Greeks he used the title '*Romanorum Imperator*' instead of the simple '*Imperator*' of his predecessors. His seals bear a legend resembling that used by Charles, '*Renovatio Imperii Romanorum;*' even the 'commonwealth,' despite the results that name had produced under Alberic and Crescentius, was to be re-established. He built a palace on the Aventine, then the most healthy and beautiful quarter of the city; he devised a regular administrative system of government for his capital—naming a patrician, a prefect, and a body of judges, who were commanded to recognize no law but Justinian's. The formula of their appointment has been

[a] Proclamation in Pertz, *M. G. H.* ii.

CHAP. IX.

preserved to us: in it the Emperor delivering to the judge a copy of the code bids him 'with this code judge Rome and the Leonine city and the whole world.' He introduced into the simple German court the ceremonious magnificence of Byzantium, not without giving offence to many of his followers[o]. His father's wish to draw Italy and Germany more closely together, he followed up by giving the chancellorship of both countries to the same churchman, by maintaining a strong force of Germans in Italy, and by taking his Italian retinue with him through the Transalpine lands. How far these brilliant and far-reaching plans were capable of realization, had their author lived to attempt it, can be but guessed at. It is reasonable to suppose that whatever power he might have gained in the South he would have lost in the North. Dwelling rarely in Germany, and in sympathies more a Greek than a Teuton, he reined in the fierce barons with no such tight hand as his grandfather had been wont to do; he neglected the schemes of northern conquest; he released the Polish dukes from the obligation of tribute. But all, save that those plans were his, is now no more than conjecture, for Otto III, 'the wonder of the world,' as his own generation called him, died childless on the threshold of manhood; the victim, if we may trust a story of the time, of the revenge of Stephania, widow of Crescentius, who ensnared him by her beauty, and slew him by a lingering poison. They carried him across the Alps with laments whose echoes sound faintly yet from the pages of monkish chroniclers, and buried him in the choir of the basilica at Aachen some fifty paces from the tomb

---

[o] 'Imperator antiquam Romanorum consuetudinem iam ex magna parte deletam suis cupiens renovare temporibus multa faciebat quæ diversi diverse sentiebant.'–Thietmar, *Chron.* ix.; ap. Pertz, *M. G. H.* t. iii.

of Charles beneath the central dome. Two years had not passed since, setting out on his last journey to Rome, he had opened that tomb, had gazed on the great Emperor, sitting on a marble throne, robed and crowned, with the Gospel-book open before him; and there, touching the dead hand, unclasping from the neck its golden cross, had taken, as it were, an investiture of Empire from his Frankish forerunner. Short as was his life and few his acts, Otto III is in one respect more memorable than any who went before or came after him. None save he desired to make the seven-hilled city again the seat of dominion, reducing Germany and Lombardy and Greece to their rightful place of subject provinces. No one else so forgot the present to live in the light of the ancient order; no other soul was so possessed by that fervid mysticism and that reverence for the glories of the past, whereon rested the idea of the mediæval Empire.

The direct line of Otto the Great had now ended, and though the Franks might elect and the Saxons accept Henry II[p], Italy was nowise affected by their acts. Neither the Empire nor the Lombard kingdom could as yet be of right claimed by the German king. Her princes placed Ardoin, marquis of Ivrea, on the vacant throne of Pavia, moved partly by the growing aversion to a Transalpine power, still more by the desire of impunity under a monarch feebler than any since Berengar. But the selfishness that had exalted Ardoin soon overthrew him. Ere long a party among the nobles, seconded by the Pope, invited Henry[q]; his strong army made opposition hopeless, and at Rome he received the im-

Italy independent.

[p] *Annales Quedlinb.*, ad ann. 1002.

[q] Henry had already entered Italy in 1004.

perial crown, A.D. 1014. It is, perhaps, more singular
that the Transalpine kings should have clung so per-
tinaciously to Italian sovereignty than that the Lombards
should have so frequently attempted to recover their
independence. For the former had often little or no
hereditary claim, they were not secure in their seat at
home, they crossed a huge mountain barrier into a land
of treachery and hatred. But Rome's glittering lure was
irresistible, and the disunion of Italy promised an easy
conquest. Surrounded by martial vassals, these Emperors
were generally for the moment supreme: once their
pennons had disappeared in the gorges of Tyrol, things
reverted to their former condition, and Tuscany was little

more dependent than France. In Southern Italy the
Greek viceroy ruled from Bari, and Rome was an outpost
instead of the centre of Teutonic power. A curious evidence of the wavering politics of the time is furnished by the
Annals of Benevento, the Lombard town which on the
confines of the Greek and Roman realms gave steady
obedience to neither. They usually date by and recognize the princes of Constantinople [r], seldom mention-
ing the Franks, till the reign of Conrad II; after him
the Western becomes *Imperator*, the Greek, appearing
more rarely, is *Imperator Constantinopolitanus*. Assailed
by the Saracens, masters already of Sicily, these regions
seemed on the eve of being lost to Christendom, and the
Romans sometimes bethought themselves of returning
under the Byzantine sceptre. As the weakness of the
Greeks in the South favoured the rise of the Norman
kingdom, so did the liberties of the northern cities shoot
up in the absence of the Emperors and the feuds of the

[r] *Annales Beneventani*, in Pertz, *M. G. H.*

princes.   Milan, Pavia, Cremona, were only the foremost among many populous centres of industry, some of them self-governing, all quickly absorbing or repelling the rural nobility, and not afraid to display by tumults their aversion to the Germans.

The reign of Conrad II, the first monarch of the great Franconian line, is remarkable for the accession to the Empire of Burgundy, or, as it is after this time more often called, the kingdom of Arles[8].   Rudolf III, the last king, had proposed to bequeath it to Henry II, and the states were at length persuaded to consent to its reunion to the crown from which it had been separated, though to some extent dependent, since the death of Lothar I (son of Lewis the Pious).   On Rudolf's death in 1032, Eudes, count of Champagne, endeavoured to seize it, and entered the north-western districts, from which he was dislodged by Conrad with some difficulty. Unlike Italy, it became an integral member of the Germanic realm: its prelates and nobles sat in imperial diets, and retained till recently the style and title of Princes of the Holy Empire.   The central government was, however, seldom effective in these outlying territories, exposed always to the intrigues, finally to the aggressions, of Capetian France.

Under Conrad's son Henry the Third the Empire attained the meridian of its power.   At home Otto the Great's prerogative had not stood so high.   The duchies, always the chief source of fear, were allowed to remain vacant or filled by the relatives of the monarch, who himself retained, contrary to usual practice, those of Franconia and (for some years) Swabia.   Abbeys and

CHAP. IX.

Conrad II.

Henry III.

8 See Appendix, Note A.

sees lay entirely in his gift. Intestine feuds were repressed by the proclamation of a public peace. Abroad, the feudal superiority over Hungary, which Henry II had gained by conferring the title of King with the hand of his sister Gisela, was enforced by war, the country made *His reform of the Pope-dom.* almost a province, and compelled to pay tribute. In Rome no German sovereign had ever been so absolute. A disgraceful contest between three claimants of the papal chair had shocked even the reckless apathy of Italy. Henry deposed them all, and appointed their successor: he became hereditary patrician, and wore constantly the green mantle and circlet of gold which were the badges of that office, seeming, one might think, to find in it some further authority than that which the imperial name conferred. The synod passed a decree granting to Henry the right of nominating the supreme pontiff; and the Roman priesthood, who had forfeited the respect of the world even more by habitual simony than by the flagrant corruption of their manners, were forced to receive German after German as their bishop, at the bidding of a ruler so powerful, so severe, and so pious. But Henry's encroachments alarmed his own nobles no less than the Italians, and the reaction, which might have been dangerous to himself, was fatal to his successor. A mere chance, as some might call it, deter-
Henry IV, mined the course of history. The great Emperor died
A.D. 1056– suddenly in A.D. 1056, and a child was left at the helm,
1106. while storms were gathering that might have demanded the wisest hand.

CHAPTER X.

STRUGGLE OF THE EMPIRE AND THE PAPACY.

REFORMED by the Emperors and their Teutonic nominees, the Papacy had resumed in the middle of the eleventh century the schemes of polity shadowed forth by Nicholas I, and which the degradation of the last age had only suspended. Under the guidance of her greatest mind, Hildebrand, the archdeacon of Rome, she now advanced to their completion, and proclaimed that war of the ecclesiastical power against the civil power in the person of the Emperor, which became the centre of the subsequent history of both. While the nature of the struggle cannot be understood without a glance at their previous connection, the vastness of the subject warns one from the attempt to draw even its outlines, and restricts our view to those relations of Popedom and Empire which arise directly out of their respective positions as heads spiritual and temporal of the universal Christian state.

The eagerness of Christianity in the age immediately following her political establishment to purchase by submission the support of the civil power, has been already remarked. The change from independence to supremacy was gradual. The tale we smile at, how Constantine,

CHAP. X.

healed of his leprosy, granted the West to bishop Sylvester, and retired to Byzantium that no secular prince might interfere with the jurisdiction or profane the neighbourhood of Peter's chair, worked great effects through the belief it commanded for many centuries. Nay more, its groundwork was true. It was the removal of the seat of government from the Tiber to the Bosphorus that made the Pope the greatest personage in the city, and in the prostration after Alaric's invasion he was seen to be so. Henceforth he alone was a permanent and effective, though still unacknowledged power, as truly superior to the revived senate and consuls of the phantom republic as Augustus and Tiberius had been to the faint continuance of their earlier prototypes. Pope Leo the First asserted the universal jurisdiction of his see [a], and his persevering successors slowly enthralled Italy, Illyricum, Gaul, Spain, Africa, dexterously confounding their undoubted metropolitan and patriarchal rights with those of œcumenical bishop, in which they were finally merged. By his writings and the fame of his personal sanctity, by the conversion of England and the introduction of an impressive ritual, Gregory the Great did more than any other pontiff to advance Rome's ecclesiastical authority. Yet his tone to Maurice of Constantinople was deferential, to Phocas adulatory; his successors were not consecrated till confirmed by the Emperor or the Exarch; one of them was dragged in chains to the Bosphorus, and banished thence to Scythia. When the iconoclastic controversy and the intervention of Pipin broke the allegiance of the Popes to the East, the Franks, as patricians

[a] 'Roma per sedem Beati Petri caput orbis effecta.'—See note *i*, p. 32.

and Emperors, seemed to step into the position which Byzantium had lost[b]. At Charles's coronation, says the Saxon poet,

'Et summus eundem
'Præsul adoravit, sicut mos debitus olim
'Principibus fuit antiquis.'

Their relations were, however, no longer the same. If the Frank vaunted conquest, the priest spoke only of free gift. What Christendom saw was that Charles was crowned by the Pope's hands, and undertook as his principal duty the protection and advancement of the Holy Roman Church. The circumstances of Otto the Great's coronation gave an even more favourable opening to sacerdotal claims, for it was a Pope who summoned him to Rome and a Pope who received from him an oath of fidelity and aid. In the conflict of three powers, the Emperor, the pontiff, and the people—represented by their senate and consuls, or by the demagogue of the hour—the most steady, prudent, and far-sighted was sure eventually to prevail. The Popedom had no minorities, as yet few disputed successions, few revolts within its own army—the host of churchmen through Europe. Boniface's conversion of Germany under its direct sanction, gave it a hold on the rising hierarchy of the greatest European state; the extension of the rule of Charles and Otto diffused in the same measure its emissaries and pretensions. The first disputes turned on the right of the prince to confirm the elected pontiff, which was afterwards supposed to have been granted by Hadrian I to

Relations of the Papacy and the Empire.

---

[b] 'Claves tibi *ad regnum* dimisimus.'—Pope Stephen to Charles Martel, in *Codex Carolinus*, ap. Muratori, *S. R. I.* iii. Some, however, prefer to read 'ad rogum.'

Charles, in the decree quoted as '*Hadrianus Papa*c.'
This '*ius eligendi et ordinandi summum pontificem,*' which
Lewis I appears as yielding by the '*Ego Ludovicus*d,' was
claimed by the Carolingians whenever they felt themselves strong enough, and having fallen into desuetude
in the troublous times of the Italian Emperors, was formally renewed to Otto the Great by his nominee Leo VIII.
We have seen it used, and used in the purest spirit, by
Otto himself, by his grandson Otto III, last of all, and
most despotically, by Henry III. Along with it there
had grown up a bold counter-assumption of the Papal
chair to be itself the source of the imperial dignity. In
submitting to a fresh coronation, Lewis the Pious admitted the invalidity of his former self-performed one :
Charles the Bald did not scout the arrogant declaration
of John VIIIe, that to him alone the Emperor owed his
crown; and the council of Paviaf, when it chose him
king of Italy, repeated the assertion. Subsequent Popes
knew better than to apply to the chiefs of Saxon and
Franconian chivalry language which the feeble Neustrian
had not resented; but the precedent remained, the wea-
pon was only hid behind the pontifical robe to be flashed
out with effect when the moment should come. There
were also two other great steps which papal power had
taken. By the invention and adoption of the False

---

c *Corpus Iuris Canonici,* Dist.
lxiii. c. 22.

d Dist. lxiii. c. 30. This decree
is, however, in all probability spu-
rious.

e ' Nos elegimus merito et ap-
probavimus una cum annisu et voto
patrum amplique senatus et gentis
togatæ,' &c., ap. Baron. *Ann. Eccl.,*

ad ann. 876.

f ' Divina vos pietas B. principum
apostolorum Petri et Pauli inter-
ventione per vicarium ipsorum
dominum Ioannem summum pontificem . . . . ad imperiale culmen
S. Spiritus iudicio provexit.'—
Concil. Ticinense, in Mur., *S. R. I.*
ii.

Decretals it had provided itself with a legal system suited to any emergency, and which gave it unlimited authority through the Christian world in causes spiritual and over persons ecclesiastical. Canonistical ingenuity found it easy in one way or another to make this include all causes and persons whatsoever : for crime is always and wrong is often sin, nor can aught be anywhere done which may not affect the clergy. On the gift of Pipin and Charles, repeated and confirmed by Lewis I, Charles II, Otto I and III, and now made to rest on the more venerable authority of the first Christian Emperor, it could found claims to the sovereignty of Rome, Tuscany, and all else that had belonged to the exarchate. Indefinite in their terms, these grants were never meant by the donors to convey full dominion over the districts —that belonged to the head of the Empire—but only as in the case of other church estates, a perpetual usufruct or *dominium utile.* They were, in fact, mere endowments. Nor had the gifts been ever actually reduced into possession : the Pope had been hitherto the victim, not the lord, of the neighbouring barons. They were not, however, denied, and might be made a formidable engine of attack : appealing to them, the Pope could brand his opponents as unjust and impious ; and could summon nobles and cities to defend him as their liege lord, just as, with no better original right, he invoked the help of the Norman conquerors of Naples and Sicily.

The attitude of the Roman Church to the imperial power at Henry the Third's death was externally respectful. The right of a German king to the crown of the city was undoubted, and the Pope was his lawful subject. Hitherto the initiative in reform had come from the civil magistrate. But the secret of the pontiff's strength lay

in this : he, and he alone, could confer the crown, and
had therefore the right of imposing conditions on its re-
cipient. Frequent interregna had weakened the claim of
the Transalpine monarch and prevented his power from
taking firm root; his title was never by law hereditary : the
holy Church had before sought and might again seek a
defender elsewhere. And since the need of such defence had originated this transference of the Empire from
the Greeks to the Franks, since to render it was the
Emperor's chief function, it was surely the Pope's duty as
well as his right to see that the candidate was capable of
fulfilling his task, to degrade him if he rejected or mis-
performed it.

Hildebran-
dine
reforms.

The first step was to remove a blemish in the constitution of the Church, by fixing a regular body to choose the
supreme pontiff. This Nicholas II did in A.D. 1059,
feebly reserving the rights of Henry IV and his successors.
Then the reforming spirit, kindled by the abuses and de-
pravity of the last century, advanced apace. It had two
main objects : the enforcement of celibacy, especially on
the secular clergy, who enjoyed in this respect considerable
freedom, and the extinction of simony. In the former,
the Emperors and a large part of the laity were not unwilling to join : the latter no one dared to defend in
theory. But when Gregory VII declared that it was sin
for the ecclesiastic to receive his benefice under conditions
from a layman, and so condemned the whole system of
feudal investitures to the clergy, he aimed a deadly blow
at all secular authority. Half of the land and wealth of
Germany was in the hands of bishops and abbots, who
would now be freed from the monarch's control to pass
under that of the Pope. In such a state of things government itself would be impossible.

Henry and Gregory already mistrusted each other: after this decree war was inevitable. The Pope cited his opponent to appear and be judged at Rome for his vices and misgovernment. The Emperor[g] replied by convoking a synod, which deposed and insulted Gregory. At once the dauntless monk pronounced Henry excommunicate, and fixed a day on which, if still unrepentant, he should cease to reign. Supported by his own princes, the monarch might have defied a mandate backed by no external force; but the Saxons, never contented since the first place had passed from their own dukes to the Franconians, only waited the signal to burst into a new revolt, whilst through all Germany the Emperor's tyranny and irregularities of life had sown the seeds of disaffection. Shunned, betrayed, threatened, he rushed into what seemed the only course left, and Canosa saw Europe's mightiest prince, titular lord of the world, a suppliant before the successor of the Apostle. Henry soon found that his humiliation had not served him; driven back into opposition, he defied Gregory anew, set up an anti-pope, overthrew the rival whom his rebellious subjects had raised, and maintained to the end of his sad and chequered life a power often depressed but never destroyed. Nevertheless had all other humiliation been spared, that one scene in the yard of the Countess Matilda's castle, an imperial penitent standing barefoot and woollen-frocked on the snow three days and nights, till the priest who sat within should admit and absolve him, was enough to mark a decisive change, and inflict an irretrievable disgrace on the crown so abased. Its wearer could no more, with the same lofty confidence, claim to be the highest power on

CHAP. X.
Henry IV and Gregory VII.

A.D. 1077.

[g] Strictly speaking, Henry was at this time only king of the Romans: he was not crowned Emperor at Rome till 1084.

earth, created by and answerable to God alone. Gregory had extorted the recognition of that absolute superiority of the spiritual dominion which he was wont to assert so sternly; proclaiming that to the Pope, as God's vicar, all mankind are subject, and all rulers responsible: so that he, the giver of the crown, may also excommunicate and depose. Writing to William the Conqueror, he says[h]: 'For as for the beauty of this world, that it may be at different seasons perceived by fleshly eyes, God hath disposed the sun and the moon, lights that outshine all others; so lest the creature whom His goodness hath formed after His own image in this world should be drawn astray into fatal dangers, He hath provided in the apostolic and royal dignities the means of ruling it through divers offices. . . . . If I, therefore, am to answer for thee on the dreadful day of judgment before the just Judge who cannot lie, the creator of every creature, bethink thee whether I must not very diligently provide for thy salvation, and whether, for thine own safety, thou oughtest not without delay to obey me, that so thou mayest possess the land of the living.'

Gregory was not the inventor nor the first propounder of these doctrines; they had been long before a part of mediæval Christianity, interwoven with its most vital doctrines. But he was the first who dared to apply them to the world as he found it. His was that rarest and grandest of gifts, intellectual courage and power of imaginative belief which, when it has convinced itself of aught, accepts it fully with all its consequences, and shrinks not from acting at once upon it. A perilous gift, as the melancholy end of his own career proved, for men were found less ready

[h] Letter of Gregory VII to William I, A.D. 1080. I quote from Migne, t. cxlviii. p. 568.

than he had thought them to follow out with unswerving consistency like his the principles which all acknowledged. But it was the very suddenness and boldness of his policy that secured the ultimate triumph of his cause, awing men's minds and making that seem realized which had been till then a vague theory. His premises once admitted,—and no one dreamt of denying them,—the reasonings by which he established the superiority of spiritual to temporal jurisdiction were unassailable. With his authority, in whose hands are the keys of heaven and hell, whose word can bestow eternal bliss or plunge in everlasting misery, no other earthly authority can compete or interfere : if his power extends into the infinite, how much more must he be supreme over things finite? It was thus that Gregory and his successors were wont to argue : the wonder is, not that they were obeyed, but that they were not obeyed more implicitly. In the second sentence of excommunication which Gregory passed upon Henry the Fourth are these words :—

'Come now, I beseech you, O most holy and blessed Fathers and Princes, Peter and Paul, that all the world may understand and know that if ye are able to bind and to loose in heaven, ye are likewise able on earth, according to the merits of each man, to give and to take away empires, kingdoms, princedoms, marquisates, duchies, countships, and the possessions of all men. For if ye judge spiritual things, what must we believe to be power over worldly things? and if ye judge the who rule over all proud princes, what can ye not do to their slaves?'

Doctrines such as these do indeed strike equally at all temporal governments, nor were the Innocents and Bonifaces of later days slow to apply them so. On the

Results of the struggle.

M

Empire, however, the blow fell first and heaviest. As when Alaric entered Rome, the spell of ages was broken, Christendom saw her greatest and most venerable institution dishonoured and helpless; allegiance was no longer undivided, for who could presume to fix in each case the limits of the civil and ecclesiastical jurisdictions? The potentates of Europe beheld in the Papacy a force which, if dangerous to themselves, could be made to repel the pretensions and baffle the designs of the strongest and haughtiest among them. Italy learned how to meet the Teutonic conqueror by gaining the papal sanction for the leagues of her cities. The German princes, anxious to narrow the prerogative of their head, were the natural allies of his enemy, whose spiritual thunders, more terrible than their own lances, could enable them to depose an aspiring monarch, or extort from him any concessions they desired. Their altered tone is marked by the promise they required from Rudolf of Swabia, whom they set up as a rival to Henry, that he would not endeavour to make the throne hereditary.

It is not possible here to dwell on the details of the great struggle of the Investitures, rich as it is in the interest of adventure and character, momentous as were its results for the future. A word or two must suffice to describe the conclusion, not indeed of the whole drama, which was to extend over centuries, but of what may be called its first act. Even that act lasted beyond the lives of the original performers. Gregory the Seventh passed away at Salerno in A.D. 1087, exclaiming with his last breath 'I have loved justice and hated iniquity, therefore I die in exile.' Nineteen years later, in A.D. 1106, Henry IV died, dethroned by an unnatural son whom the hatred of a relentless pontiff had raised in rebellion against him.] But that son, the emperor Henry the Fifth, so far from conceding the points in dispute, proved an antagonist more ruthless and not less able than his father. He claimed for his crown all the rights over ecclesiastics that his predecessors had ever enjoyed, and when at his coronation in Rome, A.D. 1112, Pope Paschal II refused to complete the rite until he should have yielded, Henry seized both Pope and cardinals and compelled them by a rigorous imprisonment to consent to a treaty which he dictated. Once set free, the Pope, as was natural, disavowed his extorted concessions, and the struggle was protracted for ten years longer, until nearly half a century had elapsed from the first quarrel between Gregory VII and Henry IV. The Concordat of Worms, concluded in A.D. 1122, was in form a compromise, designed to spare either party the humiliation of defeat. Yet the Papacy remained master of the field. The Emperor retained but one-half of those rights of investiture which had formerly been his. He could never resume the position of Henry III; his wishes or intrigues might influence the proceedings of a chapter, his oath bound him from open interference. He had entered the strife in the fulness of dignity; he came out of it with tarnished glory and shattered power. His wars had been hitherto carried on with foreign foes, or at worst with a single rebel noble; now his steadiest ally was turned into his fiercest assailant, and had enlisted against him half his court, half the magnates of his realm. · At any moment his sceptre might be shivered in his hand by the bolt of anathema, and a host of enemies spring up from every convent and cathedral.

Two other results of this great conflict ought not to pass unnoticed. The Emperor was alienated from the Church at the most unfortunate of all moments, the era

CHAP. X.

Concordat of Worms, A.D. 1122.

of the Crusades. To conduct a great religious war against the enemies of the faith, to head the church militant in her carnal as the Popes were accustomed to do in her spiritual strife, this was the very purpose for which an Emperor had been called into being; and it was indeed in these wars, more particularly in the first three of them, that the ideal of a Christian commonwealth which the theory of the mediæval Empire proclaimed, was once for all and never again realized by the combined action of the great nations of Europe. Had such an opportunity fallen to the lot of Henry III, he might have used it to win back a supremacy hardly inferior to that which had belonged to the first Carolingians. But Henry IV's proscription excluded him from all share in an enterprise which he must otherwise have led—nay, more, committed it to the guidance of his foes. The religious feeling which the Crusades evoked—a feeling which, became the origin of the great orders of chivalry, and somewhat later of the two great orders of mendicant friars—turned wholly against the opponent of ecclesiastical claims, and was made to work the will of the Holy See, which had blessed and organized the project. A century and a half later the Pope did not scruple to preach a crusade against the Emperor himself.

Again: it was now that the first seeds were sown of that fear and hatred wherewith the German people never thenceforth ceased to regard the encroaching Romish court. Branded by the Church and forsaken by the nobles, Henry IV retained the affections of the faithful burghers of Worms and Liege. It soon became the test of Teutonic patriotism to resist Italian priestcraft.

The changes in the internal constitution of Germany which the long anarchy of Henry IV's reign had produced are seen when the nature of the prerogative as it stood at the accession of Conrad II, the first Franconian Emperor, is compared with its state at Henry V's death. All fiefs are now hereditary, and when vacant can be granted afresh only by consent of the States; the jurisdiction of the crown is less wide; the idea is beginning to make progress that the most essential part of the Empire is not its supreme head but the commonwealth of princes and barons. The greatest triumph of these feudal magnates is in the establishment of the elective principle, which when confirmed by the three free elections of Lothar II, Conrad III, and Frederick I, passes into an undoubted law. The Prince-Electors are mentioned in A.D. 1156 as a distinct and important body[i]. The clergy, too, whom the policy of Otto the Great and Henry II had raised, are now not less dangerous than the dukes, whose power it was hoped they would balance; possibly more so, since protected by their sacred character and their allegiance to the Pope, while able at the same time to command the arms of their countless vassals. Nor were the two succeeding Emperors the men to retrieve those disasters. The Saxon Lothar the Second is the willing minion of the Pope; performs at his coronation a menial service unknown before, and takes a more stringent oath to defend the Holy See, that he may purchase its support against the Swabian faction in his own dominions. Conrad the Third, the first Emperor of the great house of Hohenstaufen[k], represents the anti-papal party; but

CHAP. X.

Limitations of imperial prerogative.

Lothar II, 1125-1138.

Conrad III, 1138-1152.

---

[i] 'Gradum statim post Principes Electores.'—Frederick I's Privilege of Austria, in Pertz, *M.G.H.* legg. ii.

[k] Hohenstaufen is a castle in what is now the kingdom of Würtemberg, about four miles from the Göppingen station of the railway from Stuttgart to Ulm. It stands, or rather stood, on the summit of a steep and lofty conical hill, commanding a boundless view over the

domestic troubles and an unfortunate crusade prevented him from effecting anything in Italy. He never even entered Rome to receive the crown.

great limestone plateau of the Rauhe Alp, the eastern declivities of the Schwartzwald, and the bare and tedious plains of western Bavaria. Of the castle itself, destroyed in the Peasants' War, there remain only fragments of the wall-foundations: in a rude chapel lying on the hill slope below are some strange half-obliterated frescoes; over the arch of the door is inscribed 'Hic transibat Cæsar.' Frederick Barbarossa had another famous palace at Kaiserslautern, a small town in the Palatinate, on the railway from Mannheim to Treves, lying in a wide valley at the western foot of the Hardt mountains. It was destroyed by the French: and a house of correction has been built upon its site; but in a brewery hard by may be seen some of the huge low-browed arches of its lower story.

CHAPTER XI.

THE EMPERORS IN ITALY: FREDERICK BARBAROSSA.

THE reign of Frederick the First, better known under his Italian surname Barbarossa, is the most brilliant in the annals of the Empire. Its territory had been wider under Charles, its strength perhaps greater under Henry the Third, but it never appeared in such pervading vivid activity, never shone with such lustre of chivalry, as under the prince whom his countrymen have taken to be one of their national heroes, and who is still, as the half-mythic type of Teutonic character, honoured by picture and statue, in song and in legend, through the breadth of the German lands. The reverential fondness of his annalists and the whole tenour of his life go far to justify this admiration, and dispose us to believe that nobler motives were joined with personal ambition in urging him to assert so haughtily and carry out so harshly those imperial rights in which he had such unbounded confidence. Under his guidance the Transalpine power made its greatest effort to subdue the two antagonists which then threatened and were fated in the end to destroy it— Italian nationality and the Papacy.

CHAP. XI. *Frederick of Hohenstaufen,* 1152–1189.

Even before Gregory VII's time it might have been predicted that two such potentates as the Emperor and,

His relations to the Popedom.

the Pope, closely bound together, yet each with pretensions wide and undefined, must ere long come into collision. The boldness of that great pontiff in enforcing, the unflinching firmness of his successors in maintaining, the supremacy of clerical authority, inspired their supporters with a zeal and courage which more than compensated the advantages of the Emperor in defending rights he had long enjoyed. On both sides the hatred was soon very bitter. But even had men's passions permitted a reconciliation, it would have been found difficult to bring into harmony adverse principles, each irresistible, mutually destructive. As the spiritual power, in itself purer, since exercised over the soul and directed to the highest of all ends, eternal felicity, was entitled to the obedience of all, laymen as well as clergy; so the spiritual person, to whom, according to the view then universally accepted, there had been imparted by ordination a mysterious sanctity, could not without sin be subject to the lay magistrate, be installed by him in office, be judged in his court, and render to him any compulsory service. Yet it was no less true that civil government was indispensable to the peace and advancement of society; and while it continued to subsist, another jurisdiction could not be suffered to interfere with its workings, nor one-half of the people be altogether removed from its control. Thus the Emperor and the Pope were forced into hostility as champions of opposite systems, however fully each might admit the strength of his adversary's position, however bitterly he might bewail the violence of his own partisans. There had also arisen other causes of quarrel, less respectable but not less dangerous. The pontiff demanded and the monarch refused the lands which the Countess Matilda of Tuscany had bequeathed to the

Holy See; Frederick claiming them as feudal suzerain, the Pope eager by their means to carry out those schemes of temporal dominion which Constantine's donation sanctioned, and Lothar's seeming renunciation of the sovereignty of Rome had done much to encourage. As feudal superior of the Norman kings of Naples and Sicily, as protector of the towns and barons of North Italy who feared the German yoke, the successor of Peter wore already the air of an independent potentate.

No man was less likely than Frederick to submit to these encroachments. He was a sort of imperialist Hildebrand, strenuously proclaiming the immediate dependence of his office on God's gift, and holding it every whit as sacred as his rival's. On his first journey to Rome, he refused to hold the Pope's stirrup [a], as Lothar had done, till Pope Hadrian the Fourth's threat that he would withhold the crown enforced compliance. Complaints arising not long after on some other ground, the Pope exhorted Frederick by letter to shew himself worthy of the kindness of his mother the Roman Church, who had given him the imperial crown, and would confer on him, if dutiful, benefits still greater. This word benefits—*beneficia*—understood in its usual legal sense of 'fief,' and taken in connection with the picture which had been set up at Rome to commemorate Lothar's homage, provoked angry shouts from the nobles assembled in diet at Besançon; and when the legate answered, 'From whom, then, if not from our Lord the Pope, does your king hold the Empire?' his life was not safe from their fury. On this occasion Frederick's vigour and the remonstrances of the Transalpine prelates

Contest with Hadrian IV.

[a] A great deal of importance seems to have been attached to this symbolic act of courtesy. See Art. I of the Sachsenspiegel.

obliged Hadrian to explain away the obnoxious word, and remove the picture. Soon after the quarrel was renewed by other causes, and came to centre itself round the Pope's demand that Rome should be left entirely to his government. Frederick, in reply, appeals to the civil law, and closes with the words, ʻSince by the ordination of God I both am called and am Emperor of the Romans, in nothing but name shall I appear to be ruler if the control of the Roman city be wrested from my hands.' That such a claim should need assertion marks the change since Henry III; how much more that it could not be enforced. Hadrian's tone rises into defiance; he mingles the threat of excommunication with references to the time when the Germans had not yet the Empire. ʻWhat were the Franks till Zacharias welcomed Pipin? What is the Teutonic king now till consecrated at Rome by holy hands? The chair of Peter has given, and can withdraw its gifts.'

With Pope Alexander III.

The schism that followed Hadrian's death produced a second and more momentous conflict. Frederick, as head of Christendom, proposed to summon the bishops of Europe to a general council, over which he should preside, like Justinian or Heraclius. Quoting the favourite text of the two swords, ʻOn earth,' he continues, ʻGod has placed no more than two powers: above there is but one God, so here one Pope and one Emperor. The Divine Providence has specially appointed the Roman Empire as a remedy against continued schism [b].' The plan failed; and Frederick adopted the candidate whom his own faction had chosen, while the rival claimant, Alexander III, appealed, with a confidence which the issue justified, to the support of sound churchmen through-

[b] Letter to the German bishops in Radewic; Mur., *S. R. I.*, t. vi. p. 833.

out Europe. The keen and long doubtful strife of twenty years that followed, while apparently a dispute between rival Popes, was in substance an effort by the secular monarch to recover his command of the priesthood; not less truly so than that contemporaneous conflict of the English Henry II and St. Thomas of Canterbury, with which it was constantly involved. Unsupported, not all Alexander's genius and resolution could have saved him: by the aid of the Lombard cities, whose league he had counselled and hallowed, and of the fevers of Rome, by which the conquering German host was suddenly annihilated, he won a triumph the more signal, that it was over a prince so wise and so pious as Frederick. At Venice, who, inaccessible by her position, maintained a sedulous neutrality, claiming to be independent of the Empire, yet seldom led into war by sympathy with the Popes, the two powers whose strife had roused all Europe were induced to meet by the mediation of the doge Sebastian Ziani. Three slabs of red marble in the porch of St. Mark's point out the spot where Frederick knelt in sudden awe, and the Pope with tears of joy raised him, and gave the kiss of peace. A later legend, to which poetry and painting have given an undeserved currency [c], tells how the pontiff set his foot on the neck of the prostrate king, with the words, ' The lion and the dragon shalt thou trample under feet [d].' It needed not this exaggeration to enhance the significance of that scene, even more full of meaning for the future than it was solemn and affecting to the Venetian crowd that thronged the church and the piazza. For it was the renunciation by the mightiest prince of his time of

[c] A picture in the great hall of the ducal palace (the Sala del Maggio Consiglio) represents the scene. See Rogers' Italy.
[d] Psalm xci.

CHAP. XI.

the project to which his life had been devoted : it was the abandonment by the secular power of a contest in which it had twice been vanquished, and which it could not renew under more favourable conditions.

Authority maintained so long against the successor of Peter would be far from indulgent to rebellious subjects. For it was in this light that the Lombard cities appeared to a monarch bent on reviving all the rights his predecessors had enjoyed: nay, all that the law of ancient Rome gave her absolute ruler. It would be wrong to speak of a re-discovery of the civil law. That system had never perished from Gaul and Italy, had been the groundwork of some codes, and the whole substance, modified only by the changes in society, of many others. The Church excepted, no agent did so much to keep alive the memory of Roman institutions. The twelfth century now beheld the study cultivated with a surprising increase of knowledge and ardour, expended chiefly upon the Pandects. First in Italy and the schools of the South, then in Paris and Oxford, they were expounded, commented on, extolled as the perfection of human wisdom, the sole, true, and eternal law. Vast as has been the labour and thought expended from that time to this in the elucidation of the civil law, the most competent authorities declare that in acuteness, in subtlety, in all those branches of learning which can subsist without help from historical criticism, these so-called Glossatores have been seldom equalled and never surpassed by their successors. The teachers of the canon law, who had not as yet become the rivals of the civilian, and were accustomed to recur to his books where their own were silent, spread through Europe the fame and influence of the Roman jurisprudence; while its own professors were led both by their feeling and their in-

Revival of the study of the civil law.

terest to give to all its maxims the greatest weight and the fullest application. Men just emerging from barbarism, with minds unaccustomed to create and blindly submissive to authority, viewed written texts with an awe to us incomprehensible. All that the most servile jurists of Rome had ever ascribed to their despotic princes was directly transferred to the Cæsarean majesty who inherited their name. He was 'Lord of the world,' absolute master of the lives and property of all his subjects, that is, of all men; the sole fountain of legislation, the embodiment of right and justice. These doctrines, which the great Bolognese jurists, Bulgarus, Martinus, Hugolinus, and others who constantly surrounded Frederick, taught and applied, as matter of course, to a Teutonic, a feudal king, were by the rest of the world not denied, were accepted in fervent faith by his German and Italian partisans. 'To the Emperor belongs the protection of the whole world,' says bishop Otto of Freysing. 'The Emperor is a living law upon earth [e].' To Frederick, at Roncaglia, the archbishop of Milan speaks for the assembled magnates of Lombardy: 'Do and ordain whatsoever thou wilt, thy will is law; as it is written, "Quicquid principi placuit legis habet vigorem, cum populus ei et in eum omne suum imperium et potestatem concesserit [f]." The Hohenstaufen himself was not slow to accept these magnificent ascriptions of dignity, and though modestly professing his wish to govern according to law rather than override the law, was doubtless roused by them to a more vehement assertion of a prerogative so hallowed by age and by what seemed a divine ordinance.

That assertion was most loudly called for in Italy.

[e] Document of 1230, quoted by Von Raumer, v. p. 81.

[f] Speech of archbishop of Milan, in Radewic; Mur. vi.

The Emperors might appear to consider it a conquered country without privileges to be respected, for they did not summon its princes to the German diets, and over-awed its own assemblies at Pavia or Roncaglia by the Transalpine host that followed them. Its crown, too, was theirs whenever they crossed the Alps to claim it, while the elections on the banks of the Rhine might be adorned but could not be influenced by the presence of barons from the southern kingdom [g]. In practice, however, the imperial power stood lower in Italy than in Germany, for it had been from the first intermittent, depending on the personal vigour and present armed support of each invader. The theoretic sovereignty of the Emperor-king was nowise disputed: in the cities toll and tax were of right his: he could issue edicts at the Diet, and require the tenants in chief to appear with their vassals. But the revival of a control never exercised since Henry IV's time, was felt as an intolerable hardship by the great Lombard cities, proud of riches and population equal to that of the duchies of Germany or the kingdoms of the North, and accustomed for more than a century to a turbulent independence. For republicanism and popular freedom Frederick had little sympathy. At Rome the fervent Arnold of Brescia had repeated, but with far different thoughts and hopes, the part of Crescentius [h]. The city had thrown off the yoke of its bishop, and a commonwealth under consuls and senate professed to emulate the spirit while it renewed the forms of the primitive republic. Its leaders had written to Conrad III [i], asking him to help

Rome under Arnold of Brescia.

---

[g] Frederick's election (at Frankfort) was made 'non sine quibusdam Italiæ baronibus.'—Otto Fris. i. But this was the exception.

[h] See also *post*, Chapter XVI.

[i] 'Senatus Populusque Romanus urbis et orbis totius domino Conrado.'

them to restore the Empire to its position under Constantine and Justinian; but the German, warned by St. Bernard, had preferred the friendship of the Pope. Filled with a vain conceit of their own importance, they repeated their offers to Frederick when he sought the crown from Hadrian the Fourth. A deputation, after dwelling in highflown language on the dignity of the Roman people, and their kindness in bestowing the sceptre on him, a Swabian and a stranger, proceeded, in a manner hardly consistent, to demand a largess ere he should enter the city. Frederick's anger did not hear them to the end: ' Is this your Roman wisdom? Who are ye that usurp the name of Roman dignities? Your honours and your authority are yours no longer; with us are consuls, senate, soldiers. It was not you who chose us, but Charles and Otto that rescued you from the Greek and the Lombard, and conquered by their own might the imperial crown. That Frankish might is still the same: wrench, if you can, the club from Hercules. It is not for the people to give laws to the prince, but to obey his mandate [k].' This was Frederick's version of the ' Translation of the Empire [l].'

He who had been so stern to his own capital was not likely to deal more gently with the rebels of Milan and Tortona. In the contest by which Frederick is chiefly known to history, he is commonly painted as the foreign tyrant, the forerunner of the Austrian oppressor [m], crushing under the hoofs of his cavalry the home of freedom

The Lombard Cities.

[k] Otto of Freysing.
[l] Later in his reign, Frederick condescended to negotiate with these Roman magistrates against a hostile Pope, and entered into a sort of treaty by which they were declared exempt from all jurisdiction but his own.

[m] See the first note to Shelley's *Hellas.* Sismondi is mainly answerable for this conception of Barbarossa's position.

and industry. Such a view is unjust to a great man and his cause. To the despot liberty is always licence; yet Frederick was the advocate of admitted claims; the aggressions of Milan threatened her neighbours; the refusal, where no actual oppression was alleged, to admit his officers and allow his regalian rights, seemed a wanton breach of oaths and engagements, treason against God no less than himself[n]. Nevertheless our sympathy must go with the cities, in whose victory we recognize the triumph of freedom and civilization. Their resistance was at first probably a mere aversion to unused control, and to the enforcement of imposts less offensive in former days than now, and by long dereliction apparently obsolete[o]. Republican principles were not avowed, nor Italian nationality appealed to. But the progress of the conflict developed new motives and feelings, and gave them clearer notions of what they fought for. As the Emperor's antagonist, the Pope was their natural ally: he blessed their arms, and called on the barons of Romagna and Tuscany for aid; he made 'The Church' ere long their watchword, and helped them to conclude that league of mutual support by means whereof the party of the Italian Guelfs was formed. Another cry, too, began to be heard, hardly less inspiriting than the last, the cry of freedom and municipal self-government— freedom little understood and terribly abused, self-govern-

[n] They say rebelliously, says Frederick, 'Nolumus hunc regnare super nos . . . at nos maluimus

'De tributo Cæsaris nemo cogitabat;
Omnes erant Cæsares, nemo censum dabat;
Civitas Ambrosii, velut Troia, stabat,
Deos parum, homines minus formidabat.'

honestam mortem quam ut,' &c.— Letter in Pertz. *M.G.H.* legg. ii.

Poems relating to the Emperor Frederick of Hohenstaufen, published by Grimm.

ment which the cities who claimed it for themselves refused to their subject allies, yet both of them, through their divine power of stimulating effort and quickening sympathy, as much nobler than the harsh and sterile system of a feudal monarchy as the citizen of republican Athens rose above the slavish Asiatic or the brutal Macedonian. Nor was the fact that Italians were resisting a Transalpine invader without its effect; there was as yet no distinct national feeling, for half Lombardy, towns as well as rural nobles, fought under Frederick; but events made the cause of liberty always more clearly the cause of patriotism, and increased that fear and hate of the Tedescan for which Italy has had such bitter justification.

The Emperor was for a time successful: Tortona was taken, Milan razed to the ground, her name apparently lost: greater obstacles had been overcome, and a fuller authority was now exercised than in the days of the Ottos or the Henrys. The glories of the first Frankish conqueror were triumphantly recalled, and Frederick was compared by his admirers to the hero whose canonization he had procured, and whom he strove in all things to imitate P. 'He was esteemed,' says one, 'second only to Charles in piety and justice.' 'We ordain this,' says a decree: 'Ut ad Caroli imitationem ius ecclesiarum statum reipublicæ et legum integritatem per totum imperium nostrum servaremus q.' But the hold the name of Charles had on the minds of the people, and the way in which he had become, so to speak, an eponym of Empire, has better witnesses than grave documents. A rhyming poet sings r :—

Temporary success of Frederick.

P Charles the Great was canonized by Frederick's anti-pope and confirmed afterwards.

q *Acta Concil. Hartzhem.* iii.,

quoted by Von Raumer, ii. 6.

r Poems relating to Frederick I, *ut supra.*

CHAP. XI.

' Quanta sit potentia vel laus Friderici
Cum sit patens omnibus, non est opus dici;
Qui rebelles lancea fodiens ultrici
Repræsentat Karolum dextera victrici.'

The diet at Roncaglia was a chorus of gratulations over the re-establishment of order by the destruction of the dens of unruly burghers.

Victory of the Lombard league.

This fair sky was soon clouded. From her quenchless ashes uprose Milan; Cremona, scorning old jealousies, helped to rebuild what she had destroyed, and the confederates, committed to an all but hopeless strife, clung faithfully together till on the field of Legnano the Empire's banner went down before the carroccio [*] of the free city. Times were changed since Aistulf and Desiderius trembled at the distant tramp of the Frankish hosts. A new nation had arisen, slowly reared through suffering into strength, now at last by heroic deeds conscious of itself. The power of Charles had overleaped boundaries of nature and language that were too strong for his successor, and that grew henceforth ever firmer, till they made the Empire itself a delusive name. Frederick, though harsh in war, and now balked of his most cherished hopes, could honestly accept a state of things it was beyond his power to change: he signed cheerfully and kept dutifully the peace of Constance, which left him little but a titular supremacy over the Lombard towns.

Frederick as German king.

At home no Emperor since Henry III had been so much respected and so generally prosperous. Uniting in his person the Saxon and Swabian families, he healed the long feud of Welf and Waiblingen: his prelates were faithful to him, even against Rome: no turbulent rebel

---

[*] The carroccio was a waggon with a flagstaff planted on it, which served the Lombards for a rallying-point in battle.

disturbed the public peace. Germany was proud of a
hero who maintained her dignity so well abroad, and he
crowned a glorious life with a happy death, leading the
van of Christian chivalry against the Mussulman. Frederick, the greatest of the Crusaders, is the noblest type
of mediæval character in many of its shadows, in all its
lights.

Legal in form, in practice sometimes almost absolute,
the government of Germany was, like that of other feudal
kingdoms, restrained chiefly by the difficulty of coercing
refractory vassals. All depended on the monarch's character, and one so vigorous and popular as Frederick
could generally lead the majority with him and terrify
the rest. A false impression of the real strength of his
prerogative might be formed from the readiness with
which he was obeyed. He repaired the finances of the
kingdom, controlled the dukes, introduced a more splendid ceremonial, endeavoured to exalt the central power
by multiplying the nobles of the second rank, afterwards
the 'college of princes,' and by trying to substitute the
civil law and Lombard feudal code for the old Teutonic
customs, different in every province. If not successful
in this project, he fared better with another. Since Henry
the Fowler's day towns had been growing up through
Southern and Western Germany, especially where rivers
offered facilities for trade. Cologne, Treves, Mentz,
Worms, Speyer, Nürnberg, Ulm, Regensburg, Augsburg,
were already considerable cities, not afraid to beard their
lord or their bishop, and promising before long to counter-
balance the power of the territorial oligarchy. Policy
or instinct led Frederick to attach them to the throne,
enfranchising many, granting, with municipal institutions,
an independent jurisdiction, conferring various exemptions

*The Ger-
man cities.*

N 2

CHAP. XI.

and privileges; while receiving in turn their good-will and loyal aid, in money always, in men when need should come. His immediate successors trode in his steps, and thus there arose in the state a third order, the firmest bulwark, had it been rightly used, of imperial authority; an order whose members, the Free Cities, were through many ages the centres of German intellect and freedom, the only haven from the storms of civil war, the surest hope of future peace and union. In them national congresses to this day sometimes meet: from them aspiring spirits strive to diffuse those ideas of Germanic unity and self-government, which they alone have kept alive. Out of so many flourishing commonwealths, four[t] have been spared by foreign conquerors and faithless princes. To the primitive order of German freemen, scarcely existing out of the towns, except in Swabia and Switzerland, Frederick further commended himself by allowing them to be admitted to knighthood, by restraining the licence of the nobles, imposing a public peace, making justice in every way more accessible and impartial. To the south-west of the green plain that girdles in the rock of Salzburg, the gigantic mass of the Untersberg frowns over the road which winds up a long defile to the glen and lake of Berchtesgaden. There, far up among its limestone crags, in a spot scarcely accessible to human foot, the peasants of the valley point out to the traveller the black mouth of a cavern, and tell him that within Barbarossa lies amid his knights in an enchanted sleep[u], waiting the hour

---

[t] Lübeck, Hamburg, Bremen, and Frankfort.

[Since this was first written Frankfort has been annexed by Prussia, and her three surviving sisters have, by their entrance into the North German confederation, lost something of their independence.]

[u] The legend is one which appears under various forms in many countries.

when the ravens shall cease to hover round the peak, and the pear-tree blossom in the valley, to descend with his Crusaders and bring back to Germany the golden age of peace and strength and unity. Often in the evil days that followed the fall of Frederick's house, often when tyranny seemed unendurable and anarchy endless, men thought on that cavern, and sighed for the day when the long sleep of the just Emperor should be broken, and his shield be hung aloft again as of old in the camp's midst, a sign of help to the poor and the oppressed.

CHAPTER XII.

IMPERIAL TITLES AND PRETENSIONS.

THE era of the Hohenstaufen is perhaps the fittest point at which to turn aside from the narrative history of the Empire to speak shortly of the legal position which it professed to hold to the rest of Europe, as well as of certain duties and observances which throw a light upon the system it embodied. This is not indeed the era of its greatest power : that was already past. Nor is it conspicuously the era when its ideal dignity stood highest : for that remained scarcely impaired till three centuries had passed away. But it was under the Hohenstaufen, owing partly to the splendid abilities of the princes of that famous line, partly to the suddenly-gained ascendancy of the Roman law, that the actual power and the theoretical influence of the Empire most fully coincided. There can therefore be no better opportunity for noticing the titles and claims by which it announced itself the representative of Rome's universal dominion, and for collecting the various instances in which they were (either before or after Frederick's time) more or less admitted by the other states of Europe.

The territories over which Barbarossa would have declared his jurisdiction to extend may be classed under four heads :—

First, the German lands, in which, and in which alone, the Emperor was, up till the death of Frederick the Second, effective sovereign.

Second, the non-German districts of the Holy Empire, where the Emperor was acknowledged as sole monarch, but in practice little regarded.

Third, certain outlying countries, owing allegiance to the Empire, but governed by kings of their own.

Fourth, the other states of Europe, whose rulers, while in most cases admitting the superior rank of the Emperor, were virtually independent of him.

Thus within the actual boundaries of the Holy Empire were included only districts coming under the first and second of the above classes, i.e. Germany, the northern half of Italy, and the kingdom of Burgundy or Arles— that is to say, Provence, Dauphiné, the Free County of Burgundy (Franche Comté), and Western Switzerland. Lorraine, Alsace, and a portion of Flanders were of course parts of Germany. To the north-east, Bohemia and the Slavic principalities in Mecklenburg and Pomerania were as yet not integral parts of its body, but rather dependent outliers. Beyond the march of Brandenburg, from the Oder to the Vistula, dwelt pagan Lithuanians or Prussians[a], free till the establishment among them of the Teutonic knights.

Limits of the Empire.

Hungary had owed a doubtful allegiance since the days of Otto I. Gregory VII had claimed it as a fief of the Holy See; Frederick wished to reduce it completely to subjection, but could not overcome the reluctance of his nobles. After Frederick II, by whom it was recovered from the Mongol hordes, no imperial claims were made for so many years that at last they became obsolete, and

Hungary.

---

[a] 'Pruzzi,' says the biographer of St. Adalbert, 'quorum Deus est venter et avaritia iuncta cum morte.'—*M. G. H.* t. iv.

It is curious that this non-Teutonic people should have given their name to the great German kingdom of the present.

were confessed to be so by the Constitution of Augsburg, A.D. 1566 [b].

Poland.

Under Duke Misico, Poland had submitted to Otto the Great, and continued, with occasional revolts, to obey the Empire, till the beginning of the Great Interregnum, (as it is called) in 1254. Its duke was present at the election of Richard, A.D. 1258. Thereafter Primislas called himself king, in token of emancipation, and the country became independent, though some of its provinces were long afterwards reunited to the German state. Silesia, originally Polish, was attached to Bohemia by Charles IV, and so became part of the Empire; Posen and Galicia were seized by Prussia and Austria, A.D. 1772. Down to her partition in that year, the constitution of Poland remained a copy of that which had existed in the German kingdom in the twelfth century [c].

Denmark.

Lewis the Pious had received the homage of the Danish king Harold, on his baptism at Mentz, A.D. 826; Otto the Great's victories over Harold Blue Tooth made the country regularly subject, and added the march of Schleswig to the immediate territory of the Empire: but the boundary soon receded to the Eyder, on whose banks might be seen the inscription,—

'Eidora Romani terminus imperii.'

King Peter [d] attended at Frederick I's coronation, to do

[b] Conring, *De Finibus Imperii.* It is hardly necessary to observe that the connection of Hungary with the Hapsburgs is of comparatively recent origin, and of a purely dynastic nature. The position of the archdukes of Austria as kings of Hungary had nothing to do legally with the fact that many of them were also chosen Emperors, although practically their possession of the imperial crown had greatly aided them in grasping and retaining the thrones of Hungary and Bohemia.

[c] Cf. Pfeffel, *Abrégé Chronologique.*

[d] Letter of Frederick I to Otto of Freising, prefixed to the latter's History. This king is also called Sweyn.

homage, and receive from the Emperor, as suzerain, his own crown. Since the Interregnum Denmark has been always free [e].

Otto the Great was the last Emperor whose suzerainty the French kings had admitted; nor were Henry VI and Otto IV successful in their attempts to enforce it. Boniface VIII, in his quarrel with Philip the Fair, offered the French throne, which he had pronounced vacant, to Albert I; but the wary Hapsburg declined the dangerous prize. The precedence, however, which the Germans continued to assert, irritated Gallic pride, and led to more than one contest. Blondel denies the Empire any claim to the Roman name; and in A.D. 1648 the French envoys at Münster refused for some time to admit what no other European state disputed. Till recent times the title of the Archbishop of Treves, ' Archicancellarius per Galliam atque regnum Arelatense,' preserved the memory of an obsolete supremacy which the constant aggressions of France might seem to have reversed.

No reliance can be placed on the author who tells us that Sweden was granted by Frederick I to Waldemar the Dane [f]; the fact is improbable, and we do not hear that such pretensions were ever put forth before or after.

Nor does it appear that authority was ever exercised by any Emperor in Spain. Nevertheless the choice of Alfonso X by a section of the German electors, in A.D. 1258, may be construed to imply that the Spanish kings were members of the Empire. And when, A.D. 1053, Ferdinand the Great of Castile had, in the pride of his victories over the Moors, assumed the title of 'Hispaniæ Imperator,' the remonstrance of Henry III declared the

[e] See Appendix, Note B.
[f] Albertus Stadensis apud Conringium, *De Finibus Imperii.*

rights of Rome over the Western provinces indelible, and the Spaniard, though protesting his independence, was forced to resign the usurped dignity [g].

England.

No act of sovereignty is recorded to have been done by any of the Emperors in England, though as heirs of Rome they might be thought to have better rights over it than over Poland or Denmark [h]. There was, however, a vague notion that the English, like other kingdoms, must depend on the Empire: a notion which appears in Conrad III's letter to John of Constantinople [i]; and which was countenanced by the submissive tone in which Frederick I was addressed by the Plantagenet Henry II [j]. English independence was still more compromised in the next reign, when Richard I, according to Hoveden, 'Consilio matris suæ deposuit se de regno Angliæ et tradidit illud imperatori (Henrico VI[to]) sicut universorum domino.' But as Richard was at the same time invested with the kingdom of Arles by Henry VI, his homage may have been for that fief only; and it was probably in that capacity that he voted, as a prince of the Empire,

[g] There is an allusion to this in the poems of the Cid. Arthur Duck, *De Usu et Authoritate Iuris Civilis*, quotes the view of some among the older jurists, that Spain having been, as far as the Romans were concerned, a *res derelicta*, recovered by the Spaniards themselves from the Moors, and thus acquired by *occupatio*, ought not to be subject to the Emperors.

[h] One of the greatest of English kings appears performing an act of courtesy to the Emperor which was probably construed into an acknowledgment of his own inferior position. Describing the Roman coro-nation of the Emperor Conrad II, Wippo (c. 16) tells us 'His ita peractis in duorum regum præsentia Ruodolfi regis Burgundiæ et Chnutonis regis Anglorum divino officio finito imperator duorum regum medius ad cubiculum suum honorifice ductus est.'

[i] Letter in Otto Fris. i.: 'Nobis submittuntur Francia et Hispania, Anglia et Dania.'

[j] Letter in Radewic says, 'Regnum nostrum vobis exponimus. . . Vobis imperandi cedat auctoritas, nobis non deerit voluntas obsequendi.'

at the election of Frederick II. The case finds a parallel in the claims of England over the Scottish king, doubtful, to say the least, as regards the domestic realm of the latter, certain as regards Cumbria, which he had long held from the Southern crown[k]. But Germany had no Edward I. Henry VI is said at his death to have released Richard from his submission (this too may be compared with Richard's release to the Scottish William the Lion), and Edward II declared, ' regnum Angliæ ab omni subiectione imperiali esse liberrimum[l].' Yet the idea survived : the Emperor Lewis the Bavarian, when he named Edward III his vicar in the great French war, demanded, though in vain, that the English monarch should kiss his feet[m]. Sigismund[n], visiting Henry V at London, before the meeting of the council of Constance, was met by the Duke of Gloucester, who, riding into the water to the ship where the Emperor sat, required him, at the sword's point, to declare that he did not come purposing to infringe on the king's authority in the realm of England[o]. One curious pretension of the imperial crown called forth many protests. It was declared by civilians and canonists that no public notary could have any standing, or attach any legality to the documents he drew, unless he had received his diploma from the Emperor or the Pope. A strenuous denial of a

[k] The alleged instances of homage by the Scots to the Saxon and early Norman kings are almost all complicated in some such way. They had once held also the earldom of Huntingdon from the English crown, and some have supposed (but on no sufficient grounds) that homage was also done by them for Lothian.

[l] Selden, *Titles of Honour*, part i. chap. ii.

[m] Edward refused upon the ground that he was ' *rex inunctus.*'

[n] Sigismund had shortly before given great offence in France by dubbing knights.

[o] Sigismund answered, ' Nihil se contra superioritatem regis prætexere.'

CHAP. XII.

doctrine so injurious was issued by the parliament of Scotland under James III [p].

Naples.

The kingdom of Naples and Sicily, although of course claimed as a part of the Empire, was under the Norman dynasty (A.D. 1060–1189) not merely independent, but the most dangerous enemy of the German power in Italy. Henry VI, the son and successor of Barbarossa, obtained possession of it by marrying Constantia the last heiress of the Norman kings. But both he and Frederick II treated it as a separate patrimonial state, instead of incorporating it with their more northerly dominions. After the death of Conradin, the last of the Hohenstaufen, it passed away to an Angevin, then to an Aragonese dynasty, continuing under both to maintain itself independent of the Empire, nor ever again, except under Charles V, united to the Germanic crown.

Venice.

One spot in Italy there was whose singular felicity of situation enabled her through long centuries of obscurity and weakness, slowly ripening into strength, to maintain her freedom unstained by any submission to the Frankish and Germanic Emperors. Venice glories in deducing her origin from the fugitives who escaped from Aquileia in the days of Attila: it is at least probable that her population never received an intermixture of Teutonic settlers, and continued during the ages of Lombard and Frankish rule in Italy to regard the Byzantine sovereigns as the representatives of their ancient masters. In the tenth century, when summoned to submit by Otto, they had said, 'We wish to be the servants of the Emperors of

[p] Selden, *Titles of Honour*, part i. chap. ii. Nevertheless, notaries in Scotland, as elsewhere, continued for a long time to style themselves 'Ego M. auctoritate imperiali (or papali) notarius.'

the Romans' (the Constantinopolitan), and though they overthrew this very Eastern throne in A.D. 1204, the pretext had served its turn, and had aided them in defying or evading the demands of obedience made by the Teutonic princes. Alone of all the Italian republics, Venice never, down to her extinction by France and Austria in A.D. 1796, recognized within her walls any secular authority save her own.

The East.

The kings of Cyprus and Armenia sent to Henry VI to confess themselves his vassals and ask his help. Over remote Eastern lands, where Frankish foot had never trod, Frederick Barbarossa asserted the indestructible rights of Rome, mistress of the world. A letter to Saladin, amusing from its absolute identification of his own Empire with that which had sent Crassus to perish in Parthia, and had blushed to see Mark Antony ' consulum nostrum 'q at the feet of Cleopatra, is preserved by Hoveden: it bids the Soldan withdraw at once from the dominions of Rome, else will she, with her new Teutonic defenders, of whom a pompous list follows, drive him from them with all her ancient might.

The Byzantine Emperors.

Unwilling as were the great kingdoms of Western Europe to admit the territorial supremacy of the Emperor, the proudest among them never refused, until the end of the Middle Ages, to recognize his precedence and address him in a tone of respectful deference. Very different was the attitude of the Byzantine princes, who

---

q It is not necessary to prove this letter to have been the composition of Frederick or his ministers. If it be (as it doubtless is) contemporary, it is equally to the purpose as an evidence of the feelings and ideas of the age. As a reviewer of a former edition of this book has questioned its authenticity, I may mention that it is to be found not only in Hoveden, but also in the 'Itinerarium regis Ricardi,' in Ralph de Diceto, and in the 'Chronicon Terrae Sanctae.' [See Mr. Stubbs' edition of Hoveden, vol. ii. p. 356.]

denied his claim to be an Emperor at all. The separate existence of the Eastern Church and Empire was not only, as has been said above, a blemish in the title of the Teutonic sovereigns; it was a continuing and successful protest against the whole system of an Empire Church of Christendom, centering in Rome, ruled by the successor of Peter and the successor of Augustus. Instead of the one Pope and one Emperor whom mediæval theory presented as the sole earthly representatives of the invisible head of the Church, the world saw itself distracted by the interminable feud of rivals, each of whom had much to allege on his behalf. It was easy for the Latins to call the Easterns schismatics and their Emperor an usurper, but practically it was impossible to dethrone him or reduce them to obedience: while even in controversy no one could treat the pretensions of communities who had been the first to embrace Christianity and retained so many of its most ancient forms, with the contempt which would have been felt for any Western sectaries. Seriously, however, as the hostile position of the Greeks seems to us to affect the claims of the Teutonic Empire, calling in question its legitimacy and marring its pretended universality, those who lived at the time seem to have troubled themselves little about it, finding themselves in practice seldom confronted by the difficulties it raised. The great mass of the people knew of the Greeks not even by name; of those who did, the most thought of them only as perverse rebels, Samaritans who refused to worship at Jerusalem, and were little better than infidels. The few ecclesiastics of superior knowledge and insight had their minds preoccupied by the established theory, and accepted it with too intense a belief to suffer anything else to come into collision with it: they do not

seem to have even apprehended all that was involved in
this one defect. Nor, what is still stranger, in all the
attacks made upon the claims of the Teutonic Empire,
whether by its Papal or its French antagonists, do we find
the rival title of the Greek sovereigns adduced in argument
against it. Nevertheless, the Eastern Church was then, as
she is to this day, a thorn in the side of the Papacy; and
the Eastern Emperors, so far from uniting for the good of
Christendom with their Western brethren, felt towards
them a bitter though not unnatural jealousy, lost no opportunity of intriguing for their evil, and never ceased to
deny their right to the imperial name. The coronation
of Charles was in their eyes an act of unholy rebellion;
his successors were barbarian intruders, ignorant of the
laws and usages of the ancient state, and with no claim
to the Roman name except that which the favour of an
insolent pontiff might confer. The Greeks had themselves
long since ceased to use the Latin tongue, and were
indeed become more than half Orientals in character and
manners. But they still continued to call themselves
Romans, and preserved most of the titles and ceremonies
which had existed in the time of Constantine or Justinian.
They were weak, although by no means so weak as
modern historians have been till lately wont to paint
them, and the weaker they grew the higher rose their
conceit, and the more did they plume themselves upon
the uninterrupted legitimacy of their crown, and the ceremonial splendour wherewith custom had surrounded its
wearer. It gratified their spite to pervert insultingly the
titles of the Frankish princes. Basil the Macedonian reproached Lewis II with presuming to use the name of
'Basileus,' to which Lewis retorted that he was as good
an emperor as Basil himself, but that, anyhow, *Basileus*

*Rivalry
of the two
Empires.*

was only the Greek for *rex*, and need not mean 'Emperor' at all. Nicephorus would not call Otto I anything but 'King of the Lombards [r],' Conrad III was addressed by Calo-Johannes as 'amice imperii mei Rex [s];' Isaac Angelus had the impudence to style Frederick I 'chief prince of Alemannia [t].' The great Emperor, half-resentful, half-contemptuous, told the envoys that he was 'Romanorum imperator,' and bade their master call him-

[r] Liutprand, *Legatio Constantinopolitana*. Nicephorus says, 'Vis maius scandalum quam quod se imperatorem vocat.'

[s] Otto of Freising, i.

[t] 'Isaachius a Deo constitutus Imperator, sacratissimus, excellentissimus, potentissimus, moderator Romanorum, Angelus totius orbis, heres coronæ magni Constantini, dilecto fratri imperii sui, maximo principi Alemanniæ.' A remarkable speech of Frederick's to the envoys of Isaac, who had addressed a letter to him as 'Rex Alemaniæ' is preserved by Ansbert (*Historia de Expeditione Friderici Imperatoris*):—
'Dominus Imperator divina se illustrante gratia ulterius dissimulare non valens temerarium fastum regis (*sc.* Græcorum) et usurpantem vocabulum falsi imperatoris Romanorum, hæc inter cætera exorsus est:—
"Omnibus qui sanæ mentis sunt constat, quia unus est Monarchus Imperator Romanorum, sicut et unus est pater universitatis, pontifex videlicet Romanus; ideoque cum ego Romani imperii sceptrum plusquam per annos XXX absque omnium regum vel principum contradictione tranquille tenuerim et in Romana urbe a summo pontifice imperiali benedictione unctus sim et sublimatus, quia denique Monar-

chiam prædecessores mei imperatores Romanorum plusquam per CCCC annos etiam gloriose transmiserint, utpote a Constantinopolitana urbe ad pristinam sedem imperii, caput orbis Romam, acclamatione Romanorum et principum imperii, auctoritate quoque summi pontificis et S. catholicæ ecclesiæ translatam, propter tardum et infructuosum Constantinopolitani imperatoris auxilium contra tyrannos ecclesiæ, mirandum est admodum cur frater meus dominus vester Constantinopolitanus imperator usurpet inefficax sibi idem vocabulum et glorietur stulte alieno sibi prorsus honore, cum liquido noverit me et nomine dici et re esse Fridericum Romanorum imperatorem semper Augustum."'

Isaac was so far moved by Frederick's indignation that in his next letter he addressed him as 'generosissimum imperatorem Alemaniæ,' and in a third thus:—
'Isaakius in Christo fidelis divinitus coronatus, sublimis, potens, excelsus, hæres coronæ magni Constantini et Moderator Romeon Angelus nobilissimo Imperatori antiquæ Romæ, regi Alemaniæ et dilecto fratri imperii sui, salutem,' &c., &c. (Ansbert, *ut supra*.)

self ' Romaniorum ' from his Thracian province. Though these ebullitions were the most conclusive proof of their weakness, the Byzantine rulers sometimes planned the recovery of their former capital, and seemed not unlikely to succeed under the leadership of the conquering Manuel Comnenus. He invited Alexander III, then in the heat of his strife with Frederick, to return to the embrace of his rightful sovereign, but the prudent pontiff and his synod courteously declined [u]. The Greeks were, however, too unstable and too much alienated from Latin feeling to have held Rome, could they even have seduced her allegiance. A few years later they were themselves the victims of the French and Venetian crusaders.

Though Otto the Great and his successors had dropped all titles save their highest (the tedious lists of imperial dignities were happily not yet in being), they did not therefore endeavour to unite their several kingdoms, but continued to go through four distinct coronations at the four capitals of their Empire[x]. These are concisely given in the verses of Godfrey of Viterbo, a notary of Frederick's household [y] :—

Dignities and titles.

The four crowns.

> 'Primus Aquisgrani locus est, post hæc Arelati,
> Inde Modoetiæ regali sede locari
> Post solet Italiæ summa corona dari :
> Cæsar Romano cum vult diademate fungi
> Debet apostolicis manibus reverenter inungi.'

By the crowning at Aachen, the old Frankish capital, the monarch became ' king;' formerly ' king of the Franks,' or, ' king of the Eastern Franks;' now, since Henry II's time, ' king of the Romans, always Augustus.' At Monza, (or, more rarely, at Milan) in later times, at Pavia in earlier

---

[u] Baronius, ad ann.
[x] See Appendix, Note C.

[y] Godefr. Viterb., *Pantheon*, in Mur., *S. R. I.*, tom. vii.

times, he became king of Italy, or of the Lombards [z]; at Rome he received the double crown of the Roman Empire, 'double,' says Godfrey, as 'urbis et orbis:'—

> 'Hoc quicunque tenet, summus in orbe sedet;'

though others hold that, uniting the mitre to the crown, it typifies spiritual as well as secular authority. The crown of Burgundy [a] or the kingdom of Arles, first gained by Conrad II, was a much less splendid matter, and carried with it little effective power. Most Emperors never assumed it at all, Frederick I not till late in life, when an interval of leisure left him nothing better to do. These four crowns [b] furnish matter of endless discussion to the old writers; they tell us that the Roman was golden, the German silver, the Italian iron, the metal corresponding to the dignity of each realm [c]. Others say that that of Aachen is iron, and the Italian silver, and give elaborate reasons why it should be so [d]. There seems to be no doubt that the allegory created the fact, and that all three crowns were of gold, though in that of Italy there

---

[z] Dönniges, *Deutsches Staatsrecht*, thinks that the crown of Italy, neglected by the Ottos, and taken by Henry II, was a recognition of the separate nationality of Italy. But Otto I seems to have been crowned king of Italy, and Muratori (*Ant. It.* Dissert. iii.) believes that Otto II and Otto III were likewise.

[a] See Appendix, note A.

[b] Some add a fifth crown, of Germany (making that of Aachen Frankish), which they say belonged to Regensburg.—Marquardus Freherus.

[c] 'Dy erste ist tho Aken: dar kronet men mit der Yseren Krone, so is he Konig over alle Dudesche Ryke. Dy andere tho Meylan, de is Sulvern, so is he Here der Walen. Dy drüdde is tho Rome; dy is guldin, so is he Keyser over alle dy Werlt.' — Gloss to the *Sachsenspiegel*, quoted by Pfeffinger. Similarly Peter de Andlo.

[d] Cf. Gewoldus, *De Septemviratu imperii Romani.* One would expect some ingenious allegorizer to have discovered that the crown of Burgundy must be, and therefore is, of copper or bronze, making the series complete, like the four ages of men in Hesiod. But I have not been able to find any such.

was and is inserted a piece of iron, a nail, it was believed, of the true Cross.

Why, it may well be asked, seeing that the Roman crown made the Emperor ruler of the whole habitable globe, was it thought necessary for him to add to it minor dignities which might be supposed to have been already included in it? The reason seems to be that the imperial office was conceived of as something different in kind from the regal, and as carrying with it not the immediate government of any particular kingdom, but a general suzerainty over and right of controlling all. Of this a pertinent illustration is afforded by an anecdote told of Frederick Barbarossa. Happening once to inquire of the famous jurists who surrounded him whether it was really true that he was 'lord of the world,' one of them simply assented, another, Bulgarus, answered, 'Not as respects ownership.' In this dictum, which is evidently conformable to the philosophical theory of the Empire, we have a pointed distinction drawn between feudal sovereignty, which supposes the prince original owner of the soil of his whole kingdom, and imperial sovereignty, which is irrespective of place, and exercised not over things but over men, as God's rational creatures. But the Emperor, as has been said already, was also the East Frankish king, uniting in himself, to use the legal phrase, two wholly distinct 'persons,' and hence he might acquire more direct and practically useful rights over a portion of his dominions by being crowned king of that portion, just as a feudal monarch was often duke or count of lordships whereof he was already feudal superior; or, to take a better illustration, just as a bishop may hold livings in his own diocese. That the Emperors, while continuing to be crowned at Milan and Aachen, did not call themselves

'Emperor' not assumed till the Roman coronation.

kings of the Lombards and of the Franks, was probably merely because these titles seemed insignificant compared to that of Roman Emperor.

In this supreme title, as has been said, all lesser honours were blent and lost, but custom or prejudice forbade the German king to assume it till actually crowned at Rome by the Pope[e]. Matters of phrase and title are never unimportant, least of all in an age ignorant and superstitiously antiquarian : and this restriction had the most important consequences. The first barbarian kings had been tribe-chiefs; and when they claimed a dominion which was universal, yet in a sense territorial, they could not separate their title from the spot which it was their boast to possess, and by virtue of whose name they ruled. 'Rome,' says the biographer of St. Adalbert, 'seeing that she both is and is called the head of the world and the mistress of cities, is alone able to give to kings imperial power, and since she cherishes in her bosom the body of the Prince of the Apostles, she ought of right to appoint the Prince of the whole earth[f].' The crown was therefore too sacred to be conferred by any one but the supreme Pontiff, or in any city less august than the ancient capital.

Origin and results of this practice.

Had it become hereditary in any family, Lothar I's, for instance, or Otto's, this feeling might have worn off; as it was, each successive transfer, to Guido, to Otto,

[e] Hence the numbers attached to the names of the Emperors are often different in German and Italian writers, the latter not reckoning Henry the Fowler nor Conrad I. So Henry III (of Germany) calls himself 'Imperator Henricus Secundus;' and all distinguish the years of their *regnum* from those of the *imperium.* Cardinal Baronius will not call Henry V anything but Henry III, not recognizing Henry IV's coronation, because it was performed by an antipope.

[f] Life of S. Adalbert (written at Rome early in the eleventh century, probably by a brother of the monastery of SS. Boniface and Alexius) in Pertz, *M. G. H.* iv.

to Henry II, to Conrad the Salic, strengthened it. The force of custom, tradition, precedent, is incalculable when checked neither by written rules nor free discussion. What sheer assertion will do is shewn by the success of a forgery so gross as the Isidorian decretals. No arguments are needed to discredit the alleged decree of Pope Benedict VIII [g], which prohibited the German prince from taking the name or office of Emperor till approved and consecrated by the pontiff, but a doctrine so favourable to papal pretensions was sure not to want advocacy; Hadrian IV proclaims it in the broadest terms, and through the efforts of the clergy and the spell of reverence in the Teutonic princes, it passed into an unquestioned belief. That none ventured to use the title till the Pope conferred it, made it seem in some manner to depend on his will, enabled him to exact conditions from every candidate, and gave a colour to his pretended suzerainty. Since by feudal theory every honour and estate is held from some superior, and since the divine commission has been without doubt issued directly to the Pope, must not the whole earth be his fief, and he the lord paramount, to whom even the Emperor is a vassal? This argument, which derived considerable plausibility from the rivalry between the Emperor and other monarchs, as compared with the universal and undisputed [h] authority of the Pope, was a favourite with

[g] Given by Glaber Rudolphus. It is on the face of it a most impudent forgery: 'Ne quisquam audacter Romani Imperii sceptrum præpostere gestare princeps appetat neve Imperator dici aut esse valeat nisi quem Papa Romanus morum probitate aptum elegerit, eique commiserit insigne imperiale.'

[h] Universal and undisputed in the West, which, for practical purposes, meant the world. The denial of the supreme jurisdiction of Peter's chair by the eastern churches affected very slightly the belief of

the high sacerdotal party: first distinctly advanced by Hadrian IV, when he set up the picture[i] representing Lothar's homage, which had so irritated the followers of Barbarossa, though it had already been hinted at in Gregory VII's gift of the crown to Rudolf of Suabia, with the line,—

'Petra dedit Petro, Petrus diadema Rudolfo.'

Nor was it only by putting him at the pontiff's mercy that this dependence of the imperial name on a coronation in the city injured the German sovereign[k]. With strange inconsistency it was not pretended that the Emperor's rights were any narrower before he received the rite: he could summon synods, confirm papal elections, exercise jurisdiction over the citizens: his claim of the crown itself could not, at least till the times of the Gregorys and the Innocents, be positively denied. For no one thought of contesting the right of the German nation to the Empire, or the authority of the electoral princes, strangers

Latin Christendom, just as the existence of a rival emperor at Constantinople with at least as good a legal title as the Teutonic Cæsar, was readily forgotten or ignored

'Rex venit ante fores nullo prius urbis honore;
Post homo fit Papæ, sumit quo dante coronam.'—Radewic.

[k] Mediæval history is full of instances of the superstitious veneration attached to the rite of coronation (made by the Church almost a sacrament), and to the special places where, or even utensils with which it was performed. Everyone knows the importance in France of Rheims and its sacred *ampulla;* so the Scottish king must be crowned at Scone, an old seat of Pictish

by the German and Italian subjects of the latter.

[i] Odious especially for the inscription,—

royalty—Robert Bruce risked a great deal to receive his crown there; so no Hungarian coronation was valid unless made with the crown of St. Stephen; the possession whereof is still accounted so valuable by the Austrian court.

Great importance seems to have been attached to the imperial globe (Reichsapfel) which the Pope delivered to the Emperor at his coronation.

though they were, to give Rome and Italy a master. The republican followers of Arnold of Brescia might murmur, but they could not dispute the truth of the proud lines in which the poet who sang the glories of Barbarossa[1], describes the result of the conquest of Charles the Great :—

> ' Ex quo Romanum nostra virtute redemptum
> Hostibus expulsis, ad nos iustissimus ordo
> Transtulit imperium, Romani gloria regni
> Nos penes est. Quemcunque sibi Germania regem
> Præficit, hunc dives summisso vertice Roma
> Suscipit, et verso Tiberim regit ordine Rhenus.'

But the real strength of the Teutonic kingdom was wasted in the pursuit of a glittering toy: once in his reign each Emperor undertook a long and dangerous expedition, and dissipated in an inglorious and ever to be repeated strife the forces that might have achieved conquest elsewhere, or made him feared and obeyed at home.

The title 'Holy Empire.'

At this epoch appears another title, of which more must be said. To the accustomed 'Roman Empire' Frederick Barbarossa adds the epithet of 'Holy.' Of its earlier origin, under Conrad II (the Salic), which some have supposed[m], there is no documentary trace, though there is also no proof to the contrary[n]. So far as is known it occurs first in the famous Privilege of Austria, granted by Frederick in the fourth year of his

[1] Whether the poem which passes under the name of Gunther Ligurinus be his work or that of some scholar in a later age is for the present purpose indifferent.

[m] Zedler, *Universal Lexicon*, s. v. *Reich.*

[n] It does not occur before Frederick I's time in any of the documents printed by Pertz; and this is the date which Boeclerus also assigns in his treatise, *De Sacro Imperio Romano*, vindicating the terms 'sacrum' and 'Romanum' against the aspersions of Blondel.

reign, the second of his empire, 'terram Austriæ quæ clypeus et cor sacri imperii esse dinoscitur o:' then afterwards, in other manifestos of his reign; for example, in a letter to Isaac Angelus of·Byzantium P, and in the summons to the princes to help him against Milan: 'Quia . . . . urbis et orbis gubernacula tenemus . . . . sacro imperio et divæ reipublicæ consulere debemus q;' where the second phrase is a synonym explanatory of the first. Used occasionally by Henry VI and Frederick II, it is more frequent under their successors, William, Richard, Rudolf, till after Charles IV's time it becomes habitual, for the last few centuries indispensable. Regarding the origin of so singular a title many theories have been advanced. Some declared it a perpetuation of the court style of Rome and Byzantium, which attached sanctity to the person of the monarch: thus David Blondel, contending for the honour of France, calls it a mere epithet of the Emperor, applied by confusion to his government r. Others saw in it a religious meaning, referring to Daniel's prophecy, or to the fact that the Empire was contemporary with Christianity, or to Christ's birth under it s. Strong churchmen derived it from the dependence of the imperial crown on the Pope. There were not wanting persons to maintain that it meant nothing more than great or splendid. We need not, however, be in any great doubt as to its true meaning and purport. The ascription of sacredness to the person,

o Pertz, *M. G. H.,* tom. iv. (legum ii.)
P Ibid. iv.
q Radewic. *ap.* Pertz.
r Blondellus adv. Chiffletium. Most of these theories are stated by Boeclerus. Jordanes (*Chronica*)

says, 'Sacri imperii quod non est dubium sancti Spiritus ordinatione, secundum qualitatem ipsam et exigentiam meritorum humanorum disponi.'
s Marquard Freher's notes to Peter de Andlo, book i. chap. vii.

the palace, the letters, and so forth, of the sovereign, so common in the later ages of Rome, had been partly retained in the German court. Liudprand calls Otto ' imperator sanctissimus [t].' Still this sanctity, which the Greeks above all others lavished on their princes, is something personal, is nothing more than the divinity that always hedges a king. Far more intimate and peculiar was the relation of the revived Roman Empire to the church and religion. As has been said already, it was neither more nor less than the visible Church, seen on its secular side, the Christian society organized as a state under a form divinely appointed, and therefore the name ' Holy Roman Empire' was the needful and rightful counterpart to that of ' Holy Catholic Church.' Such had long been the belief, and so the title might have had its origin as far back as the tenth or ninth century, might even have emanated from Charles himself. Alcuin in one of his letters uses the phrase ' imperium Christianum.' But there was a further reason for its introduction at this particular epoch. Ever since Hildebrand had claimed for the priesthood exclusive sanctity and supreme jurisdiction, the papal party had not ceased to speak of the civil power as being, compared with that of their own chief, merely secular, earthly, profane. It may be conjectured that to meet this reproach, no less injurious than insulting, Frederick or his advisers began to use in public documents the expression ' Holy Empire ;' thereby wishing to assert the divine institution and religious duties of the office he held. Previous Emperors had called

---

[t] So in the song on the capture of the Emperor Lewis II by Adalgisus of Benevento, we find the words, ' Ludhuicum comprenderunt sancto, pio, Augusto.' (Quoted by Gregorovius, *Geschichte der Stadt Rom im Mittelalter,* iii. p. 185.)

themselves 'Catholici,' 'Christiani,' 'ecclesiæ defensores [u];' now their State itself is consecrated an earthly theocracy. 'Deus Romanum imperium adversus schisma ecclesiæ præparavit [x],' writes Frederick to the English Henry II. The theory was one which the best and greatest Emperors, Charles, Otto the Great, Henry III, had most striven to carry out; it continued to be zealously upheld when it had long ceased to be practicable. In the proclamations of mediæval kings there is a constant dwelling on their Divine commission. Power in an age of violence sought to justify while it enforced its commands, to make brute force less brutal by appeals to a higher sanction. This is seen nowhere more than in the style of the German sovereigns: they delight in the phrases 'maiestas sacrosancta [y],' 'imperator divina ordinante providentia,' 'divina pietate,' 'per misericordiam Dei;' many of which were preserved till, like those used now by other European kings, like our own 'Defender of the Faith,' they had become at last more grotesque than solemn. The Emperor Joseph II, at the end of the eighteenth century, was 'Advocate of the Christian Church,' 'Vicar of Christ,' 'Imperial head of the faithful,' 'Leader of the Christian army,' 'Protector of Palestine, of general councils, of the Catholic faith [z].'

The title, if it added little to the power, yet certainly seems to have increased the dignity of the Empire, and by consequence the jealousy of other states, of France especially. This did not, however, go so far as to prevent its recognition by the Pope and the French king [a], and after

---

[u] Goldast, *Constitutiones.*

[x] Pertz, *M. G. H.*, legg. ii.

[y] 'Apostolic majesty' was the proper title of the king of Hungary.

The Austrian court has recently revived it.

[z] Moser. *Römische Kayser.*

[a] Urban IV used the title in

the sixteenth century it would have been a breach of diplomatic courtesy to omit it. Nor have imitators been wanting [b]: witness such titles as 'Most Christian king,' 'Catholic king,' 'Defender of the Faith [c].'

1259: Francis I (of France) calls the Empire 'sacrosanctum.'

[b] Cf. 'Holy Russia.'

[c] It is almost superfluous to observe that the beginning of the title 'Holy' has nothing to do with the beginning of the Empire itself. Essentially and substantially, the Holy Roman Empire was, as has been shewn already, the creation of Charles the Great. Looking at it more technically, as the monarchy, not of the whole West, like that of Charles, but of Germany and Italy, with a claim, which was never more than a claim, to universal sovereignty, its beginning is fixed by most of the German writers, whose practice has been followed in the text, at the coronation of Otto the Great. But the title was at least one, and probably two centuries later.

CHAPTER XIII.

FALL OF THE HOHENSTAUFEN.

IN the three preceding chapters the Holy Empire has been described in what is not only the most brilliant but the most momentous period of its history; the period of its rivalry with the Popedom for the chief place in Christendom. For it was mainly through their relations with the spiritual power, by their friendship and protection at first, no less than by their subsequent hostility, that the Teutonic Emperors influenced the development of European politics. The reform of the Roman Church which went on during the reigns of Otto I and his successors down to Henry III, and which was chiefly due to the efforts of those monarchs, was the true beginning of the grand period of the Middle Ages, the first of that long series of movements, changes, and creations in the ecclesiastical system of Europe which was, so to speak, the master current of history, secular as well as religious, during the centuries which followed. The first result of Henry III's purification of the Papacy was seen in Hildebrand's attempt to subject all jurisdiction to that of his own chair, and in the long struggle of the Investitures, which brought out into clear light the opposing pretensions of the temporal and spiritual powers. Although destined in the end to bear far other fruit, the immediate effect of this struggle was to evoke in all classes an intense religious feeling; and, in opening up new fields of ambition to the hierarchy, to stimulate wonderfully their power of political organization. It was this impulse that gave birth to the Crusades, and that enabled the Popes, stepping forth as the rightful leaders of a religious war, to bend it to serve their own ends : it was thus too that they struck the alliance—strange as such an alliance seems now—with the rebellious cities of Lombardy, and proclaimed themselves the protectors of municipal freedom. But the third and crowning triumph of the Holy See was reserved for the thirteenth century. In the foundation of the two great orders of ecclesiastical knighthood, the all-powerful all-pervading Dominicans and Franciscans, the religious fervour of the Middle Ages culminated : in the overthrow of the only power which could pretend to vie with her in antiquity, in sanctity, in universality, the Papacy saw herself exalted to rule alone over the kings of the earth. Of that overthrow, following with terrible suddenness on the days of strength and glory which we have just been witnessing, this chapter has now to speak.

CHAP. XIII.

It happened strangely enough that just while their ruin was preparing, the house of Swabia gained over their ecclesiastical foes what seemed likely to prove an advantage of the first moment. The son and successor of Barbarossa was Henry VI, a man who had inherited all his father's harshness with none of his father's generosity. By his marriage with Constance, the heiress of the Norman kings, he had become master of Naples and Sicily. Emboldened by the possession of what had been hitherto the stronghold of his predecessors' bitterest enemies, and able to threaten the Pope from south as well as north, Henry conceived a scheme which might

Henry VI, 1190–1197.

have wonderfully changed the history of Germany and Italy. He proposed to the Teutonic magnates to lighten their burdens by uniting these newly-acquired countries to the Empire, to turn their feudal lands into allodial, and to make no further demands for money on the clergy, on condition that they should pronounce the crown hereditary in his family. Results of the highest importance would have followed this change, which Henry advocated by setting forth the perils of interregna, and which he doubtless meant to be but part of an entirely new system of polity. Already so strong in Germany, and with an absolute command of their new kingdom, the Hohenstaufen might have dispensed with the renounced feudal services, and built up a firm centralized system, like that which was already beginning to develope itself in France. First, however, the Saxon princes, then some ecclesiastics headed by Conrad of Mentz, opposed the scheme; the pontiff retracted his consent, and Henry had to content himself with getting his infant son Frederick the Second chosen king of the Romans. On Henry's untimely death the election was set aside, and the contest which followed between Otto of Brunswick

Philip.
1198–1208.

and Philip of Hohenstaufen, brother of Henry the Sixth, gave the Popedom, now guided by the genius of Innocent the Third, an opportunity of extending its sway at the

Innocent III and Otto IV.

expense of its antagonist. The Pope moved heaven and earth on behalf of Otto, whose family had been the constant rivals of the Hohenstaufen, and who was himself willing to promise all that Innocent required; but Philip's personal merits and the vast possessions of his house gave him while he lived the ascendancy in Germany. His death by the hand of an assassin, while it seemed to vindicate the Pope's choice, left the Swabian party without a head, and the Papal nominee was soon recognized over the whole Empire. But Otto IV became less submissive as he felt his throne more secure. If he was a Guelf by birth, his acts in Italy, whither he had gone to receive the imperial crown, were those of a Ghibeline, anxious to reclaim the rights he had but just forsworn. The Roman Church at last deposed and excommunicated her ungrateful son, and Innocent rejoiced in a second successful assertion of pontifical supremacy, when Otto was dethroned by the youthful Frederick the Second, whom a tragic irony sent into the field of politics as the champion of the Holy See, whose hatred was to embitter his life and extinguish his house.

Upon the events of that terrific strife, for which Emperor and Pope girded themselves up for the last time, the narrative of Frederick the Second's career, with its romantic adventures, its sad picture of marvellous powers lost on an age not ripe for them, blasted as by a curse in the moment of victory, it is not necessary, were it even possible, here to enlarge. That conflict did indeed determine the fortunes of the German kingdom no less than of the republics of Italy, but it was upon Italian ground that it was fought out and it is to Italian history that its details belong. So too of Frederick himself. Out of the long array of the Germanic successors of Charles, he is, with Otto III, the only one who comes before us with a genius and a frame of character that are not those of a Northern or a Teuton[a]. There dwelt in

[a] I quote from the Liber Augustalis printed among Petrarch's works the following curious description of Frederick : 'Fuit armorum strenuus, linguarum peritus, rigorosus, luxuriosus, epicurus, nihil curans vel credens nisi temporale : fuit malleus Romanae ecclesiae.'

As Otto III had been called ' mirabilia mundi,' so Frederick II is often spoken of in his own time as ' stupor mundi Fridericus.'

him, it is true, all the energy and knightly valour of his father Henry and his grandfather Barbarossa. But along with these, and changing their direction, were other gifts, inherited perhaps from his Italian mother and fostered by his education among the orange-groves of Palermo— a love of luxury and beauty, an intellect refined, subtle, philosophical. Through the mist of calumny and fable it is but dimly that the truth of the man can be discerned, and the outlines that appear serve to quicken rather than appease the curiosity with which we regard one of the most extraordinary personages in history. A sensualist, yet also a warrior and a politician; a profound lawgiver and an impassioned poet; in his youth fired by crusading fervour, in later life persecuting heretics while himself accused of blasphemy and unbelief; of winning manners and ardently beloved by his followers, but with the stain of more than one cruel deed upon his name, he was the marvel of his own generation, and succeeding ages looked back with awe, not unmingled with pity, upon the inscrutable figure of the last Emperor who had braved all the terrors of the Church and died beneath her ban, the last who had ruled from the sands of the ocean to the shores of the Sicilian sea. But while they pitied they condemned. The undying hatred of the Papacy threw round his memory a lurid light; him and him alone of all the imperial line, Dante, the worshipper of the Empire, must perforce deliver to the flames of hell[b].

Struggle of Frederick with the Papacy.

Placed as the Empire was, it was scarcely possible for its head not to be involved in war with the constantly aggressive Popedom—aggressive in her claims of territorial dominion in Italy as well as of ecclesiastical juris-

[b] 'Quà entro è lo secondo Federico.'—<i>Inferno</i>, canto x.

diction throughout the world. But it was Frederick's peculiar misfortune to have given the Popes a hold over him which they well knew how to use. In a moment of youthful enthusiasm he had taken the cross from the hands of an eloquent monk, and his delay to fulfil the vow was branded as impious neglect. Excommunicated by Gregory IX for not going to Palestine, he went, and was excommunicated for going: having concluded an advantageous peace, he sailed for Italy, and was a third time excommunicated for returning. To Pope Gregory he was at last after a fashion reconciled, but with the accession of Innocent IV the flame burst out afresh. Upon the special pretexts which kindled the strife it is not worth while to descant: the real causes were always the same, and could only be removed by the submission of one or other combatant. Chief among them was Frederick's possession of Sicily. Now were seen the fruits which Barbarossa had stored up for his house when he gained for Henry his son the hand of the Norman heiress. Naples and Sicily had been for some two hundred years recognized as a fief of the Holy See, and the Pope, who felt himself in danger while encircled by the powers of his rival, was determined to use his advantage to the full and make it the means of extinguishing imperial authority throughout Italy. But although the struggle was far more of a territorial and political one than that of the previous century had been, it reopened every former source of strife, and passed into a contest between the civil and the spiritual potentate. The old war-cries of Henry and Hildebrand, of Barbarossa and Alexander, roused again the unquenchable hatred of Italian factions: the pontiff asserted the transference of the Empire as a fief, and declared that the power of Peter, symbolized by the two

P

keys, was temporal as well as spiritual: the Emperor appealed to law, to the indelible rights of Cæsar; and denounced his foe as the antichrist of the New Testament, since it was God's second vicar whom he was resisting. The one scoffed at anathema, upbraided the avarice of the Church, and treated her soldiery, the friars, with a severity not seldom ferocious. The other solemnly deposed a rebellious and heretical prince, offered the imperial crown to Robert of France, to the heir of Denmark, to Haco the Norse king; succeeded at last in raising up rivals in Henry of Thuringia and William of Holland. Yet throughout it is less the Teutonic Emperor who is attacked than the Sicilian king, the unbeliever and friend of Mohammedans, the hereditary enemy of the Church, the assailant of Lombard independence, whose success must leave the Papacy defenceless. And as it was from the Sicilian kingdom that the strife chiefly arose, so was the possession of the Sicilian kingdom a source rather of weakness than of strength, for it distracted Frederick's forces and put him in the false position of a liegeman resisting his lawful suzerain. Truly, as the Greek proverb says, the gifts of foes are no gifts, and bring no profit with them. The Norman kings were more terrible in their death than in their life: they had sometimes baffled the Teutonic Emperor; their heritage destroyed him.

With Frederick fell the Empire. From the ruin that overwhelmed the greatest of its houses it emerged, living indeed, and destined to a long life, but so shattered, crippled, and degraded, that it could never more be to Europe and to Germany what it once had been. In the

Conrad IV,
1250–1254.

last act of the tragedy were joined the enemy who had now blighted its strength and the rival who was destined to insult its weakness and at last blot out its name. The murder of Frederick's grandson Conradin—a hero whose youth and whose chivalry might have moved the pity of any other foe—was approved, if not suggested, by Pope Clement; it was done by the minions of Charles of France.

The Lombard league had successfully resisted Frederick's armies and the more dangerous Ghibeline nobles : their strong walls and swarming population made defeats in the open field hardly felt; and now that South Italy too had passed away from a German line—first to an Angevin, afterwards to an Aragonese dynasty—it was plain that the peninsula was irretrievably lost to the Emperors. Why, however, should they not still be strong beyond the Alps? was their position worse than that of England when Normandy and Aquitaine no longer obeyed a Plantagenet? The force that had enabled them to rule so widely would be all the greater in a narrower sphere.

So indeed it might once have been, but now it was too late. The German kingdom broke down beneath the weight of the Roman Empire. To be universal sovereign Germany had sacrificed her own political existence. The necessity which their projects in Italy and disputes with the Pope laid the Emperors under of purchasing by concessions the support of their own princes, the ease with which in their absence the magnates could usurp, the difficulty which the monarch returning found in resuming the privileges of his crown, the temptation to revolt and set up pretenders to the throne which the Holy See held out, these were the causes whose steady action laid the foundation of that territorial independence which rose into a stable fabric at the era of the Great Interregnum [b]. Frederick II had by two Pragmatic Sanctions, A.D. 1220 and 1232, granted, or rather confirmed, rights already customary, such as to give the bishops and nobles legal sovereignty in their own towns and territories, except when the Emperor should be present; and thus his direct jurisdiction became restricted to his narrowed domain, and to the cities immediately dependent on the crown. With so much less to do, an Emperor became altogether a less necessary personage; and hence the seven magnates of the realm, now by law or custom sole electors, were in no haste to fill up the place of Conrad IV, whom the supporters of his father Frederick had acknowledged. William of Holland was in the field, but rejected by the Swabian party: on his death a new election was called for, and at last set on foot. The archbishop of Cologne advised his brethren to choose some one rich enough to support the dignity, not strong enough to be feared by the electors: both requisites met in the Plantagenet Richard, earl of Cornwall, brother of the English Henry III. He received three, eventually four votes, came to Germany, and was crowned at Aachen. But three of the electors, finding that his bribe to them was lower than to the others, seceded in disgust, and chose Alfonso X of Castile [c], who, shrewder than his competitor, continued to watch the stars at Toledo, enjoying the splendours of his title while troubling himself about it no further than to issue now and then a proclamation. Meantime

*Double
election, of
Richard of
England
and Alfonso
of Castile.*

[b] The interregnum is by some reckoned as the two years before Richard's election; by others, as the whole period from the death of Frederick II or that of his son Conrad IV till Rudolf's accession in 1273.

[c] Surnamed, from his scientific tastes, 'the Wise.'

the condition of Germany was frightful. The new Didius Julianus, the chosen of princes baser than the prætorians whom they copied, had neither the character nor the outward power and resources to make himself respected. Every floodgate of anarchy was opened: prelates and barons extended their domains by war: robber-knights infested the highways and the rivers: the misery of the weak, the tyranny and violence of the strong, were such as had not been seen for centuries. Things were even worse than under the Saxon and Franconian Emperors; for the petty nobles who had then been in some measure controlled by their dukes were now, after the extinction of the great houses, left without any feudal superior. Only in the cities was shelter or peace to be found. Those of the Rhine had already leagued themselves for mutual defence, and maintained a struggle in the interests of commerce and order against universal brigandage. At last, when Richard had been some time dead, it was felt that such things could not go on for ever: with no public law, and no courts of justice, an Emperor, the embodiment of legal government, was the only resource. The Pope himself, having now sufficiently improved the weakness of his enemy, found the disorganization of Germany beginning to tell upon his revenues, and threatened that if the electors did not appoint an Emperor, he would. Thus urged, they chose, in A.D. 1272, Rudolf, count of Hapsburg, founder of the house of Austria [d].

CHAP. XIII.
State of Germany during the Interregnum.

Rudolf of Hapsburg, 1272-1292.

[d] Hapsburg is a castle in the Aargau on the banks of the Aar, and near the line of railway from Olten to Zürich, from a point on which a glimpse of it may be had. 'Within the ancient walls of Vin- donissa,' says Gibbon, ' the castle of Hapsburg, the abbey of Königsfeld, and the town of Bruck have successively arisen. The philosophic traveller may compare the monuments of Roman conquests,

From this point there begins a new era. We have seen the Roman Empire revived in A.D. 800, by a prince whose vast dominions gave ground to his claim of universal monarchy; again erected, in A.D. 962, on the narrower but firmer basis of the German kingdom. We have seen Otto the Great and his successors during the three following centuries, a line of monarchs of unrivalled vigour and abilities, strain every nerve to make good the pretensions of their office against the rebels in Italy and the ecclesiastical power. Those efforts had now failed signally and hopelessly. Each successive Emperor had entered the strife with resources scantier than his predecessors, each had been more decisively vanquished by the Pope, the cities, and the princes. The Roman Empire might, and, so far as its practical utility was concerned, ought now to have been suffered to expire; nor could it have ended more gloriously than with the last of the Hohenstaufen. That it did not so expire, but lived on six hundred years more, till it became a piece of antiquarianism hardly more venerable than ridiculous— till, as Voltaire said, all that could be said about it was that it was neither holy, nor Roman, nor an empire— was owing partly indeed to the belief, still unshaken, that it was a necessary part of the world's order, yet chiefly to its connection, which was by this time indissoluble, with the German kingdom. The Germans had confounded the two characters of their sovereign so long, and had grown so fond of the style and pretensions of a dignity whose possession appeared to exalt them above the other peoples of Europe, that it was now too late

of feudal or Austrian tyranny, of monkish superstition, and of industrious freedom. If he be truly a philosopher, he will applaud the merit and happiness of his own time.'

for them to separate the local from the universal monarch. If a German king was to be maintained at all, he must be Roman Emperor; and a German king there must still be. Deeply, nay, mortally wounded as the event proved his power to have been by the disasters of the Empire to which it had been linked, the time was by no means come for its extinction. In the unsettled state of society, and the conflict of innumerable petty potentates, no force save feudalism was able to hold society together; and its efficacy for that purpose depended, as the anarchy of the recent interregnum shewed, upon the presence of the recognized feudal head.

That head, however, was no longer what he had been. The relative position of Germany and France was now exactly the reverse of that which they had occupied two centuries earlier. Rudolf was as conspicuously a weaker sovereign than Philip III of France, as the Franconian Emperor Henry III had been stronger than the Capetian Philip I. In every other state of Europe the tendency of events had been to centralize the administration and increase the power of the monarch, even in England not to diminish it: in Germany alone had political union become weaker, and the independence of the princes more confirmed. The causes of this change are not far to seek. They all resolve themselves into this one, that the German king attempted too much at once. The rulers of France, where manners were less rude than in the other Transalpine lands, and where the Third Estate rose into power more quickly, had reduced one by one the great feudataries by whom the first Capetians had been scarcely recognized. The English kings had annexed Wales, Cumbria, and part of Ireland, had obtained a prerogative great if not uncontrolled, and

Decline of the regal power in Germany as compared with France and England.

exercised no doubtful sway through every corner of their country. Both had won their successes by the concentration on that single object of their whole personal activity, and by the skilful use of every device whereby their feudal rights, personal, judicial, and legislative, could be applied to fetter the vassal. Meantime the German monarch, whose utmost efforts it would have needed to tame his fierce barons and maintain order through wide territories occupied by races unlike in dialect and customs, had been struggling with the Lombard cities and the Normans of South Italy, and had been for full two centuries the object of the unrelenting enmity of the Roman pontiff. And in this latter contest, by which more than by any other the fate of the Empire was decided, he fought under disadvantages far greater than his brethren in England and France. William the Conqueror had defied Hildebrand, William Rufus had resisted Anselm; but the Emperors Henry the Fourth and Barbarossa had to cope with prelates who were Hildebrand and Anselm in one; the spiritual heads of Christendom as well as the primates of their special realm, the Empire. And thus, while the ecclesiastics of Germany were a body more formidable from their possessions than those of any other European country, and enjoying far larger privileges, the Emperor could not, or could with far less effect, win them over by invoking against the Pope that national feeling which made the cry of Gallican liberties so welcome even to the clergy of France.

Relations of the Papacy and the Empire.

After repeated defeats, each more crushing than the last, the imperial power, so far from being able to look down on the papal, could not even maintain itself on an equal footing. Against no pontiff since Gregory VII, had the monarch's right to name or confirm a pope, undisputed in the days of the Ottos and of Henry III, been made good. It was the turn of the Emperor to repel a similar claim of the Holy See to the function of reviewing his own election, examining into his merits, and rejecting him if unsound, that is to say, impatient of priestly tyranny. A letter of Innocent III, who was the first to make this demand in terms, was inserted by Gregory IX in his digest of the Canon Law, the inexhaustible armoury of the churchman, and continued to be quoted thence by every canonist till the end of the sixteenth century [e]. It was not difficult to find grounds on which to base such a doctrine. Gregory VII deduced it with characteristic boldness from the power of the keys, and the superiority over all other dignities which must needs appertain to the Pope as arbiter of eternal weal or woe. Others took their stand on the analogy of clerical ordination, and urged that since the Pope in consecrating the Emperor gave him a title to the obedience of all Christian men, he must have himself the right of approving or rejecting the candidate according to his merits. Others again, appealing to the Old Testament, shewed how Samuel discarded Saul and anointed David in his room, and argued that the Pope now must have powers at least equal to those of the Hebrew prophets. But the ascendancy of the doctrine dates from the time of Pope Innocent III, whose ingenuity discovered for it an historical basis. It was by the favour of the Pope, he declared, that the Empire was taken away from the Greeks

---

. [e] *Corpus Iuris Canonici*, Decr. Greg. i. 6, cap. 34, *Venerabilem:* ' Ius et authoritas examinandi personam electam in regem et pro-movendam ad imperium, ad nos spectat, qui eum inungimus, consecramus, et coronamus.'

and given to the Germans in the person of Charles [f], and the authority which Leo then exercised as God's representative must abide thenceforth and for ever in his successors, who can therefore at any time recall the gift, and bestow it on a person or a nation more worthy than its present holders. This is the famous theory of the Translation of the Empire, which plays so large a part in controversy down till the seventeenth century [g], a theory with plausibility enough to make it generally successful, yet one which to an impartial eye appears far removed from the truth of the facts [h]. Leo III did not suppose, any more than did Charles himself, that it was by his sole pontifical authority that the crown was given to the Frank; nor do we find such a notion put forward by any of his successors down to the twelfth century. Gregory VII in particular, in a remarkable letter dilating on his prerogative, appeals to the substitution by papal interference of Pipin for the last Merovingian king, and even goes back to cite the case of Theodosius humbling himself before St. Ambrose, but says never a word about this 'translatio,' excellently as it would have served his purpose.

Sound or unsound, however, these arguments did their work, for they were urged skilfully and boldly, and none

[f] 'Illis principibus,' writes Innocent, 'ius et potestatem eligendi regem [Romanorum] in imperatorem postmodum promovendum recognoscimus, ad quos de iure ac antiqua consuetudine noscitur pertinere, praesertim quum ad eos ius et potestas huiusmodi ab apostolica sede pervenerit, quae Romanum imperium in persona magnifici Caroli a Graecis transtulit in Germanos.'—Decr. Greg. i. 6, cap. 34, *Venerabilem.*

[g] Its influence, however, as Döllinger (*Das Kaiserthum Karls des Grossen und seiner Nachfolger*) remarks, first became great when this letter, some forty or fifty years after Innocent wrote it, was inserted in the digest of the canon law.

[h] Vid. supra, pp. 52-58.

denied that it was by the Pope alone that the crown could be lawfully imposed[i]. In some instances the rights claimed were actually made good. Thus Innocent III withstood Philip and overthrew Otto IV; thus another haughty priest commanded the electors to choose the Landgrave of Thuringia (A.D. 1246), and was by some of them obeyed; thus Gregory X compelled the recognition of Rudolf. The further pretensions of the Popes to the vicariate of the Empire during interregna the Germans never admitted[k]. Still their place was now generally felt to be higher than that of the monarch, and their control over the three spiritual electors and the whole body of the clergy was far more effective than his. A spark of national feeling was at length kindled by the exactions and shameless subservience to France of the papal court at Avignon[l]; and the infant democracy of industry and intelligence represented by the cities and

[i] Upon this so-called 'Translation of the Empire,' many books remain to us: many more have probably perished. A good although far from impartial summary of the controversy may be found in Vagedes, *De Ludibriis Aulæ Romanæ in transferendo Imperio Romano.*

[k] 'Vacante imperio Romano, cum in illo ad sæcularem iudicem nequeat haberi recursus, ad summum pontificem, cui in persona B. Petri terreni simul et coelestis imperii iura Deus ipse commisit, imperii prædicti iurisdictio regimen et dispositio devolvitur.'—Bull *Si fratrum* (of John XXI, in A.D. 1316), in *Bullar. Rom.* So again: 'Attendentes quod Imperii Romani regimen cura et administratio tempore quo illud vacare contingit ad

nos pertinet, sicut dignoscitur pertinere.' So Boniface VIII, refusing to recognize Albert I, because he was ugly and one-eyed (' est homo monoculus et vultu sordido, non potest esse Imperator'); and had taken a wife from the serpent brood of Frederick II (' de sanguine viperali Friderici'), declared himself Vicar of the Empire, and assumed the crown and sword of Constantine.

[l] Avignon was not yet in the territory of France: it lay within the bounds of the kingdom of Arles. But the French power was nearer than that of the Emperor; and pontiffs many of them French by extraction sympathized, as was natural, with princes of their own race.

by the English Franciscan Occam, supported Lewis IV in his conflict with John XXII, till even the princes who had risen by the help of the Pope were obliged to oppose him. The same sentiment dictated the reforms of Constance, but the imperial power which might have floated onwards and higher on the turning tide of popular opinion lacked men equal to the occasion : the Hapsburg Frederick the Third, timid and superstitious, abased himself before the Romish court, and his house has generally adhered to the alliance then struck.

CHAPTER XIV.

THE GERMANIC CONSTITUTION: THE SEVEN ELECTORS.

THE reign of Frederick the Second was not less fatal to the domestic power of the German king than to the European supremacy of the Emperor. His two Pragmatic Sanctions had conferred rights that made the feudal aristocracy almost independent, and the long anarchy of the Interregnum had enabled them not only to use but to extend and fortify their power. Rudolf of Hapsburg had striven, not wholly in vain, to coerce their insolence, but the contest between his son Albert and Adolf of Nassau which followed his death, the short and troubled reign of Albert himself, the absence of Henry the Seventh in Italy, the civil war of Lewis of Bavaria and Frederick duke of Austria, rival claimants of the imperial throne, the difficulties in which Lewis, the successful competitor, found himself involved with the Pope—all these circumstances tended more and more to narrow the influence of the crown and complete the emancipation of the turbulent nobles. They now became virtually supreme in their own domains, enjoying full jurisdiction, certain appeals excepted, the right of legislation, privileges of coining money, of levying tolls and taxes: some were without even a feudal bond to remind

CHAP. XIV.
Territorial Sovereignty of the Princes.

Adolf,
1292–1298.

Albert I,
1298–1308.

Henry VII,
1308–1314.

Lewis IV,
1314–1347.

them of their allegiance. The numbers of the immediate nobility—those who held directly of the crown—had increased prodigiously by the extinction of the dukedoms of Saxony, Franconia, and Swabia : along the Rhine the lord of a single tower was usually a sovereign prince. The petty tyrants whose boast it was that they owed fealty only to God and the Emperor, shewed themselves in practice equally regardless of both powers. Pre-eminent were the three great houses of Austria, Bavaria, and Luxemburg, this last having acquired Bohemia. A.D. 1309; next came the electors, already considered collectively more important than the Emperor, and forming ·for themselves the first considerable principalities. Brandenburg and the Rhenish Palatinate are strong independent states before the end of this period : Bohemia and the three archbishoprics almost from its beginning.

The chief object of the magnates was to keep the monarch in his present state of helplessness. Till the expenses which the crown entailed were found ruinous to its wearer, their practice was to confer it on some petty prince, such as were Rudolf and Adolf of Nassau and Gunther of Schwartzburg, seeking when they could to keep it from settling in one family. They bound the newly-elected to respect all their present immunities, including those which they had just extorted as the price of their votes; they checked all his attempts to recover lost lands or rights : they ventured at last to depose their anointed head, Wenzel of Bohemia. Thus fettered, the Emperor sought only to make the most of his short tenure, using his position to aggrandize his family and raise money by the sale of crown estates and privileges. His individual action and personal relation to the subject was replaced by a merely legal and formal one : he

Policy
of the
Emperors.

represented order and legitimate ownership, and so far was still necessary to the political system. But progresses through the country were abandoned : unlike his predecessors, who had resigned their patrimony when they assumed the sceptre, he lived mostly in his own states, often without the Empire's bounds. Frederick III never entered it for twenty-seven years.

How thoroughly the national character of the office was gone is shewn by the repeated attempts to bestow it on foreign potentates, who could not fill the place of a German king of the good old vigorous type. Not to speak of Richard and Alfonso, Charles of Valois was proposed against Henry VII, Edward III of England actually elected against Charles IV (his parliament forbade him to accept), George Podiebrad, king of Bohemia, against Frederick III. Sigismund was virtually a Hungarian king. The Emperor's only hope would have been in the support of the cities. During the thirteenth and fourteenth centuries they had increased wonderfully in population, wealth, and boldness: the Hanseatic confederacy was the mightiest power of the North, and cowed the Scandinavian kings: the towns of Swabia and the Rhine formed great commercial leagues, maintained regular wars against the counter-associations of the nobility, and seemed at one time, by an alliance with the Swiss, on the point of turning West Germany into a federation of free municipalities. Feudalism, however, was still too strong; the cavalry of the nobles was irresistible in the field, and the thoughtless Wenzel let slip a golden opportunity of repairing the losses of two centuries. After all, the Empire was perhaps past redemption, for one fatal ailment paralyzed all its efforts. The Empire was poor. The crown lands, which had

Power of the cities.

Financial distress.

suffered heavily under Frederick II, were further usurped during the confusion that followed; till at last, through the reckless prodigality of sovereigns who sought only their immediate interest, little was left of the vast and fertile domains along the Rhine from which the Saxon and Franconian Emperors had drawn the chief part of their revenue. Regalian rights, the second fiscal resource, had fared no better—tolls, customs, mines, rights of coining, of harbouring Jews, and so forth, were either seized or granted away: even the advowsons of churches had been sold or mortgaged; and the imperial treasury depended mainly on an inglorious traffic in honours and exemptions. Things were so bad under Rudolf that the electors refused to make his son Albert king of the Romans, declaring that, while Rudolf lived, the public revenue which with difficulty supported one monarch, could much less maintain two at the same time[a]. Sigismund told his Diet, 'Nihil esse imperio spoliatius, nihil egentius, adeo ut qui sibi ex Germaniæ principibus successurus esset, qui præter patrimonium nihil aliud habuerit, apud eum non imperium sed potius servitium sit futurum[b].' Patritius, the secretary of Frederick III, declared that the revenues of the Empire scarcely covered the expenses of its ambassadors[c]. Poverty such as these expressions point to, a poverty which became greater after each election, not only involved the failure

[a] Quoted by Moser, *Römische Kayser*, from *Chron. Hirsang.*: 'Regni vires temporum iniuria nimium contritæ vix uni alendo regi sufficerent, tantum abesse ut sumptus in duos reges ferre queant.'

[b] At Rupert's death, under

whom the mischief had increased greatly, there were, we are told, many bishops better off than the Emperor.

[c] 'Proventus Imperii ita minimi sunt ut legationibus vix suppetant.' —Quoted by Moser.

of the attempts which were sometimes made to recover usurped rights[d], but put every project of reform within or war without at the mercy of a jealous Diet. The three orders of which that Diet consisted, electors, princes, and cities, were mutually hostile, and by consequence selfish; their niggardly grants did no more than keep the Empire from dying of inanition.

The changes thus briefly described were in progress when Charles the Fourth, king of Bohemia, son of that blind king John of Bohemia who fell at Cressy, and grandson of the Emperor Henry VII, was chosen to ascend the throne. His skilful and consistent policy aimed at settling what he perhaps despaired of reforming, and the famous instrument which, under the name of the Golden Bull, became the corner-stone of the Germanic constitution, confessed and legalized the independence of the electors and the powerlessness of the crown. The most conspicuous defect of the existing system was the uncertainty of the elections, followed as they usually were by a civil war. It was this which Charles set himself to redress.

Charles IV (A.D. 1347–1378), and his electoral constitution.

The kingdoms founded on the ruins of the Roman Empire by the Teutonic invaders presented in their original form a rude combination of the elective with the hereditary principle. One family in each tribe had, as the offspring of the gods, an indefeasible claim to rule, but from among the members of such a family the warriors were free to choose the bravest or the most popular as king[e]. That the German crown came to be purely

German kingdom not originally elective.

---

[d] Albert I tried in vain to wrest the tolls of the Rhine from the grasp of the Rhenish electors.

[e] The Æthelings of the line of Cerdic, among the West Saxons, and the Bavarian Agilolfings, may

Q

elective, while in France, Castile, Aragon, England, and most other European states, the principle of strict hereditary succession established itself, was due to the failure of heirs male in three successive dynasties; to the restless ambition of the nobles, who, since they were not, like the French, strong enough to disregard the royal power, did their best to weaken it; to the intrigues of the churchmen, zealous for a method of appointment prescribed by their own law and observed in capitular elections; to the wish of the Popes to gain an opening for their own influence and make effective the veto which they claimed; above all, to the conception of the imperial office as one too holy to be, in the same manner as the regal, transmissible by blood. Had the German, like other feudal kingdoms, remained merely local, feudal, and national, it would without doubt have ended by becoming a hereditary monarchy. Transformed as it was by the Roman Empire, this could not be. The headship of the human race being, like the Papacy, the common inheritance of all mankind, could not be confined to any family, nor pass like a private estate by the ordinary rules of descent.

Electoral body in primitive times.

The right to choose the war-chief belonged, in the earliest ages, to the whole body of freemen. Their suffrage, which must have been very irregularly exercised, became by degrees vested in their leaders, but the assent of the multitude, although ensured already, was needed to complete the ceremony. It was thus that Henry the Fowler, and St. Henry, and Conrad the Franconian duke were chosen[f]. Though even tradition might have com-

thus be compared with the Achæmenids of Persia or the heroic houses of early Greece.

[f] Wippo, describing the election of Conrad the Franconian, says, ' Inter confinia Moguntiæ

memorated what extant records place beyond a doubt, it was commonly believed, till the end of the sixteenth century, that the elective constitution had been established, and the privilege of voting confined to seven persons, by a decree of Gregory V and Otto III, which a famous jurist describes as 'lex a pontifice de imperatorum comitiis lata, ne ius eligendi penes populum Romanum in posterum esset[g].' St. Thomas says, 'Election ceased from the times of Charles the Great to those of Otto III, when Pope Gregory V established that of the seven princes, which will last as long as the holy Roman Church, who ranks above all other powers, shall have judged expedient for Christ's faithful people[h].' Since it tended to exalt the papal power, this fiction was accepted, no doubt honestly accepted, and spread abroad by the clergy. And indeed, like so many other fictions, it had a sort of foundation in fact. The death of Otto III, the fourth

---

et Wormatiæ convenerunt cuncti primates et, ut ita dicam, vires et viscera regni.' So Bruno says that Henry IV was elected by the '*populus*.' So Gunther Ligurinus of Frederick I's election :—

'Acturi sacræ de successione coronæ
Conveniunt proceres, totius viscera regni.'

So Amandus, secretary of Frederick Barbarossa, in describing his election, says, 'Multi illustres heroes ex Lombardia, Tuscia, Ianuensi et aliis Italiæ dominiis, ac maior et potior pars principum ex Transalpino regno.'—Quoted by Mur. *Antiq.* Diss. iii. And see many other authorities to the same effect, collected by Pfeffinger, *Vitriarius illustratus*.

[g] Alciatus, *De Formula Romani Imperii*. He adds that the Gauls and Italians were incensed at the preference shewn to Germany. So too Radulfus de Columna.

[h] Quoted by Gewoldus, *De Septemviratu Sacri Imperii Romani*, himself a violent advocate of Gregory's decree, though living as late as the days of Ferdinand II. As late as A.D. 1648 we find Pope Innocent X maintaining that the sacred number *Seven* of the electors was 'apostolica auctoritate olim præfinitus.' Bull *Zelo domus* in *Bullar. Rom.*

of a line of monarchs among whom son had regularly succeeded to father, threw back the crown into the gift of the nation, and was no doubt one of the chief causes why it did not in the end become hereditary [i].

Thus, under the Saxon and Franconian sovereigns, the throne was theoretically elective, the assent of the chiefs and their followers being required, though little more likely to be refused than it was to an English or a French king; practically hereditary, since both of these dynasties succeeded in occupying it for four generations, the father procuring the son's election during his own lifetime. And so it might well have continued, had the right of choice been retained by the whole body of the aristocracy. But at the election of Lothar II, A.D. 1125, we find a certain small number of magnates exercising the so-called right of prætaxation; that is to say, choosing alone the future monarch, and then submitting him to the rest for their approval. A supreme electoral college, once formed, had both the will and the power to retain the crown in their own gift, and still further exclude their inferiors from participation. So before the end of the Hohenstaufen dynasty, two great changes had passed upon the ancient constitution. It had become a fundamental doctrine that the Germanic throne, unlike the thrones of other countries, was purely elective [k]: nor could the

Encroach-ments of the great nobles.

[i] Sometimes we hear of a decree made by Pope Sergius IV and his cardinals (of course equally fabulous with Otto's). So John Villani, iv. 2.

[k] In 1152 we read, 'Id iuris Romani Imperii apex habere dicitur ut non per sanguinis propaginem sed per principum electionem reges creentur.'—Otto Fris. Gulielmus Brito, writing not much later, says (quoted by Freher),—

'Est etenim talis dynastia Theutonicorum
Ut nullus regnet super illos, ni prius illum
Eligat unanimis cleri populique voluntas.'

influence and the liberal offers of Henry VI prevail on the princes to abandon what they rightly judged the keystone of their powers. And at the same time the right of prætaxation had ripened into an exclusive privilege of election, vested in a small body[1] : the assent of the rest of the nobility being at first assumed, finally altogether dispensed with. On the double choice of Richard and Alfonso, A.D. 1264, the only question was as to the majority of votes in the electoral college : neither then nor afterwards was there a word of the rights of the other princes, counts and barons, important as their voices had been two centuries earlier.

. The origin of that college is a matter somewhat intricate and obscure. It is mentioned A.D. 1152, and in somewhat clearer terms in 1198, as a distinct body; but without anything to shew who composed it. First in A.D. 1265 does a letter of Pope Urban IV say that by immemorial custom the right of choosing the Roman king belonged to seven persons, the seven who had just divided their votes on Richard of Cornwall and Alfonso of Castile. Of these seven, three, the archbishops of Mentz, Treves, and Cologne, pastors of the richest Transalpine sees, represented the German church : the other four ought, according to the ancient constitution, to have been the dukes of the four nations, Franks, Swabians, Saxons, Bavarians, to whom had also belonged the four great offices of the imperial household. But of these dukedoms the two first named were now extinct, and their place and power in the state, as well as the household offices they had held, had descended upon two

CHAP. XIV.

The Seven Electors.

---

[1] Innocent III, during the contest between Philip and Otto IV, speaks of 'principes ad quos principaliter spectat regis Romani electio.'

principalities of more recent origin, those, namely, of the Palatinate of the Rhine and the Margraviate of Branden-burg. The Saxon duke, though with greatly narrowed dominions, retained his vote and office of arch-marshal, and the claim of his Bavarian compeer would have been equally indisputable had it not so happened that both he and the Palsgrave of the Rhine were members of the great house of Wittelsbach. That one family should hold two votes out of seven seemed so dangerous to the state that it was made a ground of objection to the Bavarian duke, and gave an opening to the pretensions of the king of Bohemia, who, though not properly a Teutonic prince[m], might on the score of rank and power assert himself the equal of any one of the electors. The dispute between these rival claimants, as well as all the rules and requisites of the election, were settled by Charles the Fourth in the Golden Bull, thenceforward a fundamental law of the Empire. He decided in favour of Bohemia, of which he was then king; fixed Frankfort as the place of election; named the archbishop of Mentz convener of the electoral college; gave to Bohemia the first, to the Count Palatine the second place among the secular electors. A majority of votes was in all cases to be decisive. As to each electorate there was attached a great office, it was supposed that this was the title by which the vote was possessed; though it was in truth rather an effect than a cause. The three prelates were archchancellors of Germany, Gaul and Burgundy, and Italy respectively: Bohemia cupbearer, the Palsgrave seneschal, Saxony marshal, and Brandenburg chamberlain[n].

Golden Bull of Charles IV, A.D. 1356.

[m] 'Rex Bohemiæ non eligit, quia non est Teutonicus,' says a writer early in the fourteenth cen-

tury.

[n] The names and offices of the seven are concisely given in these

These arrangements, under which disputed elections became far less frequent, remained undisturbed till A.D. 1618, when on the breaking out of the Thirty Years' War the Emperor Ferdinand II by an unwarranted stretch of prerogative deprived the Palsgrave Frederick (king of Bohemia, and husband of Elizabeth, the daughter of James I of England) of his electoral vote, and transferred it to his own partisan, Maximilian of Bavaria. At the peace of Westphalia the Palsgrave was reinstated as an eighth elector, Bavaria retaining her place. The sacred number having been once broken through, less scruple was felt in making further changes. In A.D. 1692, the Emperor Leopold I conferred a ninth electorate on the house of Brunswick Lüneburg, which was then in posses-

CHAP. XIV.

Eighth Electorate.

Ninth Electorate.

lines, which appear in the treatise of Marsilius of Padua, *De Imperio Romano* :—

> ' Moguntinensis, Trevirensis, Coloniensis,
>   Quilibet Imperii sit Cancellarius horum ;
>   Et Palatinus dapifer, Dux portitor ensis,
>   Marchio præpositus cameræ, pincerna Bohemus,
>   Hi statuunt dominum cunctis per sæcula summum.'

It is worth while to place beside this the first stanza of Schiller's ballad, *Der Graf von Hapsburg*, in which the coronation feast of Rudolf is described :—

> ' Zu Aachen in seiner Kaiserpracht
>   Im alterthümlichen Saale,
>   Sass König Rudolphs heilige Macht
>   Beim festlichen Krönungsmahle.
>   Die Speisen trug der Pfalzgraf des Rheins,
>   Es schenkte der Böhme des perlenden Weins,
>   Und alle die Wähler, die Sieben,
>   Wie der Sterne Chor um die Sonne sich stellt,
>   Umstanden geschäftig den Herrscher der Welt,
>   Die Würde des Amtes zu üben.'

It is a poetical licence, however (as Schiller himself admits), to bring the Bohemian there, for King Ottocar was far away at home, mortified at his own rejection, and already meditating war.

sion of the duchy of Hanover, and succeeded to the throne of Great Britain in 1714 ; and in A.D. 1708, the assent of the Diet thereto was obtained. It was in this way that English kings came to vote at the election of a Roman Emperor.

It is not a little curious that the only potentate who still continues to entitle himself Elector º should be one who never did (and of course never can now) join in electing an Emperor, having been under the arrangements of the old Empire a simple Landgrave. In A.D. 1803, Napoleon, among other sweeping changes in the Germanic constitution, procured the extinction of the electorates of Cologne and Treves, annexing their territories to France, and gave the title of Elector, as the highest after that of king, to the duke of Würtemburg, the Margrave of Baden, the Landgrave of Hessen-Cassel, and the archbishop of Salzburg. Three years afterwards the Empire itself ended, and the title became meaningless.

As the Germanic Empire is the most conspicuous example of a monarchy not hereditary that the world has ever seen, it may not be amiss to consider for a moment what light its history throws upon the character of elective monarchy in general, a contrivance which has always had,

---

º The electoral prince (Kurfürst) of Hessen-Cassel. His retention of the title has this advantage, that it enables the Germans readily to distinguish electoral Hesse (Kur-Hessen) from the Grand Duchy (Hessen-Darmstadt) and the landgraviate (Hessen Homburg).   [Since the above was written (in 1865) this last relic of the electoral system has passed away, the Elector of Hessen having been dethroned in 186⁶, and his territories (to the great satisfaction of the inhabitants, whom he had worried by a long course of petty tyrannies) annexed to the Prussian kingdom, along with Hanover, Nassau, and the free city of Frankfort. Count Bismarck, as he raises his master nearer and nearer to the position of a Germanic Emperor, destroys one by one the historical memorials of that elder Empire which people had learned to associate with the Austrian house.]

and will probably always continue to have, seductions for a certain class of political theorists.

First of all then it deserves to be noticed how difficult, one might almost say impossible, it was found to maintain in practice the elective principle. In point of law, the imperial throne was from the tenth century to the nineteenth absolutely open to any orthodox Christian candidate. But as a matter of fact, the competition was confined to a few very powerful families, and there was always a strong tendency for the crown to become hereditary in some one of these. Thus the Franconian Emperors held it from A.D. 1024 till 1125, the Hohenstaufen, themselves the heirs of the Franconians, for a century or more; the house of Luxemburg (kings of Bohemia) enjoyed it through three successive reigns, and when in the fifteenth century it fell into the tenacious grasp of the Hapsburgs, they managed to retain it thenceforth (with but one trifling interruption) till it vanished out of nature altogether. Therefore the chief benefit which the scheme of elective sovereignty seems to promise, that of putting the fittest man in the highest place, was but seldom attained, and attained even then rather by good fortune than design.

Objects of an elective monarchy: how far attained in Germany. Choice of the fittest.

No such objection can be brought against the second ground on which an elective system has sometimes been advocated, its operation in moderating the power of the crown, for this was attained in the fullest and most ruinous measure. We are reminded of the man in the fable, who opened a sluice to water his garden, and saw his house swept away by the furious torrent. The power of the crown was not moderated but destroyed. Each successful candidate was forced to purchase his title by the sacrifice of rights which had belonged to his predecessors,

Restraint of the sovereign.

and must repeat the same shameful policy later in his reign to procure the election of his son. Feeling at the same time that his family could not make sure of keeping the throne, he treated it as a life-tenant is apt to treat his estate, seeking only to make out of it the largest present profit. And the electors, aware of the strength of their position, presumed upon it and abused it to assert an independence such as the nobles of other countries could never have aspired to.

Recognition of the popular will.

Modern political speculation supposes the method of appointing a ruler by the votes of his subjects, as opposed to the system of hereditary succession, to be an assertion by the people of their own will as the ultimate fountain of authority, an acknowledgment by the prince that he is no more than their minister and deputy. To the theory of the Holy Empire nothing could be more repugnant. This will best appear when the aspect of the system of election at different epochs in its history is compared with the corresponding changes in the composition of the electoral body which have been described as in progress from the ninth to the fourteenth century. In very early times, the tribe chose a war chief, who was, even if he belonged to the most noble family, no more than the first among his peers, with a power circumscribed by the will of his subjects. Several ages later, in the tenth and eleventh centuries, the right of choice had passed into the hands of the magnates, and the people were only asked to assent. In the same measure had the relation of prince and subject taken a new aspect. We must not expect to find, in such rude times, any very clear apprehension of the technical quality of the process, and the throne had indeed become for a season so nearly hereditary that the election was often a mere matter of form. But it seems to have been regarded, not as a delegation of authority by the nobles and people, with a power of resumption implied, but rather as their subjection of themselves to the monarch who enjoys, as of his own right, a wide and ill-defined prerogative. In yet later times, when, as has been shewn above, the assembly of the chieftains and the applauding shout of the host had been superseded by the secret conclave of the seven electoral princes, the strict legal view of election became fully established, and no one was supposed to have any title to the crown except what a majority of votes might confer upon him. Meantime, however, the conception of the imperial office itself had been thoroughly penetrated by religious ideas, and the fact that the sovereign did not, like other princes, reign by hereditary right, but by the choice of certain persons, was supposed to be an enhancement and consecration of his dignity. The electors, to draw what may seem a subtle, but is nevertheless a very real distinction, selected, but did not create. They only named the person who was to receive what it was not theirs to give. God, say the mediæval writers, not deigning to interfere visibly in the affairs of this world, has willed that these seven princes of Germany should discharge the function which once belonged to the senate and people of Rome, that of choosing his earthly viceroy in matters temporal. But it is immediately from Himself that the authority of this viceroy comes, and men can have no relation towards him except that of obedience. It was in this period, therefore, when the Emperor was in practice the mere nominee of the electors, that the belief in this divine right stood highest, to the complete exclusion of the mutual responsibility of feudalism, and still more of any notion of a devolution of authority from the sovereign people.

Conception of the electoral function.

Peace and order appeared to be promoted by the institutions of Charles IV, which removed one fruitful cause of civil war. But these seven electoral princes acquired, with their extended privileges, a marked and dangerous predominance in Germany. They were to enjoy full regalian rights in their territories [p]; causes were not to be evoked from their courts, save when justice should have been denied: their consent was necessary to all public acts of consequence. Their persons were held to be sacred, and the seven mystic luminaries of the Holy Empire, typified by the seven lamps of the Apocalypse, soon gained much of the Emperor's hold on popular reverence, as well as that actual power which he lacked. To Charles, who viewed the German Empire much as Rudolf had viewed the Roman, this result came not unforeseen. He saw in his office a means of serving personal ends, and to them, while appearing to exalt by elaborate ceremonies its ideal dignity, he deliberately sacrificed what real strength was left. The object which he sought steadily through life was the prosperity of the Bohemian kingdom, and the advancement of his own house. In the Golden Bull, whose seal bears the legend,—

'Roma caput mundi regit orbis frena rotundi [q],'

there is not a word of Rome or of Italy. To Germany he was indirectly a benefactor, by the foundation of the

[p] Goethe, whose imagination was wonderfully attracted by the splendours of the old Empire, has given in the second part of *Faust* a sort of fancy sketch of the origin of the great offices and the territorial independence of the German princes. Two lines express concisely the fiscal rights granted by the Emperor to the electors:—

'Dann Steuer Zins und Beed', Lehn und Geleit und Zoll,
Berg- Salz- und Müuz-regal euch angehören soll.'

[q] This line is said to be as old as the time of Otto III.

University of Prague, the mother of all her schools :
otherwise her bane. He legalized anarchy, and called it
a constitution. The sums expended in obtaining the
ratification of the Golden Bull, in procuring the election
of his son Wenzel, in aggrandizing Bohemia at the expense of Germany, had been amassed by keeping a
market in which honours and exemptions, with what
lands the crown retained, were put up openly to be bid
for. In Italy the Ghibelines saw, with shame and rage,
their chief hasten to Rome with a scanty retinue, and
return from it as swiftly, at the mandate of an Avignonese
Pope, halting on his route only to traffic away the last
rights of his Empire. The Guelf might cease to hate a
power he could now despise.

Thus, alike at home and abroad, the German king had
become practically powerless by the loss of his feudal
privileges, and saw the authority that had once been his
parcelled out among a crowd of greedy and tyrannical
nobles. Meantime how had it fared with the rights which
he claimed by virtue of the imperial crown?

CHAPTER XV.

THE EMPIRE AS AN INTERNATIONAL POWER.

CHAP. XV.

*Theory of
the Roman
Empire in
the four-
teenth and
fifteenth
centuries.*

THAT the Roman Empire survived the seemingly mortal wound it had received at the era of the Great Interregnum, and continued to put forth pretensions which no one was likely to make good where the Hohenstaufen had failed, has been attributed to its identification with the German kingdom, in which some life was still left. But this was far from being the only cause which saved it from extinction. It had not ceased to be upheld in the fourteenth and fifteenth centuries by the same singular theory which had in the ninth and tenth been strong enough to re-establish it in the West. The character of that theory was indeed somewhat changed, for if not positively less religious, it was less exclusively so. In the days of Charles and Otto, the Empire, in so far as it was anything more than a tradition from times gone by, rested solely upon the belief that with the visible Church there must be coextensive a single Christian state under one head and governor. But now that the Emperor's headship had been repudiated by the Pope, and his interference in matters of religion denounced as a repetition of the sin of Uzziah; now that the memory of mutual injuries had kindled an unquenchable hatred between the champions of the ecclesiastical and those of the civil power, it was natural that the latter,

while they urged, fervently as ever, the divine sanction
given to the imperial office, should at the same time be
led to seek some further basis whereon to establish its
claims. What that basis was, and how they were guided
to it, will best appear when a word or two has been said
on the nature of the change that had passed on Europe in
the course of the three preceding centuries, and the progress of the human mind during the same period.

Such has been the accumulated wealth of literature,
and so rapid the advances of science among us since the
close of the Middle Ages, that it is not now possible by
any effort fully to enter into the feelings with which the
relics of antiquity were regarded by those who saw in
them their only possession. It is indeed true that modern
art and literature and philosophy have been produced by
the working of new minds upon old materials: that in
thought, as in nature, we see no new creation. But with
us the old has been transformed and overlaid by the new
till its origin is forgotten: to them ancient books were
the only standard of taste, the only vehicle of truth, the
only stimulus to reflection. Hence it was that the most
learned man was in those days esteemed the greatest:
hence the creative energy of an age was exactly pro-
portioned to its knowledge of and its reverence for the
written monuments of those that had gone before. For
until they can look forward, men must look back: till
they should have reached the level of the old civilization,
the nations of mediæval Europe must continue to live
upon its memories. Over them, as over us, the common
dream of all mankind had power; but to them, as to
the ancient world, that golden age which seems now to
glimmer on the horizon of the future was shrouded in
the clouds of the past. It is to the fifteenth and sixteenth

CHAP. XV.

Revival of learning and litera- ture, A.D. 1100–1400.

centuries that we are accustomed to assign that new birth of the human spirit—if it ought not rather to be called a renewal of its strength and quickening of its sluggish life—with which the modern time begins. And the date is well chosen, for it was then first that the transcendently powerful influence of Greek literature began to work upon the world. But it must not be forgotten that for a long time previous there had been in progress a great revival of learning, and still more of zeal for learning, which being caused by and directed towards the literature and institutions of Rome, might fitly be called the Roman Renaissance. The twelfth century saw this revival begin with that passionate study of the legislation of Justinian, whose influence on the doctrines of imperial prerogative has been noticed already. The thirteenth witnessed the rapid spread of the scholastic philosophy, a body of systems most alien, both in subject and manner, to any-thing that had arisen among the ancients, yet one to whose development Greek metaphysics and the theology of the Latin fathers had largely contributed, and the spirit of whose reasonings was far more free than the presumèd orthodoxy of its conclusions suffered to appear. In the fourteenth century there arose in Italy the first great masters of painting and song; and the literature of the new languages, springing into the fulness of life in the Divina Commedia, adorned not long after by the names of Petrarch and Chaucer, assumed at once its place as a great and ever-growing power in the affairs of men.

Growing freedom of spirit.

Now, along with the literary revival, partly caused by, partly causing it, there had been also a wonderful stirring and uprising in the mind of Europe. The yoke of church authority still pressed heavily on the souls of men; yet some had been found to shake it off, and many more

murmured in secret. The tendency was one which
shewed itself in various and sometimes apparently opposite directions. The revolt of the Albigenses, the spread
of the Cathari and other so-called heretics, the excitement
created by the writings of Wickliffe and Huss, witnessed
to the fearlessness wherewith it could assail the dominant
theology. It was present, however skilfully disguised,
among those scholastic doctors who busied themselves
with proving by natural reason the dogmas of the Church :
for the power which can forge fetters can also break
them. It took a form more dangerous because of a more
direct application to facts, in the attacks, so often repeated
from Arnold of Brescia downwards, upon the wealth and
corruptions of the clergy, and above all of the papal
court. For the agitation was not merely speculative.
There was beginning to be a direct and rational interest
in life, a power of applying thought to practical ends,
which had not been seen before. Man's life among his
fellows was no longer a mere wild beast struggle ; man's
soul no more, as it had been, the victim of ungoverned
passion, whether it was awed by supernatural terrors or
captivated by examples of surpassing holiness. Manners
were still rude, and governments unsettled ; but society
was learning to organize itself upon fixed principles ; to
recognize, however faintly, the value of order, industry,
equality ; to adapt means to ends, and conceive of the
common good as the proper end of its own existence.
In a word, Politics had begun to exist, and with them
there had appeared the first of a class of persons whom
friends and enemies may both, though with different
meanings, call ideal politicians ; men who, however
various have been the doctrines they have held, however
impracticable many of the plans they have advanced, have

*Influence
of thought
upon the
arrange-
ments of
society.*

R

been nevertheless alike in their devotion to the highest interests of humanity, and have frequently been derided as theorists in their own age to be honoured as the prophets and teachers of the next.

Now it was towards the Roman Empire that the hopes and sympathies of these political speculators as well as of the jurists and poets of the fourteenth and fifteenth centuries were constantly directed. The cause may be gathered from the circumstances of the time. The most remarkable event in the history of the last three hundred years had been the formation of nationalities, each distinguished by a peculiar language and character, and by steadily increasing differences of habits and institutions. And as upon this national basis there had been in most cases established strong monarchies, Europe was broken up into disconnected bodies, and the cherished scheme of a united Christian state appeared less likely than ever to be realized. Nor was this all. Sometimes through race-hatred, more often by the jealousy and ambition of their sovereigns, these countries were constantly involved in war with one another, violating on a larger scale and with more destructive results than in time past the peace of the religious community; while each of them was at the same time torn within by frequent insurrections, and desolated by long and bloody civil wars. The new nationalities were too fully formed to allow the hope that by their extinction a remedy might be applied to these evils. They had grown up in spite of the Empire and the Church, and were not likely to yield in their strength what they had won in their weakness. But it still appeared possible to soften, if not to overcome, their antagonism. What might not be looked for from the erection of a presiding power common to all Europe, a power which, while

Separation of the peoples of Europe into bostile kingdoms: consequent need of an international power.

it should oversee the internal concerns of each country, not dethroning the king, but treating him as an hereditary viceroy, should be more especially charged to prevent strife between kingdoms, and to maintain the public order of Europe by being not only the fountain of international law, but also the judge in its causes and the enforcer of its sentences?

To such a position had the Popes aspired. They were indeed excellently fitted for it by the respect which the sacredness of their office commanded; by their control of the tremendous weapons of excommunication and interdict; above all, by their exemption from those narrowing influences of place, or blood, or personal interest, which it would be their chiefest duty to resist in others. And there had been pontiffs whose fearlessness and justice were worthy of their exalted office, and whose interference was gratefully remembered by those who found no other helpers. Nevertheless, judging the Papacy by its conduct as a whole, it had been tried and found wanting. Even when its throne stood firmest and its purposes were most pure, one motive had always biassed its decisions—a partiality to the most submissive. During the greater part of the fourteenth century it was at Avignon the willing tool of France: in the pursuit of a temporal principality it had mingled in and been contaminated by the unhallowed politics of Italy; its supreme council, the college of cardinals, was distracted by the intrigues of two bitterly hostile factions. And while the power of the Popes had declined steadily, though silently, since the days of Boniface the Eighth, the insolence of the great prelates and the vices of the inferior clergy had provoked throughout Western Christendom a reaction against the pretensions of all sacerdotal authority. As there is no

The Popes as international Judges.

theory at first sight more attractive than that which entrusts all government to a supreme spiritual power, which, knowing what is best for man, shall lead him to his true good by appealing to the highest principles of his nature, so there is no disappointment more bitter than that of those who find that the holiest office may be polluted by the lusts and passions of its holder; that craft and hypocrisy lead while fanaticism follows; that here too, as in so much else, the corruption of the best is worst. Some such disappointment there was in Europe now, and with it a certain disposition to look with favour on the secular power: a wish to escape from the unhealthy atmosphere of clerical despotism to the rule of positive law, harsher, it might be, yet surely less corrupting. Espousing the cause of the Roman Empire as the chief opponent of priestly claims, this tendency found it, with shrunken territory and diminished resources, fitter in some respects for the office of an international judge and mediator than it had been as a great national power. For though far less widely active, it was losing that local character which was fast gathering round the Papacy. With feudal rights no longer enforcible, and removed, except in his patrimonial lands, from direct contact with the subject, the Emperor was not, as heretofore, conspicuously a German and a feudal king, and occupied an ideal position far less marred by the incongruous accidents of birth and training, of national and dynastic interests.

Duties attributed to the Empire by the developed theory.

To that position three cardinal duties were attached. He who held it must typify spiritual unity, must preserve peace, must be a fountain of that by which alone among imperfect men peace is preserved and restored, law and justice. The first of these three objects was sought not only on religious grounds, but also from that longing for a wider brotherhood of humanity towards which, ever since the barrier between Jew and Gentile, Greek and barbarian, was broken down, the aspirations of the higher minds of the world have been constantly directed. Placed in the midst of Europe, the Emperor was to bind its tribes into one body, reminding them of their common faith, their common blood, their common interest in each other's welfare. And he was therefore above all things, pro- fessing indeed to be upon earth the representative of the Prince of Peace, bound to listen to complaints, and to redress the injuries inflicted by sovereigns or people upon each other; to punish offenders against the public order of Christendom; to maintain through the world, looking down as from a serene height upon the schemes and quarrels of meaner potentates, that supreme good without which neither arts nor letters, nor the gentler virtues of life, can rise and flourish. The mediæval Empire was in its essence what the modern despotisms that mimic it profess themselves: the Empire was peace [a]: the oldest and noblest title of its head was 'Imperator pacificus [b].'

[a] See esp. Ægidi, *Der Fürsten-rath nach dem Luneviller Frie-den*, and the passages by him quoted.

[b] The archbishop of Mentz ad-dresses Conrad II on his election thus: 'Deus quum a te multa requirat tum hoc potissimum de-siderat ut facias iudicium et iusti-tiam et pacem patriæ quæ respicit ad te, ut sis defensor ecclesiarum et clericorum, tutor viduarum et orpha-norum.'—Wippo, Vita Chuonradi, c. 3, *ap.* Pertz. So Pope Urban IV writes to Richard: 'Ut consterna-tis Imperii Romani inimicis, in pacis pulchritudine sedeat populus Chris-tianus et requie opulenta quiescat.'

Compare also the 'Edictum de crimine læsæ maiestatis' issued by Henry VII in Italy: 'Ad reprimenda multorum facinora qui ruptis to-tius debitæ fidelitatis habenis ad-versus Romanum imperium, in cuius tranquillitate totius orbis regularitas requiescit, hostili animo armati con-entur nedum humana, verum etiam divina præcepta, quibus iubetur quod omnis anima Romanorum principi sit subiecta, scelestissimis facinori-bus et rebellionibus demoliri,' &c.— Pertz, *M. G. H.*, legg. ii. p. 544.

See also a curious passage in the Life of St. Adalbert, describing the beginning of the reign at Rome of the Emperor Otto III, and his cousin,

And that he might be the peacemaker, he must be the expounder of justice and the author of its concrete embodiment, positive law; chief legislator and supreme judge of appeal, like his predecessor the compiler of the Corpus Iuris, the one and only source of all legitimate authority. In this sense, as governor and administrator, not as owner, is he, in the words of the jurists, Lord of the world; not that its soil belongs to him in the same sense in which the soil of France or England belongs to their respective kings: he is the steward of Him who has received the heathen for his possession and the uttermost parts of the earth for his inheritance. It is, therefore, by him alone that the idea of pure right, acquired not by force but by legitimate devolution from those whom God himself had set up, is visibly expressed upon earth. To find an external and positive basis for that idea is a problem which it has at all times been more easy to evade than to solve, and one peculiarly distressing to those who could neither explain the phenomena of society by reducing it to its original principles, nor inquire historically how its existing arrangements had grown up. Hence the attempt to represent human government as an emanation from divine: a view from which all the similar but far less logically consistent doctrines of divine right which have prevailed in later times are borrowed. As has been said already, there is not a trace of the notion that the Emperor reigns by an hereditary right of his own or by the will of the people, for such a theory would have seemed to the men of the middle ages an absurd and wicked perversion of the true order. Nor do his powers come to him from

Divine right of the Emperor.

and nominee Pope Gregory V: 'Lætantur cum primatibus minores civitatis: cum afflicto paupere ex- ultant agmina viduarum, quia novus imperator dat iura populis; dat iura novus papa.'

those who choose him, but from God, who uses the electoral princes as mere instruments of nomination. Having such an origin, his rights exist irrespective of their actual exercise, and no voluntary abandonment, not even an express grant, can impair them. Boniface the Eighth [c] reminds the king of France, and imperialist lawyers till the seventeenth century repeated the claim, that he, like other princes, is of right and must ever remain subject to the Roman Emperor. And the sovereigns of Europe long continued to address the Emperor in language, and yield to him a precedence, which admitted the inferiority of their own position [d].

There was in this theory nothing that was absurd, though much that was impracticable. The ideas on which it rested are still unapproached in grandeur and simplicity, still as far in advance of the average thought of Europe, and as unlikely to find men or nations fit to apply them, as when they were promulgated five hundred years ago. The practical evil which the establishment of such a universal monarchy was intended to meet, that of wars and hardly less ruinous preparations for war between the

[c] 'Imperator est monarcha omnium regum et principum terrenorum . . . . . nec insurgat superbia Gallicorum quæ dicat quod non recognoscit superiorem, mentiuntur, quia de iure sunt et esse debent sub rege Romanorum et Imperatore.'— Speech of Boniface VIII. It is curious to compare with this the words addressed nearly five centuries earlier by Pope John VIII to Lewis, king of Bavaria: 'Si sumpseritis Romanum imperium, omnia regna vobis subiecta existent.'

[d] So Alfonso, king of Naples, writes to Frederick III: 'Nos reges omnes debemus reverentiam Imperatori, tanquam summo regi, qui est Caput et Dux regum.'—Quoted by Pfeffinger, *Vitriarius illustratus*, i. 379. And Francis I (of France), speaking of a proposed combined expedition against the Turks, says, 'Cæsari nihilominus principem ea in expeditione locum non gravarer ex officio cedere.'—For a long time no European sovereign save the Emperor ventured to use the title of 'Majesty.' The imperial chancery conceded it in 1633 to the kings of England and Sweden; in 1641 to the king of France.—Zedler, *Universal Lexicon, s. v.* Majestät.

Roman
Empire
why an in-
ternational
power.

states of Europe, remains what it was then. The remedy which mediæval theory proposed has been in some measure applied by the construction and reception of international law; the greater difficulty of erecting a tribunal to arbitrate and decide, with the power of enforcing its decisions, is as far from a solution as ever.

It is easy to see how it was to the Roman Emperor, and to him only, that the duties and privileges above mentioned could be attributed. Being Roman, he was of no nation, and therefore fittest to judge between contending states, and appease the animosities of race. His was the imperial tongue of Rome, not only the vehicle of religion and law, but also, since no other was understood everywhere in Europe, the necessary medium of diplomatic intercourse. As there was no Church but the Holy Roman Church, and he its temporal head, it was by him that the communion of the saints in its outward form, its secular side, was represented, and to his keeping that the sanctity of peace must be entrusted. As direct heir of those who from Julius to Justinian had shaped the existing law of Europe [e], he was, so to speak, legality personified [f]; the only sovereign on earth who, being possessed of power by an unimpeachable title, could by his grant confer upon others rights equally valid. And as he claimed to perpetuate the greatest political system the world had known, a system which still moves the wonder of those who see before their eyes empires as much wider than the Roman as they are less symmetrical, and whose vast and complex machinery far surpassed anything the fourteenth

[e] For with the progress of society and the growth of commerce the old feudal customs were through the greater part of Western Europe, and especially in Germany, either giving way to or being remodelled and supplemented by the civil law.

[f] 'Imperator est animata lex in terris.'—Quoted by Von Raumer, v. 81.

century possessed or could hope to establish, it was not
strange that he and his government (assuming them to
be what they were entitled to be) should be taken as the
ideal of a perfect monarch and a perfect state.

Of the many applications and illustrations of these doc- *Illustra-*
trines which mediæval documents furnish, it will suffice to *tions.*
adduce two or three. No imperial privilege was prized *Right of*
more highly than the power of creating kings, for there *creating*
was none which raised the Emperor so much above them. *Kings.*
In this, as in other international concerns, the Pope soon
began to claim a jurisdiction, at first concurrent, then
separate and independent. But the older and more
reasonable view assigned it, as flowing from the possession of supreme secular authority, to the Emperor ; and
it was from him that the rulers of Burgundy, Bohemia,
Hungary, perhaps Poland and Denmark, received the
regal title[g]. The prerogative was his in the same manner
in which that of conferring titles is still held to belong to
the sovereign in every modern kingdom. And so when
Charles the Bold, last duke of French Burgundy, proposed
to consolidate his wide dominions into a kingdom, it was
from Frederick III that he sought permission to do so.
The Emperor, however, was greedy and suspicious, the
Duke uncompliant ; and when Frederick found that terms
could not be arranged between them, he stole away suddenly, and left Charles to carry back, with ill-concealed

[g] Thus we are told of the Emperor Charles the Bald, when he
confirmed the election of Boso, king
of Burgundy and Provence, 'Dedit
Bosoni Provinciam (*sc.* Carolus
Calvus), et corona in vertice capitis
imposita, eum regem appellari iussit,
ut more priscorum imperatorum
regibus videretur dominari.'—*Re-
gin. Chron.* Frederick II made
his son Enzio (that famous Enzio
whose romantic history every one
who has seen Bologna will remember) king of Sardinia, and also
erected the duchy of Austria into
a kingdom, although for some
reason the title seems never to
have been used ; and Lewis IV gave
to Humbert of Dauphiné the title
of King of Vienne, A.D. 1336.

mortification, the crown and sceptre which he had brought ready-made to the place of interview.

In the same manner, as representing what was common to and valid throughout all Europe, nobility, and more particularly knighthood, centred in the Empire. The great Orders of Chivalry were international institutions, whose members, having consecrated themselves a military priesthood, had no longer any country of their own, and could therefore be subject to no one save the Emperor and the Pope. For knighthood was constructed on the analogy of priesthood, and knights were conceived of as being to the world in its secular aspect exactly what priests, and more especially the monastic orders, were to it in its religious aspect: to the one body was given the sword of the flesh, to the other the sword of the spirit; each was universal, each had its autocratic head[h]. Singularly, too, were these notions brought into harmony with the feudal polity. Cæsar was lord paramount of the world: its countries great fiefs whose kings were his tenants in chief, the suitors of his court, owing to him homage, fealty, and military service against the infidel.

One illustration more of the way in which the empire was held to be something of and for all mankind, cannot be omitted. Although from the practical union of the imperial with the German throne none but Germans were chosen to fill it[i], it remained in point of law absolutely

[h] It is probably for this reason that the *Ordo Romanus* directs the Emperor and Empress to be crowned (in St. Peter's) at the altar of St. Maurice, the patron saint of knighthood.

[i] See especially Gerlach Buxtorff, *Dissertatio ad Auream Bullam;* and Augustinus Stenchus, *De Imperio Romano;* quoted by Marquard Freher. It was keenly debated, while Charles V and Francis I (of France) were rival candidates, whether any one but a German was eligible. By birth Charles was either a Spaniard or a Fleming; but this difficulty his partisans avoided by holding that

free from all restrictions of country or birth. In an age of the most intense aristocratic exclusiveness, the highest office in the world was the only secular one open to all Christians. The old writers, after debating at length the qualifications that are or may be desirable in an Emperor, and relating how in pagan times Gauls and Spaniards, Moors and Pannonians, were thought worthy of the purple, decide that two things, and no more, are required of the candidate for Empire: he must be free-born, and he must be orthodox [k].

It is not without a certain surprise that we see those who were engaged in the study of ancient letters, or felt indirectly their stimulus, embrace so fervently the cause of the Roman Empire. Still more difficult is it to estimate the respective influence exerted by each of the three revivals which it has been attempted to distinguish. The spirit of the ancient world by which the men who led these movements fancied themselves animated, was in

he had been, according to the civil law, *in potestate* of Maximilian his grandfather. However, to say nothing of the Guidos and Berengars of earlier days, the examples of Richard and Alfonso are conclusive as to the eligibility of others than Germans. Edward III of England was, as has been said, actually elected; Henry VIII was a candidate. And attempts were frequently made to elect the kings of France.

[k] The mediæval practice seems to have been that which still prevails in the Roman Catholic Church—to presume the doctrinal orthodoxy and external conformity of every citizen, whether lay or clerical, until the contrary be proved. Of course when heresy was rife it went hard with suspected men, unless they could either clear themselves or submit to recant. But no one was required to pledge himself beforehand, as a qualification for any office, to certain doctrines. And thus, important as an Emperor's orthodoxy was, he does not appear to have been subjected to any test, although the Pope pretended to the right of catechizing him in the faith and rejecting him if unsound. In the *Ordo Romanus* we find a long series of questions which the Pontiff was to administer, but it does not appear, and is in the highest degree unlikely, that such a programme was ever carried out.

The charge of heresy was one of the weapons used with most effect against Frederick II.

truth a pagan, or at least a strongly secular spirit, in many respects inconsistent with the associations which had now gathered round the imperial office. And this hostility did not fail to shew itself when at the beginning of the sixteenth century, in the fulness of the Renaissance, a direct and for the time irresistible sway was exercised by the art and literature of Greece, when the mythology of Euripides and Ovid supplanted that which had fired the imagination of Dante and peopled the visions of St. Francis; when men forsook the image of the saint in the cathedral for the statue of the nymph in the garden; when the uncouth jargon of scholastic theology was equally distasteful to the scholars who formed their style upon Cicero and the philosophers who drew their inspiration from Plato. That meanwhile the admirers of antiquity did ally themselves with the defenders of the Empire, was due partly indeed to the false notions that were entertained regarding the early Cæsars, yet still more to the common hostility of both sects to the Papacy. It was as successor of old Rome, and by virtue of her traditions, that the Holy See had established so wide a dominion; yet no sooner did Arnold of Brescia and his republicans arise, claiming liberty in the name of the ancient constitution of the republic, than they found in the Popes their bitterest foes, and turned for help to the secular monarch against the clergy. With similar aversion did the Romish court view the revived study of the ancient jurisprudence, so soon as it became, in the hands of the school of Bologna and afterwards of the jurists of France, a power able to assert its independence and resist ecclesiastical pretensions. In the ninth century, Pope Nicholas the First had himself judged in the famous case of Teutberga, wife of Lothar, according to the civil law:

in the thirteenth, his successors[1] forbade its study, and the canonists strove to expel it from Europe[m]. And as the current of educated opinion among the laity was beginning, however imperceptibly at first, to set against sacerdotal tyranny, it followed that the Empire would find sympathy in any effort it could make to regain its lost position. Thus the Emperors became, or might have become had they seen the greatness of the opportunity and been strong enough to improve it, the exponents and guides of the political movement, the pioneers, in part at least, of the Reformation. But the revival came too late to arrest, if not to adorn, the decline of their office. The growth of a national sentiment in the several countries of Europe, which had already gone too far to be arrested, and was urged on by forces far stronger than the theories of Catholic unity which opposed it, imprinted on the resistance to papal usurpation, and even on the instincts of political freedom, that form of narrowly local patriotism which they still retain. It can hardly be said that upon any occasion, except the gathering of the council of Constance by Sigismund, did the Emperor appear filling a truly international place. For the most part he exerted in the politics of Europe no influence greater than that of other princes. In actual resources he stood below the kings of France and England, far below his vassals the Visconti of Milan[n]. Yet this helplessness, such was men's faith or their timidity, and such their unwillingness

The doctrine of the Empire's rights and functions never carried out in fact.

---

[1] Honorius II in 1229 forbade it to be studied or taught in the University of Paris. Innocent IV published some years later a still more sweeping prohibition.

[m] See Von Savigny, *History of Roman Law in the Middle Ages,* vol. iii. pp. 81, 341-347.

[n] Charles the Bold of Burgundy was a potentate incomparably stronger than the Emperor Frederick III from whom he sought the regal title.

to make prejudice bend to facts, did not prevent his dignity from being extolled in the most sonorous language by writers whose imaginations were enthralled by the halo of traditional glory which surrounded it.

Attitude of the men of letters.

We are thus brought back to ask, What was the connection between imperialism and the literary revival?

To moderns who think of the Roman Empire as the heathen persecuting power, it is strange to find it depicted as the model of a Christian commonwealth. It is stranger still that the study of antiquity should have made men advocates of arbitrary power. Democratic Athens, oligarchic Rome, suggest to us Pericles and Brutus: the moderns who have striven to catch their spirit have been men like Algernon Sidney, and Vergniaud, and Shelley. The explanation is the same in both cases[o]. The ancient world was known to the earlier middle ages by tradition, freshest for what was latest, and by the authors of the Empire. Both presented to them the picture of a mighty despotism and a civilization brilliant far beyond their own. Writings of the fourth and fifth centuries, unfamiliar to us, were to them authorities as high as Tacitus or Livy; yet Virgil and Horace too had sung the praises of the first and wisest of the Emperors. To the enthusiasts of poetry and law, Rome meant universal monarchy[p]; to those of religion, her name called up the undimmed radiance of the Church under Sylvester and Constantine. Petrarch, the apostle of the dawning Renaissance, is excited by the least attempt to revive even the shadow of imperial greatness: as he had hailed Rienzi, he welcomes Charles IV into Italy, and execrates his departure. The following passage is taken from his letter to the Roman people

Petrarch.

[o] Cf. Sismondi, *Républiques Italiennes*, iv. chap. xxvii.
[p] See Dante, *Paradiso*, canto vi.

asking them to receive back Rienzi:—'When was there ever such peace, such tranquillity, such justice, such honour paid to virtue, such rewards distributed to the good and punishments to the bad, when was ever the state so wisely guided, as in the time when the world had obtained one head, and that head Rome; the very time wherein God deigned to be born of a virgin and dwell upon earth. To every single body there has been given a head; the whole world therefore also, which is called by the poet a great body, ought to be content with one temporal head. For every two-headed animal is monstrous; how much more horrible and hideous a portent must be a creature with a thousand different heads, biting and fighting against one another! If, however, it is necessary that there be more heads than one, it is nevertheless evident that there ought to be one to restrain all and preside over all, that so the peace of the whole body may abide unshaken. Assuredly both in heaven and in earth the sovereignty of one has always been best.'

Dante.

His passion for the heroism of Roman conquest and the ordered peace to which it brought the world, is the centre of Dante's political hopes: he is no more an exiled Ghibeline, but a patriot whose fervid imagination sees a nation arise regenerate at the touch of its rightful lord. Italy, the spoil of so many Teutonic conquerors, is the garden of the Empire which Henry is to redeem: Rome the mourning widow, whom Albert is denounced for neglecting q. Passing through purgatory, the poet sees Rudolf of Hapsburg seated gloomily apart, mourning

q 'Vieni a veder la tua Roma, che piagne
　　Vedova, sola, e dì e notte chiama:
　　" Cesare mio, ·perchè non m' accompagne?"'
　　　　　　　　　　Purgatorio, canto vi.

his sin in that he left unhealed the wounds of Italy [r]. In the deepest pit of hell's ninth circle lies Lucifer, huge, three-headed; in each mouth a sinner whom he crunches between his teeth, in one mouth Iscariot the traitor to Christ, in the others the two traitors to the first Emperor of Rome, Brutus and Cassius [s]. To multiply illustrations from other parts of the poem would be an endless task; for the idea is ever present in Dante's mind, and displays itself in a hundred unexpected forms. Virgil himself is selected to be the guide of the pilgrim through hell and purgatory, not so much as being the great poet of antiquity, as because he 'was born under Julius and lived beneath the good Augustus;' because he was divinely charged to sing of the Empire's earliest and brightest glories. Strange, that the shame of one age should be the glory of another. For Virgil's melancholy panegyrics upon the destroyer of the republic' are no more like Dante's appeals to the coming saviour of Italy than is Cæsar Octavianus to Henry count of Luxemburg.

Attitude of the Jurists.

The visionary zeal of the man of letters was seconded by the more sober devotion of the lawyer. Conqueror, theologian, and jurist, Justinian is a hero greater than either Julius or Constantine, for his enduring work bears him witness. Absolutism was the civilian's creed [t]: the phrases 'legibus solutus,' 'lex regia,' whatever else tended in the same direction, were taken to express the prerogative of him whose official style of Augustus, as well as the vernacular name of 'Kaiser,' designated the legitimate

---

[r] *Purgatorio*, canto vii.

[s] *Inferno*, canto xxxiv.

[t] Not that the doctors of the civil law were necessarily political partisans of the Emperors. Savigny says that there were on the contrary more Guelfs than Ghibelines among the jurists of Bologna.— *Roman Law in the Middle Ages*, vol. iii. p. 80.

successor of the compiler of the Corpus Juris. Since it was upon that legitimacy that his claim to be the fountain of law rested, no pains were spared to seek out and observe every custom and precedent by which old Rome seemed to be connected with her representative.

Of the many instances that might be collected, it would be tedious to enumerate more than a few. The offices of the imperial household, instituted by Constantine the Great, were attached to the noblest families of Germany. The Emperor and Empress, before their coronation at Rome, were lodged in the chambers called those of Augustus and Livia[u]; a bare sword was borne before them by the prætorian prefect; their processions were adorned by the standards, eagles, wolves and dragons, which had figured in the train of Hadrian or Theodosius[x]. The constant title of the Emperor himself, according to the style introduced by Probus, was 'semper Augustus,' or 'perpetuus Augustus,' which erring etymology translated 'at all times increaser of the Empire[y].' Edicts issued by a Franconian or Swabian sovereign were inserted as Novels[z] in the Corpus Juris, in the latest editions of which custom still allows them a place. The *pontificatus maximus* of his pagan predecessors was supposed to be preserved by the admission of each Emperor as a canon of St. Peter's at Rome and St. Mary's at Aachen[a]. Some-

[u] Cf. Palgrave, *Normandy and England*, vol. ii. (of Otto and Adelheid). The *Ordo Romanus* talks of a 'Camera Iuliæ' in the Lateran palace, reserved for the Empress.

[x] See notes to *Chron. Casin.* in Muratori, *S. R. I.* iv. 515.

[y] Zu aller Zeiten Mehrer des Reichs.

[z] *Novellæ Constitutiones.*

[a] Marquard Freher. The question whether the seven electors vote as *singuli* or as a *collegium*, is solved by shewing that they have stepped into the place of the senate and people of Rome, whose duty it was to choose the Emperor, though (it is naïvely added) the soldiers sometimes usurped it.— Peter de Andlo, *De Imperio Romano.*

times we even find him talking of his consulship[c]. Annalists invariably number the place of each sovereign from Augustus downwards[d]. The notion of an uninterrupted succession, which moves the stranger's wondering smile as he sees ranged round the magnificent Golden Hall of Augsburg the portraits of the Cæsars, laurelled, helmeted, and periwigged, from Julius the conqueror of Gaul to Joseph the partitioner of Poland, was to those generations not an article of faith only because its denial was inconceivable.

Reverence for ancient forms and phrases in the Middle Ages.

And all this historical antiquarianism, as one might call it, which gathers round the Empire, is but one instance, though the most striking, of that eager wish to cling to the old forms, use the old phrases, and preserve the old institutions to which the annals of mediæval Europe bear witness. It appears even in trivial expressions, as when a monkish chronicler says of evil bishops deposed, *Tribu moti sunt*, or talks of the 'senate and people of the Franks,' when he means a council of chiefs surrounded by a crowd of half-naked warriors. So throughout Europe charters and edicts were drawn up on Roman precedents ; the trade-guilds, though often traceable to a different source, represented the old *collegia ;* villenage was the offspring of the system of *coloni* under the later Empire. Even in remote Britain, the Teutonic invaders used Roman ensigns, and stamped their coins with Roman devices ; called themselves 'Basileis' and 'Augusti[e].' Especially did the

---

[c] Thus Charles, in a capitulary added to a revised edition of the Lombard law issued in A.D. 801, says, 'Anno consulatus nostri primo.' So Otto III calls himself 'Consul Senatus populique Romani.'

[d] Francis II, the last Emperor, was one hundred and twentieth from Augustus. Some chroniclers call Otto the Great Otto II, counting in Salvius Otho, the successor of Galba.

[e] See p. 45 and note to p. 143.

cities perpetuate Rome through her most lasting boon to the conquered, municipal self-government; those of later origin emulating in their adherence to antique style others who, like Nismes and Cologne, Zürich and Augsburg, could trace back their institutions to the *coloniæ* and *municipia* of the first centuries. On the walls and gates of hoary Nürnberg [f] the traveller still sees emblazoned the imperial eagle, with the words 'Senatus populusque Norimbergensis,' and is borne in thought from the quiet provincial town of to-day to the stirring republic of the middle ages: thence to the Forum and the Capitol of her greater prototype. For, in truth, through all that period which we call the Dark and Middle Ages, men's minds were possessed by the belief that all things continued as they were from the beginning, that no chasm never to be recrossed lay between them and that ancient world to which they had not ceased to look back. We who are centuries removed can see that there had passed a great and wonderful change upon thought, and art, and literature, and politics, and society itself : a change whose best illustration is to be found in the process whereby there arose out of the primitive basilica the Romanesque cathedral, and from it in turn the endless varieties of Gothic. But so gradual was the change that each generation felt it passing over them no more than a man feels that perpetual transformation by which his body is renewed from year to year; while the few who had learning enough to study antiquity through its contemporary records, were prevented by the utter want of criticism and of that which we call historical feeling, from seeing

---

[f] Nürnberg herself was not of Roman foundation. But this makes the imitation all the more curious. The fashion even passed from the cities to rural communities like some of the Swiss cantons. Thus we find 'Senatus populusque Uronensis.'

how prodigious was the contrast between themselves and those whom they admired. There is nothing more modern than the critical spirit which dwells upon the difference between the minds of men in one age and in another; which endeavours to make each age its own interpreter, and judge what it did or produced by a relative standard. Such a spirit was, before the last century or two, wholly foreign to art as well as to metaphysics. The converse and the parallel of the fashion of calling mediæval offices by Roman names, and supposing them therefore the same, is to be found in those old German pictures of the siege of Carthage or the battle between Porus and Alexander, where in the foreground two armies of knights, mailed and mounted, are charging each other like Crusaders, lance, in rest, while behind, through the smoke of cannon, loom out the Gothic spires and towers of the beleaguered city. And thus, when we remember that the notion of progress and development, and of change as the necessary condition thereof, was unwelcome or unknown in mediæval times, we may better understand, though we do not cease to wonder, how men, never doubting that the political system of antiquity had descended to them, modified indeed, yet in substance the same, should have believed that the Frank, the Saxon, and the Swabian ruled all Europe by a right which seems to us not less fantastic than that fabled charter whereby Alexander the Great [g] bequeathed his empire to the Slavic race for the love of Roxolana.

It is a part of that perpetual contradiction of which the history of the Middle Ages is full, that this belief had hardly any influence on practical politics. The more

[g] See Palgrave, *Normandy and England,* i. p. 379.

abjectly helpless the Emperor becomes, so much the more sonorous is the language in which the dignity of his crown is described. His power, we are told, is eternal, the provinces having resumed their allegiance after the barbarian irruptions[h]; it is incapable of diminution or injury: exemptions and grants by him, so far as they tend to limit his own prerogative, are invalid[i]: all Christendom is still of right subject to him, though it may contumaciously refuse obedience[k]. The sovereigns of Europe are solemnly warned that they are resisting the power ordained of God[l]. No laws can bind the Emperor, though he may choose to live according to them: no court can judge him, though he may condescend to be sued in his own: none may presume to arraign the

[h] Æneas Sylvius, *De Ortu et Authoritate Imperii Romani.*

[i] Thus some civilians held Constantine's Donation null; but the canonists, we are told, were clear as to its legality.

[k] 'Et idem dico de istis aliis regibus et principibus, qui negant se esse subditos regi Romanorum, ut rex Franciæ, Angliæ, et similes. Si enim fatentur ipsum esse Dominum universalem, licet ab illo universali domino se subtrahant ex privilegio vel ex præscriptione vel consimili, non ergo desunt esse cives Romani, per ea quæ dicta sunt. Et per hoc omnes gentes quæ obediunt S. matri ecclesiæ sunt de populo Romano. Et forte si quis diceret dominum Imperatorem non esse dominum et monarcham totius orbis, esset hæ-

reticus, quia diceret contra determinationem ecclesiæ et textum S. evangelii, dum dicit, "Exivit edictum a Cæsare Augusto ut describeretur universus orbis." Ita et recognovit Christus Imperatorem ut dominum.'—Bartolus, *Commentary on the Pandects*, xlviii. i. 24; *De Captivis et postliminio reversis.*

[l] Peter de Andlo, *multis locis* (see esp. cap. viii.), and other writings of the time. Cf. Dante's letter to Henry VII: 'Romanorum potestas nec metis Italiæ nec tricornis Siciliæ margine coarctatur. Nam etsi vim passa in angustum gubernacula sua contraxit undique, tamen de inviolabili iure fluctus Amphitritis attingens vix ab inutili unda Oceani se circumcingi dignatur. Scriptum est enim

"Nascetur pulchra Troianus origine Cæsar,
Imperium Oceano, famam qui terminet astris."'

So Fr. Zoannetus, in the sixteenth century, declares it to be a mortal sin to resist the Empire, as the power ordained of God.

conduct or question the motives of him who is answerable only to God[m]. So writes Æneas Sylvius, while Frederick the Third, chased from his capital by the Hungarians, is wandering from convent to convent, an imperial beggar ; while the princes, whom his subserviency to the Pope has driven into rebellion, are offering the imperial crown to Podiebrad the Bohemian king.

But the career of Henry the Seventh in Italy is the most remarkable illustration of the Emperor's position : and imperialist doctrines are set forth most strikingly in the treatise which the greatest spirit of the age wrote to herald the advent of that hero, the *De Monarchia* of Dante[n]. Rudolf, Adolf of Nassau, Albert of Hapsburg, none of them crossed the Alps or attempted to aid the Italian Ghibelines who battled away in the name of their throne. Concerned only to restore order and aggrandize his house, and thinking apparently that nothing more was to be made of the imperial crown, Rudolf was content never to receive it, and purchased the Pope's goodwill by surrendering his jurisdiction in the capital, and his claims over the bequest of the Countess Matilda. Henry the Luxemburger ventured on a bolder course ; urged perhaps only by his lofty and chivalrous spirit, perhaps in despair at effecting anything with his slender resources against the princes of Germany. Crossing from his Burgundian dominions with a scanty following of knights, and descending from the Cenis upon Turin, he found

---

[m] Æneas Sylvius Piccolomini (afterwards Pope Pius II), *De Ortu et Authoritate Imperii Romani.* Cf. Gerlach Buxtorff, *Dissertatio ad Auream Bullam.*

[n] It has hitherto been the com-mon opinion that the *De Monarchia* was written in the view of Henry's expedition. But latterly weighty reasons have been advanced for believing that its date must be placed some years later.

his prerogative higher in men's belief after sixty years of neglect than it had stood under the last Hohenstaufen. The cities of Lombardy opened their gates; Milan decreed a vast subsidy; Guelf and Ghibeline exiles alike were restored, and imperial vicars appointed everywhere : supported by the Avignonese pontiff, who dreaded the restless ambition of his French neighbour, king Philip IV, Henry had the interdict of the Church as well as the ban of the Empire at his command. But the illusion of success vanished as soon as men, recovering from their first impression, began to be again governed by their ordinary passions and interests, and not by an imaginative reverence for the glories of the past. Tumults and revolts broke out in Lombardy; at Rome the king of Naples held St. Peter's, and the coronation must take place in St. John Lateran, on the southern bank of the Tiber. The hostility of the Guelfic league, headed by the Florentines, Guelfs even against the Pope, obliged Henry to depart from his impartial and republican policy, and to purchase the aid of the Ghibeline chiefs by granting them the government of cities. With few troops, and encom- *Death of* passed by enemies, the heroic Emperor sustained an *Henry VII.* unequal struggle for a year longer, till, in A.D. 1313, he sank beneath the fevers of the deadly Tuscan summer. His German followers believed, nor has history wholly rejected the tale, that poison was given him by a Dominican monk, in sacramental wine.

Others after him descended from the Alps, but they *Later Em-* came, like Lewis the Fourth, Rupert, Sigismund, at the *perors in* behest of a faction, which found them useful tools for a *Italy.* time, then flung them away in scorn; or like Charles the Fourth and Frederick the Third, as the humble minions of a French or Italian priest. With Henry the Seventh

CHAP. XV.

ends the history of the Empire in Italy, and Dante's book is an epitaph instead of a prophecy. A sketch of its argument will convey a notion of the feelings with which the noblest Ghibelines fought, as well as of the spirit in which the Middle Age was accustomed to handle such subjects.

Dante's feelings and theories.

Weary of the endless strife of princes and cities, of the factions within every city against each other, seeing municipal freedom, the only mitigation of turbulence, vanish with the rise of domestic tyrants, Dante raises a passionate cry for some power to still the tempest, not to quench liberty or supersede local self-government, but to correct and moderate them, to restore unity and peace to hapless Italy. His reasoning is throughout closely syllogistic: he is alternately the jurist, the theologian, the scholastic metaphysician: the poet of the Divina Commedia is betrayed only by the compressed energy of diction, by his clear vision of the unseen, rarely by a glowing metaphor.

The 'De Monarchia.'

Monarchy is first proved to be the true and rightful form of government. Men's objects are best attained during universal peace: this is possible only under a monarch. And as he is the image of the Divine unity, so man is through him made one, and brought most near to God. There must, in every system of forces, be a 'primum mobile;' to be perfect, every organization must have a centre, into which all is gathered, by which all is controlled °. Justice is best secured by a supreme arbiter of disputes, himself unsolicited by ambition, since his dominion is already bounded only by ocean. Man is best and happiest when he is most free; to be free is to exist

---

° Suggesting the celestial hierarchies of Dionysius the Areopagite.

for one's own sake. To this grandest end does the monarch and he alone guide us; other forms of government are perverted [p], and exist for the benefit of some class; he seeks the good of all alike, being to that very end appointed [q].

Abstract arguments are then confirmed from history. Since the world began there has been but one period of perfect peace, and but one of perfect monarchy, that, namely, which existed at our Lord's birth, under the sceptre of Augustus; since then the heathen have raged, and the kings of the earth have stood up; they have set themselves against their Lord, and his anointed the Roman prince [r]. The universal dominion, the need for which has been thus established, is then proved to belong to the Romans. Justice is the will of God, a will to exalt Rome shewn through her whole history [s]. Her virtues deserved honour: Virgil is quoted to prove those of Æneas, who by descent and marriage was the heir of three continents: of Asia through Assaracus and Creusa; of Africa by Electra (mother of Dardanus and daughter of Atlas) and Dido; of Europe by Dardanus and Lavinia. God's favour was approved in the fall of the shields to Numa, in the miraculous deliverance of the capital from the Gauls, in the hailstorm after Cannæ. Justice is also the advantage of the state: that advantage was the constant object of the virtuous Cincinnatus, and the other heroes of the republic. They conquered the world for its own good, and

---

[p] Quoting Aristotle's *Politics*.

[q] 'Non enim cives propter consules nec gens propter regem, sed e converso consules propter cives, rex propter gentem.'

[r] 'Reges et principes in hoc unico concordantes, ut adversentur Domino suo et uncto suo Romano Principi,' having quoted 'Quare fremuerunt gentes.'

[s] Especially in the opportune death of Alexander the Great.

therefore justly, as Cicero ⸻ ; so that their sway was not so much 'imperium' a. patrocinium orbis terrarum.' Nature herself, the founta: ot all right, had, by their geographical position and by the gift of a genius so vigorous, marked them out for universal dominion :—

> 'Excudent alii spirantia mollius æra,
> Credo equidem : vivos ducent de marmore vultus ;
> Orabunt causas melius, cœlique meatus
> Describent radio, et surgentia sidera dicent :
> Tu regere imperio populos, Romane, memento ;
> Hæ tibi erunt artes ; pacisque imponere morem,
> Parcere subiectis, et debellare superbos.'

Finally, the right of war asserted, Christ's birth, and death under Pilate, ratified their government. For Christian doctrine requires that the procurator should have been a lawful judge [u], which he was not unless Tiberius was a lawful Emperor.

The relations of the imperial and papal power are then examined, and the passages of Scripture (tradition being rejected), to which the advocates of the Papacy appeal, are elaborately explained away. The argument from the sun and moon [x] does not hold, since both lights existed before man's creation, and at a time when, as still sinless, he needed no controlling powers. Else *accidentia* would

---

[t] Cic., *De Off.*, ii. 'Ita ut illud patrocinium orbis terrarum potius quam imperium poterat nominari.'

[u] 'Si Pilati imperium non de iure fuit, peccatum in Christo non fuit adeo punitum.'

[x] There is a curious seal of the Emperor Otto IV (figured in J. M. Heineccius, *De veteribus Germanorum atque aliarum nationum sigillis*), on which the sun and moon are represented over the head of the Emperor. Heineccius says he cannot

explain it, but there seems to be no reason why we should not take the device as typifying the accord of the spiritual and temporal powers which was brought about at the accession of Otto, the Guelfic leader, and the favoured candidate of Pope Innocent III.

The analogy between the lights of heaven and the princes of earth is one which mediæval writers are very fond of. It seems to have originated with Gregory VII.

have preceded *propria* in creation. The moon, too, does not receive her being nor all her light from the sun, but so much only as makes her more effective. So there is no reason why the temporal should not be aided in a corresponding measure by the spiritual authority. This difficult text disposed of, others fall more easily ; Levi and Judah, Samuel and Saul, the incense and gold offered by the Magi ʸ; the two swords, the power of binding and loosing given to Peter. Constantine's donation was illegal : no single Emperor nor Pope can disturb the everlasting foundations of their respective thrones : the one had no right to bestow, nor the other to receive, such a gift. Leo the Third gave the Empire to Charles wrongfully : ' *usurpatio iuris non facit ius.*' It is alleged that all things of one kind are reducible to one individual, and so all men to the Pope. But Emperor and Pope differ in kind, and so far as they are men, are reducible only to God, on whom the Empire immediately depends ; for it existed before Peter's see, and was recognized by Paul when he appealed to Cæsar. The temporal power of the Papacy can have been given neither by natural law, nor divine ordinance, nor universal consent : nay, it is against its own Form and Essence, the life of Christ, who said, ' My kingdom is not of this world.'

Man's nature is twofold, corruptible and incorruptible : he has therefore two ends, active virtue on earth, and the enjoyment of the sight of God hereafter ; the one to be attained by practice conformed to the precepts of philosophy, the other by the theological virtues. Hence two guides are needed, the pontiff and the Emperor, the

---

ʸ Typifying the spiritual and temporal powers. Dante meets this by distinguishing the homage paid to Christ from that which his Vicar can rightfully demand.

latter of whom, in order that he may direct mankind in accordance with the teachings of philosophy to temporal blessedness, must preserve universal peace in the world. Thus are the two powers equally ordained of God, and the Emperor, though supreme in all that pertains to the secular world, is in some things dependent on the pontiff, since earthly happiness is subordinate to eternal. ' Let Cæsar, therefore, shew towards Peter the reverence wherewith a firstborn son honours his father, that, being illumined by the light of his paternal favour, he may the more excellently shine forth upon the whole world, to the rule of which he has been appointed by Him alone who is of all things, both spiritual and temporal, the King and Governor.' So ends the treatise.

Dante's arguments are not stranger than his omissions. No suspicion is breathed against Constantine's donation; no proof is adduced, for no doubt is felt, that the Empire of Henry the Seventh is the legitimate continuation of that which had been swayed by Augustus and Justinian. Yet Henry was a German, sprung from Rome's barbarian foes, the elected of those who had neither part nor share in Italy and her capital.

CHAPTER XVI.

THE CITY OF ROME IN THE MIDDLE AGES.

'It is related,' says Sozomen in the ninth book of his Ecclesiastical History, 'that when Alaric was hastening against Rome, a holy monk of Italy admonished him to spare the city, and not to make himself the cause of such fearful ills. But Alaric answered, "It is not of my own will that I do this; there is One who forces me on, and will not let me rest, bidding me spoil Rome[a]."'

Towards the close of the tenth century the Bohemian Woitech, famous in after legend as St. Adalbert, forsook his bishopric of Prague to journey into Italy, and settled himself in the Roman monastery of Sant' Alessio. After some few years passed there in religious solitude, he was summoned back to resume the duties of his see, and laboured for awhile among his half-savage countrymen. Soon, however, the old longing came over him: he re-sought his cell upon the brow of the Aventine, and there, wandering among the ancient shrines, and taking on himself the menial offices of the convent, he abode happily for a space. At length the reproaches of his metropolitan, the archbishop of Mentz, and the express commands of

---

[a] Hist. Eccl. l. ix. c. 6: τὸν δὲ φάναι, ὡς οὐχ ἑκὼν τάδε ἐπιχειρεῖ, ἀλλά τις συνεχῶς ἐνοχλῶν αὐτὸν βιάζεται, καὶ ἐπιτάττει τὴν Ῥώμην πορθεῖν.

Pope Gregory the Fifth, drove him back over the Alps, and he set off in the train of Otto the Third, lamenting, says his biographer, that he should no more enjoy his beloved quiet in the mother of martyrs, the home of the Apostles, golden Rome. A few months later he died a martyr among the pagan Lithuanians of the Baltic[b].

Nearly four hundred years later, and nine hundred after the time of Alaric, Francis Petrarch writes thus to his friend John Colonna :—

'Thinkest thou not that I long to see that city to which there has never been any like nor ever shall be ; which even an enemy called a city of kings ; of whose people it hath been written, "Great is the valour of the Roman people, great and terrible their name ;" concerning whose unexampled glory and incomparable empire, which was, and is, and is to be, divine prophets have sung ; where are the tombs of the apostles and martyrs and the bodies of so many thousands of the saints of Christ[c] ?'

It was the same irresistible impulse that drew the warrior, the monk, and the scholar towards the mystical city which was to mediæval Europe more than Delphi had been to the Greek or Mecca to the Islamite, the Jerusalem of Christianity, the city which had once ruled the earth, and now ruled the world of disembodied spirits[d]. For

---

[b] See the two Lives of St. Adalbert in Pertz, *M. G. H.*, iv., evidently compiled soon after his death.

[c] Another letter of Petrarch's to John Colonna, written immediately after his arrival in the city, deserves to be quoted, it is so like what a stranger would now write off after his first day in Rome :—
'In præsens nihil est quod incho-are ausim, miraculo rerum tantarum et stuporis mole obrutus . . . præsentia vero, mirum dictu, nihil imminuit sed auxit omnia : vere maior fuit Roma maioresque sunt reliquiæ quam rebar : iam non orbem ab hac urbe domitum sed tam sero domitum miror. Vale.'

[d] The idea of the continuance of the sway of Rome under a new character is one which mediæval

there was then, as there is now, something in Rome to attract men of every class. The devout pilgrim came to pray at the shrine of the Prince of the Apostles, too happy if he could carry back to his monastery in the forests of Saxony or by the bleak Atlantic shore the bone of some holy martyr; the lover of learning and poetry dreamed of Virgil and Cicero among the shattered columns of the Forum; the Germanic kings, in spite of pestilence, treachery and seditions, came with their hosts to seek in the ancient capital of the world the fountain of temporal dominion. Nor has the spell yet wholly lost its power. To half the Christian nations Rome is the metropolis of religion, to all the metropolis of art. In her streets, and hers alone among the cities of the world, may every form of human speech be heard: she is more glorious in her decay and desolation than the stateliest seats of modern power.

But while men thought thus of Rome, what was Rome herself?

The modern traveller, after his first few days in Rome, when he has looked out upon the Campagna from the summit of St. Peter's, paced the chilly corridors of the Vatican, a d mused under the echoing dome of the Pantheon, when he has passed in review the monuments of regal and republican and papal Rome, begins to seek for some relics of the twelve hundred years that lie between Constantine and Pope Julius the Second. 'Where,' he asks, 'is the Rome of the Middle Ages, the Rome of Alberic and Hildebrand and Rienzi? the Rome which

writers delight to illustrate. In Appendix, Note D, there is quoted as a specimen a poem upon Rome, by Hildebert (bishop of Le Mans, and afterwards archbishop of Tours), written in the beginning of the twelfth century.

dug the graves of so many Teutonic hosts; whither the pilgrims flocked; whence came the commands at which kings bowed? Where are the memorials of the brightest age of Christian architecture, the age which reared Cologne and Rheims and Westminster, which gave to Italy the cathedrals of Tuscany and the wave-washed palaces of Venice?'

To this question there is no answer. Rome, the mother of the arts, has scarcely a building to commemorate those times, for to her they were times of turmoil and misery, times in which the shame of the present was embittered by recollections of a brighter past. Nevertheless a minute scrutiny may still discover, hidden in dark corners or disguised under an unbecoming modern dress, much that carries us back to the mediæval town, and helps us to realize its social and political condition. Therefore a brief notice of the state of Rome during the Middle Ages, with especial reference to those monuments which the visitor may still examine for himself, may not be without its use, and is at any rate no unfitting pendant to an account of the institution which drew from the city its name and its magnificent pretensions. Moreover, as will appear more fully in the sequel, the history of the Roman people is an instructive illustration of the influence of those ideas upon which the Empire itself rested, as well in their weakness as in their strength [e].

It is not from her capture by Alaric, nor even from the more destructive ravages of the Vandal Genseric, that the

---

[e] In writing this chapter I have derived much assistance from the admirable work of Ferdinand Gregorovius, *Geschichte der Stadt Rom in Mittelalter*. Unfortunately no English translation of it exists; but I am informed by the author that one is likely ere long to appear.

material and social ruin of Rome must be dated, but rather from the repeated sieges which she sustained in the war of Belisarius with the Ostrogoths. This struggle however, long and exhausting as it was, would not have proved so fatal had the previous condition of the city been sound and healthy. Her wealth and population in the middle of the fifth century were probably little inferior to what they had been in the most prosperous days of the imperial government. But this wealth was entirely gathered into the hands of a small and effeminate aristocracy. The crowd that filled her streets was composed partly of poor and idle freemen, unaccustomed to arms and debarred from political rights; partly of a far more numerous herd of slaves, gathered from all parts of the world, and morally even lower than their masters. There was no middle class, and no system of municipal institutions, for although the senate and consuls with many of the lesser magistracies continued to exist, they had for centuries enjoyed no effective power, and were nowise fitted to lead and rule the people. Hence it was that when the Gothic war and the subsequent inroads of the Lombards had reduced the great families to beggary, the framework of society dissolved and could not be replaced. In a state rotten to the core there was no vital force left for reconstruction. The old forms of political activity had been too long dead to be recalled to life: the people wanted the moral force to produce new ones, and all the authority that could be said to exist in the midst of anarchy tended to centre itself in the chief of the new religious society.

So far Rome's condition was like that of the other great towns of Italy and Gaul. But in two points her case differed from theirs, and to these the difference of

T

CHAP. XVI.
*Peculiari-
ties in the
position
of Rome.*

her after fortunes may be traced. Her bishop had no temporal potentate to overshadow his dignity or check his ambition, for the vicar of the Eastern court lived far away at Ravenna, and seldom interfered except to ratify a papal election or punish a more than commonly outrageous sedition. Her population received an all but imperceptible infusion of that Teutonic blood and those Teutonic customs by whose stern discipline the inhabitants of northern Italy were in the end renovated. Everywhere the old institutions had perished of decay: in Rome alone there was nothing except the ecclesiastical system out of which new ones could arise. Her condition was therefore the most pitiable in which a community can find itself, one of struggle without purpose or progress. The citizens were divided into three orders: the military class, including what was left of the ancient aristocracy; the clergy, a host of priests, monks and nuns, attached to the countless churches and convents; and the people or *plebs*, as they are called, a poverty-stricken rabble without trade, without industry, without any municipal organization to bind them together. Of these two latter classes the Pope was the natural leader, the first was divided into factions headed by some three or four of the great families, whose quarrels kept the town in incessant bloodshed. The internal history of Rome from the sixth to the twelfth century is an obscure and tedious record of the contest of these factions with each other, and of the aristocracy as a whole with the slowly growing power of the Church.

*Her condi-
tion in the
ninth and
tenth cen-
turies.*

The revolt of the Romans from the Iconoclastic Emperors of the East, followed as it was by the reception of the Franks as patricians and emperors, is an event of the highest importance in the history of Italy and of the popedom. In the domestic constitution of Rome it made

little change. With the instinct of a profound genius,
Charles the Great saw that Rome, though it might be
ostensibly the capital, could not be the real centre of his
dominions. He continued to reside in Germany, and did
not even build a palace at Rome. For a time the awe of
his power, the presence of his *missus* or lieutenant, and
the occasional visits of his successors Lothar and Lewis II
to the city, repressed her internal disorders. But after
the death of the prince last named, and still more after
the dissolution of the Carolingian Empire itself, Rome
relapsed into a state of profligacy and barbarism to which,
even in that age, Europe supplied no parallel, a barbarism
which had inherited all the vices of civilization without
any of its virtues. The papal office in particular seems
to have lost its religious character, as it had certainly lost
all claim to moral purity. For more than a century the
chief priest of Christendom was no more than a tool of
some ferocious faction among the nobles. Criminal
means had raised him to the throne; violence, sometimes
going the length of mutilation or murder, deprived him of
it. The marvel is, a marvel in which papal historians
have not unnaturally discovered a miracle, that after
sinking so low, the Papacy should ever have risen again.
Its rescue and exaltation to the pinnacle of glory was
accomplished not by the Romans but by the efforts of
the Transalpine Church, aiding and prompting the Saxon
and Franconian Emperors. Yet even the religious reform
did not abate intestine turmoil, and it was not till the
twelfth century that a new spirit began to work in politics,
which ennobled if it could not heal the sufferings of the
Roman people.

Ever since the time of Alberic their pride had revolted
against the haughty behaviour of the Teutonic emperors.

T 2

CHAP. XVI.

Growth of a republican feeling: hostility to the Popes.

From still earlier times they had been jealous of sacerdotal authority, and now watched with alarm the rapid extension of its influence. The events of the twelfth century gave these feelings a definite direction. It was the time of the struggle of the Investitures, in which Hildebrand and his disciples had been striving to draw all the things of this world as well as of the next into their grasp. It was the era of the revived study of Roman law, by which alone the extravagant pretensions of the decretalists could be resisted. The Lombard and Tuscan towns had become flourishing municipalities, independent of their bishops, and at open war with their Emperor.

Arnold of Brescia.

While all these things were stirring the minds of the Romans, Arnold of Brescia came preaching reform, denouncing the corrupt life of the clergy, not perhaps, like some others of the so-called schismatics of his time, denying the need of a sacerdotal order, but at any rate urging its restriction to purely spiritual duties. On the minds of the Romans such teaching fell like the spark upon dry grass; they threw off the yoke of the Pope[f], drove out the imperial prefect, reconstituted the senate and the equestrian order, appointed consuls, struck their own coins, and professed to treat the German Emperors as their nominees and dependants. To have successfully imitated the republican constitution of the cities of northern Italy would have been much, but with this they were not content. Knowing in a vague ignorant way that there had been a Roman republic before there was a Roman empire, they fed their vanity with visions of a

---

[f] Republican forms of some sort had existed before Arnold's arrival, but we hear the name of no other leader mentioned; and doubtless it was by him chiefly that the spirit of hostility to the clerical power was infused into the minds of the Romans.

renewal of all their ancient forms, and saw in fancy their senate and people sitting again upon the Seven Hills and ruling over the kings of the earth. Stepping, as it were, into the arena where Pope and Emperor were contending for the headship of the world, they rejected the one as a priest, and declaring the other to be only their creature, they claimed as theirs the true and lawful inheritance of the world-dominion which their ancestors had won. Antiquity was in one sense on their side, and to us now it seems less strange that the Roman people should aspire to rule the earth than that a German barbarian should rule it in their name. But practically the scheme was absurd, and could not maintain itself against any serious opposition. As a modern historian aptly expresses it, 'they were setting up ruins:' they might as well have raised the broken columns that strewed their Forum and hoped to rear out of them a strong and stately temple. The reverence which the men of the Middle Ages felt for Rome was given altogether to the name and to the place, nowise to the people. As for power, they had none: so far from holding Italy in subjection, they could scarcely maintain themselves against the hostility of Tusculum. But it would have been well worth the while of the Teutonic Emperors to have made the Romans their allies, and bridled by their help the temporal ambition of the Popes. The offer was actually made to them, first to Conrad the Third, who seems to have taken no notice of it; and afterwards, as has been already stated, to Frederick the First, who repelled in the most contumelious fashion the envoys of the senate. Hating and fearing the Pope, he always respected him: towards the Romans he felt all the contempt of a feudal king for burghers, and of a German warrior for Italians. At the demand of

CHAP. XVI.

Short-sighted policy of the Emperors.

Pope Hadrian, whose foresight thought' no heresy so dangerous as one which threatened the authority of the clergy, Arnold of Brescia was seized by the imperial prefect, put to death, and his ashes cast into the Tiber, lest the people should treasure them up as relics. But the martyrdom of their leader did not quench the hopes of his followers. The republican constitution continued to exist, and rose from time to time, during the weakness or the absence of the Popes, into a brief and fitful activity[g]. Once awakened, the idea, seductive at once to the imagination of the scholar and the vanity of the Roman citizen, could not wholly disappear, and two centuries after Arnold's time it found a more brilliant if less disinterested exponent in the tribune Nicholas Rienzi.

Character and career of the tribune Rienzi.

The career of this singular personage is misunderstood by those who suppose him to have been possessed of profound political insight, a republican on modern principles. He was indeed, despite his overweening conceit, and what seems to us his charlatanry, both a patriot and a man of genius, in temperament a poet, filled with soaring ideas. But those ideas, although dressed out in gaudier colours by his lively fancy, were after all only the old ones, memories of the long-faded glories of the heathen republic, and a series of scornful contrasts levelled at her present oppressors, both of them shewing no vista of future peace except through the revival of those ancient names to which there were no things to correspond. It

[g] The series of papal coins is interrupted (with one or two slight exceptions) from A.D. 984 (not long after the time of Alberic) to A.D. 1304. In their place we meet with various coins struck by the municipal authorities, some of which bear on the obverse the head of the Apostle Peter, with the legend Roman. Pricipe: on the reverse the head of the Apostle Paul, legend, Senat. Popul. Q. R. Gregorovius, *ut supra.*

was by declaiming on old texts and displaying old monuments that the tribune enlisted the support of the Roman populace, not by any appeal to democratic principles; and the whole of his acts and plans, though they astonished men by their boldness, do not seem to have been regarded as novel or impracticable [h]. In the breasts of men like Petrarch, who loved Rome even more than they hated her people, the enthusiasm of Rienzi found a sympathetic echo: others scorned and denounced him as an upstart, a demagogue, and a rebel. Both friends and enemies seem to have comprehended and regarded as natural his feelings and designs, which were altogether those of his age. Being, however, a mere matter of imagination, not of reason, having no anchor, so to speak, in realities, no true relation to the world as it then stood, these schemes of republican revival were as transient and unstable as they were quick of growth and gay of colour. As the authority of the Popes became consolidated, and free municipalities disappeared elsewhere throughout Italy, the dream of a renovated Rome at length withered up and fell and died. Its last struggle was made in the conspiracy of Stephen Porcaro, in the time of Pope Nicholas the Fifth; and from that time onward there was no question of the supremacy of the bishop within his holy city.

[h] Rienzi called himself Augustus as well as tribune; 'tribuno Augusto de Roma.' (He pretended, or his friends pretended for him—it was at any rate believed—that he was an illegitimate son of the Emperor Henry the Seventh) He cited, on his appointment, the Pope and cardinals to appear before the people of Rome and give an account of their conduct; and after them the Emperor. 'Ancora citao lo Bavaro (Lewis the Fourth). Puoi citao li elettori de lo imperio in Alemagna, e disse "Voglio vedere che rascione haco nella elettione," che trovasse scritto che passato alcuno tempo la elettione recadeva a li Romani.'—*Vita di Cola di Rienzi*, c. xxvi (written by a contemporary). I give the spelling as it stands in Muratori's edition.

Causes of the failure of the struggle for independence.

It is never without a certain regret that we watch the disappearance of a belief, however illusive, around which the love and reverence for mankind once clung. But this illusion need be the less regretted that it had only the feeblest influence for good on the state of mediæval Rome. During the three centuries that lie between Arnold of Brescia and Porcaro, the disorders of Rome were hardly less violent than they had been in the Dark Ages, and to all appearance worse than those of any other European city. There was a want not only of fixed authority, but of those elements of social stability which the other cities of Italy possessed. In the greater republics of Lombardy and Tuscany the bulk of the population were artizans, hard working orderly people; while above them stood a prosperous middle class, engaged mostly in commerce, and having in their system of trade-guilds an organization both firm and flexible. It was by foreign trade that Genoa, Venice, and Pisa became great, as it was the wealth acquired by manufacturing industry that enabled Milan and Florence to overcome and incorporate the territorial aristocracies which surrounded them.

Rome possessed neither source of riches. She was ill-placed for trade; having no market she produced no goods to be disposed of, and the unhealthiness which long neglect had brought upon her Campagna made its fertility unavailable. Already she stood as she stands now, lonely and isolated, a desert at her very gates. As there was no industry, so there was nothing that deserved to be called a citizen class. The people were a mere rabble, prompt to follow the demagogue who flattered their vanity, prompter still to desert him in the hour of danger. Superstition was with them a matter of national

Internal condition of the city. The people.

pride, but they lived too near sacred things to feel much reverence for them: they ill-treated the Pope and fleeced the pilgrims who crowded to their shrines: they were probably the only community in Europe who sent no recruit to the armies of the Cross. Priests, monks, and all the nondescript hangers on of an ecclesiastical court formed a large part of the population; while of the rest many were supported in a state of half mendicancy by the countless religious foundations, themselves enriched by the gifts or the plunder of Latin Christendom. The noble families were numerous, powerful, ferocious; they were surrounded by bands of unruly retainers, and waged a constant war against each other from their castles in the adjoining country or in the streets of the city itself. Had things been left to take their natural course, one of these families, the Colonna, for instance, or the Orsini, would probably have ended by overcoming its rivals, and have established, as was the case in the republics of Romagna and Tuscany, a 'signoria' or local tyranny, like those which had once prevailed in the cities of Greece. But the presence of the sacerdotal power, as it had hindered the growth of feudalism, so also it stood in the way of such a development as this, and in so far aggravated the confusion of the city. Although the Pope was not as yet recognized as legitimate sovereign, he was not only the most considerable person in Rome, but the only one whose authority had anything of an official character. But the reign of each pontiff was short; he had no military force, he was frequently absent from his see. He was, moreover, very often a member of one of the great families, and, as such, no better than a faction leader at home, while venerated by the rest of Europe as the universal priest.

The nobility.

The bishop.

It remains only to speak of the person who should have been to Rome what the national king was to the cities of France, or England, or Germany, that is to say, of the Emperor. As has been said already, his power was a mere chimera, chiefly important as furnishing a pretext to the Colonna and other Ghibeline chieftains for their opposition to the papal party. Even his abstract rights were matter of controversy. The Popes, whose predecessors had been content to govern as the lieutenants of Charles and Otto, now maintained that Rome as a spiritual city could not be subject to any temporal jurisdiction, and that she was therefore no part of the Roman Empire, though at the same time its capital. Not only, it was urged, had Constantine yielded up Rome to Sylvester and his successors, Lothar the Saxon had at his coronation formally renounced his sovereignty by doing homage to the pontiff and receiving the crown as his vassal. The Popes felt then as they feel now, that their dignity and influence would suffer if they should even appear to admit in their place of residence the jurisdiction of a civil potentate, and although they could not secure their own authority, they were at least able to exclude any other. Hence it was that they were so uneasy whenever an Emperor came to them to be crowned, that they raised up difficulties in his path, and endeavoured to be rid of him

as soon as possible. And here something must be said of the programme, as one may call it, of these imperial visits to Rome, and of the marks of their presence which the Germans left behind them, remembering always that after the time of Frederick the Second it was rather the exception than the rule for an Emperor to be crowned in his capital at all.

The traveller who enters Rome now, if he comes, as he

most commonly does, by way of Civita Vecchia, slips in by the railway before he is aware, is huddled into a vehicle at the terminus, and set down at his hotel in the middle of the modern town before he has seen anything at all. If he comes overland from Tuscany along the bleak road that passes near Veii and crosses the Milvian bridge, he has indeed from the slopes of the Ciminian range a splendid prospect of the sea-like Campagna, girdled in by glittering hills, but of the city he sees no sign, save the pinnacle of St. Peter's, until he is within the walls. Far otherwise was it in the Middle Ages. Then travellers of every grade, from the humble pilgrim to the new-made archbishop who came in the pomp of a lengthy train to receive from the Pope the pallium of his office, approached from the north or north-east side; following a track along the hilly ground on the Tuscan side of the Tiber until they halted on the brow of Monte Mario [i]—the Mount of Joy—and saw the city of their solemnities lie spread before them, from the great pile of the Lateran far away upon the Cœlian hill, to the basilica of St. Peter's at their feet. They saw it not, as now, a sea of billowy cupolas, but a mass of low red-roofed houses, varied by tall brick towers, and at rarer intervals by masses of ancient ruin, then larger far than now; while over all rose those two monuments of the best of the heathen Emperors, monuments that still look down, serenely changeless, on the armies of new nations and the festivals of a new religion—the columns of Marcus Aurelius and Trajan.

Their approach.

---

[i] The Germans called this hill, which is the highest in or near Rome, conspicuous from a beautiful group of stone-pines upon its brow, Mons Gaudii; the origin of the Italian name, Monte Mario, is not known, unless it be, as some think, a corruption of Mons Malus.

It was on this hill that Otto the Third hanged Crescentius and his followers.

Their entrance.

From Monte Mario the Teutonic host descended, when they had paid their orisons, into the Neronian field, the piece of flat land that lies outside the gate of St. Angelo. Here it was the custom for the elders of the Romans to meet the elected Emperor, present their charters for confirmation, and receive his oath to preserve their good customs[j]. Then a procession was formed : the priests and monks, who had come out with hymns to greet the Emperor, led the way; the knights and soldiers of Rome, such as they were, came next; then the monarch, followed by a long array of Transalpine chivalry. Passing into the city they advanced to St. Peter's, where the Pope, surrounded by his clergy, stood on the great staircase of the basilica to welcome and bless the Roman king. On the next day came the coronation, with ceremonies too elaborate for description[k], ceremonies which, we may well believe, were seldom duly completed. Far more usual were other rites, of which the book of ritual makes no mention, unless they are to be counted among the 'good customs of the Romans;' the clang of war bells, the battle cry of German and Italian combatants. The Pope, when he could not keep the Emperor from entering Rome, required him to leave the bulk of his host without the walls, and if foiled in this, sought his safety in raising up plots and seditions against his too powerful friend. The Roman

Hostility of Pope and people to the Germans.

[j] I quote this from the *Ordo Romanus* as it stands in Muratori's third Dissertation in the *Antiquitates Italiae medii aevi.*

[k] Great stress was laid on one part of the procedure,—the holding by the Emperor of the Pope's stirrup for him to mount, and the leading of his palfrey for some distance. Frederick Barbarossa's omission of this mark of respect when Pope Hadrian IV met him on his way to Rome, had nearly caused a breach between the two potentates, Hadrian absolutely refusing the kiss of peace until Frederick should have gone through the form, which he was at last forced to do in a somewhat ignominious way.

people, on the other hand, violent as they often were against the Pope, felt nevertheless a sort of national pride in him. Very different were their feelings towards the Teutonic chieftain, who came from a far land to receive in their city, yet without thanking them for it, the ensign of a power which the prowess of their forefathers had won. Despoiled of their ancient right to choose the universal bishop, they clung all the more desperately to the belief that it was they who chose the universal prince ; and were mortified afresh when each successive sovereign contemptuously scouted their claims, and paraded before their eyes his rude barbarian cavalry. Thus it was that a Roman sedition was the all but invariable accompaniment of a Roman coronation. The three revolts against Otto the Great have been already described. His grandson Otto the Third, in spite of his passionate fondness for the city, was met by the same faithlessness and hatred, and departed at last in despair at the failure of his attempts at conciliation[1]. A century afterwards Henry the Fifth's coronation produced violent tumults, which ended in his seizing the Pope and cardinals in St. Peter's, and keeping them prisoners till they submitted to his terms. Remembering this, Pope Hadrian the Fourth would fain have forced the troops of Frederick Barbarossa to remain without the walls, but the

[1] A remarkable speech of expostulation made by Otto III to the Roman people (after one of their revolts) from the tower of his house on the Aventine has been preserved to us. It begins thus : ' Vosne estis mei Romani ? Propter vos quidem meam patriam, propinquos quoque reliqui; amore vestro Saxones et cunctos Theotiscos, sanguinem meum, proieci ; vos in remotas partes imperii nostri adduxi, quo patres vestri cum orbem ditione premerent numquam pedem posuerunt ; scilicet ut nomen vestrum et gloriam ad fines usque dilatarem ; vos filios adoptavi: vos cunctis prætuli.'— *Vita S. Bernwardi ;* in Pertz, *M. G. H.,* t. iv.

(It is from this form ' Theotiscus ' that the Italian ' Tedesco ' seems to have been derived.)

rapidity of their movements disconcerted his plans and anticipated the resistance of the Roman populace. Having established himself in the Leonine city [m], Frederick barricaded the bridge over the Tiber, and was duly crowned in St. Peter's. But the rite was scarcely finished when the Romans, who had assembled in arms on the Capitol, dashed over the bridge, fell upon the Germans, and were with difficulty repulsed by the personal efforts of Frederick. Into the city he did not venture to pursue them, nor was he at any period of his reign able to make himself master of the whole of it. Finding themselves similarly baffled, his successors at last accepted their position, and were content to take the crown on the Pope's conditions and depart without further question.

Memorials of the Germanic Emperors in Rome.

Coming so seldom and remaining for so short a time, it is not wonderful that the Teutonic Emperors should, in the seven centuries from Charles the Great to Charles the Fifth, have left fewer marks of their presence in Rome than Titus or Hadrian alone have done; fewer and less considerable even than those which tradition attributes to those whom it calls Servius Tullius and the elder Tarquin. Those monuments which do exist are just sufficient to make the absence of all others more conspicuous. The

Of Otto the Third.

most important dates from the time of Otto the Third, the only Emperor who attempted to make Rome his permanent residence. Of the palace, probably nothing more than a tower, which he built on the Aventine, no trace has been discovered; but the church, founded by him to receive the ashes of his friend the martyred St. Adalbert, may still be seen upon the island in the Tiber. Having

[m] The Leonine city, so called from Pope Leo IV, lay between the Vatican and St. Peter's and the river.

received from Benevento relics suppósed to be those of Bartholomew the Apostle [n], it became dedicated to that saint, and is now the church of San Bartolommeo in Isola, whose quaintly picturesque bell-tower of red brick, now grey with extreme age, looks out from among the orange trees of a convent garden over the swift-eddying yellow waters of the Tiber.

Otto the Second, son of Otto the Great, died at Rome, and lies buried in the crypt of St. Peter's, the only Emperor who has found a resting-place among the graves of the Popes [o]. His tomb is not far from that of his nephew Pope Gregory the Fifth: it is a plain one of roughly chiselled marble. The lid of the superb porphyry sarcophagus in which he lay for a time now serves as the great font of St. Peter's, and may be seen in the baptismal chapel, on the left of the entrance of the church, not far from the tombs of the Stuarts. Last of all must be mentioned a curious relic of the Emperor Frederick the Second, the prince whom of all others one would least expect to see honoured in the city of his foes. It is an inscription in the palace of the Conservators upon the Capitoline hill, built into the wall of the great staircase, and relates the victory of Frederick's army over the

---

[n] It would seem that Otto was deceived, and that in reality they are the bones of St. Paulinus of Nola.

[o] The only other of the Teutonic Emperors buried in Italy were, so far as I know, Lewis the Second (whose tomb, with an inscription commemorating his exploits, is built into the wall of the north aisle of the famous church of S. Ambrose at Milan), Henry the Sixth and Frederick the Second, who lie at Palermo, Conrad IV, buried at Foggia, and Henry the Seventh. whose sarcophagus may be seen in the Campo Santo of Pisa, a city always conspicuous for her zeal on the imperial side.

Six Emperors lie buried at Speyer, three or four at Prague, two at Aachen, two at Bamberg, one at Innsbruck, one at Magdeburg, one at Quedlinburg, two at Munich, and most of the later ones at Vienna.

Milanese, and the capture of the carroccio [p] of the rebel city, which he sends as a trophy to his faithful Romans. These are all or nearly all the traces of her Teutonic lords that Rome has preserved till now. Pictures indeed there are in abundance, from the mosaic of the Scala Santa at the Lateran [q] and the curious frescoes in the church of Santi Quattro Incoronati [r], down to the paintings of the Sistine antechapel and the Stanze of Raphael in the Vatican, where the triumphs of the Popedom over all its foes are set forth with matchless art and equally matchless unveracity. But these are mostly long subsequent to the events they describe, and these all the world knows.

Associations of the highest interest would have attached to the churches in which the imperial coronation was performed—a ceremony which, whether we regard the dignity of the performers or the splendour of the adjuncts, was probably the most imposing that modern Europe has known. But old St. Peter's disappeared in the end of the fifteenth century, not long after the last Roman coronation, that of Frederick the Third, while the basilica of St. John Lateran, in which Lothar the Saxon and Henry the Seventh were crowned, has been so wofully modernized that we can hardly figure it to ourselves as the same building [s].

[p] See note 8, p. 178.

[q] See p. 117.

[r] These highly curious frescoes are in the chapel of St. Sylvester attached to the very ancient church of Quattro Santi on the Cœlian hill, and are supposed to have been executed in the time of Pope Innocent III. They represent scenes in the life of the Saint, more particularly the making of the famous donation to him by Constantine, who submissively holds the bridle of his palfrey.

[s] The last imperial coronation, that of Charles the Fifth, took place in the church of St. Petronius at Bologna, Pope Clement VII being unwilling to receive Charles in Rome. It is a grand church, but the choir, where the ceremony took place, seems to have been 'restored,' that is to say modernized, since Charles' time.

Bearing in mind what was the social condition of Rome during the middle ages, it becomes easier to understand the architectural barrenness which at first excites the visitor's surprise. Rome had no temporal sovereign, and there were therefore only two classes who could build at all, the nobles and the clergy. Of these, the former had seldom the wealth, and never the taste, which would have enabled them to construct palaces graceful as the Venetian or massively grand as the Florentine and Genoese. Moreover, the constant practice of domestic war made defence the first object of a house, beauty and convenience the second. The nobility, therefore, either adapted ancient edifices to their purpose or built out of their materials those huge square towers of brick, a few of which still frown over the narrow streets in the older parts of Rome. We may judge of their number from the statement that the senator Brancaleone destroyed one hundred and forty of them. With perhaps no more than one exception, that of the so-called House of Rienzi, these towers are the only domestic buildings in the city older than the middle of the fifteenth century. The vast palaces to which strangers now flock for the sake of the picture galleries they contain, have been most of them erected in the sixteenth or seventeenth centuries, some even later. Among the earliest is that Palazzo Cenci [u], whose gloomy low-browed arch so powerfully affected the imagination of Shelley.

It was no want of wealth that hampered the architectural efforts of the clergy, for vast revenues flowed in upon them from every corner of Christendom. A good

CHAP. XVI.
Causes of the want of mediaeval monuments in Rome.

Barbarism of the aristocracy.

[u] The name of Cenci is a very old one at Rome: it is supposed to be an abbreviation of Crescentius. We hear in the eleventh century of a certain Cencius, who on one occasion made Gregory VII prisoner.

U

Ambition, weakness, and corruption of the clergy.

deal was actually spent upon the erection or repairs of churches and convents, although with a less liberal hand than that of such great Transalpine prelates as Hugh of Lincoln or Conrad of Cologne. But the Popes always needed money for their projects of ambition, and in times when disorder or corruption were at their height the work of building stopped altogether. Thus it was that after the time of the Carolingians scarcely a church was erected until the beginning of the twelfth century, when the reforms of Hildebrand had breathed new zeal into the priesthood. The Babylonish captivity of Avignon, as it was called, with the great schism of the West that followed upon it, was the cause of a second similar intermission, which lasted nearly a century and a half.

At every time, however, even when his work went on most briskly, the labours of the Roman architect took the direction of restoring and readorning old churches rather *Tendency of the Roman builders to adhere to the ancient manner.* than of erecting new ones. While the Transalpine countries, except in a few favoured spots, such as Provence and part of the Rhineland, remained during several ages with few and rudely built stone churches, Rome possessed, as the inheritance of the earlier Christian centuries, a profusion of houses of worship, some of them still unsurpassed in splendour, and far more than adequate to the needs of her diminished population. In repairing these from time to time, their original form and style of work were usually as far as possible preserved, while in constructing new ones, the abundance of models beautiful in themselves and hallowed as well by antiquity as by religious feeling, enthralled the invention of the workman, bound him down to be at best a faithful imitator, and forbade him to deviate at pleasure from the old established manner. Thus it befel that while his brethren throughout the rest of Europe were passing by successive steps from the old Roman and Byzantine styles to Romanesque, and from Romanesque to Gothic, the Roman architect scarcely departed from the plan and arrangements of the primitive basilica. This is one chief reason why there is so little of Gothic work in Rome, so little even of Romanesque like that of Pisa. What there is appears chiefly in the pointed window, more rarely in the arch, seldom or never in spire or tower or column. Only one of the existing churches of Rome is Gothic throughout, and that, the Dominican church of S. Maria sopra Minerva, was built by foreign monks. In some of the other churches, and especially in the cloisters of the convents, instances may be observed of the same style: in others slight traces, by accident or design almost obliterated [x].

The mention of obliteration suggests a third cause of the comparative want of mediæval buildings in the city— the constant depredations and changes of which she has been the subject. Ever since the time of Constantine Rome has been a city of destruction, and Christians have vied with pagans, citizens with enemies, in urging on the

[x] Thus in the church of San Lorenzo without the walls there are several pointed windows, now bricked up; and similar ones may be seen in the church of Ara Cœli on the summit of the Capitol. So in the apse of St. John Lateran there are three or four windows of Gothic form: and in its cloister, as well as in that of St. Paul without the walls, a great deal of beautiful Lombard work. The elegant porch of the church of Sant' Antonio Abate is Lombard. In the apse of the church of San Giovanni e Paolo on the Cœlian hill there is an ex-ternal arcade exactly like those of the Duomo at Pisa. Nor are these the only instances.

The ruined chapel attached to the fortress of the Caetani family— the family to which Boniface the Eighth belonged, and whose head is now the first of the Roman nobility—is a pretty little building, more like northern Gothic than anything within the walls of Rome. It stands upon the Appian Way, opposite the tomb of Cæcilia Metella, which the Caetani used as a stronghold.

*By the
Romans of
the Middle
Ages.*

*By modern
restorers of
churches.*

fatal work.   Her siege and capture by Robert Guiscard [y],
the ally of Hildebrand against Henry the Fourth, was far
more ruinous than the attacks of the Goths or Vandals:
and itself yields in atrocity to the sack of Rome in
A.D. 1526 by the soldiers of the Catholic king and most
pious Emperor Charles the Fifth [z].   Since the days of the
first barbarian invasions the Romans have gone on building with materials taken from the ancient temples, theatres,
law-courts, baths and villas, stripping them of their gorgeous casings of marble, pulling down their walls for the
sake of the blocks of travertine, setting up their own hovels
on the top or in the midst of these majestic piles.   Thus
it has been with the memorials of paganism: a somewhat
different cause has contributed to the disappearance of the
mediæval churches.   What pillage, or fanaticism, or the
wanton lust of destruction did in the one case, the osten-
tatious zeal of modern times has done in the other.   The
era of the final establishment of the Popes as temporal
sovereigns of the city, is also that of the supremacy of
the Renaissance style in architecture.   After the time of
Nicholas the Fifth, the pontiff against whom, it will be
remembered, the spirit of municipal freedom made its last
struggle in the conspiracy of Porcaro, nothing was built in
Gothic, and the prevailing enthusiasm for the antique pro-

[y] A good deal of the mischief
done by Robert Guiscard, from
which the parts of the city lying
beyond the Coliseum towards the
river and St. John Lateran never
recovered, is attributed to the Saracenic troops in his service. Saracen
pirates are said to have once before
sacked Rome. Genseric was not
a heathen, but he was a furious
Arian, which, as far as respect to
the churches of the orthodox went,

was nearly the same thing. He is
supposed to have carried off the
seven-branched candlestick and
other vessels of the Temple, which
Titus had brought from Jerusalem
to Rome.

[z] We are told that one cause of
the ferocity of the German part of
the army of Charles was their anger
at the ruinous condition of the imperial palace.

duced a corresponding dislike to everything mediæval, a dislike conspicuous in men like Julius the Second and Leo the Tenth, from whom the grandeur of modern Rome may be said to begin. Not long after their time the great religious movement of the sixteenth century, while triumphing in the north of Europe, was in the south met and overcome by a counter-reformation in the bosom of the old church herself, and the construction or restoration of ecclesiastical buildings became again the passion of the devout[a]. No employment, whether it be called an amusement or a duty, could have been better suited to the court and aristocracy of Rome. They were indolent; wealthy, and fond of displaying their wealth; full of good taste, and anxious, especially when advancing years had chased away youth's pleasures, to be full of good works also. Popes and cardinals and the heads of the great families vied with one another in building new churches and restoring or enlarging those they found till little of the old was left; raising over them huge cupolas, substituting massive pilasters for the single-shafted columns, adorning the interior with a profusion of rare marbles, of carving and gilding, of frescoes and altar-pieces by the best masters of the sixteenth and seventeenth centuries. None but a bigoted mediævalist can refuse to acknowledge the warmth of tone, the repose, the stateliness, of the churches of modern Rome; but even in the midst of admiration the sated eye turns away from the wealth of ponderous ornament, and we long for the clear pure colour, the

[a] Under the influence, partly of this anti-pagan spirit, partly of his own restless vanity, partly of a passion to be doing something, Pope Sixtus the Fifth did a great deal of mischief in the way of destroying or spoiling the monuments of antiquity.

CHAP. XVI.

Existing
relics of the
Dark and
Middle
Ages.

The Mo-
saics.

The Bell-
towers.

simple yet grand proportions that give a charm to the buildings of an earlier age.

Few of the ancient churches have escaped untouched; many have been altogether rebuilt. There are also some, however, in which the modernizers of the sixteenth and subsequent centuries have spared two features of the old structure, its round apse or tribune and its bell-tower. The apse has its interior usually covered with mosaics, exceedingly interesting, both from the ideas they express and as the only monuments of pictorial art that remain to us from the Dark Ages. To speak of them, however, as they deserve to be spoken of, would involve a digression for which there is no space here. The campanile or bell-tower is a quaint little square brick tower, of no great height, usually standing detached from the church, and having in its topmost, sometimes also in its other upper stories, several arcade windows, divided by tiny marble pillars b. What with these campaniles, then far more numerous than they are now, and with the huge brick

b These campaniles are generally supposed to date from the ninth and tenth centuries. I am informed, however, by Mr. J. H. Parker, of Oxford, whose antiquarian skill is well known, that he is led to believe by an examination of their mouldings that few or none, unless it be that of San Prassede, are older than the twelfth century.

This of course applies only to the existing buildings. The type of tower may be, and indeed no doubt is, older.

Somewhat similar towers may be observed in many parts of the Italian Alps, especially in the wonderful mountain land north of Venice, where such towers are of all dates from the eleventh or twelfth down to the nineteenth century, the ancient type having in these remote valleys been adhered to because the builder had no other models before him. In the valley of Cimolais I have seen such a campanile in course of erection, precisely similar to others in the neighbouring villages some eight centuries old.

The very curious round towers of Ravenna, some four or five of which are still standing, seem to have originally had similar windows, though these have been all, or nearly all, stopped up. The Roman towers are all square.

fortresses of the nobles, towers must have held in the landscape of the mediæval city very much the part which domes do now. Although less imposing, they were probably more picturesque, the rather as in the earlier part of the Middle Ages the houses and churches, which are now mostly crowded together on the flat of the Campus Martius, were scattered over the heights and slopes of the Cœlian, Aventine, and Esquiline hills[c]. Modern Rome lies chiefly on the opposite or north-eastern side of the Capitol, and the change from the old to the new site of the city, which can hardly be said to have distinctly begun before the destruction of the south-western part of the town by Robert Guiscard, was not completed until the sixteenth century. In A.D. 1536 the Capitol was rebuilt by Michael Angelo, in anticipation of the entry of Charles the Fifth, upon foundations that had been laid by the first Tarquin; and the palace of the Senator, the greatest municipal edifice of Rome, which had hitherto looked towards the Forum and the Coliseum, was made to front in the direction of St. Peter's and the modern town.

The Rome of to-day is no more like the city of Rienzi than she is to the city of Trajan; just as the Roman church of the nineteenth century differs profoundly, however she may strive to disguise it, from the church of Hildebrand. But among all their changes, both church and city have kept themselves wonderfully free from the intrusion of foreign, at least of Teutonic, elements, and have

Changed aspect of the city of Rome.

---

[c] The Palatine hill seems to have been then, as it is for the most part now, a waste of stupendous ruins. In the great imperial palace upon its northern and eastern sides was the residence of an official of the Eastern court in the beginning of the eighth century. In the time of Charles, some seventy years later, this palace was no longer habitable.

CHAP. XVI.

*Analogy
between her
architecture
and her
civil and
ecclesiasti-
cal consti-
tution.*

faithfully preserved at all times something of an old Roman character. Latin Christianity inherited from the imperial system of old that firmly knit yet flexible organization, which was one of the grand secrets of its power: the great men whom mediæval Rome gave to or trained up for the Papacy were, like their progenitors, administrators, legislators, statesmen; seldom enthusiasts themselves, but perfectly understanding how to use and guide the enthusiasm of others—of the French and German crusaders, of men like Francis of Assissi and Dominic and Ignatius. Between Catholicism in Italy and Catholicism in Germany or England there was always, as there is still, a very perceptible difference. So also, if

the analogy be not too fanciful, was it with Rome the city. Socially she seemed always drifting towards feudalism; yet she never fell into its grasp. Materially, her architecture was at one time considerably influenced by Gothic forms, yet Gothic never became, as in the rest of Europe, the dominant style. It approached Rome late, and departed from her early, so that we scarcely notice its presence, and seem to pass almost without a break from the old Romanesque [d] to the Græco-Roman of the Renaissance. Thus regarded, the history of the city, both in her political state and in her buildings, is seen to be intimately connected with that of the Holy Empire itself. The Empire in its title and its pretensions expressed the idea of the permanence of the institutions of the ancient world; Rome the city had, in externals at least, carefully preserved their traditions: the names of her magistracies, the character of her buildings, all spoke of antiquity, and gave it a strange and shadowy life in the midst of new races and new forms of faith.

[d] Such as we see it in the later and lesser churches of basilica form.

In its essence the Empire rested on the feeling of the unity of mankind; it was the perpetuation of the Roman dominion by which the old nationalities had been destroyed, with the addition of the Christian element which had created a new nationality that was also universal. By the extension of her citizenship to all her subjects heathen Rome had become the common home, and, figuratively, even the local dwelling-place of the civilized races of man. By the theology of the time Christian Rome had been made the mystical type of humanity, the one flock of the faithful scattered over the whole earth, the holy city whither, as to the temple on Moriah, all the Israel of God should come up to worship. She was not merely an image of the mighty world, she was the mighty world itself in miniature. The pastor of her local church is also the universal bishop; the seven suffragans who consecrate him are the overseers of petty sees in Ostia, Antium, and the like, towns lying close round Rome: the cardinal priests and deacons who join these seven in electing him derive their title to be princes of the Church, the supreme spiritual council of the Christian world, from the incumbency of a parochial cure within the precincts of the city. Similarly, her ruler, the Emperor, is ruler of mankind; he is chosen by the acclamations of her people [e]: he can be lawfully crowned nowhere but in one

---

[e] It was thus that most of the earlier Teutonic Emperors, and notably Charles and Otto, professed to have obtained the crown; although practically it was partly a matter of conquest and partly of private arrangement with the Pope. In later times, the seven Germanic princes were recognized as the legally qualified electoral body, but their appearance on the stage was a result of the confusion of the German kingdom with the Roman Empire, and in strictness they had nothing to do with the Roman crown at all. The right to bestow it could only—on principle—belong to some Roman authority, and those who felt the difficulty were driven to suppose a formal cession

of her basilicas. She is, like Jerusalem of old, the mother of us all.

There is yet another way in which the record of the domestic contests of Rome throws light upon the history of the Empire. From the eleventh century to the fifteenth her citizens ceased not to demand in the name of the old republic their freedom from the tyranny of the nobles and the Pope, and their right to rule over the world at large. These efforts—selfish and fantastic we may call them, yet men like Petrarch did not disdain to them their sympathy—issued from the same theories and were directed to the same ends as those which inspired Otto the Third and Frederick Barbarossa and Dante himself. They witness to the same incapacity to form any ideal for the future except a revival of the past; the same belief that one universal state is both desirable and possible, but possible only through the means of Rome: the same refusal to admit that a right which has once existed can ever be extinguished. In the days of the Renaissance these notions were passing silently away: the succeeding century brought with it misfortunes that broke the spirit of the nation. Italy was the battle-field of Europe: her wealth became the prey of a rapacious soldiery: the last and greatest of her republics was enslaved by an unfeeling Emperor, and handed over as the pledge of amity to a selfish Medicean Pope. When the hope of independence had been lost, the people turned away from politics to live for art and literature, and found, before many generations had passed, how little such exclusive devotion could com-

Extinction of the Florentine republic, A.D. 1530.

of their privilege by the Roman people to the seven electors. See p. 227 *supra:* and cf. Matthew Villani (iv. 77), 'Il popolo Romano, non da se, ma la chiesa per lui, concedette la elezione degli Imperadori a sette principi della Magna.'

pensate for the departure of freedom, and a national spirit, and the activity of civic life. A century after the golden days of Ariosto and Raphael, Italian literature had become frigid and affected, while Italian art was dying of mannerism.

At length, after long ages of sloth, the stagnant waters were troubled. The Romans, who had lived in listless contentment under the paternal sway of the Popes, received new ideas from the advent of the revolutionary armies of France, and have found the Papal system, since its re-establishment fifty years ago as a modern bureaucratic depotism, far less tolerable than it was of yore. Our own days have seen the name of Rome become again a rallying-cry for the patriots of Italy, but in a sense most unlike the old one. The contemporaries of Arnold and Rienzi desired freedom only as a step to universal domination: their descendants, more wisely, yet not more from patriotism than from a pardonable civic pride, seek only to be the capital of the Italian kingdom. Dante prayed for a monarchy of the world, a reign of peace and Christian brotherhood: those who invoke his name as the earliest prophet of their creed strive after an idea that never crossed his mind—the national union of Italy [f].

Plain common-sense politicians in other countries do not understand this passion for Rome as a capital, and think it their duty to lecture the Italians on their flightiness. The latter do not themselves pretend that the shores of the Tiber are a suitable site for a capital: Rome is lonely, unhealthy, and in a bad strategical position; she has no particular facilities for trade: her people, with

[f] That which Dante, Arnold of Brescia, and the rest really have in common with the modern Italian 'party of movement' is their hostility to the temporal power of the Popes.

some fine qualities, are less orderly and industrious than the Tuscans or the Piedmontese. Nevertheless all Italy cries with one voice for Rome, firmly believing that national life can never thrill with a strong and steady pulsation till the ancient capital has become the nation's heart. They feel that it is owing to Rome—Rome pagan as well as Christian—that they once played so grand a part in the drama of European history, and that they have now been able to attain that fervid sentiment of unity which has brought them at last together under one government. Whether they are right, whether if right they are likely to be successful, need not be inquired here. But it deserves to be noted that this enthusiasm for a famous name—for it is nothing more—is substantially the same feeling as that which created and hallowed the Holy Empire of the Middle Ages. The events of the last few years on both sides of the Atlantic have proved that men are not now, any more than they ever were, chiefly governed by calculations of material profit and loss. Sentiments, fancies, theories, have not lost their power; the spirit of poetry has not wholly passed away from politics. And strange as seems to us the worship paid to the name of mediæval Rome by those who saw the sins and the misery of her people, it can hardly have been an intenser feeling than is the imaginative reverence wherewith the Italians of to-day look on the city whence, as from a fountain, all the streams of their national life have sprung, and in which, as in an ocean, they are all again to mingle.

CHAPTER XVII.

THE RENAISSANCE: CHANGE IN THE CHARACTER
OF THE EMPIRE.

In Frederick the Third's reign the Empire sank to its lowest point. It had shot forth a fitful gleam under Sigismund, who in convoking and presiding over the council of Constance had revived one of the highest functions of his predecessors. The precedents of the first great œcumenical councils, and especially of the council of Nicæa, had established the principle that it belonged to the Emperor, even more properly than to the Pope, to convoke ecclesiastical assemblies from the whole Christian world[a]. The tenet commended 'itself to the reforming party in the church, headed by Gerson, the chancellor of Paris, whose aim it was, while making no changes in matters of faith, to correct the abuses which had grown up in discipline and government, and limit the power of the Popes by exalting the authority of general councils, to whom there was now attributed an immunity from error superior even to that which resided in the successor of Peter. And although it was only the sacerdotal body, not the whole Christian people, who were thus made the exponents of the universal religious con-

[a] See Dean Stanley's *Lectures on the History of the Eastern Church*, Lecture II.

sciousness, the doctrine was nevertheless a foreshadowing of that fuller freedom which was soon to follow. The existence of the Holy Empire and the existence of general councils were, as has been already remarked, necessary parts of one and the same theory [b], and it was therefore more than a coincidence that the last occasion on which the whole of Latin Christendom met to deliberate and act as a single commonwealth [c] was also the last on which that commonwealth's lawful temporal head appeared in the exercise of his international functions. Never afterwards was he, in the eyes of Europe, anything more than a German monarch.

Weakness of Germany as compared with the other states of Europe. Albert II. 1438–1440. Frederick III. 1440–1493.

It might seem doubtful whether he would long remain a monarch at all. When in A.D. 1493 the calamitous reign of Frederick the Third ended, it was impossible for the princes to see with unconcern the condition into which their selfishness and turbulence had brought the Empire. The time was indeed critical. Hitherto the Germans had been protected rather by the weakness of their enemies than by their own strength. From France there had been little to fear while the English menaced her on one side and the Burgundian dukes on the other : from England still less while she was torn by the strife of York and Lancaster. But now throughout Western Europe the power of the feudal oligarchies was broken; and its chief countries were being, by the establishment of fixed rules of succession and the absorption of the smaller into the

[b] It is not without interest to observe that the council of Basel shewed signs of reciprocating imperial care by claiming those very rights over the Empire to which the Popes were accustomed to pretend.

[c] The councils of Basel and Florence were not recognized from first to last by all Europe, as was the council of Constance. When the assembly of Trent met, the great religious schism had already made a general council, in the true sense of the word, impossible.

larger principalities, rapidly built up into compact and aggressive military monarchies. Thus Spain became a great state by the union of Castile and Aragon, and the conquest of the Moors of Granada. Thus in England there arose the popular despotism of the Tudors. Thus France, enlarged and consolidated under Lewis the Eleventh and his successors, began to acquire that predominant influence on the politics of Europe which her commanding geographical position, the martial spirit of her people, and, it must be added, the unscrupulous ambition of her rulers, have secured to her in every succeeding century. Meantime there had appeared in the far East a foe still more terrible. The capture of Constantinople gave the Turks a firm hold on Europe, and inspired them with the hope of effecting in the fifteenth century what Abderrahman and his Saracens had so nearly effected in the eighth—of establishing the faith of Islam through all the provinces that obeyed the Western as well as the Eastern Cæsars. The navies of the Ottoman Sultans swept the Mediterranean; their well-appointed armies pierced Hungary and threatened Vienna.

Nor was it only that formidable enemies had arisen without: the frontiers of Germany herself were exposed by the loss of those adjoining territories which had formerly owned allegiance to the Emperors. Poland, once tributary, had shaken off the yoke at the interregnum, and had recently wrested Prussia and Lusatz from the Teutonic knights. Bohemia, where German culture had struck deeper roots, remained a member of the Empire; but the privileges she had obtained from Charles the Fourth, and the subsequent acquisition of Silesia and Moravia, made her virtually independent. The restless Hungarians

Loss of imperial territories.

avenged their former vassalage to Germany by frequent inroads on her eastern border.

Imperial power in Italy ended with the life of Henry the Seventh. Rupert did indeed cross the Alps, but it was as the hireling of Florence; Frederick the Third received the Lombard crown, but it no longer conveyed the slightest power. In the beginning of the fourteenth century Dante still hopes the renovation of his country from the action of the Teutonic Emperors. Some fifty years later Matthew Villani sees clearly that they do not and cannot reign to any purpose south of the Alps [d]. Nevertheless the phantom of imperial authority lingers on for a time. It is put forward by the Ghibeline tyrants of the cities to justify their attacks on their Guelfic neighbours: even resolute republicans like the Florentines do not yet venture altogether to reject it, however unwilling to permit its exercise. Before the middle of the fifteenth century, the names of Guelf and Ghibeline had ceased to have any sense or meaning; the Pope was no longer the protector nor the Emperor the assailant of municipal freedom, for municipal freedom itself had well-nigh disappeared. But the old war-cries of the Church and the Empire were still repeated as they had been three centuries before, and the rival principles that had once enlisted the

---

[d] 'E pero venendo gl' imperadori della Magna col supremo titolo, e volendo col senno e colla forza della Magna reggiere gli Italiani, non lo fanno e non lo possono fare.'—M. Villani, iv. 77. Matthew Villani's etymology of the two great faction names of Italy is worth quoting, as a fair sample of the skill of mediævals in such matters:—'La Italia tutta e divisa mistamente in due parti, l'una che seguita ne' fatti del mondo la santa chiesa—e questi son dinominati Guelfi; cioè, guardatori di fè. E l' altra parte seguitano lo 'mperio o fedele o enfedele che sia delle cose del mondo a santa chiesa. E chiamansi Ghibellini, quasi guida belli; cioè, guidatori di battaglie.'

noblest spirits of Italy on one or other side had now sunk into a pretext for wars of aggrandizement or of mere unmeaning hate. That which had been remarked long before in Greece was seen to be true here; the spirit of faction outlived the cause of faction, and became itself the new and prolific source of a useless, endless strife.

After Frederick the Third no Emperor was crowned in Rome, and almost the only trace of that connection between Germany and Italy to maintain which so much had been risked and lost, was to be found in the obstinate belief of the Hapsburg Emperors, that their own claims, though often purely dynastic and personal, could be enforced by an appeal to the imperial rights of their predecessors. Because Barbarossa had overrun Lombardy with a Transalpine host they fancied themselves entitled to demand duchies for themselves and their relatives, and to entangle the Empire in wars wherein no interest but their own was involved.

The kingdom of Arles, if it had never added much strength to the Empire, had been useful as an outwork against France. And thus its loss—Dauphiné passing over, partly in A.D. 1350, finally in 1457, Provence in 1486—proved a serious calamity, for it brought the French nearer to Switzerland, and opened to them a tempting passage into Italy. The Emperors did not for a time expressly renounce their feudal suzerainty over these lands, but if it was hard to enforce a feudal claim over a rebellious landgrave in Germany, how much harder to control a vassal who was also the mightiest king in Europe.

On the north-west frontier, the fall in A.D. 1477 of the great principality which the dukes of French Burgundy were building up, was seen with pleasure by the Rhinelanders whom Charles the last duke had incessantly alarmed. But the only effect of its fall was to leave France and Germany directly confronting each other, and it was soon seen that the balance of strength lay on the side of the less numerous but better organized and more active nation.

Switzer-land. Switzerland, too, could no longer be considered a part of the Germanic realm. The revolt of the Forest Cantons, in A.D. 1313, was against the oppressions practised in the name of Albert count of Hapsburg, rather than against the legitimate authority of Albert the Emperor. But although several subsequent sovereigns, and among them conspicuously Henry the Seventh and Sigismund, favoured the Swiss liberties, yet while the antipathy between the Confederates and the territorial nobility gave a peculiar direction to their policy, the accession of new cantons to their body, and their brilliant success against Charles the Bold in A.D. 1477, made them proud of a separate national existence, and not unwilling to cast themselves loose from the stranded hulk of the Empire. Maximilian tried to reconquer them, but after a furious struggle, in which the valleys of Western Tyrol were repeatedly laid waste by the peasants of the Engadin, he was forced to give way, and in A.D. 1500 recognized them by treaty as practically independent. Not, however, till the peace of Westphalia, in A.D. 1648, was the Swiss Confederation in the eye of public law a sovereign state, and even after that date some of the towns continued to stamp their coins with the double eagle of the Empire.

Internal weakness. If those losses of territory were serious, far more serious was the plight in which Germany herself lay. The country had now become not so much an empire as an aggregate of very many small states, governed by sovereigns who would neither remain at peace with each other nor combine against a foreign enemy, under the nominal presidency of an Emperor who had little lawful authority, and could not exert what he had [e].

There was another cause, besides those palpable and obvious ones already enumerated, to which this state of things must be ascribed. That cause is to be found in the theory which regarded the Empire as an international power, supreme among Christian states. From the day when Otto the Great was crowned at Rome, the characters of German king and Roman Emperor were united in one person, and it has been shewn how that union tended more and more to become a fusion. If the two offices, in their nature and origin so dissimilar, had been held by different persons, the Roman Empire would most probably have soon disappeared, while the German kingdom grew into a robust national monarchy. Their connection gave a longer life to the one and a feebler life to the other, while at the same time it transformed both. So long as Germany was only one of the many countries that bowed beneath their sceptre it was possible for the Emperors, though we need not suppose they troubled themselves with speculations on the matter, to distinguish their imperial authority, as international and more than half religious, from their royal, which was, or was meant to be, exclusively local and feudal. But when within the narrowed bounds of Germany these international functions had ceased to have any meaning, when the rulers of

Influence of the theory of the Empire as an international power upon the Germanic constitution.

---

[e] 'Nam quamvis Imperatorem et regem et dominum vestrum esse fateamini, precario tamen ille imperare videtur: nulla ei potentia est; tantum ei paretis quantum vultis, vultis autem minimum.'— Æneas Sylvius to the princes of Germany, quoted by Hippolytus a Lapide.

England, Spain, France, Denmark, Hungary, Poland, Italy, Burgundy, had in succession repudiated their control, and the Lord of the World found himself obeyed by none but his own people, he would not sink from being lord of the world into a simple Teutonic king, but continued to play in the more contracted theatre the part which had belonged to him in the wider. Thus did Germany instead of Europe become the sphere of his international jurisdiction; and her electors and princes, originally mere vassals, no greater than a Count of Champagne in France, or an Earl of Chester in England, stepped into the place which it had been meant that the several monarchs of Christendom should fill. If the power of their head had been what it was in the eleventh century, the additional dignity so assigned to them might have signified very little. But coming in to confirm and justify the liberties already won, this theory of their relation to the sovereign had a great though at the time scarcely perceptible influence in changing the German Empire, as we may now begin to call it, from a state into a sort of confederation or body of states, united indeed for some of the purposes of government, but separate and independent for others more important. Thus, and that in its ecclesiastical as well as its civil organization, Germany became a miniature of Christendom f. The Pope, though he retained the wider sway which his rival had lost, was in an especial manner the head of the German clergy, as the Emperor was of the laity: the three Rhenish prelates sat in the supreme college beside the four temporal electors: the nobility of prince-bishops and abbots

---

f See Ægidi, *Der Fürstenrath nach dem Luneviller Frieden;* a book which throws more light than any other with which I am acquainted on the inner nature of the Empire.

was as essential a part of the constitution and as influential in the deliberations of the Diet as were the dukes, counts, and margraves of the Empire. The world-embracing Christian state was to have been governed by a hierarchy of spiritual pastors, whose graduated ranks of authority should exactly correspond with those of the temporal magistracy, who were to be like them endowed with worldly wealth and power, and to enjoy a jurisdiction co-ordinate although distinct. This system, which it was in vain attempted to establish in Europe during the eleventh and twelfth centuries, was in its main features that which prevailed in the Germanic Empire from the fourteenth century onwards. And conformably to the analogy which may be traced between the position of the archdukes of Austria in Germany and the place which the four Saxon and the two first Franconian Emperors had held in Europe, both being recognized as leaders and presidents in all that concerned the common interest, in the one case of the Christian, in the other of the whole German people, while neither of them had any power of direct government in the territories of local kings and lords; so the plan by which those who chose Maximilian emperor sought to strengthen their national monarchy was in substance that which the Popes had followed when they conferred the crown of the world on Charles and Otto. The pontiffs then, like the electors now, finding that they could not give with the title the power which its functions demanded, were driven to the expedient of selecting for the office persons whose private resources enabled them to sustain it with dignity. The first Frankish and the first Saxon Emperors were chosen because they were already the mightiest potentates in Europe; Maximilian because he was the strongest of the German princes. The parallel

Position of the Emperor in Germany, compared with that of his predecessors in Europe.

may be carried one step further. Just as under Otto and his successors the Roman Empire was Teutonized, so now under the Hapsburg dynasty, from whose hands the sceptre departed only once thenceforth, the Teutonic Empire tends more and more to lose itself in an Austrian monarchy.

Beginning of the Hapsburg influence in Germany.

Of that monarchy and of the power of the house of Hapsburg, Maximilian was, even more than Rudolph his ancestor, the founder [g]. Uniting in his person those wide domains through Germany which had been dispersed among the collateral branches of his house, and claiming by his marriage with Mary of Burgundy most of the territories of Charles the Bold, he was a prince greater than any who had sat on the Teutonic throne since the death of Frederick the Second. But it was as archduke of Austria, count of Tyrol, duke of Styria and Carinthia, feudal superior of lands in Swabia, Alsace, and Switzerland, that he was great, not as Roman Emperor. For just as from him the Austrian monarchy begins, so with him the Holy Empire in its old meaning ends. That strange system of doctrines, half religious half political, which had supported it for so many ages, was growing obsolete, and the theory which had wrought such changes on Germany and Europe, passed ere long so completely from remembrance that we can now do no more than call up a faint and wavering image of what it must once have been.

Character of the epoch of Maximilian.

For it is not only in imperial history that the accession of Maximilian is a landmark. That time—a time of

[g] The two immediately preceding Emperors, Albert II (1438-1439) and Frederick III, father of Maximilian (1439-1493), had been Hapsburgs. It is nevertheless from Maximilian that the ascendancy of that family must be dated.

change and movement in every part of human life, a time when printing had become common, and books were no longer confined to the clergy, when drilled troops were replacing the feudal militia, when the use of gunpowder was changing the face of war—was especially marked by one event, to which the history of the world offers no parallel before or since, the discovery of America. The cloud which from the beginning of things had hung thick and dark round the borders of civilization was suddenly lifted : the feeling of mysterious awe with which men had regarded the firm plain of earth and her encircling ocean ever since the days of Homer, vanished when astronomers and geographers taught them that she was an insignificant globe, which, so far from being the centre of the universe, was itself swept round in them otion of one of the least of its countless systems. The notions that had hitherto prevailed regarding the life of man and his relations to nature and the supernatural, were rudely shaken by the knowledge that was soon gained of tribes in every stage of culture and living under every variety of condition, who had developed apart from all the influences of the Eastern hemisphere. In A.D. 1453 the capture of Constantinople and extinction of the Eastern Empire had dealt a fatal blow to the prestige of tradition and an immemorial name : in A.D. 1492 there was disclosed a world whither the eagles of all-conquering Rome had never winged their flight. No one could now have repeated the arguments of the *De Monarchia.*

Another movement, too, widely different, but even more momentous, was beginning to spread from Italy beyond the Alps. Since the barbarian tribes settled in the Roman provinces, no change had come to pass in Europe at all comparable to that which followed the diffusion of the

CHAP. XVII.

The discovery of America.

The Renaissance.

new learning in the latter half of the fifteenth century. Enchanted by the beauty of the ancient models of art and poetry, more particularly those of the Greeks, men came to regard with aversion and contempt all that had been done or produced from the days of Trajan to those of Pope Nicholas the Fifth. The Latin style of the writers who lived after Tacitus was debased: the architecture of the Middle Ages was barbarous: the scholastic philosophy was an odious and unmeaning jargon: Aristotle himself, Greek though he was, Aristotle who had been for three centuries more than a prophet or an apostle, was hurled from his throne, because his name was associated with the dismal quarrels of Scotists and Thomists. That spirit, whether we call it analytical or sceptical, or earthly, or simply secular, for it is more or less all of these—the spirit which was the exact antithesis of mediæval mysticism, had swept in and carried men away, with all the force of a pent-up torrent. People were content to gratify their tastes and their senses, caring little for worship, and still less for doctrine: their hopes and ideas were no longer such as had made their forefathers crusaders or ascetics: their imagination was possessed by associations far different from those which had inspired Dante: they did not revolt against the church, but they had no enthusiasm for her, and they had enthusiasm for whatever was fresh and graceful and intelligible. From all that was old and solemn, or that seemed to savour of feudalism or monkery, they turned away, too indifferent to be hostile. And so, in the midst of the Renaissance, so, under the consciousness that former things were passing from the earth, and a new order opening, so, with the other beliefs and memories of the Middle Age, the shadowy rights of the Roman

Empire melted away in the fuller modern light. Here and there a jurist muttered that no neglect could destroy its universal supremacy, or a priest declaimed to listless hearers on its duty to protect the Holy See; but to Germany it had become an ancient device for holding together the discordant members of her body, to its possessors an engine for extending the power of the house of Hapsburg.

Empire henceforth German.

Henceforth, therefore, we must look upon the Holy Roman Empire as lost in the German; and after a few faint attempts to resuscitate old-fashioned claims, nothing remains to indicate its origin save a sounding title and a precedence among the states of Europe. It was not that the Renaissance exerted any direct political influence either against the Empire or for it; men were too busy upon statues and coins and manuscripts to care what befel Popes or Emperors. It acted rather by silently withdrawing the whole system of doctrines upon which the Empire had rested, and thus leaving it, since it had previously no support but that of opinion, without any support at all.

Attempts to reform the Germanic Constitution.

During Maximilian's eventful reign several efforts were made to construct a new constitution, but it is to German, rather than to imperial history that they properly belong. Here, indeed, the history of the Holy Empire might close, did not the title unchanged beckon us on, and were it not that the events of these later centuries may in their causes be traced back to times when the name of Roman was not wholly a mockery. It may be enough to remark that while the preservation of peace and the better administration of justice were in some measure attained by the Public Peace and Imperial Chamber, established in A.D. 1495, schemes still more important

CHAP. XVII.

failed through the bad constitution of the Diet, and the unconquerable jealousy of the Emperor and the Estates. Maximilian refused to have his prerogative, indefinite though weak, restricted by the appointment of an administrative council[h], and when the Estates extorted it from him, did his best to ensure its failure. In the Diet, which consisted of three colleges, electors, princes, and cities, the lower nobility and knights of the Empire were unrepresented, and resented every decree that affected their position, refusing to pay taxes in voting which they had no voice. The interests of the princes and the cities were often irreconcilable, while the strength of the crown would not have been sufficient to make its adhesion to the latter of any effect. The policy of conciliating the commons, which Sigismund had tried, succeeding Emperors seldom cared to repeat, content to gain their point by raising factions among the territorial magnates, and so to stave off the unwelcome demand for reform. After many earnest attempts to establish a representative system, such as might resist the tendency to local independence and cure the evils of separate administration, the hope so often baffled died

Causes of the failure of the projects of reform.

away. Forces were too nearly balanced: the sovereign could not extend his personal control, nor could the reforming party limit him by a strong council of government, for such a measure would have equally trenched on the independence of the states. So ended the first great effort for German unity, interesting from its bearing on the events and aspirations of our own day; interesting, too, as giving the most convincing proof of the decline of the imperial office. For the projects of reform did not propose to effect their objects by restoring to Maximilian

[h] Reichsregiment.

the authority his predecessors had once enjoyed, but by setting up a body which would resemble far more nearly the senate of a federal state than the administrative council which surrounds a monarch. The existing system developed itself further : relieved from external pressure, the princes became more despotic in their own territories : distinct codes were framed, and new systems of administration introduced : the insurgent peasantry were crushed down with more confident harshness. Already had leagues of princes and cities · been formed[i] (that of Swabia was one of the strongest forces in Germany, and often the monarch's firmest support) ; now alliances begin to be contracted with foreign powers, and receive a direction of formidable import from the rivalry which the pretensions on Naples and Milan of Charles the Eighth and Lewis the Twelfth of France kindled between their house and the Austrian. It was no slight gain to have friends in the heart of the enemy's country, such as French intrigue found in the Elector Palatine and the count of Würtemberg.

Nevertheless this was also the era of the first conscious feeling of German nationality, as distinct from imperial. Driven in on all hands, with Italy and the Slavic lands and Burgundy hopelessly lost, Teutschland learnt to separate itself from Welschland[k]. The Empire became

Germanic nationality.

---

[i] Wenzel had encouraged the leagues of the cities, and incurred thereby the hatred of the nobles.

[k] The Germans, like our own ancestors, called foreign, *i. e.* non-Teutonic nations, Welsh. Yet apparently not all such nations, but only those which they in some way associated with the Roman Empire, the Cymry of Roman Britain, the Romanized Kelts of Gaul, the Italians, the Roumans or Wallachs of Transylvania and the Principalities. It does not appear that either the Magyars or any Slavonic people were called by any form of the name Welsh.

the representative of a narrower but more practicable national union. It is not a mere coincidence that at this date there appear several notable changes of style. 'Nationis Teutonicæ' (Teutscher Nation) is added to the simple 'sacrum imperium Romanum.' The title of 'Imperator electus,' which Maximilian obtains leave from Pope Julius the Second to assume, when the Venetians prevent him from reaching his capital, marks the severance of Germany from Rome. No subsequent Emperor received his crown in the ancient capital (Charles the Fifth was indeed crowned by the Pope's hands, but the ceremony took place at Bologna, and was therefore of at least questionable validity); each assumed after his German coronation[1] the title of Emperor Elect[m], and employed this in all documents issued in his name. But the word 'elect' being omitted when he was addressed by others, partly from motives of courtesy, partly because the old rules regarding the Roman coronation were forgotten, or remembered only by antiquaries, he was never called, even when formality was required, anything but

[1] The German crown was received at Aachen, the ancient Frankish capital, where may still be seen, in the gallery of the basilica, the marble throne on which the Emperors from the days of Charles to those of Ferdinand I were crowned. It was upon this chair that Otto III had found the body of Charles seated, when he opened his tomb in A.D. 1001. After Ferdinand I, the coronation as well as the election took place at Frankfort. An account of the ceremony may be found in Goethe's *Wahrheit und Dichtung*. Aachen, though it remained and indeed is still a German town, lay in too remote a corner of the country to be a convenient capital, and was moreover in dangerous proximity to the West Franks, as stubborn old Germans continue to call them. As early as A.D. 1353 we find bishop Leopold of Bamberg complaining that the French had arrogated to themselves the honours of the Frankish name, and called themselves 'reges Franciæ,' instead of 'reges Franciæ occidentalis.'—Lupoldus Bebenburgensis, apud Schardium, *Sylloge Tractatuum*.

[m] Erwählter Kaiser. See Appendix, Note C.

Emperor. The substantial import of another title now first introduced is the same. Before Otto the First, the Teutonic king had called himself either 'rex' alone, or 'Francorum orientalium rex,' or 'Francorum atque Saxonum rex:' after A.D. 962, all lesser dignities had been merged in the 'Romanorum Imperator[n].' To this Maximilian appended 'Germaniæ rex.' or, adding Frederick the Second's bequest[o], 'König in Germanien und Jerusalem.' It has been thought that from a mixture of the title King of Germany, and that of Emperor, has been formed the phrase 'German Emperor,' or less correctly, 'Emperor of Germany[p].' But more probably the terms 'German Emperor' and 'Emperor of Germany' are nothing but convenient corruptions of the technical description of the Germanic sovereign[q].

That the Empire was thus sinking into a merely German power cannot be doubted. But it was only natural that those who lived at the time should not discern the tendency of events. Again and again did the restless and sanguine Maximilian propose the recovery of Burgundy and Italy,—his last scheme was to adjust the relations of Papacy and Empire by becoming Pope himself: nor were successive Diets less zealous to check private war, still the scandal of Germany, to set right

[n] Romanorum rex (after Henry II) till the coronation at Rome.

[o] But the Emperor was only one of many claimants to this kingdom; they multiplied as the prospect of regaining it died away.

[p] The latter does not occur, even in English books, till comparatively recent times. English writers of the seventeenth century always call him 'The Emperor,' pure and simple, just as they invariably say 'the French king.' But the phrase 'Empereur d'Almayne' may be found in very early French writers.

[q] See Moser, *Römische Kayser;* Goldast's and other collections of imperial edicts and proclamations.

the gear of the imperial chamber, to make the imperial officials permanent, and their administration uniform throughout the country. But while they talked the heavens darkened, and the flood came and destroyed them all.

CHAPTER XVIII.

THE REFORMATION AND ITS EFFECTS UPON THE EMPIRE.

THE Reformation falls to be mentioned here, of course not as a religious movement, but as the cause of political changes, which still further rent the Empire, and struck at the root of the theory by which it had been created and upheld. Luther completed the work of Hildebrand. Hitherto it had seemed not impossible to strengthen the German state into a monarchy, compact if not despotic; the very Diet of Worms, where the monk of Wittenberg proclaimed to an astonished church and Emperor that the day of spiritual tyranny was past, had framed and presented a fresh scheme for the construction of a central council of government. The great religious schism put an end to all such hopes, for it became a source of political disunion far more serious and permanent than any that had existed before, and it taught the two factions into which Germany was henceforth divided to regard each other with feelings more bitter than those of hostile nations.

The breach came at the most unfortunate time possible. After an election, more memorable than any preceding, an election in which Francis the First of France and Henry the Eighth of England had been his competitors,

Accession of Charles V (1519-1558).

a prince had just ascended the imperial throne who united dominions vaster than any Europe had seen since the days of his great namesake. Spain and Naples, Flanders, and other parts of the Burgundian lands, as well as large regions in Eastern Germany, obeyed Charles: he drew inexhaustible revenues from a new empire beyond the Atlantic. Such a power, directed by a mind more resolute and profound than that of Maximilian his grandfather, might have well been able, despite the stringency of his coronation engagements [a], and the watchfulness of the electors [b], to override their usurped privileges, and make himself practically as well as officially the head of the nation. Charles the Fifth, though from the coldness of his manner [c] and his Flemish speech never a favourite among the Germans, was in point of fact far stronger than Maximilian or any other Emperor who had reigned for three centuries. In Italy he succeeded, after long struggles with the Pope and the French, in rendering himself supreme: England he knew how to lead, by flattering Henry and cajoling Wolsey: from no state but France had he serious opposition to fear. To this strength his imperial dignity was indeed a mere accident: its sources were the infantry of Spain, the looms of Flanders, the sierras of Peru. But the conquest once achieved, might could lose itself in right; and as an earlier Charles had veiled the terror of the Frankish

[a] The so-called 'Wahlcapitulation.'

[b] The electors long refused to elect Charles, dreading his great hereditary power, and were at last induced to do so only by their overmastering fear of the Turks.

[c] Nearly all the Hapsburgs seem to have wanted that sort of genial heartiness which, apt as it is to be stifled by education in the purple, has nevertheless been possessed by several other royal lines, greatly contributing to their vitality; as for instance by more than one prince of the houses of Brunswick and Hohenzollern.

sword under the mask of Roman election, so might his
successor sway a hundred provinces with the sole name
of Roman Emperor, and transmit to his race a dominion
as wide and more enduring.

One is tempted to speculate as to what might have
happened had Charles espoused the reforming cause.
His reverence for the Pope's person is sufficiently seen
in the sack of Rome and the captivity of Clement; the
traditions of his office might have led him to tread in the
steps of the Henrys and the Fredericks, into which even
the timid Lewis the Fourth and the unstable Sigismund
had sometimes ventured; the awakening zeal of the
German people, exasperated by the exactions of the
Romish court, would have strengthened his hands, and
enabled him, while moderating the excesses of change, to
fix his throne on the deep foundations of national love.
It may well be doubted—Englishmen at least have reason
for the doubt—whether the Reformation would not have
lost as much as it could have gained by being entangled
in the meshes of royal patronage. But, setting aside
Charles's personal leaning to the old faith, and forgetting
that he was king of the most bigoted race of Europe, his
position as Emperor made him almost perforce the
Pope's ally. The Empire had been called into being
by Rome, had vaunted the protection of the Apostolic
See as its highest earthly privilege, had latterly been
wont, especially in Hapsburg hands, to lean on the
papacy for support. Itself founded entirely on prescription and the traditions of immemorial reverence, how
could it abandon the cause which the longest prescription
and the most solemn authority had combined to consecrate? With the German clergy, despite occasional
quarrels, it had been on better terms than with the lay

Attitude of Charles towards the religious movement.

Y

aristocracy; their heads had been the chief ministers of the crown; the advocacies of their abbeys were the last source of imperial revenue to disappear. To turn against them now, when furiously assailed by heretics; to abrogate claims hallowed by antiquity and a hundred laws, would be to pronounce its own sentence, and the fall of the eternal city's spiritual dominion must involve the fall of what still professed to be her temporal. Charles would have been glad to see some abuses corrected; but a broad line of policy was called for, and he cast in his lot with the Catholics [d].

Ultimate failure of the repressive policy of Charles.

Of many momentous results only a few need be noticed here. The reconstruction of the old imperial system, upon the basis of Hapsburg power, proved in the end impossible. Yet for some years it had seemed actually accomplished. When the Smalkaldic league had been dissolved and its leaders captured, the whole country lay prostrate before Charles. He overawed the Diet at Augsburg by the Spanish soldiery: he forced formularies of doctrine upon the vanquished Protestants : he set up and pulled down whom he would throughout Germany, amid

[d] See this brought out with great force in the very interesting work of Padre Tosti, *Prolegomeni alla Storia Universale della Chiesa*, from which I quote one passage, which bears directly on the matter in hand: 'Il grido della riforma clericale aveva un eco terribile in tutta la compagnia civile dei popoli: essa percuoteva le cime del laicale potere, e rimbalzava per tutta la gerarchia sociale. Se l' imperatore Sigismondo nel concilio di Costanza non avesse fiutate queste consequenze nella eresia di Hus e di Girolamo di Praga, forse non av- rebbe con tanto zelo mandati alle fiamme que' novatori. Rotto da Lutero il vincolo di suggezione al Papa ed ai preti in fatti di religione, avvenne che anche quello che sommetteva il vassallo al barone, il barone al imperadore si allentasse. Il popolo con la Bibbia in mano era prete, vescovo, e papa ; e se prima contristato della prepotenza di chi gli soprastava, ricorreva al successore di San Pietro, ora ricorreva a se stesso, avendogli commesse Fra Martino le chiavi del regno dei Cieli.'—vol. ii. pp. 398, 9.

the muttered discontent of his own partisans. Then, as in the beginning of the year 1552, he lay at Innsbruck, fondly dreaming that his work was done, waiting the spring weather to cross to Trent, where the Catholic fathers had again met to settle the world's faith for it, news was suddenly brought that North Germany was in arms, and that the revolted Maurice of Saxony had seized Donauwerth, and was hurrying through the Bavarian Alps to surprise his sovereign. Charles rose and fled southwards over the snows of the Brenner, then eastwards, under the blood-red cliffs of dolomite that wall in the Pusterthal, far away into the valleys of Carinthia: the council of Trent broke up in consternation : Europe saw and the Emperor acknowledged that in his fancied triumph over the spirit of revolution he had done no more than block up for the moment an irresistible torrent. When this last effort to produce religious uniformity by violence had failed as hopelessly as the previous devices of holding discussions of doctrine and calling a general council, a sort of armistice was agreed to in 1554, which lasted in mutual fear and suspicion for more than sixty years. Four years after this disappointment of the hopes and projects which had occupied his busy life, Charles, weighed down by cares and with the shadow of coming death already upon him, resigned the sovereignty of Spain and the Indies, of Flanders and Naples, into the hands of his son Philip the Second; while the imperial sceptre passed to his brother Ferdinand, who had been some time before *Ferdi-* chosen King of the Romans. Ferdinand was content to *nand I,* leave things much as he found them, and the amiable *1558-1564.* Maximilian II, who succeeded him, though personally *Maximilian* well inclined to the Protestants, found himself fettered by *II.* his position and his allies, and could do little or nothing *1564-1576.*

CHAP. XVIII.

*Destruction
of the
Germanic
state-sys-
tem.*

to quench the flame of religious and political hatred.
Germany remained divided into two omnipresent factions,
and so further than ever from harmonious action, or
a tightening of the long-loosened bond of feudal allegiance.   The states of either creed being gathered into
a league, there could no longer be a recognized centre of
authority for judicial or administrative purposes.   Least
of all could a centre be sought in the Emperor, the leader
of the papal party, the suspected foe of every Protestant.
Too closely watched to do anything of his own authority,
too much committed to one party to be accepted as
a mediator by the other, he was driven to attain his own
objects by falling in with the schemes and furthering the
selfish ends of his adherents, by becoming the accomplice
or the tool of the Jesuits.   The Lutheran princes addressed themselves to reduce a power of which they had
still an over-sensitive dread, and found when they exacted
from each successive sovereign engagements more stringent than his predecessor's, that in this, and this alone,
their Catholic brethren were not unwilling to join them.
Thus obliged to strip himself one by one of the ancient
privileges of his crown, the Emperor came to have little
influence on the government except that which his intrigues might exercise.   Nay, it became almost impossible
to maintain a government at all.   For when the Reformers found themselves outvoted at the Diet, they
declared that in matters of religion a majority ought not
to bind a minority.   As the measures were few which
did not admit of being reduced to this category, for whatever benefited the Emperor or any other Catholic prince
injured the Protestants, nothing could be done save by
the assent of two bitterly hostile factions.   Thus scarce
anything was done; and even the courts of justice were

stopped by the disputes that attended the appointment of every judge or assessor.

In the foreign politics of Germany another result followed. Inferior in military force and organization, the Protestant princes at first provided for their safety by forming leagues among themselves. The device was an old one, and had been employed by the monarch himself before now, in despair at the effete and cumbrous forms of the imperial system. Soon they began to look beyond the Vosges, and found that France, burning heretics at home, was only too happy to smile on free opinions elsewhere. The alliance was easily struck; Henry the Second assumed in 1552 the title of 'Protector of the Germanic liberties,' and a pretext for interference was never wanting in future.

Alliance of the Protestants with France.

These were some of the visible political consequences of the great religious schism of the sixteenth century. But beyond and above them there was a change far more momentous than any of its immediate results. There is perhaps no event in history which has been represented in so great a variety of lights as the Reformation. It has been called a revolt of the laity against the clergy, or of the Teutonic races against the Italians, or of the kingdoms of Europe against the universal monarchy of the Popes. Some have seen in it only a burst of long-repressed anger at the luxury of the prelates and the manifold abuses of the ecclesiastical system; others a renewal of the youth of the church by a return to primitive forms of doctrine. All these indeed to some extent it was; but it was also something more profound, and fraught with mightier consequences than any of them. It was in its essence the assertion of the principle of individuality—that is to say, of true spiritual freedom. Hitherto

The Reformation spirit, and its influence upon the Empire.

the personal consciousness had been a faint and broken reflection of the universal; obedience had been held the first of religious duties; truth had been conceived as a something external and positive, which the priesthood who were its stewards were to communicate to the passive layman, and whose saving virtue lay not in its being felt and known by him to be truth, but in a purely formal and unreasoning acceptance. The great principles which mediæval Christianity still cherished were obscured by the limited, rigid, almost sensuous forms which had been forced on them in times of ignorance and barbarism. That which was in its nature abstract, had been able to survive only by taking a concrete expression. The universal consciousness became the Visible Church: the Visible Church hardened into a government and degenerated into a hierarchy. Holiness of heart and life was sought by outward works, by penances and pilgrimages, by gifts to the poor and to the clergy, wherein there dwelt often little enough of a charitable mind. The presence of divine truth among men was symbolized under one aspect by the existence on earth of an infallible Vicar of God, the Pope; under another, by the reception of the present Deity in the sacrifice of the mass; in a third, by the doctrine that the priest's power to remit sins and administer the sacraments depended upon a transmission of miraculous gifts which can hardly be called other than physical. All this system of doctrine, which might, but for the position of the church as a worldly and therefore obstructive power, have expanded, renewed, and purified itself during the four centuries that had elapsed since its completion[e], and thus remained in harmony with the growing intelligence

[e] It was not till the end of the eleventh century that transubstantiation was definitely established as a dogma.

of mankind, was suddenly rent in pieces by the convulsion of the Reformation, and flung away by the more religious and more progressive peoples of Europe. That which was external and concrete, was in all things to be superseded by that which was inward and spiritual. It was proclaimed that the individual spirit, while it continued to mirror itself in the world-spirit, had nevertheless an independent existence as a centre of self-issuing force, and was to be in all things active rather than passive. Truth was no longer to be truth to the soul until it should have been by the soul recognized, and in some measure even created; but when so recognized and felt, it is able under the form of faith to transcend outward works and to transform the dogmas of the understanding; it becomes the living principle within each man's breast, infinite itself, and expressing itself infinitely through his thoughts and acts. He who as a spiritual being was delivered from the priest, and brought into direct relation with the Divinity, needed not, as heretofore, to be enrolled a member of a visible congregation of his fellows, that he might live a pure and useful life among them. Thus by the Reformation the Visible Church as well as the priesthood lost that paramount importance which had hitherto belonged to it, and sank from being the depositary of all religious tradition, the source and centre of religious life, the arbiter of eternal happiness or misery, into a mere association of Christian men, for the expression of mutual sympathy and the better attainment of certain common ends. Like those other doctrines which were now assailed by the Reformation, this mediæval view of the nature of the Visible Church had been naturally, and so, it may be said, necessarily developed between the third and the twelfth century, and must therefore have represented the thoughts and satisfied the wants of those times. By the Visible Church the flickering lamp of knowledge and literary culture, as well as of religion, had been fed and tended through the long night of the Dark Ages. But, like the whole theological fabric of which it formed a part, it was now hard and unfruitful, identified with its own worst abuses, capable apparently of no further development, and unable to satisfy minds which in growing stronger had grown more conscious of their strength. Before the awakened zeal of the northern nations it stood a cold and lifeless system, whose organization as a hierarchy checked the free activity of thought, whose bestowal of worldly power and wealth on spiritual pastors drew them away from their proper duties, and which by maintaining alongside of the civil magistracy a co-ordinate and rival government, maintained also that separation of the spiritual element in man from the secular, which had been so complete and so pernicious during the Middle Ages, which debases life, and severs religion from morality.

Consequent effect upon the Empire.   The Reformation, it may be said, was a religious movement : and it is the Empire, not the Church, that we have here to consider. The distinction is only apparent. The Holy Empire is but another name for the Visible Church. It has been shewn already how mediæval theory constructed the State on the model of the Church ; how the Roman Empire was the shadow of the Popedom—designed to rule men's bodies as the pontiff ruled their souls. Both alike claimed obedience on the ground that Truth is One, and that where there is One faith there must be One government [f]. And, therefore, since it was this very principle of Formal Unity that the Reformation overthrew, it became

---

[f] See the passages quoted in note [m], p. 98 ; and note [s], p. 110.

a revolt against despotism of every kind; it erected the
standard of civil as well as of religious liberty, since both
of them are needed, though needed in a different measure,
for the worthy development of the individual spirit. The
Empire had never been conspicuously the antagonist of
popular freedom, and was, even under Charles the Fifth,
far less formidable to the commonalty than were the petty
princes of Germany. But submission, and submission on
the ground of indefeasible transmitted right, upon the
ground of Catholic traditions and the duty of the Christian magistrate to suffer heresy and schism as little as the
parallel sins of treason and rebellion, had been its constant claim and watchword. Since the days of Julius
Cæsar it had passed through many phases, but in none of
them had it ever been a constitutional monarchy, pledged
to the recognition of popular rights. And hence the
indirect tendency of the Reformation to narrow the province of government and exalt the privileges of the subject
was as plainly adverse to the Empire as the Protestant
claim of the right of private judgment was to the pretensions of the Papacy and the priesthood.

The remark must not be omitted in passing, how much *Immediate*
less than might have been expected the religious move- *influence of*
the Refor-
ment did at first actually effect in the way of promoting *mation on*
either political progress or freedom of conscience. The *political*
and religi-
habits of centuries were not to be unlearnt in a few years, *ous liberty.*
and it was natural that ideas struggling into existence
and activity should work erringly and imperfectly for a
time. By a few inflammable minds liberty was carried
into antinomianism, and produced the wildest excesses of
life and doctrine. Several fantastic sects arose, refusing
to conform to the ordinary rules without which human
society could not subsist. But these commotions neither

Conduct of the Protestant States.

spread widely nor lasted long. Far more pervading and more remarkable was the other error, if that can be called an error which was the almost unavoidable result of the circumstances of the time. The principles which had led the Protestants to sever themselves from the Roman Church, should have taught them to bear with the opinions of others, and warned them from the attempt to connect agreement in doctrine or manner of worship with the necessary forms of civil government. Still less ought they to have enforced that agreement by civil penalties; for faith, upon their own shewing, had no value save when it was freely given. A church which does not claim to be infallible is bound to allow that some part of the truth may possibly be with its adversaries: a church which permits or encourages human reason to apply itself to revelation has no right first to argue with people and then to punish them if they are not convinced. But whether it was that men only half saw what they had done, or that finding it hard enough to unrivet priestly fetters, they welcomed all the aid a temporal prince could give, the result was that religion, or rather religious creeds, began to be involved with politics more closely than had ever been the case before. Through the greater part of Christendom wars of religion raged for a century or more, and down to our own days feelings of theological antipathy continue to affect the relations of the powers of Europe. In almost every country the form of doctrine which triumphed associated itself with the state, and maintained the despotic system of the Middle Ages, while it forsook the grounds on which that system had been based. It was thus that there arose National Churches, which were to be to the several countries of Europe that which the Church Catholic had been to the world at large; churches, that is to say, each of which was to be co-extensive with its respective state, was to enjoy landed wealth and exclusive political privilege, and was to be armed with coercive powers against recusants. It was not altogether easy to find a set of theoretical principles on which such churches might be made to rest, for they could not, like the old church, point to the historical transmission of their doctrines; they could not claim to have in any one man or body of men an infallible organ of divine truth; they could not even fall back upon general councils, or the argument, whatever it may be worth, '*Securus iudicat orbis terrarum.*' But in practice these difficulties were soon got over, for the dominant party in each state, if it was not infallible, was at any rate quite sure that it was right, and could attribute the resistance of other sects to nothing but moral obliquity. The will of the sovereign, as in England, or the will of the majority, as in Holland, Scandinavia, and Scotland, imposed upon each country a peculiar form of worship, and kept up the practices of mediæval intolerance without their justification. Persecution, which might be at least excused in an infallible Catholic and Apostolic Church, was peculiarly odious when practised by those who were not catholic, who were no more apostolic than their neighbours, and who had just revolted from the most ancient and venerable authority in the name of rights which they now denied to others. If union with the visible church by participation in a material sacrament be necessary to eternal life, persecution may be held a duty, a kindness to perishing souls. But if the kingdom of heaven be in every sense a kingdom of the spirit, if saving faith be possible out of one visible body and under a diversity of external forms, persecution becomes at once a crime and a folly. Therefore the intolerance of Protestants, if the forms it took were less cruel than those practised by the Roman Catholics, was also far less defensible; for it had seldom anything better to allege on its behalf than motives of political expediency, or, more often, the mere headstrong passion of a ruler or a faction to silence the expressions of any opinions but their own. To enlarge upon this theme, did space permit it, would not be to digress from the proper subject of this narrative. For the Empire, as has been said more than once already, was far less an institution than a theory or doctrine. And hence it is not too much to say, that the ideas which have but recently ceased to prevail regarding the duty of the magistrate to compel uniformity in doctrine and worship by the civil arm, may all be traced to the relation which that doctrine established between the Roman Church and the Roman Empire; to the conception, in fact, of an Empire Church itself.

Two of the ways in which the Reformation affected the Empire have been now described: its immediate political results, and its far more profound doctrinal importance, as implanting new ideas regarding the nature of freedom and the province of government. A third, though apparently almost superficial, cannot be omitted. Its name *Influence* *of the Re-* *formation* and its traditions, little as they retained of their former *on the name* magic power, were still such as to excite the antipathy of *and asso-* *ciations of* the German reformers. The form which the doctrine of *the Empire.* the supreme importance of one faith and one body of the faithful had taken was the dominion of the ancient capital of the world through her spiritual head, the Roman bishop, and her temporal head, the Emperor. As the names of Roman and Christian had been once convertible, so long afterwards were those of Roman and Catholic. The Reformation, separating into its parts what had hitherto been one conception, attacked Roman- ism but not Catholicity, and formed religious communities which, while continuing to call themselves Christian, re- pudiated the form with which Christianity had been so long identified in the West. As the Empire was founded upon the assumption that the limits of Church and State are exactly co-extensive, a change which withdrew half of its subjects from the one body while they remained members of the other, transformed it utterly, destroyed the meaning and value of its old arrangements, and forced the Emperor into a strange and incongruous position. To his Protestant subjects he was merely the head of the administration, to the Catholics he was also the Defender and Advocate of their church. Thus from being chief of the whole state he became the chief of a party within it, the Corpus Catholicorum, as opposed to the Corpus Evangelicorum ; he lost what had been hitherto his most holy claim to the obedience of the subject; the awakened feeling of German nationality was driven into hostility to an' institution whose title and history bound it to the centre of foreign tyranny. After exulting for seven cen- turies in the heritage of Roman rule, the Teutonic nations cherished again the feelings with which their ancestors had resisted Julius Cæsar and Germanicus. Two mutually repugnant systems could not exist side by side without striving to destroy one another. The instincts of theo- logical sympathy overcame the duties of political alle- _giance, and men who were subjects both of the Empire and of their local prince, gave all their loyalty to him who espoused their doctrines and protected their worship. For in North Germany, princes as well as people were mostly Lutheran : in the southern and especially the south-eastern lands, where the magnates held to the old

CHAP. XVIII.

faith, Protestants were scarcely to be found except in the free cities. The same causes which injured the Emperor's position in Germany swept away the last semblance of his authority through other countries. In the great struggle which followed, the Protestants of England and France, of Holland and Sweden, thought of him only as the ally of Spain, of the Vatican, of the Jesuits; and he of whom it had been believed a century before that by nothing but his existence was the coming of Antichrist on earth delayed, was in the eyes of the northern divines either Antichrist himself or Antichrist's foremost champion. The earthquake that opened a chasm in Germany was felt through Europe; its states and peoples marshalled themselves under two hostile banners, and with the Empire's expiring power vanished that united Christendom it had been created to lead [g].

Troubles of Germany.

Some of the effects thus sketched began to shew themselves as early as that famous Diet of Worms, from Luther's appearance at which, in A.D. 1521, we may date the beginning of the Reformation. But just as the end of the religious conflict in England can hardly be placed earlier than the Revolution of 1688, nor in France than the Revocation of the Edict of Nantes in 1685, so it was not till after more than a century of doubtful strife that the new order of things was fully and finally established in Germany. The arrangements of Augsburg,

Rudolf II, 1576-1612.

like most treaties on the basis of *uti possidetis*, were no

---

[g] Henry VIII of England when he rebelled against the Pope called himself King of Ireland (his predecessors had used only the title 'Dominus Hiberniæ') without asking the Emperor's permission, in order to shew that he repudiated the temporal as well as the spiritual dominion of Rome.

So the Statute of Appeals is careful to deny and reject the authority of 'other foreign potentates,' meaning, no doubt, the Emperor as well as the Pope.

better than a hollow truce, satisfying no one, and consciously made to be broken. The church lands which Protestants had seized, and Jesuit confessors urged the Catholic princes to reclaim, furnished an unceasing ground of quarrel: neither party yet knew the strength of its antagonists sufficiently to abstain from insulting or persecuting their modes of worship, and the smouldering hate of half a century was kindled by the troubles of Bohemia into the Thirty Years' War.

The imperial sceptre had now passed from the indolent and vacillating Rudolf II (1576-1612), the corrupt and reckless policy of whose ministers had done much to exasperate the already suspicious minds of the Protestants, into the firmer grasp of Ferdinand the Second[h]. Jealous, bigoted, implacable, skilful in forming and concealing his plans, resolute to obstinacy in carrying them out in action, the house of Hapsburg could have had no abler and no more unpopular leader in their second attempt to turn the German Empire into an Austrian military monarchy. They seemed for a time as near to the accomplishment of the project as Charles the Fifth had been. Leagued with Spain, backed by the Catholics of Germany, served by such a leader as Wallenstein, Ferdinand proposed nothing less than the extension of the Empire to its old limits, and the recovery of his crown's full prerogative over all its vassals. Denmark and Holland were to be attacked by sea and land: Italy to be reconquered with the help of Spain : Maximilian of Bavaria and Wallenstein to be rewarded with principalities in Pomerania and Mecklenburg. The latter general was all but master of Northern Germany when the successful resistance of Stralsund turned the wavering balance of

---

[h] Matthias, brother of Rudolf II, reigned from 1612 till 1619.

Margin notes:

CHAP. XVIII.

Matthias,
1612-1619.

Thirty Years' War,
1618-1648.

Ferdinand II, A.D.
1619-37.

Plans of Ferdinand II.

CHAP. XVIII.

the war. Soon after (A.D. 1630), Gustavus Adolphus crossed the Baltic, and saved Europe from an impending reign of the Jesuits. Ferdinand's high-handed proceedings had already alarmed even the Catholic princes. Of his own authority he had put the Elector Palatine and other magnates to the ban of the Empire: he had transferred an electoral vote to Bavaria; had treated the districts overrun by his generals as spoil of war, to be portioned out at his pleasure; had unsettled all possession by requiring the restitution of church property occupied since A.D. 1555. The Protestants were helpless; the Catholics, though they complained of the flagrant illegality of such conduct, did not dare to oppose it: the rescue of Germany was the work of the Swedish king. In four campaigns he destroyed the armies and the prestige of the Emperor; devastated his lands, emptied his treasury, and left him at last so enfeebled that no subsequent successes could make him again formidable. Such, nevertheless, was the selfishness and apathy of the Protestant princes, divided by the mutual jealousy of the Lutheran and the Calvinist party—some, like the Saxon elector, most inglorious of his inglorious house, bribed by the cunning Austrian; others afraid to stir lest a reverse should expose them unprotected to his vengeance— that the issue of the long protracted contest would have gone against them but for the interference of France. It was the leading principle of Richelieu's policy to depress the house of Hapsburg and keep Germany disunited: hence he fostered Protestantism abroad while trampling it down at home. The triumph he did not live to see was sealed in A.D. 1648, on the utter exhaustion of all the combatants, and the treaties of Münster and Osnabrück were thenceforward the basis of the Germanic constitution.

Gustavus Adolphus.

Ferdinand III, 1637-1658.

The peace of Westphalia.

CHAPTER XIX.

THE PEACE OF WESTPHALIA: LAST STAGE IN THE DECLINE OF THE EMPIRE.

THE Peace of Westphalia is the first, and, with the exception perhaps of the Treaties of Vienna in 1815, the most important of those attempts to reconstruct by diplomacy the European states-system which have played so large a part in modern history. It is important, however, not as marking the introduction of new principles, but as winding up the struggle which had convulsed Germany since the revolt of Luther, sealing its results, and closing definitively the period of the Reformation. Although the causes of disunion which the religious movement called into being had now been at work for more than a hundred years, their effects were not fully seen till it became necessary to establish a system which should represent the altered relations of the German states. It may thus be said of this famous peace, as of the other so-called 'fundamental law of the Empire,' the Golden Bull, that it did no more than legalize a condition of things already in existence, but which by being legalized acquired new importance. To all parties alike the result of the Thirty Years' War was thoroughly unsatisfactory: to the Protestants, who had lost Bohemia, and still were obliged to hold an inferior place in the electoral college

z

and in the Diet: to the Catholics, who were forced to permit the exercise of heretical worship, and leave the church lands in the grasp of sacrilegious spoilers: to the princes, who could not throw off the burden of imperial supremacy: to the Emperor, who could turn that supremacy to no practical account.   No other conclusion was possible to a contest in which every one had been vanquished and no one victorious ; which had ceased because while the reasons for war continued the means of war had failed.   Nevertheless, the substantial advantage remained with the German princes, for they gained the formal recognition of that territorial independence whose origin may be placed as far back as the days of Frederick the Second, and the maturity of which had been hastened by the events of the last preceding century.   It was, indeed, not only recognized but justified as rightful and necessary.   For while the political situation, to use a current phrase, had changed within the last two hundred years, the eyes with which men regarded it had changed still more.   Never by their fiercest enemies in earlier times, not once by the Popes or Lombard republicans in the heat of their strife with the Franconian and Swabian Cæsars, had the Emperors been reproached as mere German kings, or their claim to be the lawful heirs of Rome denied.   The Protestant jurists of the sixteenth or rather of the seventeenth century were the first persons who ventured to scoff at the pretended lordship of the world, and declare their Empire to be nothing more than a German monarchy, in dealing with which no superstitious reverence need prevent its subjects from making the best terms they could for themselves, and controlling a sovereign whose religious predilections made him the friend of their enemies.

It is very instructive to turn suddenly from Dante or Peter de Andlo to a book published shortly before A.D. 1648, under the name of Hippolytus a Lapide [a], and notice the matter-of-fact way, the almost contemptuous spirit in which, disregarding the traditional glories of the Empire, he comments on its actual condition and prospects. Hippolytus, the pseudonym which the jurist Chemnitz assumed, urges with violence almost superfluous, that the Germanic constitution must be treated entirely as a native growth: that the 'lex regia' (so much discussed and so often misunderstood) and the whole system of Justinianean absolutism which the Emperor had used so dexterously, were in their applications to Germany not merely incongruous but positively absurd. With eminent learning, Chemnitz examines the early history of the Empire, draws from the unceasing contests of the monarch with the nobility the unexpected moral that the power of the former has been always dangerous, and is now more dangerous than ever, and then launches out into a long invective against the policy of the Hapsburgs, an invective which the ambition and harshness of the late Emperor made only too plausible. The one real remedy for the evils that menace Germany he states concisely—'domus Austriacæ extirpatio:' but, failing this, he would have the Emperor's prerogative restricted in every way, and provide means for resisting or dethroning him. It was by these views, which seem to have made a profound impression in Germany, that the states, or rather France and Sweden acting on their behalf, were guided in the negotiations of Osnabrück and Münster. By extorting a full recognition of the sovereignty of all the princes, Catholics and Protestants alike, in their

---

[a] *De Ratione Status in Imperio nostro Romano-Germanico.*

CHAP. XIX.
*Rights of
the Em-
peror and
the Diet, as
settled in*
A.D. 1648.

respective territories, they bound the Emperor from any direct interference with the administration, either in particular districts or throughout the Empire. All affairs of public importance, including the rights of making war or peace, of levying contributions, raising troops, building fortresses, passing or interpreting laws, were henceforth to be left entirely in the hands of the Diet. The Aulic Council, which had been sometimes the engine of imperial oppression, and always of imperial intrigue, was so restricted as to be harmless for the future. The 'reservata' of the Emperor were confined to the rights of granting titles and confirming tolls. In matters of religion, an exact though not perfectly reciprocal equality was established between the two chief ecclesiastical bodies, and the right of 'Itio in partes,' that is to say, of deciding questions in which religion was involved by amicable negotiations between the Protestant and Catholic states, instead of by a majority of votes in the Diet, was definitely conceded. Both Lutherans and Calvinists were declared free from all jurisdiction of the Pope or any Catholic prelate. Thus the last link which bound Germany to Rome was snapped, the last of the principles by virtue of which the Empire had existed was abandoned. For the Empire now contained and recognized as its members persons who formed a visible body at open war with the Holy Roman Church; and its constitution admitted schismatics to a full share in all those civil rights which, according to the doctrines of the early Middle Age, could be enjoyed by no one who was out of the communion of the Catholic Church. The Peace of Westphalia was therefore an abrogation of the sovereignty of Rome, and of the theory of Church and State with which the name of Rome was associated. And in this light was it regarded by Pope Innocent the Tenth, who commanded his legate to protest against it, and subsequently declared it void by the bull ' Zelo domus Dei [b].'

The transference of power within the Empire, from its head to its members, was a small . matter compared with the losses which the Empire suffered as a whole. The real gainers by the treaties of Westphalia were those who had borne the brunt of the battle against Ferdinand the Second and his son. To France were ceded Brisac, the Austrian part of Alsace, and the lands of the three bishoprics in Lorraine—Metz, Toul, and Verdun, which her armies had seized in A.D. 1552 : to Sweden, northern Pomerania, Bremen, and Verden. There was, however, this difference between the position of the two, that whereas Sweden became a member of the German Diet for what she received (as the king of Holland was, until 1866-7, a member for Dutch Luxemburg, and as the kings of Denmark, up till the accession of the present sovereign, were for Holstein), the acquisitions of France were delivered over to her in full sovereignty, and for ever severed from the Germanic body. And as it was by their aid that the liberties of the Protestants had been won, these two states obtained at the same time what was more valuable than territorial accessions—the right of inter-

Loss of imperial territories.

[b] Even then the Roman pontiffs had lapsed into that scolding, anile tone (so unlike the fiery brevity of Hildebrand, or the stern precision of Innocent III) which is now seldom absent from their public utterances. Pope Innocent the Tenth pronounces the provisions of the treaty, ' ipso iure nulla, irrita, invalida, iniqua, iniusta, damnata, reprobata, inania, viribusque et effectu vacua, omnino fuisse, esse, et perpetuo fore.' In spite of which they were observed.

This bull may be found in vol. xvii. of the *Bullarium*. It bears date Nov. 20th, A.D. 1648.

CHAP. XIX.

fering at imperial elections, and generally whenever the provisions of the treaties of Osnabrück and Münster, which they had guaranteed, might be supposed to be endangered. The bounds of the Empire were further narrowed by the final separation of two countries, once integral parts of Germany, and up to this time legally members of her body. Holland and Switzerland were, in A.D. 1648, declared independent.

Germany after the Peace.

The Peace of Westphalia is an era in imperial history not less clearly marked than the coronation of Otto the Great, or the death of Frederick the Second. As from the days of Maximilian it had borne a mixed or transitional character, well expressed by the name Romano-Germanic, so henceforth it is in everything but title purely and solely a German Empire. Properly, indeed, it was no longer an Empire at all, but a Confederation, and that of the loosest sort. For it had no common treasury, no efficient common tribunals c, no means of coercing a refractory member d; its states were of different religions, were governed according to different forms, were administered judicially and financially without any regard to each other. The traveller in Central Germany now is amused to find, every hour or two, by the change in the soldiers' uniforms, and the colour of the stripes on the railway fences, that he has passed out of one and into another of its miniature kingdoms. Much more surprised

---

c The Imperial Chamber (Kammergericht) continued, with frequent and long interruptions, to sit while the Empire lasted. But its slowness and formality passed that of any other legal body the world has yet seen, and it had no power to enforce its sentences.

The Aulic council was little more efficient, and was generally disliked as the tool of imperial intrigue.

d The 'matricula' specifying the quota of each state to the imperial army could not be any longer employed.

and embarrassed would he have been a century ago, when, instead of the present thirty-two there were three hundred petty principalities between the Alps and the Baltic, each with its own laws, its own courts (in which the ceremonious pomp of Versailles was faintly reproduced), its little armies, its separate coinage, its tolls and custom-houses on the frontier, its crowd of meddlesome and pedantic officials, presided over by a prime minister who was generally the unworthy favourite of his prince and the pensioner of some foreign court. This vicious system, which paralyzed the trade, the literature, and the political thought of Germany, had been forming itself for some time, but did not become fully established until the Peace of Westphalia, by emancipating the princes from imperial control, had made them despots in their own territories. The impoverishment of the inferior nobility and the decline of the commercial cities caused by a war that had lasted a whole generation, removed every counterpoise to the power of the electors and princes, and made absolutism supreme just where absolutism wants all its justification, in states too small to have any public opinion, states in which everything depends on the monarch, and the monarch depends on his favourites. After A.D. 1648 the provincial estates or parliaments became obsolete in most of these principalities, and powerless in the rest. Germany was forced to drink to its very dregs the cup of feudalism, feudalism from which all the feelings that once ennobled it had departed.

It is instructive to compare the results of the system of feudality in the three chief countries of modern Europe. In France, the feudal head absorbed all the powers of the state, and left to the aristocracy only a few privileges, odious indeed, but politically worthless. In England,

CHAP. XIX.

Number of petty independent states: effects of such a system on Germany.

Feudalism in France, England, Germany.

the mediæval system expanded into a constitutional monarchy, where the oligarchy was still strong, but the commons had won the full recognition of equal civil rights. In Germany, everything was taken from the sovereign, and nothing given to the people; the representatives of those who had been fief-holders of the first and second rank before the Great Interregnum were now independent potentates; and what had been once a monarchy was now an aristocratic federation. The Diet, originally an assembly of magnates meeting from time to time like our early English Parliaments, became in A.D. 1654 a permanent body, at which the electors, princes, and cities were represented by their envoys. In other words, it was now not a national council, but an international congress of diplomatists.

Causes of the con- tinuance of the Empire.

Where the sacrifice of imperial, or rather federal, rights to state rights was so complete, we may wonder that the farce of an Empire should have been retained at all. A mere German Empire would probably have perished; but the Teutonic people could not bring itself to abandon the venerable heritage of Rome. Moreover, the Germans were of all European peoples the most slow-moving and long-suffering; and as, if the Empire had fallen, something must have been erected in its place, they preferred to work on with the clumsy machine so long as it would work at all. Properly speaking, it has no history after this; and the history of the particular states of Germany which takes its place is one of the dreariest chapters in the annals of mankind. It would be hard to find, from the Peace of Westphalia to the French Revolution, a single grand character or a single noble enterprise; a single sacrifice made to great public interests, a single instance in which the welfare of nations was preferred to the selfish passions of their princes. The military history of those times will always be read with interest; but free and progressive countries have a history of peace not less rich and varied than that of war; and when we ask for an account of the political life of Germany in the eighteenth century, we hear nothing but the scandals of buzzing courts, and the wrangling of diplomatists at never-ending congresses.

Useless and helpless as the Empire had become, it was not without its importance to the neighbouring countries, with whose fortunes it had been linked by the Peace of Westphalia. It was the pivot on which the political system of Europe was to revolve: the scales, so to speak, which marked the equipoise of power that had become the grand object of the policy of all states. This modern caricature of the plan by which the theorists of the fourteenth century had proposed to keep the world at peace, used means less noble and attained its end no better than theirs had done. No one will deny that it was and is desirable to prevent a universal monarchy in Europe. But it may be asked whether a system can be considered successful which allowed Frederick of Prussia to seize Silesia, which did not check the aggressions of Russia and France upon their neighbours, which was for ever bartering and exchanging lands in every part of Europe without thought of the inhabitants, which permitted and has never been able to redress that greatest of public misfortunes, the partitionment of Poland. And if it be said that bad as things have been under this system, they would have been worse without it, it is hard to refrain from asking whether any evils could have been greater than those which the people of Europe have suffered through constant wars with each other, and through the

CHAP. XIX.

The Empire and the Balance of power.

Position of the Empire in Europe.

withdrawal, even in time of peace, of so large a part of their population from useful labour to be wasted in maintaining a standing army.

The result of the extended relations in which Germany now found herself to Europe, with two foreign kings never wanting an occasion, one of them never the wish, to interfere, was that a spark from her set the Continent ablaze, while flames kindled elsewhere were sure to spread hither. Matters grew worse as her princes inherited or created so many thrones abroad. The Duke of Holstein acquired Denmark, the Count Palatine Sweden, the Elector of Saxony Poland, the Elector of Hanover England, the Archduke of Austria Hungary and Bohemia, while the Elector (originally Margrave) of Brandenburg obtained, on the strength of non-imperial territories to the north-eastward which had come into his hands, the style and title of King of Prussia. Thus the Empire seemed again about to embrace Europe; but in a sense far different from that which those words would have expressed under Charles and Otto. Its history for a century and a half is a dismal list of losses and disgraces. The chief external danger was from French influence, for a time supreme, always menacing. For though Lewis the Fourteenth, on whom, in A.D. 1658, half the electoral college wished to confer the imperial crown, was before the end of his life an object of intense hatred, officially entitled 'Hereditary enemy of the Holy Empire e,' France had nevertheless a strong party among the princes always at her beck. The Rhenish and Bavarian electors were her favourite tools. The '*réunions*' begun in A.D. 1680, a pleasant euphemism for robbery in time of peace, added Strasburg and other places in Alsace, Lorraine, and

e *Erbfeind des heiligen Reichs.*

Franche Comté to the monarchy of Lewis, and brought him nearer the heart of the Empire; his ambition and cruelty were witnessed to by repeated wars, and by the devastation of the Rhine countries; the ultimate though short-lived triumph of his policy was attained when Marshal Belleisle dictated the election of Charles VII in A.D. 1742. In the Turkish wars, when the princes left Vienna to be saved by the Polish Sobieski, the Empire's weakness appeared in a still more pitiable light. There was, indeed, a complete loss of hope and interest in the old system. The princes had been so long accustomed to consider themselves the natural foes of a central government, that a request made by it was sure to be disregarded; they aped in their petty courts the pomp and etiquette of Vienna or Paris, grumbling that they should be required to garrison the great frontier fortresses which alone protected them from an encroaching neighbour. The Free Cities had never recovered the famines and sieges of the Thirty Years' War: Hanseatic greatness had waned, and the southern towns had sunk into languid oligarchies. All the vigour of the people in a somewhat stagnant age either found its sphere in rising states like the Prussia of Frederick the Great, or turned away from politics altogether into other channels. The Diet had become contemptible from the slowness with which it moved, and its tedious squabbles on matters the most frivolous. Many sittings were consumed in the discussion of a question regarding the time of keeping Easter, more ridiculous than that which had distracted the Western churches in the seventh century, the Protestants refusing to reckon by the reformed calendar because it was the work of a Pope. Collective action through the old organs was confessed impossible, when the common object of

CHAP. XIX.

Weakness and stagnation of Germany.

C IAP. XIX.

defence against France was sought by forming a league under the Emperor's presidency, and when at European congresses the Empire was not represented at all [f]. No change could come from the Emperor, whom the capitulation of A.D. 1658 deposed *ipso facto* if he violated its provisions. As Dohm [g] said, to keep him from doing harm, he was kept from doing anything.

Leopold I, 1658-1705. Joseph I, 1705-1711. Charles VI, 1711-1742.

Yet little was lost by his inactivity, for what could have been hoped from his action? From the election of Albert the Second, A.D. 1437, to the death of Charles the Sixth, A.D. 1742, the sceptre had remained in the hands of one family. So far from being fit subjects for undistinguishing invective, the Hapsburg Emperors may be contrasted favourably with the contemporary dynasties of France, Spain, or England. Their policy, viewed as a whole from the days of Rudolf downwards, had been neither conspicuously tyrannical, nor faltering, nor dishonest. But it had been always selfish. Entrusted with an office which might, if there be any power in those memories of the past to which the champions of hereditary monarchy so constantly appeal, have stirred their sluggish souls with some enthusiasm for the heroes on whose throne they sat, some wish to advance the glory and the happiness of Germany, they had cared for nothing, sought nothing, used the Empire as an instrument for nothing but the attainment of their own personal or dynastic ends. Placed on the eastern verge of Germany, the Hapsburgs had added to their ancient lands in Austria proper and Tyrol, non-German territories far more extensive, and had thus become the chiefs of a separate and independent state. They endeavoured to reconcile its interests with

The Hapsburg Emperors and their policy.

[f] Only the envoys of the several states were present at Utrecht in 1713.   [g] Quoted by Ludwig Haüsser, *Deutsche Geschichte.*

the interests of the Empire, so long as it seemed possible to recover part of the old imperial prerogative. But when such hopes were dashed by the defeats of the Thirty Years' War, they hesitated no longer between an elective crown and the rule of their hereditary states, and comported themselves thenceforth in European politics not as the representatives of Germany, but as heads of the great Austrian monarchy. There would have been nothing culpable in this had they not at the same time continued to entangle Germany in wars with which she had no concern: to waste her strength in tedious combats with the Turks, or plunge her into a new struggle with France, not to defend her frontiers or recover the lands she had lost, but that some scion of the house of Hapsburg might reign in Spain or Italy. Watching the whole course of their foreign policy, marking how in A.D. 1736 they had bartered away Lorraine for Tuscany, a German for a non-German territory, and seeing how at home they opposed every scheme of reform which could in the least degree trench upon their own prerogative, how they strove to obstruct the imperial chamber lest it should interfere with their own Aulic council, men were driven to separate the body of the Empire from the imperial office and its possessors [h], and when plans for reinvigorating the one failed, to leave the others to their fate. Still the old line clung to the crown with that Hapsburg gripe which has almost passed into a proverb. Odious as Austria was, no one could despise her, or fancy it easy to shake her commanding position in Europe. Her alliances were fortunate: her designs were steadily pursued: her dismembered territories always returned to her. Though

Causes of the long retention of the throne by Austria.

[h] The distinction is well expressed by the German 'Reich' and 'Kaiserthum,' to which we have unfortunately no terms to correspond.

the throne continued strictly elective, it was impossible not to be influenced by long prescription. Projects were repeatedly formed to set the Hapsburgs aside by electing a prince of some other line[i], or by passing a law that there should never be more than two, or four, successive Emperors of the same house. France[k] ever and anon renewed her warnings to the electors, that their freedom was passing from them, and the sceptre becoming hereditary in one haughty family. But it was felt that a change would be difficult and disagreeable, and that the heavy expense and scanty revenues of the Empire required to be supported by larger patrimonial domains than most German princes possessed. The heads of states like Prussia and Hanover, states whose size and wealth would have made them suitable candidates, were Protestants, and so excluded both by the connexion of the imperial office with the Church, and by the majority of Roman Catholics in the electoral college[l], who, however jealous they might be of Austria, were led both by habit and sympathy to rally round her in moments of peril. The

[i] So the Elector of Saxony proposed in 1532 that Albert II, Frederick III, and Maximilian having been all of one house, Charles V's successor should be chosen from some other.—Moser, *Römische Kayser*. See the various attempts of France in Moser. The coronation engagements (Wahlcapitulation) of every Emperor bound him not to attempt to make the throne hereditary in his family.

[k] In 1658 France offered to subsidize the Elector of Bavaria if he would become Emperor.

[l] Whether an Evangelical was eligible for the office of Emperor was a question often debated, but never actually raised by the candidature of any but a Roman Catholic prince. The 'exacta æqualitas' conceded by the Peace of Westphalia might appear to include so important a privilege. But when we consider that the peculiar relation in which the Emperor stood to the Holy Roman Church was one which no heretic could hold, and that the coronation oaths could not have been taken by, nor the coronation ceremonies (among which was a sort of ordination) performed upon a Protestant, the conclusion must be unfavourable to the claims of any but a Catholic.

one occasion on which these considerations were disregarded shewed their force. On the extinction of the male line of Hapsburg in the person of Charles the Sixth, the intrigues of the French envoy, Marshal Belleisle, procured the election of Charles Albert of Bavaria, who stood first among the Catholic princes. His reign was a succession of misfortunes and ignominies. Driven from Munich by the Austrians, the head of the Holy Empire lived in Frankfort on the bounty of France, cursed by the country on which his ambition had brought the miseries of a protracted war [m]. The choice in 1745 of Duke Francis of Lorraine, husband of the archduchess of Austria and queen of Hungary, Maria Theresa, was meant to restore the crown to the only power capable of wearing it with dignity: in Joseph the Second, her son, it again rested on the brow of a Hapsburg [n]. In

CHAP. XIX.

Charles VII, 1742-1745.

Francis I, 1745-1765.

[m] 'The bold Bavarian, in a luckless hour,
Tries the dread summits of Cæsarian power.
With unexpected legions bursts away,
And sees defenceless realms receive his sway. . . .
The baffled prince in honour's flattering bloom
Of hasty greatness finds the fatal doom;
His foes' derision and his subjects' blame,
And steals to death from anguish and from shame.'
JOHNSON, *Vanity of Human Wishes.*

[n] The following nine reasons for the long continuance of the Empire in the House of Hapsburg are given by Pfeffinger (*Vitriarius Illustratus*), writing early in the eighteenth century :—

1. The great power of Austria.
2. Her wealth, now that the Empire was so poor.
3. The majority of Catholics among the electors.
4. Her fortunate matrimonial alliances.
5. Her moderation.
6. The memory of benefits conferred by her.
7. The example of evils that had followed a departure from the blood of former Cæsars.
8. The fear of the confusion that would ensue if she were deprived of the crown.
9. Her own eagerness to have it.

the war of the Austrian succession, which followed on the death of Charles the Sixth, the Empire as a body took no part; in the Seven Years' War its whole might broke in vain against one resolute member. Under Frederick the Great Prussia approved herself at least a match for France and Austria leagued against her, and the semblance of unity which the predominance of a single power had hitherto given to the Empire was replaced by the avowed rivalry of two military monarchies. The Emperor Joseph the Second, a sort of philosopher-king, than whom few have more narrowly missed greatness, made a desperate effort to set things right, striving to restore the disorded finances, to purge and vivify the Imperial Chamber. Nay, he renounced the intolerant policy of his ancestors, quarrelled with the Pope[o], and presumed to visit Rome, whose streets heard once more the shout that had been silent for three centuries, 'Evviva il nostro imperatore! Siete a casa vostra: siete il padrone[p].' But his indiscreet haste was met by a sullen resistance, and he died disappointed in plans for which the time was not yet ripe, leaving no result save the league of princes which Frederick the Great had formed to oppose his designs on Bavaria. His successor, Leopold the Second, abandoned the projected reforms, and a calm, the calm before the hurricane, settled down again upon Germany. The existence of the Empire was almost forgotten by its subjects: there was nothing to remind them of it but a feudal investiture now and then at Vienna (real

---

[o] The Pope undertook a journey to Vienna to mollify Joseph, and met with a sufficiently cold reception. When he saw the famous minister Kaunitz and gave him his hand to kiss, Kaunitz took it and shook it.

[p] 'You are in your own house: be the master.'

feudal rights were obsolete q); a concourse of solemn old
lawyers at Wetzlar puzzling over interminable suits r; and
some thirty diplomatists at Regensburg s, the relics of that
Imperial Diet where once a hero-king, a Frederick or a
Henry, enthroned amid mitred prelates and steel-clad
barons, had issued laws for every tribe from the Mediterranean to the Baltic t. The solemn triflings of this so-
called 'Diet of Deputation' have probably never been
equalled elsewhere u. Questions of precedence and title,
questions whether the envoys of princes should have
chairs of red cloth like those of the electors, or only of
the less honourable green, whether they should be served
on gold or on silver, how many hawthorn boughs should
be hung up before the door of each on May-day; these,
and such as these, it was their chief employment not to
settle but to discuss. The pedantic formalism of old
Germany passed that of Spaniards or Turks; it had now
crushed under a mountain of rubbish whatever meaning
or force its old institutions had contained. It is the
penalty of greatness that its form should outlive its substance: that gilding and trappings should remain when
that which they were meant to deck and clothe has departed. So our sloth or our timidity, not seeing that
whatever is false must be also bad, maintains in being
what once was good long after it has become helpless and
hopeless: so now at the close of the eighteenth century,

CHAP. XIX.

The Diet.

---

q Joseph II was foiled in his
attempt to assert them.

r Goethe spent some time in
studying law at Wetzlar among
those who practised in the Kammergericht.

s Cf. Pütter, *Historical Develope-
ment of the Political Constitution of
the German Empire*, vol. iii.

t Frederick the Great said of
the Diet, 'Es ist ein Schattenbild,
eine Versammlung aus Publizisten
die mehr mit Formalien als mit
Sachen sich beschäftigen, und, wie
Hofhunde, den Mond anbellen.'

u Cf. Haüsser, *Deutsche Geschichte*; Introduction.

*Feelings
of the
German
people.*

strings of sounding titles were all that was left of the Empire which Charles had founded, and Frederick adorned, and Dante sung.

The German mind, just beginning to put forth the blossoms of its wondrous literature, turned away in disgust from the spectacle of ceremonious imbecility more than Byzantine. National feeling seemed gone from princes and people alike. Lessing, who did more than any one else to create the German literary spirit, says, ' Of the love of country I have no conception : it appears to me at best a heroic weakness which I am right glad to be without [x].' The Emperor Joseph II writes to his brother of France : ' You must know that the annihilation of German nationality is a necessary leading principle of my policy [y].' There were nevertheless persons who saw how fatal such a system was, lying like a nightmare on the people's soul. Speaking of the union of princes formed by Frederick of Prussia to preserve the existing condition of things, Johannes von Müller writes [z] : ' If the German Union serves for nothing better than to maintain the *status quo*, it is against the eternal order of God, by which neither the physical nor the moral world remains for a moment in the *status quo*, but all is life and motion and progress. To exist without law or justice, without security from arbitrary imposts, doubtful whether we can preserve from day to day our honours, our liberties, our rights, our lives, helpless before superior force, without a beneficial connexion between our states, without a national spirit at all, this is the *status quo* of our nation. And it was this that the Union was meant to confirm. If it be this and

[x] Quoted by Haüsser.
[y] Rotteck and Welcker, *Staats Lexikon*, s. v. ' Deutsches Reich.'

[z] *Deutschlands Erwartungen vom Fürstenbunde*, quoted in the *Staats Lexikon*.

nothing more, then bethink you how when Israel saw that
Rehoboam would not hearken, the people gave answer to
the king and spake, " What portion have we in David, or
what inheritance in the son of Jesse? to your tents, O
Israel : David, see to thine own house." See then to your
own houses, ye princes.'

Nevertheless, though the Empire stood like a corpse
brought forth from some Egyptian sepulchre, ready to
crumble at a touch, there seemed no reason why it should
not stand so for centuries more. Fate was kind, and slew
it in the light.

CHAPTER XX.

FALL OF THE EMPIRE.

GOETHE has described the uneasiness with which, in the days of his childhood, the burghers of his native Frankfort saw the walls of the Roman Hall covered with the portraits of Emperor after Emperor, till space was left for few, at last for one [a]. In A.D. 1792 Francis the Second mounted the throne of Augustus, and the last place was filled. Three years before there had arisen on the western horizon a little cloud, no bigger than a man's hand, and now the heaven was black with storms of ruin. There was a prophecy [b], dating from the first days of the Empire's decline, that when all things were falling to ruin, and wickedness rife in the world, a second Frankish Charles should rise as Emperor to purge and heal, to bring back peace and purify religion. If this was not exactly the mission of the new ruler of the West Franks, he was at least anxious to tread in the steps and revive the glories of the hero whose crown he professed to have inherited. It were a task superfluously easy to shew how delusive is that minute historical parallel of which every Parisian was full in A.D. 1804, the parallel between the heir of a long

---

[a] *Wahrheit und Dichtung*, book i. The Römer Saal is still one of the sights of Frankfort. The portraits, however, which one now sees in it, seem to be all or nearly all of them modern; and few have any merit as works of art.

[b] *Jordanis Chronica*, ap. Schardium, *Sylloge Tractatuum*.

line of fierce Teutonic chieftains, whose vigorous genius had seized what it could of the monkish learning of the eighth century, and the son of the Corsican lawyer, with all the brilliance of a Frenchman and all the resolute profundity of an Italian, reared in, yet only half believing, the ideas of the Encyclopædists, swept up into the seat of absolute power by the whirlwind of a revolution. Alcuin and Talleyrand are not more unlike than are their masters. But though in the characters and temper of the men there is little resemblance, though their Empires agree in this only, and hardly even in this, that both were founded on conquest, there is nevertheless a sort of grand historical similarity between their positions. Both were the leaders of fiery and warlike nations, the one still untamed as the creatures of their native woods, the other drunk with revolutionary fury. Both aspired to found, and seemed for a time to have succeeded in founding, universal monarchies. Both were gifted with a strong and susceptible imagination, which if it sometimes overbore their judgment, was yet one of the truest and highest elements of their greatness. As the one looked back to the kings under the Jewish theocracy and the Emperors of Christian Rome, so the other thought to model himself after Cæsar and Charlemagne. For, useful as was the fancied precedent of the title and career of the great Carolingian to a chief determined to be king, yet unable to be king after the fashion of the Bourbons, and seductive as was such a connexion to the imaginative vanity of the French people, it was no studied purpose or simulating art that led Napoleon to remind his subjects so frequently of the hero he claimed to represent. No one who reads the records of his life can doubt that he believed, as fully as he believed anything, that the same destiny which had made France

CHAP. XX.
*Napoleon,
Emperor of
the West.*

*Belief of
Napoleon
that he was
the successor*

the centre of the modern world had also appointed him to sit on the throne and carry out the projects of Charles the Frank, to rule all Europe from Paris, as the Cæsars had ruled it from Rome [c]. It was in this belief that he went to the ancient capital of the Frankish Emperors to receive there the Austrian recognition of his imperial title : that he talked of 'revendicating' Catalonia and Aragon, because they had formed a part of the Carolingian realm, though they had never obeyed the descendants of Hugh Capet : that he undertook a journey to Nimeguen, where he had ordered the ancient palace to be restored, and inscribed on its walls his name below that of Charles : that he summoned the Pope to attend his coronation as Stephen had come ten centuries before to instal Pipin in the throne of the last Merovingian [d]. The same desire

[c] In an address by Napoleon to the Senate in 1804, bearing date 10th Frimaire (1st Dec.), are the words, ' Mes descendans conserveront longtemps ce trône, le premier de l'univers.' Answering a deputation from the department of the Lippe, Aug. 8th, 1811, ' La Providence, qui a voulu que je rétablisse le trône de Charlemagne, vous a fait naturellement rentrer, avec la Hollande et les villes anséatiques, dans le sein de l'Empire.'—Œuvres de Napoléon, tom. v. p. 521.

' Pour le Pape, je suis Charlemagne, parce que, comme Charlemagne, je réunis la couronne de France à celle des Lombards, et que mon Empire confine avec l'Orient.' (Quoted by Lanfrey, Vie de Napoleon, iii. 417.)

' Votre Sainteté est souveraine de Rome, mais j'en suis l'Empereur.' (Letter of Napoleon to Pope- Pius, Feb. 13th, 1806. Lanfrey.)

' Dites bien,' says Napoleon to Cardinal Fesch, ' que je suis Charlemagne, leur Empereur [of the Papal Court] que je dois être traité de même. Je fais connaitre au Pape mes intentions en peu de mots, s'il n' y acquiesce pas, je le réduirai à la même condition qu' il était avant Charlemagne.' (Lanfrey, Vie de Napoleon, iii. 420.)

[d] Napoleon said on one occasion, ' Je n' 'ai pas succédé a Louis Quatorze, mais a Charlemagne.'— Bourrienne, Vie de Napoléon, iv. In 1804, shortly before he was crowned, he had the imperial insignia of Charles brought from the old Frankish capital, and exhibited them in a jeweller's shop in Paris, along with those which had just been made for his own coronation ;—(Bourrienne, ut supra.) Somewhat in the same spirit in which he

to be regarded as lawful Emperor of the West shewed
itself in his assumption of the Lombard crown at Milan;
in the words of the decree by which he annexed Rome to
the Empire, revoking 'the donations which my predecessors, the French Emperors, have made [e];' in the title
'King of Rome,' which he bestowed on his ill-fated son,
in imitation of the German 'King of the Romans [f].' We
are even told that it was at one time his intention to eject
the Hapsburgs, and be chosen Roman Emperor in their
stead. Had this been done, the analogy would have been
complete between the position which the French ruler
held to Austria now, and that in which Charles and Otto
had stood to the feeble Cæsars of Byzantium. It was
curious to see the head of the Roman church turning
away from his ancient ally to the reviving power of France
—France, where the Goddess of Reason had been worshipped eight years before—just as he had sought the help
of the first Carolingians against his Lombard enemies [g].
The difference was indeed great between the feelings
wherewith Pius the Seventh addressed his 'very dear
son in Christ,' and those that had pervaded the intercourse of Pope Hadrian the First with the son of Pipin;
just as the contrast is strange between the principles that
shaped Napoleon's policy and the vision of a theocracy
that had floated before the mind of Charles. Neither

Attitude of the Papacy towards Napoleon.

---

displayed the Bayeux tapestry, in
order to incite his subjects to the
conquest of England.

e . ' Je n' ai pu concilier ces grands
intérêts (of political order and the
spiritual authority of the Pope) qu'
en annulant les donations des Em-
pereurs Français, mes predecesseurs,
et en réunissant les états romains à
la France.'—Proclamation issued

in 1809 : *Œuvres*, iv.

f See Appendix, Note C.

g Pope Pius VII wrote to the
First Consul, ' Carissime in Christo
Fili noster .... tam perspecta sunt
nobis tuæ voluntatis studia erga nos,
ut *quotiescunque* ope aliqua in rebus
nostris indigemus, eam a te fidenter
petere non dubitare debeamus.'—
Quoted by Ægidi.

CHAP. XX.

comparison is much to the advantage of the modern; but Pius might be pardoned for catching at any help in his distress, and Napoleon found that the protectorship of the church strengthened his position in France, and gave him dignity in the eyes of Christendom [h].

The French Empire.

A swift succession of triumphs had left only one thing still preventing the full recognition of the Corsican warrior as sovereign of Western Europe, and that one was the existence of the old Romano-Germanic Empire. Napoleon had not long assumed his new title when he began to mark a distinction between 'la France' and 'l'Empire Française.' France had, since A.D. 1792, advanced to the Rhine, and, by the annexation of Piedmont, had over-stepped the Alps; the French Empire included, besides the kingdom of Italy, a mass of dependent states, Naples, Holland, Switzerland, and many German principalities, the allies of France in the same sense in which the 'socii populi Romani' were allies of Rome [i]. When the last of Pitt's coalitions had been destroyed at Austerlitz, and Austria had made her submission by the peace of Pres-burg, the conqueror felt that his hour was come. He had now overcome two Emperors, those of Austria and Russia, claiming to represent the old and the new Rome

[h] Let us place side by side the letters of Hadrian to Charles in the *Codex Carolinus*, and the following preamble to the Concordat of A.D. 1801, between the First Consul and the Pope (which I quote from the *Bullarium Romanum*), and mark the changes of a thousand years.

'Gubernium reipublicæ [Gallicæ] recognoscit religionem Catholicam Apostolicam Romanam eam esse religionem quam longe maxima pars civium Gallicæ reipublicæ profitetur.

'Summus pontifex pari modo recognoscit eandem religionem maximam utilitatem maximumque decus percepisse et hoc quoque tempore præstolari ex catholico cultu in Gallia constituto, necnon ex peculiari eius professione quam faciunt reipublicæ consules.'

[i] Cf. Heeren, *Political System*, vol. iii. 273.

respectively, and had in eighteen months created more kings than the occupants of the Germanic throne in as many centuries. It was time, he thought, to sweep away obsolete pretensions, and claim the sole inheritance of that Western Empire, of which the titles and ceremonies of his court presented a grotesque imitation [k]. The task was an easy one after what had been already accomplished. Previous wars and treaties had so redistributed the territories and changed the constitution of the Germanic Empire that it could hardly be said to exist in anything but name. In French history Napoleon appears as the restorer of peace, the rebuilder of the shattered edifice of social order: the author of a code and an administrative system which the Bourbons who dethroned him were glad to preserve. Abroad he was the true child of the Revolution, and conquered only to destroy. It was his mission—a mission more beneficent in its result than in its means [l]—to break up in Germany and Italy the abominable system of petty states, to reawaken the spirit of the people, to sweep away the relics of an effete feudalism, and leave the ground clear for the growth of newer and better forms of political life. Since A.D. 1797, when Austria at Campo Formio perfidiously exchanged the Netherlands for Venetia, the work of destruction had gone on apace. All the German sovereigns west of the Rhine had been dispossessed, and their territories incorporated with France, while the rest of the country had been revolutionized by the arrange-

CHAP. XX.

Napoleon in Germany.

---

[k] He had arch-chancellors, arch-treasurers, and so forth. The Legion of Honour, which was thought important enough to be mentioned in the coronation oath, was meant to be something like the mediæval orders of knighthood: whose connexion with the Empire has already been mentioned.

[l] Napoleon's feelings towards Germany may be gathered from the phrase he once used, ' Il faut depayser l'Allemagne.'

ments of the peace of Luneville and the 'Indemnities,' dictated by the French to the Diet in February 1803. New kingdoms were erected, electorates created and extinguished, the lesser princes mediatized, the free cities occupied by troops and bestowed on some neighbouring potentate. More than any other change, the secularization of the dominions of the prince-bishops and abbots proclaimed the fall of the old constitution, whose principles had required the existence of a spiritual alongside of the temporal aristocracy. The Emperor Francis, partly foreboding the events that were at hand, partly in order to meet Napoleon's assumption of the imperial name by depriving that name of its peculiar meaning, began in A.D. 1805 to style himself 'Hereditary Emperor of Austria,' while retaining at the same time his former title [m]. The next act of the drama was one in which we may more readily pardon the ambition of a foreign conqueror than the traitorous selfishness of the German princes, who broke every tie of ancient friendship and duty to grovel at his throne. By the Act of the Confederation [n] of the Rhine, signed at Paris, July 12th, 1806, Bavaria, Würtemberg, Baden, and several other states,

The Confederation of the Rhine.

[m] Thus in documents issued by the Emperor during these two years he is styled 'Roman Emperor Elect, Hereditary Emperor of Austria' (erwählter Römischer Kaiser, Erbkaiser von Oesterreich).

[n] This Act of Confederation of the Rhine (Rheinbund) is printed in Koch's *Traités* (continued by Schöll), vol. viii., and Meyer's *Corpus Iuris Confœderationis Germanicæ,* vol. i. It has every appearance of being a translation from the French, and was no doubt originally drawn up in that language. Napoleon is called in one place 'Der nämliche Monarch, dessen Absichten sich stets mit den wahren Interessen Deutschlands übereinstimmend gezeigt haben.' The phrase 'Roman Empire' does not occur: we hear only of the 'German Empire,' 'body of German states' (Staatskörper), and so forth. This Confederation of the Rhine was eventually joined by every German State except Austria, Prussia, Electoral Hesse, and Brunswick.

sixteen in all, withdrew from the body and repudiated the laws of the Empire, while on August 1st the French envoy at Regensburg announced to the Diet that his master, who had consented to become Protector of the Confederate princes, no longer recognized the existence of the Empire. Francis the Second resolved at once to anticipate this new Odoacer, and by a declaration, dated August 6th, 1806, resigned the imperial dignity. His deed states that finding it impossible, in the altered state of things, to fulfil the obligations imposed by his capitulation, he considers as dissolved the bonds which attached him to the Germanic body, releases from their allegiance the states who formed it, and retires to the government of his hereditary dominions under the title of 'Emperor of Austria °.' Throughout, the term 'German Empire' (*Deutsches Reich*) is employed. But it was the crown of Augustus, of Constantine, of Charles, of Maximilian, that Francis of Hapsburg laid down, and a new era in the world's history was marked by the fall of its most venerable institution. One thousand and six years after Leo the Pope had crowned the Frankish king, eighteen hundred and fifty-eight years after Cæsar had conquered at Pharsalia, the Holy Roman Empire came to its end.

There was a time when this event would have been thought a sign that the last days of the world were at

CHAP. XX.

Abdication of the Emperor Francis II.

End of the Empire.

° *Histoire des Traités*, vol. viii. The original may be found in Meyer's *Corpus Iuris Confœderationis Germanicæ*, vol. i. p. 70. It is a document in no way remarkable, except from the ludicrous resemblance which its language suggests to the circular in which a tradesman, announcing the dissolution of an old partnership, solicits, and hopes by close attention to merit, a continuance of his customers' patronage to his business, which will henceforth be carried on under the name of, &c., &c.

hand. But in the whirl of change that had bewildered men since A.D. 1789, it passed almost unnoticed. No one could yet fancy how things would end, or what sort of a new order would at last shape itself out of chaos. When Napoleon's universal monarchy had dissolved, and old landmarks shewed themselves again above the receding waters, it was commonly supposed that the Empire would be re-established on its former footing [p]. Such was indeed the wish of many states, and among them of Hanover, representing Great Britain [q]. Though a simple revival of the old Romano-Germanic Empire was plainly out of the question, it still appeared to them that Germany would be best off under the presidency of a single head, entrusted with the ancient office of maintaining peace among the members of the confederation. But the new kingdoms, Bavaria especially, were unwilling to admit a superior; Prussia, elated at the glory she had won in the war of independence, would have disputed the crown with Austria; Austria herself cared little to resume an office shorn of much of its dignity, with duties to perform and no resources to enable her to discharge them. Use was therefore made of an expression in the Peace of Paris which spoke of uniting Germany by a federative bond [r], and the Congress of Vienna was decided by the wishes of Austria to establish a Confederation. Thus

Congress of Vienna.

[p] Koch (Schöll), *Histoire des Traités*, vol. xi. p. 257, *sqq.;* Haüsser, *Deutsche Geschichte*, vol. iv.

[q] Great Britain had refused in 1806 to recognize the dissolution of the Empire. And it may indeed be maintained that in point of law the Empire was never extinguished at all, but lives on as a disembodied spirit to this day. For it is clear that, technically speaking, the abdication of a sovereign can destroy only his own rights, and does not dissolve the state over which he presides.

[r] 'Les états d'Allemagne seront independans et unis par un lien federatif.'—*Histoire des Traités*, xi. p. 257.

was brought about the present German federal constitution, which is itself confessed, by the attempts so often made to reform it, to be a mere temporary expedient, oppressive in the hands of the strong, and useless for the protection of the weak. Of late years, one school of liberal politicians, justly indignant at their betrayal by the princes after the enthusiastic uprising of A.D. 1814, has aspired to the restoration of the Empire, either as an hereditary kingdom in the Prussian or some other family, or in a more republican fashion under a head elected by the people [s]. The obstacles in the way of such plans are evidently very great; but even were the horizon more clear than it is, this would not be the place from which to scan it [t].

[s] The late king of Prussia was actually elected Emperor by the revolutionary Diet at Frankfort in 1848. He refused the crown.

[t] [Since the above was written (in A.D. 1865) sudden and momentous changes have been effected in Germany by the war of 1866; the Prussian kingdom has been enlarged by the annexation of Hanover, Hessen-Cassel, Nassau, and Frankfort; the establishment of the North German Confederation has brought all the states north of the Main under Prussian control; while even the potentates of the south have virtually accepted the hegemony of the house of Hohenzollern. It was the author's intention to have added here a chapter examining these changes by the light of the past history of Germany and the Empire, and tracing out the causes to which the success of Prussia is to be ascribed. But at this moment (July 15th, 1870) the French Emperor declares war against Prussia, and there rises to meet the challenge an united German people,—united for the time, at least, by the folly of the enemy who has so long plotted for and profited by its disunion. Whatever the result of the struggle may be, it is almost certain to alter still further the internal constitution of Germany; and there is therefore little use in discussing the existing system, and tracing the progress hitherto of a development which, if not suddenly arrested, is likely to be greatly accelerated by the events which we see passing.

CHAPTER XXI.

CONCLUSION.

AFTER the attempts already made to examine separately each of the phases of the Empire, little need be said, in conclusion, upon its nature and results in general. A general character can hardly help being either vague or false. For the aspects which the Empire took are as many and as various as the ages and conditions of society during which it continued to exist. Among the exhausted peoples around the Mediterranean, whose national feeling had died out, whose faith was extinct or turned to superstition, whose thought and art was a faint imitation of the Greek, there arises a huge despotism, first of a city, then of an administrative system, which presses with equal weight on all its subjects, and becomes to them a religion as well as a government. Just when the mass is at length dissolving, the tribes of the North come down, too rude to maintain the institutions they found subsisting, too few to introduce their own, and a weltering confusion follows, till the strong hand of the first Frankish Emperor raises the fallen image and bids the nations bow down to it once more. Under him it is for some brief space a theocracy; under his German successors the first of feudal kingdoms, the centre of European chivalry. As feudalism wanes, it is again trans-

formed, and after promising for a time to become an
hereditary Hapsburg monarchy, sinks at last into the
presidency, not more dignified than powerless, of an international league. To us moderns, a perpetuation under
conditions so diverse of the same name and the same
pretensions, appears at first sight absurd, a phantom too
vain to impress the most superstitious mind. Closer
examination will correct such a notion. No power was
ever based on foundations so sure and deep as those
which Rome laid during three centuries of conquest and
four of undisturbed dominion. If her empire had been
an hereditary or local kingdom, it might have fallen with
the extinction of the royal line, the conquest of the tribe,
the destruction of the city to which it was attached.
But it was not so limited. It was imperishable because
it was universal; and when its power had ceased, it was
remembered with awe and love by the races whose separate existence it had destroyed, because it had spared the
weak while it smote down the strong; because it had
granted equal rights to all, and closed against none of
its subjects the path of honourable ambition. When the
military power of the conquering city had departed, her
sway over the world of thought began: by her the theories
of the Greeks had been reduced to practice; by her the
new religion had been embraced and organized; her
language, her theology, her laws, her architecture made
their way where the eagles of war had never flown, and
with the spread of civilization have found new homes
on the Ganges and the Mississippi.

Nor is such a claim of government prolonged under
changed conditions by any means a singular phenomenon.
Titles sum up the political history of nations, and are as
often causes as effects: if not insignificant now, how

CHAP. XXI.

*Perpetua-
tion of the
name of
Rome.*

*Parallel
instances.*

CHAP. XXI. much less so in ages of ignorance and unreason. It would be an instructive, if it were not a tedious task, to examine the many pretensions that are still put forward to represent the Empire of Rome, all of them baseless, *Claims to* none of them effectless. Austria clings to a name which *represent* seems to give her a sort of precedence in Europe, and *the Roman* was wont, while she held Lombardy, to justify her position *Empire.* there by invoking the feudal rights of the Hohenstaufen. *Austria.* With no more legal right than the prince of Reuss or the landgrave of Homburg might pretend to, she has assumed the arms and devices of the old Empire, and being almost the youngest of European monarchies, is respected as the *France.* oldest and most conservative. Bonapartean France, as the self-appointed heir of the Carolingians, grasped for a time the sceptre of the West, and still aspires to hold the balance of European politics, and be recognized as the leader and patron of the so-called Latin races on both sides of the Atlantic [a]. Professing the creed of Byzan- *Russia.* tium, Russia claims the crown of the Byzantine Cæsars, and trusts that the capital which prophecy has promised for a thousand years will not be long withheld. The doctrine of Panslavism, under an imperial head of the whole Eastern church, has become a formidable engine of aggression in the hands of a crafty and warlike des- *Greece.* potism. Another testimony to the enduring influence of old political combinations is supplied by the eagerness with which modern Hellas has embraced the notion of gathering all the Greek races into a revived Empire of *The Turks.* the East, with its capital on the Bosphorus. Nay, the intruding Ottoman himself, different in faith as well as in blood, has more than once declared himself the repre-

[a] See Louis Napoleon's letter to General Forey, explaining the object of the expedition to Mexico.

sentative of the Eastern Cæsars, whose dominion he extinguished. Solyman the Magnificent assumed the name of Emperor, and refused it to Charles the Fifth: his successors were long preceded through the streets of Constantinople by twelve officers, bearing straws aloft, a faint semblance of the consular fasces that had escorted a Quinctius or a Fabius through the Roman forum. Yet in no one of these cases has there been that apparent legality of title which the shouts of the people and the benediction of the pontiff conveyed to Charles and Otto[b].

These examples, however, are minor parallels: the complement and illustration of the history of the Empire is to be found in that of the Holy See. The Papacy, whose spiritual power was itself the offspring of Rome's temporal dominion, evoked the phantom of her parent, used it, obeyed it, rebelled and overthrew it, in its old age once more embraced it, till in its downfall she has heard the knell of her own approaching doom[c].

Parallel of the Papacy.

Both Papacy and Empire rose in an age when the human spirit was utterly prostrated before authority and tradition, when the exercise of private judgment was impossible to most and sinful to all. Those who believed the miracles recorded in the *Acta Sanctorum*, and did not question the Isidorian decretals, might well recognize as ordained of God the twofold authority of Rome, founded, as it seemed to be, on so many texts of Scripture, and confirmed by five centuries of undisputed possession. Both sanctioned and satisfied the passion of the Middle

---

[b] One may also compare the retention of the office of consul at Rome till the time of Justinian: indeed it even survived his formal abolition. The relinquishment of the title 'King of Great Britain, France, and Ireland,' seriously distressed many excellent persons.

[c] I speak, of course, of the Papacy as an autocratic power claiming a more than spiritual authority.

Ages for unity. Ferocity, violence, disorder, were the conspicuous evils of that time: hence all the aspirations of the good were for something which, breaking the force of passion and increasing the force of sympathy, should teach the stubborn wills to sacrifice themselves in the view of a common purpose. To those men, moreover, unable to rise above the sensuous, not seeing the true connexion or the true difference of the spiritual and the secular, the idea of the Visible Church was full of awful meaning. Solitary thought was helpless, and strove to lose itself in the aggregate, since it could not create for itself that which was universal. The schism that severed a man from the congregation of the faithful on earth was hardly less dreadful than the heresy which excluded him from the company of the blessed in heaven. He who kept not his appointed place in the ranks of the church militant had no right to swell the rejoicing anthems of the church triumphant. Here, as in so many other cases, the continued use of traditional language seems to have prevented us from seeing how great is the difference between our own times and those in which the phrases we repeat were first used, and used in full sincerity. Whether the world is better or worse for the change which has passed upon its feelings in these matters is another question: all that it is necessary to note here is that the change is a profound and pervading one. Obedience, almost the first of mediæval virtues, is now often spoken of as if it were fit only for slaves or fools. Instead of praising, men are wont to condemn the submission of the individual will, the surrender of the individual belief, to the will or the belief of the community. Some persons declare variety of opinion to be a positive good. The great mass have certainly no longing for an abstract unity of faith. They have no horror of schism. They do not, cannot, understand the intense fascination which the idea of one all-pervading church exercised upon their mediæval forefathers. A life in the church, for the church, through the church; a life which she blessed in mass at morning and sent to peaceful rest by the vesper hymn; a life which she supported by the constantly recurring stimulus of the sacraments, relieving it by confession, purifying it by penance, admonishing it by the presentation of visible objects for contemplation and worship,—this was the life which they of the Middle Ages conceived of as the rightful life for man; it was the actual life of many, the ideal of all. The unseen world was so unceasingly pointed to, and its dependence on the seen so intensely felt, that the barrier between the two seemed to disappear. The church was not merely the portal to heaven; it was heaven anticipated; it was already self-gathered and complete. In one sentence from a famous mediæval document may be found a key to much which seems strangest to us in the feelings of the Middle Ages: 'The church is dearer to God than heaven. For the church does not exist for the sake of heaven, but conversely, heaven for the sake of the church [d].'

Again, both Empire and Papacy rested on opinion rather than on physical force, and when the struggle of the eleventh century came, the Empire fell, because its rival's hold over the souls of men was firmer, more direct, enforced by penalties more terrible than the death of the

[d] 'Ipsa enim ecclesia charior Deo est quam cœlum. Non enim propter cœlum ecclesia, sed e converso propter ecclesiam cœlum.' From the tract entitled 'A Letter of the four Universities to Wenzel and Urban VIII,' quoted in an earlier chapter.

body. The ecclesiastical body under Alexander and Innocent was animated by a loftier spirit and more wholly devoted to a single aim than the knights and nobles who followed the banner of the Swabian Cæsars. Its allegiance was undivided; it comprehended the principles for which it fought: they trembled at even while they resisted the spiritual power.

Papacy and Empire compared as perpetuations of a name.

Both sprang from what might be called the accident of name. The power of the great Latin patriarchate was a Form: the ghost, it has been said, of the older Empire, favoured in its growth by circumstances, but really vital because capable of wonderful adaptation to the character and wants of the time. So too, though far less perfectly, was the Empire. Its Form was the tradition of the universal rule of Rome; it met the needs of successive centuries by civilizing barbarous peoples, by maintaining unity in confusion and disorganization, by controlling brute violence through the sanctions of a higher power, by being made the keystone of a gigantic feudal arch, by assuming in its old age the presidency of a European confederation. And the history of both, as it shews the power of ancient names and forms, shews also within what limits such a perpetuation is possible, and how it sometimes deceives men, by preserving the shadow while it loses the substance. This perpetuation itself, what is it but the expression of the belief of mankind, a belief incessantly corrected yet never weakened, that their old institutions do and may continue to subsist unchanged, that what has served their fathers will do well enough for them, that it is possible to make a system perfect and abide in it for ever? Of all political instincts this is perhaps the strongest; often useful, often grossly abused, but never so natural and so fitting as when it leads men who feel themselves inferior to their predecessors, to save what they can from the wreck of a civilization higher than their own. It was thus that both Papacy and Empire were maintained by the generations who had no type of greatness and wisdom save that which they associated with the name of Rome. And therefore it is that no examples shew so convincingly how hopeless are all such attempts to preserve in life a system which arose out of ideas and under conditions that have passed away. Though it never could have existed save as a prolongation, though it was and remained through the Middle Ages an anachronism, the Empire of the tenth century had little in common with the Empire of the second. Much more was the Papacy, though it too hankered after the forms and titles of antiquity, in reality a new creation. And in the same proportion as it was new, and represented the spirit not of a past age but of its own, was it a power stronger and more enduring than the Empire. More enduring, because younger, and so in fuller harmony with the feelings of its contemporaries: stronger, because at the head of the great ecclesiastical body, in and through which, rather than through secular life, all the intelligence and political activity of the Middle Ages sought its expression. The famous simile of Gregory the Seventh is that which best describes the Empire and the Popedom. They were indeed the 'two lights in the firmament of the militant church,' the lights which illumined and ruled the world all through the Middle Ages. And as moonlight is to sunlight, so was the Empire to the Papacy. The rays of the one were borrowed, feeble, often interrupted: the other shone with an unquenchable brilliance that was all her own.

The Empire, it has just been said, was never truly

mediæval. Was it then Roman in anything but name? and was that name anything better than a piece of fantastic antiquarianism? It is easy to draw a comparison between the Antonines and the Ottos which should shew nothing but unlikeness. What the Empire was in the second century every one knows. In the tenth it was a feudal monarchy, resting on a strong territorial oligarchy. Its chiefs were barbarians, the sons of those who had destroyed Varus and baffled Germanicus, sometimes unable even to use the tongue of Rome. Its powers were limited. It could scarcely be said to have a regular organization at all, whether judicial or administrative. It was consecrated to the defence, nay, it existed by virtue of the religion which Trajan and Marcus had persecuted. Nevertheless, when the contrast has been stated in the strongest terms, there will remain points of resemblance. The thoroughly Roman idea of universal denationalization survived, and drew with it that of a certain equality among all free subjects. It has been remarked already, that the world's highest dignity was for many centuries the only civil office to which any free-born Christian was legally eligible. And there was also, during the earlier ages, that indomitable vigour which might have made Trajan or Severus seek their true successors among the woods of Germany rather than in the palaces of Byzantium, where every office and name and custom had floated down from the court of Constantine in a stream of unbroken legitimacy. The ceremonies of Henry the Seventh's coronation would have been strange indeed to Caius Julius Cæsar Octavianus Augustus; but how much nobler, how much more Roman in force and truth than the childish and unmeaning forms with which a Palæologus was installed! It was not in purple buskins that the dignity of the Luxemburger lay[e]. To such a boast the Germanic Empire had long ere its death lost right: it had lived on, when honour and nature bade it die: it had become what the Empire of the Moguls was, and that of the Ottomans is now, a curious relic of antiquity, over which the imaginative might muse, but which the mass of men would push aside with impatient contempt. But institutions, like men, should be judged by their prime.

The comparison of the old Roman Empire with its Germanic representative raises a question which has been a good deal canvassed of late years. That wonderful system which Julius Cæsar and his subtle nephew erected upon the ruins of the republican constitution of Rome has been made the type of a certain form of government and of a certain set of social as well as political arrangements, to which, or rather to the theory whereof they are a part, there has been given the name of Imperialism. The sacrifice of the individual to the mass, the concentration of all legislative and judicial powers in the person of the sovereign, the centralization of the administrative system, the maintenance of order by a large military force, the substitution of the influence of public opinion for the control of representative assemblies, are commonly taken, whether rightly or wrongly, to characterize that theory. Its enemies cannot deny that it has before now given and may again give to nations a sudden and violent access of aggressive energy; that it has often achieved the glory (whatever that may be) of war and conquest; that it has a better title to respect in the ease with which it may be made, as it was by the Flavian and Antonine Cæsars of old, and at the beginning of this century by Napoleon in France, the instrument of comprehensive

'Imperialism:' Roman, French, and mediæval.

[e] Von Raumer, *Geschichte der Hohenstaufen,* v.

CHAP. XXI.

reforms in law and government. The parallel between the Roman world under the Cæsars and the French people now is indeed less perfect than those who dilate upon it fancy. That equalizing despotism which was a good to a medley of tribes, the force of whose national life had spent itself and left them languid, yet restless, with all the evils of isolation and none of its advantages, is not necessarily a good to a country already the strongest and most united in Europe, a country where the administration is only too perfect, and the pressure of social uniformity only too strong. But whether it be a good or an evil, no one can doubt that France represents, and has always represented, the imperialist spirit of Rome far more truly than those whom the Middle Ages recognized as the legitimate heirs of her name and dominion. In the political character of the French people, whether it be the result of the five centuries of Roman rule in Gaul, or rather due to the original instincts of the Gallic race, is to be found their claim, a claim better founded than any which Napoleon put forward, to be the Romans f of the modern world. The tendency of the Teuton was and is to the independence of the individual life, to the mutual repulsion, if the phrase may be permitted, of the social atoms, as contrasted with Keltic and so-called Romanic peoples, among which the unit is more completely absorbed in the mass, who live possessed by a common idea which they are driven to realize in the concrete. Teutonic states have been little more successful than their neighbours in the establishment of free constitutions. Their assemblies meet, and vote, and are dissolved, and nothing comes of it : their citizens endure without greatly resent-

Political character of the Teutonic and Gallic races.

f Meaning thereby not the citizens of Rome in her republican days, but the Italo-Hellenic subjects of the Roman Empire.

ing outrages that would raise the more excitable French or Italians in revolt. But, whatever may have been the form of government, the body of the people have in Germany always enjoyed a freedom of thought which has made them comparatively careless of politics; and the absolutism of the Elbe is at this day no more like that of the Seine than a revolution at Dresden is to a revolution at Paris. The rule of the Hohenstaufen had nothing either of the good or the evil of the imperialism which Tacitus painted, or of that which the panegyrists of the present system in France paint in colours somewhat different from his.

There was, nevertheless, such a thing as mediæval imperialism, a theory of the nature of the state and the best form of government, which has been described once already, and need not be described again. It is enough to say, that from three leading principles all its properties may be derived. The first and the least essential was the existence of the state as a monarchy. The second was the exact coincidence of the state's limits, and the perfect harmony of its workings with the limits and the workings of the church. The third was its universality. These three were vital. Forms of political organization, the presence or absence of constitutional checks, the degree of liberty enjoyed by the subject, the rights conceded to local authorities, all these were matters of secondary importance. But although there brooded over all the shadow of a despotism, it was a despotism not of the sword but of law; a despotism not chilling and blighting, but one which, in Germany at least, looked with favour on municipal freedom, and everywhere did its best for learning, for religion, for intelligence; a despotism not hereditary, but one which constantly maintained in theory

Essential principles of the mediæval Empire.

the principle that he should rule who was found the fittest. To praise or to decry the Empire as a despotic power is to misunderstand it altogether. We need not, because an unbounded prerogative was useful in ages of turbulence, advocate it now; nor need we, with Sismondi, blame the Frankish conqueror because he granted no 'constitutional charter' to all the nations that obeyed him. Like the Papacy, the Empire expressed the political ideas of a time, and not of all time: like the Papacy, it decayed when those ideas changed; when men became more capable of rational liberty; when thought grew stronger, and the spiritual nature shook itself more free from the bonds of sense.

Influence of the Holy Empire on Germany.

The influence of the Empire upon Germany is a subject too wide to be more than glanced at here. There is much to make it appear altogether unfortunate. For many generations the flower of Teutonic chivalry crossed the Alps to perish by the sword of the Lombards, or the deadlier fevers of Rome. Italy terribly avenged the wrongs she suffered. Those who destroyed the national existence of another people forfeited their own: the German kingdom, crushed beneath the weight of the Roman Empire, could never recover strength enough to form a compact and united monarchy, such as arose elsewhere in Europe: the race whom their neighbours had feared and obeyed till the fourteenth century saw themselves, down even to our own day, the prey of intestine feuds and their country the battlefield of Europe. Spoiled and insulted by a neighbour restlessly aggressive and superior in all the arts of success, they came to regard France as the persecuted Slave regards them. The want of national union and political liberty from which Germany has suffered, and to some extent suffers still, cannot be attributed

to the differences of her races; for, conspicuous as that
difference was in the days of Otto the Great, it was no
greater than in France, where intruding Franks, Goths,
Burgundians, and Northmen were mingled with primitive
Kelts and Basques; not so great as in Spain, or Italy, or
Britain. Rather is it due to the decline of the central
government, which was induced by its strife with the
Popedom, its endless Italian wars, and the passion for
universal dominion which made it the assailant of all the
neighbouring countries. The absence or the weakness
of the monarch enabled his feudal vassals to establish
petty despotisms, debarring the nation from united political action, and greatly retarding the emancipation of
the commons. Thus, while the princes became shame-
lessly selfish, justifying their resistance to the throne
as the defence of their own liberty—liberty to oppress
the subject—and ready on the least occasion to throw
themselves into the arms of France, the body of the
people were deprived of all political training, and have
found the lack of such experience impede their efforts
to this day.

For these misfortunes, however, there has not been
wanting some compensation. The inheritance of the
Roman Empire made the Germans the ruling race of
Europe, and the brilliance of that glorious dawn can
never fade entirely from their name. A peaceful people
now, peaceful in sentiment even now when they have
become a great military power, submissive to paternal
government, and given to the quiet enjoyments of art,
music, and meditation, they delight themselves with
memories of the time when their conquering chivalry
was the terror of the Gaul and the Slave, the Lombard
and the Saracen. The national life received a keen

stimulus from the sense of exaltation which victory brought, and from the intercourse with countries where the old civilization had not wholly perished. It was this con-nexion with Italy that raised the German lands out of barbarism, and did for them the work which Roman con-quest had performed in Gaul, Spain, and Britain. From the Empire flowed all the richness of their mediæval life and literature: it first awoke in them a consciousness of national existence; its history has inspired and served as material to their poetry; to many ardent politicians the splendours of the past have become the beacon of the future [g]. There is a bright side even to their political disunion. When they complain that they are not a na-tion, and sigh for the harmony of feeling and singleness of aim which their great rival displays, the example of the Greeks may comfort them. To the variety which so many small governments have produced may be partly attributed the breadth of development in German thought and literature, by virtue of which it transcends the French hardly less than the Greek surpassed the Roman. Paris no doubt is great, but a country may lose as well as gain by the predominance of a single city; and Germany need not mourn that she alone among modern states has not and never has had a capital.

The merits of the old Empire were not long since the subject of a brisk controversy among several German professors of history [h]. The spokesmen of the Austrian or Roman Catholic party, a party which ten years ago was not less powerful in some of the minor South Ger-

---

[g] Take, among many instances, those of the preface to Giesebrecht, *Die Deutsche Kaiserzeit*; and Rot-teck and Welcker's *Staats Lexikon*. The German newspapers are indeed sufficient illustration.

[h] See especially Von Sybel, *Die Deutsche Nation und das Kaiser-reich*; and the answers of Ficker and Von Wydenbrugk.

man States than in Vienna, claimed for the Hapsburg monarchy the honour of being the legitimate representative of the mediæval Empire, and declared that only by again accepting Hapsburg leadership could Germany win back the glory and the strength that once were hers. The North German liberals ironically applauded the comparison. 'Yes,' they replied, 'your Austrian Empire, as it calls itself, is the true daughter of the old despotism : not less tyrannical, not less aggressive, not less retrograde ; like its progenitor, the friend of priests, the enemy of free thought, the trampler upon the national feeling of the peoples that obey it. It is you whose selfish and antinational policy blasts the hope of German unity now, as Otto and Frederick blasted it long ago by their schemes of foreign conquest. The dream of Empire has been our bane from first to last.' It is possible, one may hope, to escape the alternative of admiring the Austrian Empire or denouncing the Holy Roman. Austria has indeed, in some things, but too faithfully reproduced the policy of the Saxon and Swabian Cæsars. Like her, they oppressed and insulted the Italian people : but it was in the defence of rights which the Italians themselves admitted. Like her, they lusted after a dominion over the races on their borders, but that dominion was to them a means of spreading civilization and religion in savage countries, not of pampering upon their revenues a hated court and aristocracy. Like her, they strove to maintain a strong government at home, but they did it when a strong government was the first of political blessings. Like her, they gathered and maintained vast armies; but those armies were composed of knights and barons who lived for war alone, not of peasants torn away from useful labour and condemned to the cruel task of perpetuating their own bondage by crushing the aspirations of another nationality. They sinned grievously, no doubt, but they sinned in the dim twilight of a half-barbarous age, not in the noonday blaze of modern civilization. The enthusiasm for mediæval faith and simplicity which was so fervid some years ago has run its course, and is not likely soon to revive. He who reads the history of the Middle Ages will not deny that its heroes, even the best of them, were in some respects little better than savages. But when he approaches more recent times, and sees how, during the last three hundred years, kings have dealt with their subjects and with each other, he will forget the ferocity of the Middle Ages, in horror at the heartlessness, the treachery, the injustice all the more odious because it sometimes wears the mask of legality, which disgraces the annals of the military monarchies of Europe. With regard, however, to the pretensions of modern Austria, the truth is that this dispute about the worth of the old system has no bearing upon them at all. The day of imperial greatness was already past when Rudolf the first Hapsburg reached the throne; while during what may be called the Austrian period, from Maximilian to Francis II, the Holy Empire was to Germany a mere clog and incumbrance, which the unhappy nation bore because she knew not how to rid herself of it. The Germans are welcome to appeal to the old Empire to prove that they were once a united people. Nor is there any harm in their comparing the politics of the twelfth century with those of the nineteenth, although to argue from the one to the other seems to betray a want of historical judgment. But the one thing which is wholly absurd is to make Francis Joseph of Austria the successor of Frederick of Hohenstaufen, and justify the most sordid and ungenial of modern despotisms by the example of the mirror of mediæval chivalry, the noblest creation of mediæval thought.

We are not yet far enough from the Empire to comprehend or state rightly its bearing on European progress. The mountain lies behind us, but miles must be traversed before we can take in at a glance its peaks and slopes and buttresses, picture its form, and conjecture its height. Of the perpetuation among the peoples of the West of the arts and literature of Rome it was both an effect and a cause, a cause only less powerful than the church. It would be endless to shew in how many ways it affected the political institutions of the Middle Ages, and through them of the whole civilized world. Most of the attributes of modern royalty, to take the most obvious instance, belonged originally and properly to the Emperor, and were borrowed from him by other monarchs. The once famous doctrine of divine right had the same origin. To the existence of the Empire is chiefly to be ascribed the prevalence of Roman law through Europe, and its practical importance in our own days. For while in Southern France and Central Italy, where the subject population greatly outnumbered their conquerors, the old system would have in any case survived, it cannot be doubted that in Germany, as in England, a body of customary Teutonic law would have grown up, had it not been for the notion that since the German monarch was the legitimate successor of Justinian, the Corpus Juris must be binding on all his subjects. This strange idea was received with a faith so unhesitating that even the aristocracy, who naturally disliked a system which the Emperors and the cities favoured, could not but admit its validity, and before the end of the Middle Ages Roman law pre-

Bearing of the Empire upon the progress of European civilization.

Influence upon modern jurisprudence.

vailed through all Germany [1]. When it is considered how great are the services which German writers have rendered and continue to render to the study of scientific jurisprudence, this result will appear far from insignificant. But another of still wider import followed. When by the Peace of Westphalia a crowd of petty principalities were recognized as practically independent states, the need of a code to regulate their intercourse became pressing. That code Grotius and his successors formed out of what was then the private law of Germany, which thus became the foundation whereon the system of international jurisprudence has been built up during the last two centuries. That system is, indeed, entirely a German creation, and could have arisen in no country where the law of Rome had not been the fountain of legal ideas and the groundwork of positive codes. In Germany, too, was it first carried out in practice, and that with a success which is the best, some might say the only, title of the later Empire to the grateful remembrance of mankind. Under its protecting shade small princedoms and free cities lived unmolested beside states like Saxony and Bavaria; each member of the Germanic body feeling that the rights of the weakest of his brethren were also his own.

Influence of the Empire upon the history of the Church.

The most important chapter in the history of the Empire is that which describes its relation to the Church and the Papacy. Of the ecclesiastical power it was alternately the champion and the enemy. In the ninth and tenth centuries the Emperors extended the dominion of Peter's chair: in the tenth and eleventh they rescued it from an abyss of guilt and shame to be the instrument of

[1] Modified of course by the canon law, and not superseding the feudal law of land.

their own downfall. The struggle which Gregory the Seventh began, although it was political rather than religious, awoke in the Teutonic nations a hostility to the pretensions of the Romish court. That struggle ended, with the death of the last Hohenstaufen, in the victory of the priesthood, a victory whose abuse by the insolent and greedy pontiffs of the fourteenth and fifteenth centuries made it more ruinous than a defeat. The anger which had long smouldered in the breasts of the northern nations of Europe burst out in the sixteenth with a violence which alarmed those whom it had hitherto defended, and made the Emperors once more the allies of the Popedom, and the partners of its declining fortunes. But the nature of that alliance and of the hostility which had preceded it must not be misunderstood. It is a natural, but not the less a serious error to suppose, as modern writers often seem to do, that the pretensions of the Empire and the Popedom were mutually exclusive; that each claimed all the rights, spiritual and secular, of a universal monarch. So far was this from being the case, that we find mediæval writers and statesmen, even Emperors and Popes themselves, expressly recognizing a divinely appointed duality of government—two potentates, each supreme in the sphere of his own activity, Peter in things eternal, Cæsar in things temporal. The relative position of the two does indeed in course of time undergo a signal alteration. In the days of Charles, the barbarous age of modern Europe, when men were and could not but be governed chiefly by physical force, the Emperor was practically, if not theoretically, the grander figure. Four centuries later, in the era of Pope Innocent the Third, when the power of ideas had grown stronger in the world, and was able to resist or to bend to its service the arms

c c

and the wealth of men, we see the balance inclined the other way. Spiritual authority is conceived of as being of a nature so high and holy that it must inspire and guide the civil administration. But it is not proposed to supplant that administration nor to degrade its head: the great struggle of the eleventh and two following centuries does not aim at the annihilation of one or other power, but turns solely upon the character of their connexion. Hildebrand, the typical representative of the Popedom, requires the obedience of the Emperor on the ground of his own personal responsibility for the souls of their common subjects: he demands, not that the functions of temporal government shall be directly committed to himself, but that they shall be exercised in conformity with the will of God, whereof he is the exponent. The imperialist party had no means of meeting this argument, for they could not deny the spiritual supremacy of the Pope, nor the transcendant importance of eternal salvation. They could therefore only protest that the Emperor, being also divinely appointed, was directly answerable to God, and remind the Pope that his kingdom was not of this world. There was in truth no way out of the difficulty, for it was caused by the attempt to sever things that admit of no severance, life in the soul and life in the world, life for the future and life in the present. What it is most pertinent to remark is that neither combatant pushed his theory to extremities, since he felt that his adversary's title rested on the same foundations as his own. The strife was keenest at the time when the whole world believed fervently in both powers; the alliance came when faith had forsaken the one and grown cold towards the other; from the Reformation onwards Empire and Popedom fought no longer for supremacy, but for

existence. One is fallen already, the other shakes with
every blast.

Nor was that which may be called the inner life of the
Empire less momentous in its influence upon the minds
of men than were its outward dealings with the Roman
church upon her greatness and decline. In the Middle
Ages, men conceived of the communion of the saints as
the formal unity of an organized body of worshippers,
and found the concrete realization of that conception in
their universal religious state, which was in one aspect,
the Church; in another, the Empire. Into the meaning
and worth of the conception, into the nature of the connexion which subsists or ought to subsist between the
Church and the State, this is not the place to inquire.
That the form which it took in the Middle Ages was
always imperfect and became eventually rigid and un-
progressive was sufficiently proved by the event. But by
it the European peoples were saved from the isolation,
and narrowness, and jealous exclusiveness which had
checked the growth of the earlier civilizations of the
world, and which we see now lying like a weight upon
the kingdoms of the East: by it they were brought into
that mutual knowledge and co-operation which is the
condition if it be not the source of all true culture and
progress. For as by the Roman Empire of old the
nations were first forced to own a common sway, so by
the Empire of the Middle Ages was preserved the feeling
of a brotherhood of mankind, a commonwealth of the
whole world, whose sublime unity transcended every minor
distinction.

As despotic monarchs claiming the world for their
realm, the Teutonic Emperors strove from the first against
three principles, over all of which their forerunners of

CHAP. XXI.

*Ennobling
influence
of the con-
ception of
the World
Empire.*

the elder Rome had triumphed,—those of Nationality, Aristocracy, and Popular Freedom. Their early struggles were against the first of these, and ended with its victory in the emancipation, one after another, of England, France, Poland, Hungary, Denmark, Burgundy, and Italy. The second, in the form of feudalism, menaced even when seeming to embrace and obey them, and succeeded, after the Great Interregnum, in destroying their effective strength in Germany. Aggression and inheritance turned the numerous independent principalities thus formed out of the greater fiefs, into a few military monarchies, resting neither on a rude loyalty, like feudal kingdoms, nor on religious duty and tradition, like the Empire, but on physical force, more or less disguised by legal forms. That the hostility to the Empire of the third was accidental rather than necessary is seen by this, that the very same monarchs who strove to crush the Lombard and Tuscan cities favoured the growth of the free towns of Germany. Asserting the rights of the individual in the sphere of religion, the Reformation weakened the Empire by denying the necessity of external unity in matters spiritual : the extension of the same principle to the secular world, whose fulness is still withheld from the Germans, would have struck at the doctrine of imperial absolutism had it not found a nearer and deadlier foe in the actual tyranny of the princes. It is more than a coincidence, that as the proclamation of the liberty of thought had shaken it, so that of the liberty of action made by the revolutionary movement, whose beginning the world saw and understood not in 1789, whose end we see not yet, should have indirectly become the cause which overthrew the Empire.

Its fall in the midst of the great convulsion that changed

the face of Europe marks an era in history, an era whose
character the events of every year are further unfolding:
an era of the destruction of old forms and systems and
the building up of new. The last instance is the most
memorable. Under our eyes, the work which Theodoric
and Lewis the Second, Guido and Ardoin and the second
Frederick essayed in vain, has been achieved by the
steadfast will of the Italian people. The fairest province
of the Empire, for which Franconian and Swabian battled
so long, is now a single monarchy under the Burgundian
count, whom Sigismund created imperial vicar in Italy,
and who wants only the possession of the capital to be
able to call himself 'king of the Romans' more truly
than Greek or Frank or Austrian has done since Constantine forsook the Tiber for the Bosphorus. No longer
the prey of the stranger, Italy may forget the past, and
sympathize, as she has now indeed, since the fortunate
alliance of 1866, begun to sympathize, with the efforts
after national unity of her ancient enemy—efforts confronted by so many obstacles that a few years ago they
seemed all but hopeless. On the new shapes that may
emerge in this general reconstruction it would be idle
to speculate. Yet one prediction may be ventured. No
universal monarchy is likely to arise. More frequent intercourse, and the progress of thought, have done much
to change the character of national distinctions, substituting for ignorant prejudice and hatred a genial sympathy and the sense of a common interest. They have
not lessened their force. No one who reads the history
of the last three hundred years, no one, above all, who
studies attentively the career of Napoleon, can believe
it possible for any state, however great her energy and
material resources, to repeat in modern Europe the part

CHAP. XXI.

*Relations of
the Empire
to the na-
tionalities
of Europe.*

of ancient Rome: to gather into one vast political body races whose national individuality has grown more and more marked in each successive age. Nevertheless, it is in great measure due to Rome and to the Roman Empire of the Middle Ages that the bonds of national union are on the whole both stronger and nobler than they were ever before. The latest historian of Rome, after summing up the results to the world of his hero's career, closes his treatise with these words: 'There was in the world as Cæsar found it the rich and noble heritage of past centuries, and an endless abundance of splendour and glory, but little soul, still less taste, and, least of all, joy in and through life. Truly it was an old world, and even Cæsar's genial patriotism could not make it young again. The blush of dawn returns not until the night has fully descended. Yet with him there came to the much-tormented races of the Mediterranean a tranquil evening after a sultry day; and when, after long historical night, the new day broke once more upon the peoples, and fresh nations in free self-guided movement began their course towards new and higher aims, many were found among them in whom the seed of Cæsar had sprung up, many who owed him, and who owe him still, their national individuality [k].' If this be the glory of Julius, the first great founder of the Empire, so is it also the glory of Charles, the second founder, and of more than one amongst his Teutonic successors. The work of the mediæval Empire was self-destructive; and it fostered, while seeming to oppose, the nationalities that were destined to replace it. It tamed the barbarous races of the North, and forced them within the pale of

[k] Mommsen, *Römische Geschichte*, iii. *sub fin.*

civilization. It preserved the arts and literature of antiquity. In times of violence and oppression, it set before its subjects the duty of rational obedience to an authority whose watchwords were peace and religion. It kept alive, when national hatreds were most bitter, the notion of a great European Commonwealth. And by doing all this, it was in effect abolishing the need for a centralizing and despotic power like itself: it was making men capable of using national independence aright: it was teaching them to rise to that conception of spontaneous activity, and a freedom which is above law but not against it, to which national independence itself,· if it is to be a blessing at all, must be only a means. Those who mark what has been the tendency of events since A.D. 1789, and who remember how many of the crimes and calamities of the past are still but half redressed, need not be surprised to see the so-called principle of nationalities advocated with honest devotion as the final and perfect form of political development. But such undistinguishing advocacy is after all only the old error in a new shape. If all other history did not bid us beware the habit of taking the problems and the conditions of our own age for those of all time, the warning which the Empire gives might alone be warning enough. From the days of Augustus down to those of Charles the Fifth the whole civilized world believed in its existence as a part of the eternal fitness of things, and Christian theologians were not behind heathen poets in declaring that when it perished the world would perish with it. Yet the Empire is gone, and the world remains, and hardly notes the change.

This is but a small part of what might be said upon an almost inexhaustible theme: inexhaustible not from its

CHAP. XXI.

*Difficulties
arising
from the
nature of
the subject.*

extent but from its profundity: not because there is so much to say, but because, pursue we it never so far, more will remain unexpressed, since incapable of expression. For that which it is at once most necessary and least possible to do, is to look at the Empire as a whole: a single institution, in which centres the history of eighteen centuries—whose outer form is the same, while its essence and spirit are constantly changing. It is when we come to consider it in this light that the difficulties of so vast a subject are felt in all their force. Try to explain in words the theory and inner meaning of the Holy Empire, as it appeared to the saints and poets of the Middle Ages, and that which we cannot but conceive as noble and fertile in its life, sinks into a heap of barren and scarcely intelligible formulas. Who has been able to describe the Papacy in the power it once wielded over the hearts and imaginations of men? Those persons, if such there still be, who see in it nothing but a gigantic upas-tree of fraud and superstition, planted and reared by the enemy of mankind, are hardly further from entering into the mystery of its being than the complacent political philosopher, who explains in neat phrases the process of its growth, analyses it as a clever piece of mechanism, enumerates and measures the interests it appealed to, and gives, in conclusion, a sort of tabular view of its results for good and for evil. So, too, is the Holy Empire above all description or explanation; not that it is impossible to discover the beliefs which created and sustained it, but that the power of those beliefs cannot be adequately apprehended by men whose minds have been differently trained, and whose imaginations are fired by different ideals. Something, yet still how little, we should know of it if we knew what were the thoughts of Julius Cæsar when he laid the

foundations on which Augustus built : of Charles, when
he reared anew the stately pile : of Barbarossa and his
· grandson, ·when they strove to avert the surely coming
ruin. Something more succeeding generations will know,
who will judge the Middle Ages more fairly than we, still
living in the midst of a reaction against all that is mediæval, can hope to do, and to whom it will be given to
see and understand new forms of political life, whose
nature we cannot so much as conjecture. Seeing more
than we do, they will also see some things less distinctly.
The Empire which to us still looms largely on the
horizon of the past, will to them sink lower and lower as
they journey onwards into the future. But its importance
in universal ·history it can never lose. For into it all the
life of the ancient world was gathered : out of ·it all the
life of the modern world arose.

THE END.

APPENDIX.

NOTE A.

ON THE BURGUNDIES.

IT would be hard to mention any geographical name which, by its application at different times to different districts, has caused, and continues to cause, more confusion than this name Burgundy. There may, therefore, be some use in a brief statement of the more important of those applications. Without going into the minutiæ of the subject, the following may be given as the ten senses in which the name is most frequently to be met with:—

I. The kingdom of the Burgundians (*regnum Burgundionum*), founded A.D. 406, occupying the whole valley of the Saone and lower Rhone, from Dijon to the Mediterranean, and including also the western half of Switzerland. It was destroyed by the sons of Clovis in A.D. 534.

II. The kingdom of Burgundy (*regnum Burgundiæ*), mentioned occasionally under the Merovingian kings as a separate principality, confined within boundaries apparently somewhat narrower than those of the older kingdom last named.

III. The kingdom of Provence or Burgundy (*regnum Provinciæ seu Burgundiæ*)—also, though less accurately, called the kingdom of Cis-Jurane Burgundy—was founded by Boso in A.D. 877, and included Provence, Dauphiné, the southern part of Savoy, and the country between the Saone and the Jura*(the Free County)*.

IV. The kingdom of Trans-Jurane Burgundy (*regnum Iurense, Burgundia Transiurensis*), founded by Rudolf in A.D. 888, recognized in the same year by the Emperor Arnulf, included the northern part of Savoy, and all Switzerland between the Reuss and the Jura.

V. The kingdom of Burgundy or Arles (*regnum Burgundiæ, regnum Arelatense*), formed by the union, under Conrad the Pacific, in A.D. 937, of the kingdoms described above as III and IV. On the death, in 1032, of the last independent king, Rudolf III, it came partly by bequest, partly by conquest, into the hands of the Emperor Conrad II (the Salic), and thenceforward formed a part of the Empire. In the thirteenth century, France began to absorb it, bit by bit, and has now (since the annexation of Savoy in 1861) acquired all except the Swiss portion of it.

VI. The Lesser Duchy (*Burgundia Minor*), (Klein Burgund), corresponded very nearly with what is now Switzerland west of the Reuss, including the Valais. It was Trans-Jurane Burgundy (IV) *minus* the parts of Savoy which had belonged to that kingdom. It disappears from history after the extinction of the house of Zahringen in the thirteenth century. Legally it was part of the Empire till A.D. 1648, though practically independent long before that date.

VII. The Free County or Palatinate of Burgundy (Franche Comté), (Freigrafschaft), (called also Upper Burgundy), to which the name of Cis-Jurane Burgundy originally and properly belonged, lay between the Saone and the Jura. It formed a part of III and V, and was therefore a fief of the Empire. The French dukes of

Burgundy were invested with it in A.D. 1384, and in 1678 it was annexed to the crown of France.

VIII. The Landgraviate of Burgundy (Landgrafschaft) was in Western Switzerland, on both sides of the Aar, between Thun and Solothurn. It was a part of the Lesser Duchy (VI), and, like it, is hardly mentioned after the thirteenth century.

IX. The Circle of Burgundy (Kreis Burgund), an administrative division of the Empire, was established by Charles V in 1548; and included the Free County of Burgundy (VII) and the seventeen provinces of the Netherlands, which Charles inherited from his grandmother Mary, daughter of Charles the Bold.

X. The Duchy of Burgundy (Lower Burgundy), (Bourgogne), the most northerly part of the old kingdom of the Burgundians, was always a fief of the crown of France, and a province of France till the Revolution. It was of this Burgundy that Philip the Good and Charles the Bold were Dukes. They were also Counts of the Free County (VII).

The most copious and accurate information regarding the obscure history of the Burgundian kingdoms (III, IV, and V) is to be found in the contributions of Baron Frederic de Gingins la Sarraz, a Vaudois historian, to the *Archiv für Schweizer Geschichte*. See also an admirable article in the *National Review* for October 1860, entitled 'The Franks and the Gauls.'

NOTE B.

ON THE RELATIONS TO THE EMPIRE OF THE KINGDOM OF DENMARK, AND THE DUCHIES OF SCHLESWIG AND HOLSTEIN.

THE history of the relations of Denmark and the Duchies to the Romano-Germanic Empire is a very small part of the great Schleswig-Holstein controversy. But having been unnecessarily mixed up with two questions properly quite distinct,—the first, as to the relation of Schleswig to Holstein, and of both jointly to the Danish crown; the second, as to the diplomatic engagements which the Danish kings have in recent times contracted with the German powers,—it has borne its part in making the whole question the most intricate and interminable that has vexed Europe for two centuries and a half. Setting aside irrelevant matter, the facts as to the Empire are as follows :—

I. The Danish kings began to own the supremacy of the Frankish Emperors early in the ninth century. Having recovered their independence in the confusion that followed the fall of the Carolingian dynasty, they were again subdued by Henry the Fowler and Otto the Great, and continued tolerably submissive till the death of Frederick II and the period of anarchy which followed. Since that time Denmark has been always independent, although her king was, until the treaty of A.D. 1865, a member of the German Confederation for Holstein.

II. Schleswig was in Carolingian times Danish; the Eyder being, as Eginhard tells us, the boundary between Saxonia Transalbiana (Holstein), and the Terra Nortmannorum (wherein lay the town of Sliesthorp), inhabited by the Scandinavian heathen. Otto the Great conquered all Schleswig, and, it is said, Jutland also, and added the southern part of Schleswig to the immediate territory of the Empire, erecting it into a margraviate. So it remained till the days of Conrad II, who made the Eyder again the boundary, retaining of course his suzerainty over the kingdom of Denmark as a whole. But by this time the colonization of Schleswig by the Germans had begun; and ever since the numbers of the Danish population seem to have steadily declined, and the mass of the people to have grown more and more disposed to sympathize with their southern rather than their northern neighbours.

III. Holstein always was an integral part of the Empire, as it is at this day of the North German Bund.

NOTE C.

ON CERTAIN IMPERIAL TITLES AND CEREMONIES.

THIS subject is a great deal too wide and too intricate to be more than touched upon here. But a few brief statements may have their use; for the practice of the Germanic Emperors varied so greatly from time to time, that the reader becomes hopelessly perplexed without some clue. And if there were space to explain the causes of each change of title, it would be seen that the subject, dry as it may appear, is very far from being a barren or a dull one.

I. TITLES OF EMPERORS.

Charles the Great styled himself ' Carolus serenissimus Augustus, a Deo coronatus, magnus et pacificus imperator, Romanum (*or* Romanorum) gubernans imperium, qui et per misericordiam Dei rex Francorum et Langobardorum.'

Subsequent Carolingian Emperors were usually entitled simply ' Imperator Augustus.' Sometimes 'rex Francorum et Langobardorum' was added [a].

Conrad I and Henry I (the Fowler) were only German kings.

A Saxon Emperor was, before his coronation at Rome, ' rex,' or ' rex Francorum Orientalium,' or ' Francorum atque Saxonum rex;' after it, simply ' Imperator Augustus.' Otto III is usually said to have introduced the form ' Romanorum Imperator Augustus,' but some authorities state that it occurs in documents of the time of Lewis I.

[a] Waitz (*Deutsche Verfassungsgeschichte*) says that the phrase 'semper Augustus' may be found in the times of the Carolingians, but not in official documents.

Henry II and his successors, not daring to take the title of Emperor till crowned at Rome (in conformity with the superstitious notion which had begun with Charles the Bald), but anxious to claim the sovereignty of Rome, as indissolubly attached to the German crown, began to call themselves 'reges Romanorum.' The title did not, however, become common or regular till the time of Henry IV, in whose proclamations it occurs constantly.

From the eleventh century till the sixteenth, the invariable practice was for the monarch to be called 'Romanorum rex semper Augustus,' till his coronation at Rome by the Pope; after it, 'Romanorum Imperator semper Augustus.'

In A.D. 1508, Maximilian I, being refused a passage to Rome by the Venetians, obtained a bull from Pope Julius II permitting him to call himself 'Imperator electus' (erwählter Kaiser). This title Ferdinand I (brother of Charles V) and all succeeding Emperors took immediately upon their German coronation, and it was till A.D. 1806 their strict legal designation[b], and was always employed by them in proclamations or other official documents. The term 'elect' was however omitted, even in formal documents when the sovereign was addressed or spoken of in the third person; and in ordinary practice he was simply 'Roman Emperor.'

Maximilian added the title 'Germaniæ rex,' which had never been known before, although the phrase 'rex Germanorum' may be found employed once or twice in early times. 'Rex Teutonicorum,' 'regnum Teutonicum[c],'

---

[b] There is some reason to think that towards the end of the Empire people had begun to fancy that 'erwählter' did not mean 'elect,' but 'elective.' Cf. note [m], p. 362.

[c] These expressions seem to have been intended to distinguish the kingdom of the Eastern or Germanic Franks from that of the Western or Gallicized Franks

occur often in the tenth and eleventh centuries. A great many titles of less consequence were added from time to time. Charles the Fifth had seventy-five, not, of course, as Emperor, but in virtue of his vast hereditary possessions [d].

It is perhaps worth remarking that the word Emperor has not at all the same meaning now that it had even so lately as two centuries ago. It is now a commonplace, not to say vulgar, title, somewhat more pompous than that of King, and supposed to belong especially to despots. It is given to all sorts of barbarous princes, like those of China and Abyssinia, in default of a better name. It is peculiarly affected by new dynasties; and has indeed grown so fashionable, that what with Emperors of Brazil, of Hayti, and of Mexico, the good old title of King seems in a fair way to become obsolete [e]. But in former times there was, and could be but one Emperor; he was always mentioned with a certain reverence: his name summoned up a host of thoughts and associations, which we cannot comprehend or sympathize with. His office, unlike that of modern Emperors, was by its very nature elective, and not hereditary; and, so far from resting on conquest or the will of the people, rested on and represented

---

(Francigenæ), which having been for some time 'regnum Francorum Occidentalium,' grew at last to be simply 'regnum Franciæ,' the East Frankish kingdom being swallowed up in the Empire.

[d] It is right to remark that what is stated here can be taken as only generally and probably true: so great are the discrepancies among even the most careful writers on the subject, and so numerous the forgeries of a later age, which are to be found among the genuine documents of the early Empire. Goldast's *Collections*, for instance, are full of forgeries and anachronisms. Detailed information may be found in Pfeffinger, Moser, and Pütter, and in the host of writers to whom they refer.

[e] We in England may be thought to have made some slight movement in the same direction by calling the united great council of the Three Kingdoms the Imperial Parliament.

pure legality. War could give him nothing which law had not given him already: the people could delegate no power to him who was their lord and the viceroy of God.

II. THE CROWNS.

Of the four crowns something has been said in the text. They were those of Germany, taken at Aachen; of Burgundy, at Arles; of Italy, sometimes at Pavia, more usually at Milan or Monza; of the world, at Rome.

The German crown was taken by every Emperor after the time of Otto the Great; that of Italy by every one, or almost every one, who took the Roman down to Frederick III, by none after him; that of Burgundy, it would appear, by four Emperors only, Conrad II, Henry III, Frederick I, and Charles IV. The imperial crown was received at Rome by most Emperors till Frederick III; after him by none save Charles V, who obtained both it and the Italian at Bologna in a somewhat informal manner. But down to A.D. 1806, every Emperor bound himself by his capitulation to proceed to Rome to receive it.

It should be remembered that none of these inferior crowns was necessarily connected with that of the Roman Empire, which might have been held by a simple knight without a foot of land in the world. For as there had been Emperors (Lothar I, Lewis II, Lewis of Provence (son of Boso), Guy, Lambert, and Berengar) who were not kings of Germany, so there were several (all those who preceded Conrad II) who were not kings of Burgundy, and others (Arnulf, for example) who were not kings of Italy. And it is also worth remarking, that although no crown save the German was assumed by the successors of Charles V, their wider rights remained in full force, and were never subsequently relinquished. There was nothing, except the practical difficulty and absurdity of such a project, to prevent Francis II from having himself crowned at Arles [f], Milan, and Rome.

III. The King of the Romans (Römischer König).

It has been shewn above how and why, about the time of Henry II, the German monarch began to entitle himself 'Romanorum rex.' Now it was not uncommon in the Middle Ages for the heir-apparent to a throne to be crowned during his father's lifetime, that at the death of the latter he might step at once into his place. (Coronation, it must be remembered, which is now merely a spectacle, was in those days not only a sort of sacrament, but a matter of great political importance.) This plan was specially useful in an elective monarchy, such as Germany was after the twelfth century, for it avoided the delays and dangers of an election while the throne was vacant. But as it seemed against the order of nature to have two Emperors at once [g], and as the sovereign's authority in Germany depended not on the Roman but on the German coronation, the practice came to be that each Emperor during his own life procured, if he could, the election of his successor, who was crowned at Aachen, in later times at Frankfort, and took the title of 'King

---

[f] Although to be sure the Burgundian dominions had all passed from the Emperor to France, the kingdom of Sardinia, and the Swiss Confederation.

[g] Nevertheless, Otto II was crowned Emperor, and reigned for some time along with his father, under the title of 'Co-Imperator.'

So Lothar I was associated in the Empire with Lewis the Pious, as Lewis himself had been crowned in the lifetime of Charles. Many analogies to the practice of the Romano-Germanic Empire in this respect might be adduced from the history of the old Roman, as well as of the Byzantine Empire.

of the Romans.' During the presence of the Emperor in Germany he exercised no more authority than a Prince of Wales does in England, but on the Emperor's death he succeeded at once, without any second election or coronation, and assumed (after the time of Ferdinand I) the title of ' Emperor Elect [h].' Before Ferdinand's time, he would have been expected to go to Rome to be crowned there. While the Hapsburgs held the sceptre, each monarch generally contrived in this way to have his son or some other near relative chosen to succeed him. But many were foiled in their attempts to do so; and, in such cases, an election was held after the Emperor's death, according to the rules laid down in the Golden Bull.

The first person who thus became king of the Romans in the lifetime of an Emperor seems to have been Henry VI, son of Frederick I.

It was in imitation of this title that Napoleon called his son king of Rome.

---

[h] Maximilian had obtained this title, ' Emperor Elect,' from the Pope. Ferdinand took it as bf right, and his successors followed the example.

NOTE D.

Lines contrasting the Past and Present of Rome.

Dum simulacra mihi, dum numina vana placebant,
　　Militia, populo, mœnibus alta fui :
At simul effigies arasque superstitiosas
　　Deiiciens, uni sum famulata Deo,
Cesserunt arces, cecidere palatia divûm,
　　Servivit populus, degeneravit eques.
Vix scio quæ fuerim, vix Romæ Roma recordor ;
　　Vix sinit occasus vel meminisse mei.
Gratior hæc iactura mihi successibus illis ;
　　Maior sum pauper divite, stante iacens :
Plus aquilis vexilla crucis, plus Cæsare Petrus,
　　Plus cinctis ducibus vulgus inerme dedit.
Stans domui terras, infernum diruta pulso,
　　Corpora stans, animas fracta iacensque rego.
Tunc miseræ plebi, modo principibus tenebrarum
　　Impero : tunc urbes, nunc mea regna polus.

Written by Hildebert, bishop of Le Mans, and afterwards archbishop of Tours (born A.D. 1057). Extracted
from his works as printed by Migne, *Patrologiæ Cursus
Completus*[1].

[1] See note ᵈ, p. 270.

INDEX.

G.

LaVergne, TN USA
16 April 2010
179535LV00003B/13/P